With the Best of Intentions

How Philanthropy Is Reshaping K–12 Education

With the Best of Intentions

How Philanthropy Is Reshaping K–12 Education

Edited by
Frederick M. Hess

HARVARD EDUCATION PRESS

Cambridge, Massachusetts

Library of Congress Control Number 2005931448

Paperback ISBN 1-891792-65-2
Library Edition ISBN 1-891792-66-0

Published by Harvard Education Press,
an imprint of the Harvard Education Publishing Group

Harvard Education Press
8 Story Street
Cambridge, MA 02138

Cover Design: Alyssa Morris

The typefaces used in this book are ITC Stone Serif for text and ITC Stone Sans for display.

Contents

Preface

I never intended to study philanthropy. Why then is my name on the jacket of a book on that very subject? The answer is revealing. What I am interested in is education and school reform, and in one project after another I have seen the push and pull of philanthropic giving. In some sense, giving in K–12 schooling is like the "dark matter" that physicists study: We think it's there, it seems to matter, and we see traces of its influence, but we're not sure how much there is, where it is, what it does, or how it works.

In examining a variety of educational questions—including urban reform, school choice, accountability, teacher licensure, and school leadership—I've seen firsthand how intertwined reform efforts and philanthropic giving are. There's no ready way to separate them. So I found myself gradually encroaching upon the subject until, by early 2004, I was examining the role of educational donors.

At that time, I was astonished by how little information I could locate on educational giving. My research assistants and I had great trouble finding data on the national picture, detailing the role of givers in influential reforms, or documenting the role of funders in particular initiatives or locales. Adopting the approach employed so devilishly by Tom Sawyer when he found himself with a fence to paint, I sought to convince nearly a dozen of the researchers and analysts I most admire to investigate and sketch key pieces of the story. Intrigued by the topic, these scholars generously agreed. In this volume, you will find the fruits of their contribution.

The research was initially unveiled at a research conference at the American Enterprise Institute in April 2005. There, an estimable collection of discussants and an audience packed with leading funders offered invaluable insights and comments that helped to refine the analyses. I want to thank the following discussants who participated: Arlene Ackerman, superintendent of the San Francisco Unified School District; Alan Bersin, then-superintendent of San Diego City Schools; Daniel Fallon of Carnegie Corporation of New York; Michael Feinberg, cofounder of the Knowledge Is Power Program

Foundation; Chester E. Finn, Jr., of the Thomas B. Fordham Foundation; Susan Fuhrman, dean of the University of Pennsylvania's Graduate School of Education; Howard Fuller of Marquette University; James A. Kelly, former head of the National Board for Professional Teaching Standards; Wendy Kopp, founder of Teach For America; Bruno V. Manno of The Annie E. Casey Foundation; Lawrence C. Patrick, III, of the Black Alliance for Educational Options; William Porter, executive director of Grantmakers for Education; Stefanie Sanford of the Bill & Melinda Gates Foundation; Warren Simmons, executive director of the Annenberg Institute for School Reform at Brown University; and Kim Smith, CEO of the NewSchools Venture Fund.

I want to thank AEI, and particularly its president, Chris DeMuth, for the resources and support that enabled me to pursue this line of scholarship. I also want to offer special thanks to my assistants at AEI, especially Morgan Goatley, who was instrumental in coordinating the research effort and ensuring the quality of the volume that you hold in your hands. Other staff members who provided valuable assistance include Rachel Hoff, Emily Kluver, Michael Ruderman, and Juliet Squire. Finally, I'd like to thank my publisher Doug Clayton for his guidance, advice, and support, and his colleagues at HEP, including Caroline Chauncey and Dody Riggs.

Frederick M. Hess

Introduction

Frederick M. Hess

From the Gates Foundation high school initiative to the Annenberg Challenge, from the Children's Scholarship Fund to the Broad Prize for Urban Education, philanthropic efforts are playing a catalytic role in contemporary school reform. Yet, even as philanthropy has helped define effective practice, forge school-community relationships, shape policy agendas, and anoint hot new icons, it remains little understood.

Philanthropy constitutes only a fraction of 1 percent of total U.S. K–12 spending, but the realities of school budgeting and public policy mean that this money can have a vastly disproportionate impact on the direction of America's schools. Educational philanthropy has often disappointed, but neither the reasons nor the consequences for that are well understood. How much does educational philanthropy matter? What kinds of reforms do donors support? How does this money affect our schools? How might this money be invested more effectively—from the point of view of either donors or recipients? Such questions are critical for practitioners, policymakers, and philanthropists. These are the kinds of questions that this volume addresses.

Philanthropy is a sprawling enterprise. The Foundation Center in Washington, D.C., estimates that there are more than 60,000 foundations in the United States, and that about one-fourth of all foundation giving goes to K–12 schooling or higher education. The vast majority of these givers are small local enterprises giving to local efforts.[1] This volume does not focus on that mass of small givers—instead, the contributors focus on the role of the big donors. The 30 largest philanthropies in K–12 education appear to account for more than half of all giving to public schooling, and it is primarily these large donors who seek to influence the larger world of American schooling.

The bulk of educational philanthropy has traditionally been a localized affair, even when large foundations are involved. Donors give to their alma maters, to schools their children or family members attend, to libraries, and to neighborhood schools. The result has been a wealth of small-scale giving, guided by personal history and relationships and with limited attention to outcomes or the impact of giving.

Nonetheless, throughout the 20th century, foundations influenced public policy in an array of fields. Early in the century, when government was more limited in size and scope, foundations sometimes played a role in establishing and supporting institutions like hospitals and libraries. In the case of education, philanthropy played a prominent role in influencing policy and forging institutions. Andrew Carnegie founded the Carnegie Foundation for the Advancement of Teaching in 1905. Among its contributions was the creation of the Educational Testing Service in 1948. John D. Rockefeller gave $33 million to found the General Education Board (GEB) in 1902. The GEB proceeded to underwrite a slate of national activity, including teacher training, the development of state education departments, and initiatives to improve educational opportunities for black students in the South. The Ford Foundation, launched by Henry Ford in 1936, helped support the creation of the Advanced Placement program in 1955 and, in the 1960s, sponsored the Comprehensive School Improvement Program to award money for curriculum and teacher development. Leslie Lenkowsky's chapter in this volume discusses a number of such historical efforts, though he points out that the first donor-funded "systemic" reform efforts did not emerge until the 1980s.

While leading foundations have always played a national role, it is fair to say that the ranks and ambition of these have grown in the past two decades—dramatically so in the past five to ten years. This development has been driven by broader developments in the world of education policy. The 1983 release of the influential report *A Nation at Risk* and the ongoing transition of America to a service-based economy gave K–12 education an unprecedented, sustained national salience. This new focus fostered a nationalization of education policy, marked by heightened presidential attention and ultimately the 2001 passage of the far-reaching No Child Left Behind Act. Fueled by frustration with the results of curricular and teacher quality reforms that states pursued in response to *A Nation at Risk*, structural reforms like test-based accountability, school choice, and alternative teacher licensure made enormous gains after 1990. All of this took place against a backdrop of eroding public faith in K–12 schooling, with the percentage of Americans reporting a "great deal" or "quite a lot" of confidence in the nation's schools falling from 58 percent in 1973 to 41 percent in 2004.[2] The changed environment encouraged many educational givers—and especially professional foundation staff—to view their role in a new light. In this volume, Richard Colvin reports that the new givers were far more likely to see themselves combating a pressing national problem than serving as publicly minded local patrons. The result has been a heightened focus on systematic impact and replicable models, and a shift away from the emphasis on piecemeal accomplishments that characterized earlier eras.

There is good reason for philanthropists to play this more ambitious role. As Alexis de Tocqueville observed nearly two centuries ago, the genius of the American system resides in its ability to nurture ingenuity, foster voluntary cooperation, and provide opportunities for individual and entrepreneurial initiative. Too often, the bureaucracy and regulation that suffuse public schooling stifle these impulses. Philanthropic giving can help break this stranglehold, nurturing entrepreneurial efforts that cannot find a foothold in the traditional system and pressing for policy change intended to transform a creaking edifice. Many philanthropic efforts will come to naught, and some will be wrong-headed, but the very infusion of energy and ideas is critical to ensuring that new and promising programs can earn a trial and a democratic hearing. For good or ill, the most significant new ventures of the past two decades—including Teach For America, KIPP public schools, the National Board for Professional Teaching Standards, New Leaders for New Schools, and the Milwaukee Parental Choice Program—were only made possible by philanthropic support.

Federal law restricts the types of activities in which tax-exempt foundations can engage. Explicitly "political" efforts to lobby public officials or become involved in electoral policies are prohibited, though private foundations may fund groups that engage in lobbying. These restrictions are quite limited, however, and leave foundations free to play an aggressive role in shaping public policy. In general, as James Ferris has noted for the Center on Philanthropy and Public Policy, "Despite widely held perceptions in the foundation community, federal law provides considerable latitude for private foundations to engage in public policy work. . . . Foundations can play an important role in framing issues, developing public will, supporting advocacy organizations, and funding policy implementation and evaluation."[3] The challenge of high-impact giving has not been finding ways to stretch the boundaries of the legally permissible but learning to give more effectively. The contributors to this volume do not explore the statutory and legal environment of giving. Rather, their analyses examine what we are learning about how, when, and why philanthropic giving makes a difference for schooling.

The contributions here are significant because the field of educational philanthropy has received such limited scrutiny to date. Aside from a few careful histories of select foundations and the impact they have had, like Harvard

University professor Ellen Condliffe Lagemann's two volumes on Carnegie Corporation or Gerald Jonas's 1989 book *The Circuit Riders: Rockefeller Money and the Rise of Modern Science*, educational philanthropy has received limited scholarly attention.[4] Even policy thinkers have paid surprisingly little notice to the topic, with the handful of works characterizing the results of much traditional K–12 philanthropy as disappointing and hindered by insufficient attention to strategy or results.[5] Finally, a few specialized organizations and institutes, like The Center for Effective Philanthropy, Grantmakers for Education, and The Philanthropy Roundtable, have provided valuable briefs and reports that offer practical advice for donors, but these are naturally limited in their ability to provide wide-ranging, exhaustive, or skeptical analysis.[6]

This volume seeks to extend and expand the existing body of knowledge. Providing a far-reaching depiction of K–12 philanthropy, how it works, and why it matters, the contributors necessarily work in broad strokes and with proximate data. What they offer here is intended to serve as a first cut rather than the final word on the subject.

THE ANNENBERG CHALLENGE

Perhaps the most famous contemporary gift to K–12 schooling is the Annenberg Challenge, known both as an exemplar of ambitious giving and as a cautionary tale. At a December 1993 White House ceremony, former ambassador Walter Annenberg pledged $500 million dollars over five years to help improve the nation's most troubled public school systems. The grant still represents the single largest gift ever made to American public schooling and has supported reform efforts in nearly two dozen communities, including New York, Chicago, Philadelphia, Houston, and Los Angeles. Participating districts were required to secure matching funds, generating more than $600 million in additional giving.[7]

At the launch, Annenberg explained, "I felt I had to drop a bomb on the situation to show the public what needs to be done." Vartan Gregorian, then president of Brown University, institutional home to the Annenberg Challenge, declared that the gift would help "rekindle the notion of school reform." While there is no definitive way to assess the Annenberg Challenge's impact or results, and while Gregorian and other officials have mounted an impassioned defense of the effort, it is widely regarded as a disappointment. Michael Casserly, executive director of the Council of the Great City Schools, has observed, "The best I can say about Annenberg was that it provided us a terrific bad example. The grants were poorly conceived, poorly managed, and . . . disconnected from any ability to drive any broader policy changes. The lesson is: Don't do that again." An independent evaluation of Annenberg Challenge efforts in New York, Philadelphia, and Chicago concluded that the results demonstrated that "good intentions and a generous checkbook are clearly not enough to transform American education."[8]

Whatever its accomplishments or limitations, the Annenberg Challenge was historically significant for at least two reasons. First, the scope, publicness, and broad ambition of Ambassador Annenberg's bold effort to radically improve urban schooling across the nation set a new standard for givers and raised important questions about public-private relationships.

Second, the widespread perception that Annenberg did not achieve its goals spurred a new focus on "leveraged" strategic giving that directly addressed the institutional, statutory, and organizational hurdles thought to have tripped up the Annenberg initiative. In Annenberg's wake, there was a changing of the guard in the world of educational philanthropy, as a new generation of activist, hands-on donors like the Gates Foundation, The Walton Family Foundation, the Milken Family Foundation, and The Broad Foundation entered the world of K–12 giving.

THE EMERGENCE OF NEW GIVERS

Since the late 1990s, established education givers like the Ford, Carnegie, and Rockefeller foundations have cut back their role in K–12 schooling, while new entrants like the Gates, Broad, and Walton foundations have moved to the forefront. In 1998, the top four foundations in total giving to elementary and secondary education were the Annenberg Foundation, Lilly Endowment Inc., The David and Lucile Packard Foundation, and W. K. Kellogg Foundation. Emphasizing measures like curricular reform, professional development, and community participation, these four foundations accounted for about 30 percent of all giving by the top 50 education donors. That same year, four of the five leading grant recipients were Annenberg Challenge affiliates.[9]

Just four years later, in 2002, the top two givers were the Bill & Melinda Gates Foundation and The Walton Family Foundation. That year, Gates and Walton alone accounted for about 25 percent of giving by the top 50 education givers. In 1998, Gates was not among the top 50 givers to K–12 education, and Walton had ranked 26th among education funders.[10] In 2002, the top recipient of foundation giving in K–12 philanthropy was the Children's Scholarship Fund, an organization that provides private school tuition to low-income children.[11]

Meanwhile, traditionally prominent K–12 funders were scaling back their efforts. The Packard Foundation ranked third among the top 50 givers in

1998, The Pew Charitable Trusts ranked fifth, and The Rockefeller Foundation ranked sixteenth. By 2002, Packard and Rockefeller had dropped entirely off the top 50 list, while The Pew Charitable Trusts fell back eight places to thirteenth. Packard and Pew announced that they were shifting their emphasis from K–12 education to pre-K, while The Rockefeller Foundation cut its K–12 spending to less than $5 million a year.[12]

The new donors—typically men who made their fortunes as entrepreneurs and hands-on corporate leaders in the new economy—exhibit little patience for educational bureaucracies, traditional approaches to giving, or pleas to give the public schools more time. Instead, they have supported endeavors like charter schools and nontraditional programs for recruiting or recognizing teachers. New givers like The Broad Foundation, discussed by Dan Katzir and Wendy Hassett in this volume, have adopted a hands-on approach to giving and imported a "private sector" mindset regarding results, accountability, and rapid execution.

Adopting a new theory of hands-on giving flavored by their experiences in the world of entrepreneurial, high-tech competition, these new entrants have adopted new strategies and are actively involved with their grantees. What does this mean for schools, educators, and public policy?

In answering that question, it is vital to understand, as Jay Greene explains in this volume, that total philanthropic giving amounts to well under 1 percent of what the nation spends on public K–12 schooling each year. Because taxpayers provide almost the entirety of public school funding, donor-initiated reforms will ultimately stand or fall on their ability to reshape public institutions or redirect public expenditures. As philanthropists seek to alter public policy, however, they find themselves increasingly engaged in an enterprise that can be regarded as public rather than private.

PHILANTHROPY AND PUBLIC POLICY

Even those who don't follow education have seen in recent years how philanthropic giving has impacted the nation's education agenda. We read stories in papers like the *New York Times, Chicago Tribune*, and *USA Today* that bear such headlines as "A Booster Shot for Chicago's Public Schools," "Foundation Awards Aim to Boost Stature of Urban School Districts," "Redesigning the American Teacher," and "Taking a Corporate Approach to Remaking Education." Meanwhile, in January and February 2005, for instance, the education newspaper *Education Week* ran stories with such headlines as "Teacher-Pay Plan in Denver Gets Foundation Boost," "Philadelphia Lands Grant for

Principal-Training Effort," and "Five Cities Receive Grants to Tackle Dropout Problem."

The most visible and significant contemporary effort is the Gates Foundation's ambitious effort to reshape the American high school. Founded by the world's richest man, Microsoft cofounder Bill Gates, and his wife Melinda French Gates, the Gates Foundation had risen to become the nation's biggest education giver by the beginning of the 21st century. In February 2005, after several years of prominent Gates Foundation support for high school reform initiatives across the country, Gates delivered a keynote speech to the nation's governors at a National Governors Association conference. Garnering headlines like "Mr. Gates Goes to Washington" on the *New York Times* editorial page and "Summit Underscores Gates Foundation's Emergence as a Player" on page one of *Education Week*, he told the assembled governors, "Training the workforce of tomorrow with the high schools of today is like trying to teach kids about today's computers on a 50-year-old mainframe. It's the wrong tool for the times."[13] The governors embraced Gates's message, with more than a dozen signing up after the conference for the Gates-backed American Diploma Project network.

As foundations seek to change public policy or spending, they wade into the public debate. Gates's effort on this front has been far from unique. In spring 2005, Jim Barksdale, the former chief executive officer of the Internet firm Netscape Communications and a native Mississippian, announced that he would give $50 million to support student achievement in Mississippi—if state lawmakers agreed to multiple conditions, including increasing state spending on K–12 education by more than $200 million. Barksdale's proposal would have provided $5,000 awards to students from eligible schools if they graduated high school and, again, if they graduated from college. However, Barksdale said he would only make the gift if the state legislature approved the requested spending to "fully fund" the K–12 system, gave teachers a raise, and enacted an annual audit of how schools spent federal child-care money. In early summer, Barksdale withdrew his proposal, announcing that the state's $2.2 billion budget for elementary and secondary education was $87.7 million short of being "fully funded."[14]

In one much-discussed example in 2002, three major Pittsburgh foundations suspended their support for the Pittsburgh Public Schools because, in the words of one funder, "the system is so dysfunctional that we cannot put money into it." The three givers—the Heinz Endowments, the Grable Foundation, and the Pittsburgh Foundation—had given the school system nearly $12 million over the previous five years. While the $2.4 million a year in question amounted to less than 1 percent of the district's annual budget, the action attracted national attention and provoked local unrest. The president of the school board, Jean Fink, protested, "I can't tell them what to do, and they shouldn't tell me what to do." However, Mayor Tom Murphy announced, "The action of the foundation community is a wake-up call." Within a month, Murphy had launched a Mayor's Commission on Public Education to recommend system reforms. In 2003, the commission issued a scathing report that called for substantial reforms in policy, governance, and operations. The next year, a new board majority began to implement many of the recommendations, and the three foundations resumed their district support.[15]

A MORE "PUBLIC" ROLE

The activities of Gates, Barksdale, or the Heinz, Grable, and Pittsburgh foundations are important for how we think about the role and rights of philanthropists. Most of us regard philanthropic giving as a private affair. If a donor in Baltimore or Fresno wishes to give money for a local park, library, or school, our instinct is to appreciate the largesse and leave it at that. We don't want to prod regarding the giver's beliefs, "larger agenda," or plans for future giving. Out of appreciation for the gift, in order to encourage others to give, and out of simple courtesy, we offer thanks and move on.

When donors are not giving simple gifts to a school or district but are advocating particular policies or models of reform—especially when they dangle large sums contingent upon public officials adopting those proposals—the role of the philanthropist has changed. No longer merely a private citizen making a private contribution, donors are now engaged in an effort to reshape public education, alter public policy, and redirect public expenditures. "Reform-oriented" giving pulls donors—willingly or not—into a larger, more public world.

This new role carries the reciprocal obligation that donors embrace transparency and accept scrutiny of aims, activities, and methods. In a democratic nation it is altogether proper that private efforts to reshape public institutions—even for the most beneficent of purposes—be accorded the same hard look that greets any policy proposal.

That is the democratic compact. Such scrutiny can help citizens, policymakers, and practitioners consider the merits of philanthropic efforts, debate their effects, and learn from their results. The conversation will provide a useful check on philanthropic agendas and provide useful feedback on the acceptance and implementation of various reforms. Addressing the implications of these developments requires an informed public conversation that establishes the facts and then enables reformers, policymakers, donors, parents, and citizens to grapple with them. Unfortunately, the debates today are clouded by ambiguity surrounding even the most elemental facts.

THE ABSENCE OF SCRUTINY

This dearth of knowledge is due in large part to media coverage and scholarly analysis that have failed to ask hard questions, challenge assumptions, or shine much of a light on philanthropic activity.

In late 2003, the Texas education commissioner called a Gates Foundation initiative in the state "probably the most significant education reform ever undertaken in the state of Texas."[16] Given Texas's dramatic and much-debated legacy of school reform during the past two decades—including a nationally influential accountability system and controversial "Robin Hood" finance regime—that's a bold claim. Such hyperbole, however, is unexceptional when characterizing philanthropic gifts. After all, there's no harm in being effusive and complimentary when it comes to someone giving away money. Even stories in unsentimental newspapers like the *Washington Post*, *Chicago Tribune*, and the *New York Times* routinely carry upbeat headlines like "Grant Helps Principals Get Plugged In," "Devotion Pays Off for Two Teachers," and "Financier Uses Scholarships to Spur Action."

The reaction to Gates's 2005 speech to the nation's governors was instructive. Whereas public pronouncements on high school reform by a political figure, union leader, or school reformer would typically be treated with some skepticism, Gates received no such scrutiny. Of the 44 newspaper stories turned up by a search conducted three months after the Gates speech, not one questioned his assessment or critiqued his recommendations. Illustrative was an Associated Press wire service story that ran two months after the Gates speech, which depicted Gates as a tough talker who was also willing to "put his money where his mouth is." The article was headlined, "Public Schools, Private Billions and the Best of Intentions," and began, "Bill Gates raised some hackles with his withering assessment of American high schools, but at least the billionaire founder of Microsoft is putting his money where his mouth is." The story reported that the mother of a student in one small high school supported by Gates "credits the Gates program with giving [her son] the confidence to chase his dream and scholarships to finance it."[17]

Such headlines and stories are not unique to one foundation, but reflect the kid-glove treatment philanthropists habitually receive from the press and the education community. One has to search hard to find even obliquely critical accounts. One examination in early 2005 assessed how the educational activities of the Annenberg Challenge, The Broad Foundation, The Walton Family Foundation, Milken Family Foundation, and Gates Foundation were depicted in major national media from 1995 to 2005. The researchers searched the *New York Times*, *Los Angeles Times*, *Washington Post*, *Chicago Tribune*, *Newsweek*, and the Associated Press, coding each article on the five foundations as either positive, negative, balanced, or primarily factual. Of the 146 articles, editorials, and op-eds found, 67 simply discussed facts—usually these focused on the size of a grant and its purpose. Of the other 79 stories, 65 were positive, just five were critical, and the remaining nine were balanced. In other words, there were 13 positive articles for every critical account.[18]

There are several reasons for this gentle treatment. One is the natural inclination of journalists to frame stories about generous gifts in a positive manner. Another is the routine tendency of newspapers to write positively about professionally endorsed school reforms. A third is that reporters have a difficult time finding local educators or scholars who will publicly criticize philanthropic initiatives.

If the disinterested media go easy on foundations, leaders in the education and policy worlds are even more hesitant to look askance. For instance, while dozens of books have been written in recent years on Bill Gates, Microsoft, Wal-Mart, and many of the companies and individuals that have spurred the new educational philanthropy, not a single book has been written that examines their philanthropic efforts or their foundations. In truth, researchers have reasons of their own for being cautious when the question is the design or outcomes of philanthropic initiatives.

First, philanthropists are, almost by definition, worthy of praise. After all, they are giving money away in an effort to help others.

Second, academics, activists, and the policy community live in a world where philanthropists are royalty—where philanthropic support is often the ticket to tackling big projects, making a difference, and maintaining one's livelihood. Even individuals and organizations financed by government grants, tuition, endowment, or interest groups are eager to be on good terms with the philanthropic community.

Third, even if scholars themselves are insulated enough to risk being impolitic, they routinely collaborate with school districts, policymakers, and colleagues who desire philanthropic support. Offending a major giver may make it harder for otherwise blunt scholars to collaborate with skittish colleagues, public officials, or educators. In fact, even the perception that a reformer or scholar has offended a significant donor may leave school districts or researchers hesitant to work with the presumed offender—in order to ensure that they are not rendered guilty through association. The irony is that leading experts on high schools, school choice, or urban school reform, for instance, tend to avoid commenting starkly on major philanthropic efforts in those very areas.

All of this results in an amiable conspiracy of silence. The usual scolds choose to give philanthropic efforts only a pro forma glance while training their fire on other, less sympathetic targets.

WHAT WE DON'T KNOW

Both because of this restrained treatment and because foundations are understandably reluctant to subject their private workings to public scholarship, we don't really know how much money foundations give, what it gets spent on, how they decide what to fund, how they think about strategy, or what lessons they have drawn from experience.

We also don't know much about the role or effects of K–12 philanthropy. How much is there? How much is given to urban school districts? What kinds of measures does this funding support? What reforms do foundation staff favor? What role have philanthropists played in advancing reforms like school choice or teacher quality or in seeking to promote research and policy? How does education giving in the United States compare with that in other nations? What are the practical challenges that bedevil funders? What effect does philanthropic giving have on the reform strategies of school systems? In the chapters that follow, the authors will tackle these and similar questions.

When it comes to these topics, confusion and misinformation abound. To take just one example, it is shockingly hard to get a straightforward determination of how much philanthropic support there is for K–12 schooling. As Jay Greene points out later in this volume, the *New York Times* reported in 2004 that schools get about $9 billion a year in donations (equal to about 2 percent of total public school spending). The National PTA claimed it gave $10 billion to public schools that year. However, based on a survey of the nation's largest school districts and an analysis of giving by leading foundations, Greene places total giving at closer to $1.3 billion. In light of the Greene analysis, one is surprised by an Associated Press story in 2005 that reported the Gates Foundation had "invested $2.3 billion since 2000 in new visions of education," primarily in "smaller schools and more personalized instruction." In fact, if one takes Greene's calculations as a rough guide, giving of that scope would have represented about 50 percent of all K–12 giving in that period—and is probably at least two or three times what Gates actually contributed.[19] Similarly, Lynn Jenkins and Don McAdams explain that they had trouble determining how much giving there is to school districts in Charlotte, Houston, and San Diego.

THE NEED FOR PUBLIC SCRUTINY

Now, it is not as if today's foundations are unconcerned with data. As contributors to this volume like Richard Colvin, Wendy Hassett, and Dan Katzir point out, many of today's philanthropists are intensely interested in the measurable outcomes of their efforts. They have made increasing efforts to hire leading social scientists to evaluate the effectiveness of grants. Those who steer foundations also make concerted efforts at disciplined self-appraisal, engaging in extensive assessments, holding retreats, and convening working groups to evaluate their giving. This is all laudable and sensible. It does not, however, serve the purposes of public scrutiny. Conversations typically take place privately and away from public view, reassuring foundation officials that they've heard the array of arguments, sorted through options, and made the best decision they can.

While useful, these exercises are inherently limited. Open, public exchanges are the forum in which discussions can most effectively change the way options are weighed and reframe the context in which decisions are made. The groups convened by foundations tend to include, naturally enough, their friends, allies, and grantees. Such groups are less likely than outsiders to offer a radically different take on strategy or thinking—especially given the sensible disinclination of grantees to offend their benefactors. As one grantee explained of a leading local foundation, "Because it is such a huge player in the community, the foundation's grant recipients and those who ever hope to be, never criticize its processes, programs or expenditures for fear of losing support. Consequently, our relationship with the foundation tends to function within narrow ranges of hope, fear, and supplication."[20]

In short, it is in the interest of both philanthropists and the larger public that skeptical observers step forward and offer gimlet-eyed assessments of philanthropic initiatives. The need is not for more hired evaluations or strategic assessments but for rigorous debate over objectives, strategies, and results. Of course, such debate will inevitably entail critiques that some donors or grantees will regard as misguided, incomplete, or unfair.

Only such scrutiny, however, will flag blind spots or ineffective spending. The point is not that skeptics or naysayers are necessarily right, but that efforts to change public policy or balky organizations will enjoy mixed results and encounter complications. Skeptics are useful precisely because they raise unpleasant issues and challenge the comfort, hubris, and groupthink that are so much a part of human nature. In this volume, a number of leading thinkers on school reform, philanthropy, and public policy have turned their own gimlet eyes on K–12 giving. Not only do their analyses hold vital lessons and raise crucial questions for philanthropists, policymakers, and the public, but my hope is that they help to trigger an honest, open, and sustained conversation about the nature of K–12 philanthropy.

OVERVIEW OF THE BOOK

The analyses here are not intended to provide the last word on these vital issues—rather, they very deliberately seek to break new ground on questions that have been rarely examined. The authors, a mix of researchers and practitioners with a combination of research acumen, educational and philanthropic expertise, and practical experience, bring an array of intellectual and experiential orientations to the subject. Their efforts do not "answer" questions about how philanthropy influences or should influence our schools, but they do offer a comprehensive set of rigorous, provocative, and sometimes conflicting takes on the nature, role, and results of K–12 philanthropy.

The chapters are linked by two premises. The first is that policymakers, practitioners, philanthropists, and scholars will benefit from a clearer and more systematic understanding of the extent, nature, and effects of K–12 philanthropy. The second is that it is possible to approach the giving, pursuit, and utilization of educational philanthropy more effectively than has been the norm.

With that as an introduction, allow me to briefly sketch the topics of the 11 chapters to follow. The chapters fall into three sections: the first four chapters sketch the landscape of educational philanthropy, the next four examine several philanthropic models of reform, and the third offers some food for thought drawn from experience. I'll close the volume by providing some concluding reflections regarding the lessons learned, the implications for research, and the questions posed for philanthropists, practitioners, and policymakers.

The four chapters in Section I explore the landscape of education philanthropy. In chapter 1, Richard Lee Colvin of the Hechinger Institute provides a sweeping tour of the "new" education givers. He reports that some of the nation's most successful and innovative business leaders are spending hundreds of millions of dollars on innovative projects intended to help public schools better serve disadvantaged students. He argues that foundations traditionally tried to achieve this goal mainly by getting the government to spend more money on compensatory programs, but today's givers are more geared to helping school districts improve their performance. The new givers are promoting more effective leadership, better use of data, choice and competition, school restructuring, and the improvement of teaching. Agnostic about whether students will be best served by existing school districts and schools of education or by new arguments, they are looking for answers wherever they can find them.

In chapter 2, Jay P. Greene of the University of Arkansas examines the amount of money flowing to K–12 schooling and the purposes for which it is given. Greene examined the 2002 IRS filings from each of the 30 leading givers (the most recent year for which data were available) and surveyed the nation's 100 largest school districts in order to estimate total giving and giving to particular kinds of reform. He argues that philanthropic giving has the potential to spark widespread reform, but most current educational philanthropy is unlikely to have far-reaching effects. He concludes that philanthropists simply don't give enough to reshape the education system on their own. To make a real difference, Greene argues that funders must support programs that redirect how future public education dollars are spent. In analyzing patterns of giving, however, he concludes that only a small portion of current giving funds these types of high-leverage reforms.

In chapter 3, Leslie Lenkowsky of Indiana University provides a history of educational philanthropy. He explains that, apart from religion, education has traditionally received more philanthropic support than any other social endeavor. He argues that donors—"new" or old—have always followed five principal avenues when making grants to elementary and secondary schooling. With tongue only slightly in cheek, he depicts the five avenues as seeking to create better schools, create better teachers, create better curricula, create better communities, and create better children. In general, in education as in other areas of philanthropy, the most successful philanthropic ventures have been focused and persistent, willing to support unconventional methods, and possessed of a clear and convincing educational vision.

In chapter 4, Tom Loveless of the Brookings Institution examines the educational views of program officers at education philanthropies. He reports the results of a 2005 survey that employed a Public Agenda instrument previously used to study the educational beliefs of parents, students, teachers, and education professors. Loveless asks how the views of foundation education officers compare to those of parents, teachers, and education professors and finds that education program officers disagree with the general public, parents, and K–12 teachers on the most serious problems facing schools and the best way to address them. In particular, program officers are much more dismissive of discipline, basic skills, and student accountability than parents or teachers. Rather surprisingly, Loveless finds that program officers are even more skeptical of skills and discipline than are the nation's famously progressive education professors.

Section II examines four different approaches to funding reform. In chapter 5, Lynn Jenkins and Donald R. McAdams study the role and impact of philanthropy given to support districtwide reform initiatives in three urban school districts—Charlotte-Mecklenburg Schools, Houston Independent School District, and the San Diego City Schools. Jenkins and McAdams report how each district attracted philanthropic support for an ambitious reform initiative and then analyze the giving and the role it played in supporting or complicating district efforts. Though some of this funding was actively sought by the district to support a particular reform strategy, more often initiatives were launched because funders promised to finance them. Significantly, no one in these large districts was systematically evaluating, overseeing, or coordinating the various philanthropy-funded efforts. Jenkins and McAdams conclude that philanthropy may represent just a small share of districts' total budgets but that, like a small rudder turning a large ship, it can have an outsized impact.

In chapter 6, Jane Hannaway and Kendra Bischoff examine the role of philanthropy in supporting two nationally known efforts to improve the teaching force. They tell the stories of the National Board for Professional Teaching Standards and Teach For America—two ventures that have successfully catalyzed policy debates and altered the traditional teacher labor market. Although the two efforts reflect different approaches and have survived in very different ways, both began as radical, outside-the-system solutions designed to tackle ingrained institutional problems. Most relevant here is that both ventures were made possible by philanthropic support, drew heavily on such backing in their initial years, and were shaped in important ways by funders and the need to attract support. Hannaway and Bischoff conclude that these cases teach that philanthropy is not only helpful for reform, but it may well be essential.

In chapter 7, Bryan C. Hassel and Amy Way assess the extent and nature of financial support for school choice by leading donors. Building on Jay Greene's analysis, they examined the IRS filings of the 50 leading philanthropies in 2002 and categorized giving to five different types of choice-based reform. In total, the foundations awarded about $280 million in choice-related grants in 2002—about 36 percent of their total K–12 giving. Philanthropists support school choice in a variety of ways; the major focus is on

building individual schools and charter networks that will increase the supply of choice options. Hassel and Way conclude that effective choice-based
reform will require a focus on creating high-quality options for students and
expanding the scale of such options, but ask whether the necessary number
of donors will be willing to support these often controversial reforms.

In chapter 8, Andrew J. Rotherham takes up the question of philanthropic
support for educational research, policy, and advocacy. He notes that philanthropists have normally devoted a small share of their giving to these
activities, leaving them on the sidelines in debates about how educational
resources are spent and what kinds of policies should govern schooling.
This means their grantees often face a hostile political and policy environment that can undermine programs and new ventures. Rotherham explores
the reasons for today's giving patterns and shows examples of how strategic
grantmaking can, and has, changed education policy.

Section III provides some hard-won insights on the nature and impact of
giving. In chapter 9, Wendy Hassett and Dan Katzir offer a firsthand look
from inside one of the leading "new" givers. Katzir has been engaged in The
Broad Foundation since its 1999 launch, and in this chapter, he and Hassett
describe some of the experiences and lessons they have learned. Eli Broad,
a businessman committed to structural change in urban education, is one
of the influential, entrepreneurial, new philanthropists discussed by Colvin
in chapter 1. Hassett and Katzir discuss the experiences of launching a K–12
educational philanthropy, The Broad Foundation's theory of action, and how
the foundation approaches grantmaking. They draw on their successes and
missteps to provide six lessons learned so far and to anticipate the challenges
ahead.

In chapter 10, Stephen P. Heyneman draws on international experiences
with educational philanthropy and development loans to explore the lessons for domestic philanthropy. He reports that private U.S. foundations
donated about $2.5 billion to activities outside the country in 2000 (the
most recent year for which data were available), with about 14 percent of
that amount supporting educational activities. Philanthropy in nations outside of the United States is far more prevalent and visible, with international
giving in low-income countries constituting as much as a third of the local
gross domestic product. This reality can place the "philanthropists" in a position of considerable power and raises important questions about grantor-
grantee relationships. Heyneman closes by asking the provocative question
of whether private philanthropy is a sign of entrepreneurial enterprise or of
failed public responsibility.

In chapter 11, Peter Frumkin argues that even focused and hard-charging donors have often failed to develop clear plans or objectives for their giving. Noting the disappointing track record of philanthropic efforts to push new interventions, systems, and practices, he sketches three critical dilemmas that donors must address: the needs to achieve some clarity about the theory of change that guides their philanthropy, to ground their work in a clear and plausible model of scale, and to select and pursue an appropriate engagement level with recipient organizations. Frumkin suggests that donors committed to making a difference in public school reform must work to address these conceptual and practical challenges if they are to overcome the substantial obstacles to change.

Finally, in the conclusion, I identify key findings and highlight five challenges that loom for philanthropists, policymakers, practitioners, and the public. With that, shall we begin?

The Landscape of K–12 Giving

CHAPTER 1

A New Generation of Philanthropists and Their Great Ambitions

Richard Lee Colvin

In February of 2005, in a speech in the nation's capital that drew 45 of the nation's governors, as well as an ample contingent of the nation's education policy elite, Microsoft chairman Bill Gates issued a jeremiad on the state of the American high school, contending that this venerable institution was not only obsolete but also a threat to the nation's economic and political well-being. Pronouncements that public education in general and high schools in particular turn out badly prepared graduates, perpetuate inequities, and generally operate in ways counter to the nation's interests had become commonplace during the previous several decades. But coming from Gates, whose prodigious wealth and aggressive tactics propelled one of the nation's best-known business narratives, the words took on new meaning. Stories in the *New York Times, Los Angeles Times, Washington Post*, and many other newspapers, most written not by education reporters but by Washington-based political and legislative correspondents, repeated Gates's assertions in an unquestioning, almost awestruck tone that conveyed a clear if implicit subtext: If high schools were bad enough for Bill Gates to declare them a disaster, then it must be so.

"Our high schools are obsolete," Gates wrote in a version of his remarks reprinted on op-ed pages in a number of cities. "By obsolete, I don't just mean that they're broken, flawed or under-funded, although I could not argue with any of those descriptions. What I mean is that . . . even when they work exactly as designed, our high schools cannot teach our kids what they need to know."

"This is an economic disaster," he said, one that is ruining children's lives and "is offensive to our values."[1]

It was publicity even the world's richest man could not buy.

What enabled Gates to speak authoritatively on the issue rested on more than his wealth, celebrity, business acumen, or even his company's need to hire well-trained workers. It also came from the education-related philanthropy of the Bill & Melinda Gates Foundation, the richest in the world. In 1999, the foundation announced that it would spend $1 billion over 20 years on college and graduate school scholarships for thousands of African American, Hispanic, and Native American students. Around the same time, the foundation began spending what would eventually add up to $400 million on principal and teacher training, mostly in the use of technology. Then, in 2002, the foundation decided to abandon the latter two efforts and to intervene in students' lives prior to college by focusing attention on improving high schools. The foundation's strategy evolved, but it eventually could be summed up by Tom Vander Ark, the foundation's executive director of education, as seeking to transform high schools into "learning communities" based on a new set of "three Rs": academic rigor, relevance to students' lives, and supportive relationships among students, teachers, and families. Between 2002 and 2005, the foundation gave out more than $1.2 billion to create about 820 new high schools and to break up about 750 large, comprehensive high schools into smaller schools and academies. The immediate goal of those projects was to raise academic achievement and student engagement in hopes of elevating from 65 percent to at least 80 percent the percentage of American students graduating from high school. The longer-term goals were even more ambitious: to reduce the need for college remediation, boost college graduation rates, expand the number of workers holding good jobs, and increase civic and political involvement.

Foundations usually test a promising school model or teaching method by backing a few demonstration projects. It is hoped and assumed—almost always wrongly—that school districts or states will seize on a proven concept and invest in replicating it. But rather than leave that dynamic to chance, the Gates Foundation identified successful model schools and invested in replicating them. As a result, idiosyncratic schools such as the New Country Day School in Wisconsin or the Big Picture Company in Rhode Island, both places where students learn almost entirely through hands-on projects and tests and textbooks are eschewed, as well as the highly traditional and private Cristo Rey schools, would gain national visibility. With such lofty educational and social changes on the agenda, the foundation needed partners. That was why it brought together 13 other foundations and funded more than 100 intermediary organizations to do the day-to-day work. The foundation's leaders were aware, however, that even Gates's wealth and the contributions of partners would not be sufficient to alter the high school experience for large numbers of students. For that to occur, the public purse would have to open. "In the narrowest sense, it's a $10 billion to $20 billion problem that we're attacking, and over time we might contribute a tenth of the solutions it will require," Vander Ark said in an interview.

Spending for public education rose sharply during the late 1990s and early 2000s, and by 2005 was estimated at nearly $500 billion annually. Around the same time, foundations of all sizes, local, national, and regional, were spending about $1.5 billion per year, with corporate and individual donations adding tens or even hundreds of millions more. The work of foundations, understandably, tends to vary by size and type. Local foundations mainly invest in scholarships, building programs, teacher awards, and teacher-led projects. Corporate giving generally falls along the same lines. But national foundations, which make up but a fraction of the 65,000 or so U.S. foundations, have more expansive ambitions. They seek not just to help students or teachers in one school or district, but to affect the direction and quality of education as an enterprise. Such foundations represent but a handful, but that list, in the first few years of the 21st century, grew longer with the addition of Gates and a number of other innovative and wealthy business leaders. As the Gates example makes plain, if private philanthropy is to have a broad and lasting impact it must bring about changes in the spending and impact of public dollars. Almost all of the billions spent on schools, however, is already spoken for, claimed by current teachers and the always escalating costs of salaries, health benefits, books, supplies, and maintenance. That leaves precious few public dollars available for experimentation, or what in private industry would be called R&D, research and development. That is where foundations—especially those that are thoughtful, strategic, and focused—can have an outsized impact relative to their spending.

THE ROLE OF PHILANTHROPY

American philanthropy has played many important roles in K–12 education since at least the late 1880s: creating new schools, underwriting research, funding scholarships, testing hypotheses, generating new curricula, setting agendas, bolstering training, and building a case for policy changes. Indeed, the large, comprehensive, multipurpose American high school that Gates wanted to see dismantled emerged from the efforts of a coalition of progressive political forces, business leaders, educators, and philanthropists, including Carnegie Corporation of New York, at the time the nation's most well-endowed foundation. In 1959, Carnegie commissioned the former president of Harvard, James B. Conant, to analyze American high schools; Conant concluded that most were far too small, with graduating classes of fewer than 100. He recommended that high schools have no more than 400 students, of which only about a third to a quarter of whom needed to take academically rigorous classes. The rest, it was thought, could do nicely if they developed readily marketable skills and good personal habits. By the time Gates spoke, of course, many high schools had five or even, in Los Angeles and a few other fast-growing cities, ten times as many students as Conant recommended. Carnegie had by then joined with Gates in the effort to make schools smaller and more academically demanding.

An enduring theme of the work of philanthropists has been to seek to level the educational playing field by helping schools compensate for social and economic disparities. "You need excellence everywhere, not just excellence somewhere," said Janice Petrovich, the director of education programs for the Ford Foundation, which has long been a major funder in education. "Our concern is, who is benefiting? Are the poorest of the poor benefiting? We're supposed to worry about them. We're a philanthropy."

So widespread, and so sought after, is private money in education that few educators or educational institutions can claim to stand apart from the chase for money. Indeed, I direct an organization at Teachers College, Columbia University, supported by the likes of The Broad Foundation, Carnegie Corporation of New York, Ford, The Pew Charitable Trusts, the Ewing Marion Kauffman Foundation, and The Wallace Foundation, among others. That means that this chapter can hardly be said to be a disinterested overview of education philanthropy. That is not an admission; it is nothing more than a rather transparent attempt at transparency. But it makes the point that critical or even disinterested reviews of the impact of philanthropy are rare. Few academics or educators want to look gift horses—or billionaires—in the mouth. Indeed, foundations themselves usually underwrite evaluations of their work. Although those hired to do such work attempt to use rigorous evaluative methods and to embrace frankness, such reviews always carry a whiff of insider trading.

PHILANTHROPY'S ACCOMPLISHMENTS

Undeniably, however, foundations have left a lasting mark on American schools. Indeed, many of the features of public schools that are taken for granted can be traced back to foundation-funded projects. For example, thousands of schools for African American students across the Jim Crow South, many of them still standing today, were built with the backing and encouragement of the Rosenwald Fund, one of the earliest and most important foundations in education. Philanthropist Grace Dodge founded Teachers College in 1887 to train teachers in pedagogy to serve the children of immigrants. That led to the creation of schools and colleges of education nationally. The Ford Foundation promoted the employment of classroom aides, National Merit Scholarships, and funded the development of Advanced Placement classes and tests. The National Board of Professional Teaching Standards grew out of a report underwritten by Carnegie, which also gave $1 million a year over 11 years to get it established. Carnegie also funded the Educational Testing Service, with the aim of developing objective ways to measure academic merit, which led to SAT tests. Another Carnegie-supported effort was the creation of middle schools to replace junior highs, and Lilly and the Edna McConnell Clark Foundation invested heavily in their spread. The academic-standards movement drew crucial support from The Pew Charitable Trusts and the John D. and Catherine T. MacArthur Foundation. Beginning in 1970, Ford and later Carnegie, The Spencer Foundation, The Rockefeller Foundation, and others supported research, analysis, and advocacy that led to a wave of lawsuits in California, New Jersey, Texas, Kentucky, New York, Ohio, and elsewhere that challenged, on constitutional grounds, disparities of resources and tax rates between rich and poor communities. Those lawsuits led to a dramatic expansion of the state role in the financing of schools and a large increase in spending on education overall. All of these developments are frequently cited as examples of philanthropy's potential to be a catalyst for change.

But the environment within which both the public schools and philanthropy operate underwent dramatic changes in the 25 years before 2005. The 1983 *A Nation at Risk* report issued by the Reagan administration decried a "rising tide of mediocrity" and prompted the formation of more than 250 task forces to examine every aspect of education. The task forces touched off waves of reform: widespread increases in graduation requirements, a movement to professionalize teaching, school-based management, standards, systemic reform, and accountability. In the 1990s, policies designed to give parents alternatives to their neighborhood schools and inject competition into the education environment altered school enrollment patterns in many communities.

Foundations financed aspects of many of these reforms or funded research or advocacy related to them. Yet, little progress was made. That left many in the foundation world uneasy. Foundations could point to achievements—schools that had been started, programs that had materialized according to plan, curricula that had been developed, training that had been held, spending that had increased, and policies that had changed. But despite good intentions, many hundreds of millions of dollars, and a lot of hard work, it was difficult to conclude that foundations had had a large, positive effect on the academic achievement of American students. Meanwhile, the world of private philanthropy was coming under greater scrutiny and facing demands for accountability—from Congress, from impatient boards of directors, and even from educators, who chafed at the sometimes demanding requirements that foundations placed on them in order to receive funding. Beginning in 2000, a number of foundations that had previously been prominent in elementary and secondary education, such as Pew, The David and Lucile Packard Foundation, The Atlantic Philanthropies, Ford, Lilly, and Clark, reduced their involvement or shifted their support to higher education, prekindergarten, or afterschool programs. In some cases, the shift reflected a change in program officers, strategy, or the value of the foundation's endowment after the sharp fall in the stock market. There was, however, also a sense of unease and frustration that more had not been accomplished. "Large public systems are slow to reform, if not inherently intractable," said Michael Bailin, president of the Clark foundation.[2] After three decades of trying to reform public-sector systems, including schools, he recommended that the foundation serve children directly by underwriting organizations in a few communities that provide afterschool services. Changing public systems, he said, is "a battle of Homeric proportions fought with Lilliputian resources."[3]

Still, many philanthropists, like Americans in general, continued to see the public schools as one of the few institutions that has the scope and the potential to bring about social change. Indeed, the stakes for American education had probably never been higher. Demographic, technological, and economic changes in the United States and worldwide had made education more valuable for individuals, and for the nation's economic well-being, than ever before. It was that last development, brought into focus with stories of outsourcing jobs and the multiplying number of engineers and scientists emerging from universities across India and Asia, that motivated Gates and others to remain committed to addressing the problems of the public schools. Bill Porter, executive director of Grantmakers for Education, said far more philanthropists are entering the scene than are leaving. Moreover, education-related philanthropy was expected to swell. The Future of Philanthropy Project, a foundation-funded analysis of private giving, estimated that the number of foundations in the United States would increase by 50 percent between 2000 and 2020 to 100,000, as the parents of the baby-boom generation passed their wealth on to their children and the baby boomers themselves retired.[4]

In September 2004, six months before Gates spoke, billionaire businessman and philanthropist Eli Broad stood before a crowd gathered in the towering, wood-paneled atrium of the Walt Disney Concert Hall in downtown Los Angeles and made a similarly dire assessment of American education. "Public education is in many ways in a crisis that we can no longer ignore," Broad told the several hundred people crowded into the light-filled space that had been built largely because of his leadership and his giving. The problem, he said, was that the global economy had become more competitive and U.S. public schools weren't doing an adequate job of preparing many of their graduates, particularly the poor or immigrants, to compete in that world.

"We risk not only a lower standard of living and a weaker economy," Broad warned darkly. "We're in danger of becoming a second-class nation. I see the stakes as incredibly high. We're headed in the wrong direction."

"It's up to everyone," he said, "to take responsibility and get involved."

To that end, Broad and his wife Edythe, beginning in 1999, began contributing hundreds of millions of dollars to the education foundation that bears the family name. By the end of 2004, the foundation had assets worth $540 million and had rocketed into position as one of the nation's best-funded philanthropies in the field of education. In its first six years, the foundation had committed about $135 million to its initiatives. The foundation's focus is one of the most intractable problems in American education; remedying the ills of urban school districts that have largely been abandoned by the middle and upper classes. Although a number of foundations that have been active for a long time are continuing to press for more funding for such districts, The Broad Foundation has adopted a different strategy, focused more on improving the organizational capacity of the systems. The foundation has launched projects that identify new sources of leadership talent, develop alternative training methods, create tools to better analyze data, and work with school board members to help those sometimes obstructionist bodies become more focused on student learning than on petty power plays. "We did not see anyone addressing issues of governance, management, and labor relations," the foundation's literature explained.[5]

NEW GIVERS

Broad and Gates were but two of a rapidly growing group of new philanthropists who, in the late 1990s and early 2000s, began looking to find a niche in education where they could make a difference. They included:

Jim Barksdale, former chief operating officer of Netscape, and his late wife gave $100 million in 2000 to improve reading instruction in Mississippi and, in the spring of 2005, offered another $50 million for scholarships if the state legislature came up with the money to fully fund the state's schools.[6] The foundation established by Michael Dell, founder of computer retailing giant Dell Inc., and his wife Susan now has assets worth $1.2 billion and has begun partnering with Gates on high school reform. The foundation also is a major donor to Advancement Via Individual Determination, a program that began in San Diego that boosts college enrollment among middling students with potential by helping them succeed in advanced classes. The San Francisco-based Pisces Foundation, endowed by Donald Fisher, founder and chairman emeritus of the Gap clothing chain, and his wife Doris was by 2005 the biggest single supporter of Teach For America (TFA), a nonprofit that has, improbably, made teaching in poverty-ridden urban schools one of the most popular career choices of students at Ivy League colleges. Pisces also gave about $35 million to fund the national expansion of the instructionally demanding Knowledge Is Power Program charter schools, which serve mostly low-income students. Overall, the foundation is spending about $20 million a year to "leverage change in public education—especially in schools serving disadvantaged students—through large strategic investments in a small number of initiatives that bolster student achievement."[7] That rate of spending was about the same as the venerable Carnegie Corporation and put the foundation in the top 10 or so givers to K–12 education, based on 2002 figures from the Foundation Center.[8]

Financier and buyout specialist Theodore J. Forstmann gave $50 million of his own money and raised tens of millions more for scholarships to help poor kids attend private schools. Through their family foundation, Lowell and Michael Milken, the innovative Los Angeles-based financiers, spent more than $100 million by 2005 to make teaching more attractive by recognizing excellence and developing a program that based teacher pay on performance. David Packard, a former classics professor and film buff and an heir to the fortune of the cofounder of Hewlett Packard, broke away from his family's foundation to expend nearly $75 million on helping a small number of California school districts respond to the state's demanding reading standards. The Stupski Foundation, established by Larry Stupski, former vice chairman of the Charles Schwab investment brokerage, and his wife Joyce employed consultants that included a half-dozen former superintendents to help school districts improve their management techniques and use of research. The spending of the foundation, which is an operating rather than a grantmaking outfit, put it among the top 20 donors to education. One of the largest donors during the first years of the 21st century was The Walton Family Foundation, started by Sam and Helen Walton, the founders of Wal-Mart. Starting in 1998, the foundation gave an estimated $284 million to K–12 education, the bulk of that to support charter schools and tuition vouchers for low-income students.[9]

As is clear from just this partial list, many of the newcomers were in the West, far from the old-money power centers in the East. While some, like Gates, were well known, many others had a low public profile. A number of the individual donors did not come from money but had attended public schools and amassed fortunes. These same observations could be made about philanthropy in general. The 1980s and 1990s saw an explosion of wealth, much of it concentrated in a small group of the super rich. Having amassed fortunes too large to spend, this new stratum of society wanted to make a difference and became active in the whole gamut of charitable causes, including education. In many cases, they disrupted old-money ways of doing things, bringing to bear a flashier, more entrepreneurial, more aggressive approach to both giving money and insisting on results.

In education, this newer group of givers shared a belief that public education had not done well by disadvantaged students—hardly a radical claim. But as is obvious from the focus of their giving, they were less likely than donors of previous generations to think that the solution to that problem lay solely or even primarily in spending more money on education or even in making the allocation of resources more equitable, as had such foundations as Ford, Carnegie, Rockefeller, and others. They were willing to invest in something new—such as Teach For America, an institute to train school boards, or charter schools—rather than supporting only what already existed. The new philanthropists tended instead to believe that in addition to securing adequate financial resources, schools should embrace accountability and overhaul basic functions. Relatively young, many of these philanthropists were personally involved in overseeing their grants and believed good leadership, effective management, compensation based on performance, competition, the targeting of resources, and accountability for results all could pay dividends for education as well as for foundations. These givers closely monitored the impact of their generosity, keeping track not only of, say, how many principals were trained or schools were launched, but also whether students' academic performance improved as a result. Many, but not all, pursued their agendas very publicly, which was something of a departure for philanthropists, who have tended to stay in the background and let their grantees set their own goals and bask in the spotlight.

"These are people who made money challenging the status quo," said Barry Munitz, president and CEO of the J. Paul Getty Trust, referring to the new philanthropists on the scene. "These high-net-worth, first-generation folks . . . approach their gift-giving the way they approached their investing—due diligence, measures of accountability, a lot of involvement, each with an agenda. It's very different from spending money on the system and standing back and letting it work."

The bottom line for all foundations is to do good, to expand what's known, and to improve on what is already known. But to achieve those goals, especially in the area of education, foundations have to fight long odds. They have to overcome the inertia of bureaucracies and nudge them in a new direction. They have to recognize that their resources, although large, are no match for the public resources that always will finance the bulk of the education enterprise. They have to be strategic, monitor progress, maneuver through risky and challenging political environments, and know which battles to fight and which ones to avoid.

"The pressure is on all of us to be more outcomes oriented," said Kim Smith, CEO of the NewSchools Venture Fund, which has funneled about $35 million from Broad and other foundations into 22 innovative education organizations. "Practitioners, funders, entrepreneurs, it doesn't matter. Everyone has to move in that direction."

It's not easy for foundations to manage the tradeoffs between aggressively pushing school districts in a certain direction and respecting the wishes of a community and its leadership; between demanding quick results and acknowledging the complexity of school reform; between investing in something new and injecting operating resources into a project already underway.

Robert Schwartz, a former program officer for education at Pew who became a member of the faculty at the Harvard Graduate School of Education, said in an interview that "from the point of view of the folks carrying out the reform work, a lot of these new players are much tougher to deal with. They tend to be more intrusive, ask much tougher questions, have a much more hands-on relationship. They bring a degree of impatience which, in my mind, is mostly healthy. But it's a very different orientation, a very different conception of what the work is."

THE LARGEST EDUCATION GIFT EVER

In thinking about these dilemmas, many in the philanthropic world continue to cite the 1993 Annenberg Challenge as an example of what they want to avoid. The $500 million "Challenge" issued by former ambassador and publishing mogul Walter Annenberg is still the largest philanthropic gift ever given to American public education. It was matched by more than $600 million in goods and services from the local communities that were recipients, making the total value $1.1 billion.

Annenberg wanted his gift to inspire Americans and American educators to get involved in fixing the problems of the public schools. Like some of the philanthropists coming into education today, Annenberg made the announcement of his gift very publicly, in a ceremony at the White House. Like some of the new philanthropists, Annenberg also wanted to be involved in deciding which communities participated. The money went to nine large city school systems, a consortium of rural schools, two national school-reform groups, and projects designed to boost arts education in New York and other cities. Rather than going to the school districts themselves, most of the money was given to intermediary groups that worked with school districts to increase professional development, improve governance, and develop standards, or on other issues. The details differed from city to city, on the theory that local groups knew best what their local schools needed. And to make sure that communities backed the efforts, applicants had to show that they could raise a matching amount locally.

In some ways, the amount of money involved was both too much and too little. "The main lesson I draw from Annenberg is that you can't responsibly invest anything like that amount of money with virtually no staff," Robert Schwartz said. But others contend that the foundation diluted the effect of the money by spreading it too widely. "We spread ourselves too thin," Harold Williams, president emeritus of the J. Paul Getty Trust and a board member of the Los Angeles organization that was spawned by the Annenberg grant, ruefully remarked. "If we had taken on fewer school families and focused our dollars and human resources on those, we would have accomplished more."[10]

Guilbert C. Hentschke, dean of the school of education at the University of Southern California, one of the main partners in the Challenge, has studied the impact of philanthropy on education. He said that the Annenberg grant met "the classic definition of a professional reform," meaning that it mostly paid for more of what was already going on in the schools. For the most part, he said, "the school districts and the schools gobbled up those grants like lunch and they were ready for the next one." What may have been needed instead, Hentschke said, was a "radical" reform that started with an empty slate and redesigned the most basic operations of the schools.

That is a common criticism of the Challenge, and it reflects both the high hopes that the enormous sum of money involved would have a dramatic effect and the disappointment that it did not. The foundation commissioned a series of postmortems on the Challenge that, in their own way, offer a roadmap for philanthropy in education. The summation concluded that the Challenge had a number of positive effects. Among them: 86 Bay Area schools gained more ground than non-Annenberg schools; teachers in Philadelphia schools received four more days of professional development sessions each year; and the New York city schools spent more than $75 million of its own money for lessons in music, dance, and the visual arts. In Boston, the Challenge invigorated an organization known as the Boston Plan for Excellence in the Public Schools. Nevertheless, the analysis concluded, schools in urban districts "remain beset with difficulties."[11] One of the lessons of the Challenge, the report said, was that "even large gifts like ours are no substitute for adequate, equitable, and reliable funding."

Vartan Gregorian, who as president of Brown University oversaw the Challenge on behalf of Annenberg, responded to some of those criticisms in an article printed in April 2005. Now president of Carnegie, Gregorian wrote that the Challenge invested in a wide variety of reforms that were already underway, attempting to infuse them with new capital and new energy. He said the Challenge tried to create "among its 18 sites a 'research and development laboratory,' not only for America's educators but also for the philanthropists and other investors who would follow in its footsteps."[12] He said the Challenge made a point of gathering and analyzing extensive data on its efforts, data it published "without bias or prejudice," and that it was one of the first philanthropies to "embrace the concept of complete transparency."

"Without the inspiration of the Annenberg Challenge I would not have recommended to the board, as president of Carnegie Corporation of New York, that the foundation invest an average of $20 million a year focused on reform of K–12 education . . . if I had not seen what was accomplished by the Challenge," Gregorian wrote.

Indeed, Gregorian said, Gates and Broad and other philanthropists "are using information and lessons learned from the Challenge to identify their own priorities, set their goals, and implement their grant programs in education."[13]

HIGH SCHOOLS

In 2002, the Gates Foundation decided to drop earlier efforts involving professional development and technology and focus on "the most difficult problem in education"—remaking high schools. The foundation soon became the leading force attacking the problem. But it was not the first. Carnegie, Ford, and Annenberg had previously tried to address the fact that in most high schools only a small percentage of students are on an academic track. But no foundation had ever had the resources to pursue that agenda so aggressively and on so many fronts at once. The idea of smaller, personalized schools did not begin with Gates, however. In fact, a consortium of foundations fostered small schools in New York City in the early 1990s with support from the Annenberg Foundation, and that group, New Visions for Public Schools, became a Gates partner. Rather than giving grants directly to school districts, the foundation joined forces with 100 intermediary organizations, such as New Visions, in 200 cities. The Gates money leveraged the involvement of Carnegie, the Open Society Institute, Annenberg, Ford, and others. Carnegie alone put in $60 million for its Schools for a New Society high school redesign effort. "It would be difficult, impractical, expensive, and ineffective for us to do this work ourselves," Vander Ark said.

Though the Gates's high school efforts often were described as promoting smaller high schools, the foundation actually has fostered a rich variety of school types and philosophies. About 75 percent of the schools are traditionally operated public schools, but 20 percent of them are charter schools and 5 percent are private. The foundation's goal, Vander Ark said, is not to create small schools, something that is often misunderstood. The goal is to improve college enrollment and graduation in any way possible. "We're not ideological about attacking the problem," Vander Ark said. "We're trying to attack it in many different ways." In December 2004 the foundation announced it would devote $100 million, matched by $25 million from other sources, to open 20 new "early college" high schools. Such schools help students see that attending a four-year college is a bona fide possibility by making it possible for them to graduate from high school with a semester or more of college credit. "Affluent kids have increasingly, over the past 30 years, had access to college experiences in high school, and poor kids haven't," Vander Ark said. "This new investment is creating new options for urban kids and demonstrating that they can and should be doing rigorous work when they're 17 or 18," Vander Ark said. He acknowledged that the concept is new and unproven, but said it was an example of a "bold initiative" that the foundation's vast resources allow it to make.

Vander Ark said that despite its willingness to experiment, the foundation believes that all effective schools have some elements in common. Such
schools should have high expectations for all students, a "common intellectual mission," a positive school culture, and time for teachers to work
together as teams and take responsibility for groups of students. But it was
not enough to start a few or even many successful schools. That is why the
foundation began working to make sure certain "mission critical" policies
were in place in order to guarantee that success pervaded entire systems and
states. Those policies included academic standards and high school graduation requirements aligned with college entrance requirements and valid, reliable assessments to give teachers timely feedback on their students' learning.
States had to collect and disseminate extensive data about the performance
of schools and intervene swiftly in those that fail. Dollars should be distributed according to the needs of the students, not according to the wealth of
their parents or the value of the neighborhood real estate. College scholarships should be distributed according to financial need rather than students'
grades and SAT scores. Finally, parents and students should not be locked
into attending neighborhood schools and should instead be able to select
from a "portfolio" of schools to find the one that would best meet each student's individual needs.

To bring those policies about, the Gates Foundation began paying far
more attention to advocacy and to investing in research. The foundation
financed research projects on graduation rates and school choice and opened
a lobbying operation in Washington, D.C. It began pushing states to develop
policies that were supportive of its "early college" high school initiative. In
February 2005, at the National Governors Association meeting, Bill Gates
announced $15 million in competitive grants to states willing to pursue such
policies. Five other foundations agreed to put up another $6 million, with
the total amount to be matched by the states.

Besides wanting more low-income and African American students to be
well prepared to succeed in college, Vander Ark said the foundation had
another goal, one in keeping with the R&D mission of philanthropy. "Second only to changing the educational experiences of young people, the next
most important thing that Bill and Melinda's contribution should do is help
the field to learn from success, and most importantly, learn from failure,"
he said. "At the end of this decade . . . there should be a body of knowledge about high schools that simply didn't exist previously." To that end,
the foundation supported evaluations of its work by such respected organizations as the American Institutes for Research and SRI International. The
investigators working on the projects said it was too early to measure the aca-

demic impact of the new and newly constituted schools, but they reported that preliminary surveys showed that teachers were spending more time teaching. They also reported that the positive effects of small school size dissipate as schools that started out with one grade add more grades—teacher collaboration goes down, the intense workload drives teachers away, principals move on, and not all of the schools remain academically distinct from other schools. Even so, the new small schools demonstrated more rigor and relevance to students and more productive relationships between teachers and students than did comparable conventional schools.[14] Other evidence, however, indicated that many large schools that had been broken up into smaller schools, as opposed to starting from scratch, were struggling. "We've funded 750 high school improvement efforts and we still don't know very much about how to reform a large struggling high school," Vander Ark said. "That's a whole body of work that we still have a lot to learn about. You can call that a whole body of work at risk."

In response, foundation leaders said they would shift their attention away from converting existing high schools and more toward starting new high schools, such as those being developed in collaboration with the College Board, the organization that administers the SAT and Advanced Placement tests. Given the attention paid to the work of the Gates Foundation by educators and journalists, it is interesting that this change in strategy did not seem to garner more notice. When the nation's largest foundation acknowledges in a number of public forums that its strategy for reforming hundreds of high schools may not work, it would seem noteworthy. This is a good example of how few pay attention, even though foundations must change the spending of public dollars in order to achieve their ambitious goals.

Despite its visibility and size, the Gates Foundation and its partners weren't alone in working on improving high schools. In 2005, the James Irvine Foundation, which invests only in California, launched a five-year, $70 million initiative to help adolescents and young adults not intending to go to a four-year college find their way in the world. Anne Stanton, the foundation's program officer for education, said she worried that disadvantaged students, particularly those whose first language is not English, were getting the message that if they didn't want to go to four-year college they would not have a viable future. She said that misconception was causing more students to become discouraged and to drop out of high school. That's why the foundation decided to support high schools that offer high-quality career-oriented programs. "I don't think the one-size-fits-all model works," she said. "We have to show [kids] there are viable pathways so that [they] can create [their] own sense of a future."

LEADERSHIP, MANAGEMENT, AND GOVERNANCE

Eli Broad credited the principal of a successful school in Inglewood, California, a school that successfully taught low-income students and students whose first language was not English, with helping him understand the importance of principals. The school's veteran principal did not embrace California's prevailing bilingual education philosophy, taught children to read using phonics lessons when phonics lessons were virtually taboo, and used the demanding Saxon math curriculum. The lesson Broad took away was not that a particular curriculum was better than another, but that a good principal could motivate his or her staff to work hard to achieve ambitious goals. As a philanthropist, then, he could bring his money to bear to help make sure more public schools had principals like the one he admired.

Dan Katzir, the managing director of Broad's education foundation, said that when the foundation was getting off the ground, staff members spent nine months looking across the country for successful programs that tried to identify, train, mentor, and support principals, superintendents, and school board members. "Eli said, 'Find the best and we'll invest in those,'" Katzir recalled. "We looked at a ton of investments and we didn't find any good ones." So the foundation started such enterprises itself. "We told Eli that we would have to be the ones to incubate promising new practices," Katzir said. "We'd have to be the catalyst or instigator." That led the foundation to support a number of what Katzir called branded flagship initiatives, such as The Broad Center for the Management of School Systems and The Broad Institute for School Boards. In such instances the majority of the funding, if not all of it, came from the foundation, but the entities maintained independent legal status.

Beyond its education agenda, Broad's foundation is considered a leading practitioner of a form of philanthropy that some have called venture philanthropy or social entrepreneurship, or, sometimes, engaged philanthropy. The labels imply a role that is more aggressive, more "muscular" some have said, than that assumed by many philanthropies in the past. As with venture capitalists, this self-described group of philanthropists identifies a niche in the broad area of education reform, seeks out innovative or entrepreneurial approaches to solving that problem, analyzes their prospects, works to develop the capacity of the enterprise to better ensure its success, and then closely monitors progress toward agreed-upon targets. Should those targets be missed, a grant may be delayed, and if missed repeatedly, new management may be brought in or financial support withdrawn altogether.

The Broad Foundation's largest investment, a $20 million-plus stake in SchoolMatters.com, a project of Standard & Poor's School Evaluation Services unit that marries information about how schools spend their money with academic indicators, occurred because Broad read about the then-fledgling enterprise in *Forbes* magazine and became intrigued. Broad and the leaders of his foundation helped broker a partnership with the Gates Foundation, and the service was expanded nationally in the winter of 2005. That role, too, is one that the newer philanthropists seem to relish, helping promising organizations grow and flourish.

Broad was a major supporter of Teach For America and gave almost $9 million to the principal-preparation program called New Leaders for New Schools, an organization similar to Teach For America in that it recruits nationally and provides an alternative to attending a university preparation program. New Leaders gives its recruits a year of training, focusing on developing management skills as well as instruction, while paying them a stipend.

Katzir said the foundation evaluates its investments in a variety of ways but, ultimately, expects its work to produce gains in student achievement. In the case of the principal-preparation programs, for example, the foundation expects that schools led by program graduates will not only perform better than they did before but that they will perform better than similar schools.

Another major foundation that has invested heavily—even more heavily than Broad—in improving the skills of principals and superintendents is The Wallace Foundation. But compared to Broad, Wallace has pursued a more traditional agenda, underwriting efforts to change state policy and to improve training programs. In 2000, the foundation committed $150 million over five years to improving leadership at the school and district levels and is now underwriting a wide variety of programs—leadership academies, university–school district partnerships, research, changes in what it takes to become certified as a principal, superintendent training—in 24 states. Wallace and Broad and Dell, as well as the Annenberg Foundation and others, are also underwriting the New York City Leadership Academy, an expensive undertaking that pays aspiring principals full salaries as they train for a year to take jobs heading up schools in the city. Some critics have said that because not everyone who goes through the program becomes a principal, each principal it places costs more than $300,000. The foundation disputes that figure. But it's clear the approach is expensive.

For the most part, however, Wallace did not set up new organizations to carry out its agenda. Instead, Wallace solicited proposals from states, districts, and universities. Richard Laine, a former high-ranking official with the Illinois State Board of Education and an expert on equity in school finance, joined the foundation in 2002 to head up its education programs. He emphasized that the foundation's goals were much more ambitious than just improving the training of principals. The whole system of training, supporting, and promoting principals had to change. Put a well-trained principal in a bad system, he was fond of saying, and "the system will win every time."

"We cannot train our way out of the current problem if what we hope to achieve is all kids learning at high standards," Laine said. "An example of why that's so is relatively easy to see. Look at where the human capital is, where the teachers with the greatest talents are, and where the kids with the greatest needs are." He said the best, most experienced teachers are not generally assigned to the schools with the greatest needs. Training better principals who simply wind up working in the most advantaged schools wouldn't do much to reduce educational inequities.

What's needed, he said, are policies that give the best teachers and principals incentives to work in the most demanding schools, let principals have more control of their school budgets, and more latitude to hire and evaluate teachers. Laine said The Wallace Foundation is not in favor of "blowing up the system" in order to bring about such changes. It does not, for example, support publicly funded vouchers to try to force the system to reform itself by creating competition. "You can't stretch the system too far, or else the people won't listen to it and the learning process shuts down," he said. On the other hand, he added, "also don't put us in the 'just put more money in the system' camp. We're somewhere in the middle because we've begun to articulate this notion of leadership and the need for systemic change."

TEACHING

Improving teaching has long been high on the agenda of many foundations. "It really all boils down to good teaching," said Janice Petrovich of the Ford Foundation. "If you can figure out how to do that, you'll make a difference."

That, however, has long proven difficult to do on a large scale and over time. But that hasn't stopped foundations from trying a variety of strategies. Some seek to build the capacity of the current system by investing in professional development sessions on particular topics or improving schools of education. Others try to change the way the system works by developing new approaches to hiring, compensating, and evaluating teachers.

Carnegie initiated a $65 million program it called Teachers for a New Era with the intent of overhauling teacher training in schools of education. It was joined in the effort by Annenberg, Ford, and Rockefeller. As of 2003, 11 education schools had received five-year grants, which they had to match. Each was to develop a teacher-preparation program mimicking the clinical training of doctors and focusing on helping teachers learn how to improve students' academic achievement. The participating schools, which included such prestigious institutions as Stanford University, Boston College, Bank Street College in New York City, and Michigan State University, also were required to evaluate their programs based on the effectiveness of their graduates.

By contrast, Broad, Stupski, Pisces, Carnegie, The Atlantic Philanthropies, and other foundations backed Teach For America, the program that by 2005 had placed more than 12,000 graduates of top-notch schools in classrooms in urban school districts. Although many of those teachers, like teachers generally, did not remain in teaching, many remained active in education in other roles—founding charter schools, working on policy issues, becoming principals, and so on. The organization won financial support from many school districts and the U.S. Department of Education, as well as foundations, meaning that private money had brought about a change in the spending of public money. An independent evaluation of the program found that students who have TFA fellows as teachers do slightly better than those with teachers from other backgrounds, especially in math. But many in schools of education see TFA as a threat. Linda Darling-Hammond, a Stanford professor, has written several reports that cast doubt on the effectiveness of TFA fellows. Those studies were dismissed by most observers, but they demonstrate that such new approaches face opposition from the education establishment.

The Milken Family Foundation has pursued a dual strategy for improving teaching. The foundation's National Educator Awards identify outstanding teachers from each state and award each one $25,000 at a surprise ceremony at their school. In addition, however, the foundation tried to change how teachers are trained, promoted, evaluated and compensated with a program it calls the Teacher Advancement Project or TAP. TAP, which in 2005 was in place in about 85 schools, provides willing teachers with extra training, and those who choose to be rigorously evaluated earn higher salaries. In the spring of 2005, the foundation decided to spin TAP off into an independent charitable organization. The idea was that if the organization were independent, other foundations and states would be more likely to support it financially. In announcing the new arrangement, Lowell Milken, who created it, said the foundation would spend another $5 million on top of the $18 million it had spent up to that point. In addition, The Broad Foundation announced it would pitch in $5.3 million over five years to spread TAP to urban school districts.

"We are hell bent on figuring out a way of creating the proper incentives and putting them into practice to attract talented people into the profession," Lowell Milken said. TAP is a "culmination or consolidation of the different ideas we've had over two decades to address the most critical need in education—how to attract, retain, and motivate the educators we need. Until we figure out a way to get talented people into the classrooms of America, we're not going to achieve the intended results."

But Milken said the foundation didn't want to impose the program on schools that didn't want it. "A lot of reforms imposed on schools don't work," Milken said. "You have to have buy-in, consistency of policies, effective design, effective implementation, adequate resources. You have to listen, have to be willing to modify the reform if necessary, but you have to be firm in your basic principles. We also believe you have to start on a demonstration basis, have to prove what you are offering works."

Another foundation committed to improving teaching is The William and Flora Hewlett Foundation, where Mike Smith is in charge of education programs. Smith is one of the most highly respected thinkers in the field, a former acting deputy secretary of education in the Clinton administration, former dean of the Stanford School of Education, and perhaps the leading proponent of what's known as "systemic" reform in education. Earlier in his career, Smith and a coauthor wrote influential papers arguing that teaching, textbooks, and tests ought to be aligned with state standards and that schools should be provided with the financial resources they needed to meet those expectations. His work has had a powerful influence on the drive to create academic content and performance standards and on the development of measures of school accountability.

Smith said academic content and performance standards have become well engrained in American public education. But, he added, the standards movement that he had a hand in launching "really doesn't touch the classroom in a deep way. What's arisen in the last five or six years as an issue is the quality of the teacher and whether we have the capacity and smarts and knowledge to improve that." He observed that about 8 percent of the nation's teachers leave the field each year. That rapid turnover creates a disincentive to invest in their training because many of them will be gone within a few years. But it also represents an opportunity for districts, states, and foundations to influence the training of the new teachers coming into the classroom, he said. He noted that about half of the $36 million or so he has to spend on K–12 education annually goes to "trying to figure out ways of improving instruction in inner-city schools."

Hewlett helped finance an effort in San Diego, where Alan Bersin was superintendent for seven years, to help teachers improve through coaching. "We will have made a difference if we hear that the nature of their professional development has influenced the quality of their instruction, and what's being studied is whether the quality of instruction influences student achievement," Smith said. "If we can show that, then we'll have a model that we can show is working." Unfortunately, however, Hewlett and the other foundations involved in that district's reform efforts, including Gates and Broad, encountered a very real example of how district politics can thwart reforms. After fighting Bersin at every turn, the teachers union spent $250,000 in the fall of 2004 to oust board members who had supported him. Bersin announced in the spring of 2005 that he would leave at the end of June that year.

On another front, Hewlett put about $10 million a year toward developing "formative assessments," which are tests or other exercises that reveal what students know and can help teachers tailor their lessons to better serve them. To help teachers with that process, the foundation supported the development of wireless, hand-held devices that teachers could use to enter data about students' performance in reading or math and then use a computer to analyze it and track it over time. The foundation also has worked on a service called Teachscape, which would deliver streaming video of exemplary lessons to a teacher's computer. "What it comes down to is that you want to enable teachers to gather information on a regular basis, not yearly or every trimester," Smith said. "A lot of these steps people have used at various times but all of them haven't been put together into a system."

The Barksdale Reading Institute was set up to bring a systematic approach to teaching reading to the lowest achieving and most poverty-stricken elementary schools in Mississippi. On average, 95 percent of the students in the schools were poor and 75 percent of them came from single-family homes. To participate, schools had to agree to release their teachers for two hours a week to work with one of 11 regional reading coordinators employed by the institute. The institute also paid for additional tutoring, supplemental materials, and training for parents to help them learn to read to their children. The institute's approach to teaching was based on authoritative, widely accepted reading research. Teachers were encouraged to move away from whole-group instruction, use data to diagnose the needs of individual students, and provide one-on-one tutoring, which the institute also provided. But the institute's efforts were not uniformly welcomed. Universities in Mississippi refused to use the institute's comprehensive approach to teaching reading in their teacher-preparation courses. Professors were especially resistant to teaching teachers how to use phonics to help students identify words that they did not know. In response, the institute distanced itself from the universities and began working exclusively with the teachers after they were on the job. They met resistance there as well.

"What we've run into is a lot of teachers who say either explicitly or tacitly, 'I know how to teach kids to read, I've been doing it for 20 years,'" said Claiborne Barksdale, who runs the Institute for his brother. "I say, half jestingly, that they would love to have us give them a check in August and come back in May to see if it works."

Despite the resistance, Barksdale said foundations must work with teachers if they are to make a difference. "What we were doing at first was just nibbling at the edges and ignoring core instruction," Barksdale said. "A lot of foundations are afraid to get inside the classroom and it's understandable. It's a sensitive threshold. But it's absolutely essential because that's where it's going on. If you don't cross that threshold, you don't know what's going on and you don't sufficiently affect the end delivery of the product."

Barksdale said the schools the institute has worked with have made statistically significant gains, but that the gains were not big enough to have much effect on the students' academic prospects. "We're hitting singles and doubles, we're not yet hitting home runs," he said.

"The $100 million question in our case is, 'Are we getting sufficient return on investment? Could Jim have taken his dollars and done something else, in housing or medicine or something else in Mississippi, and get a bigger bang for his buck?' That's a continual question."

What seems to matter the most, Barksdale said, is the talent and commitment of the principal. That suggests that foundations, if they are to be successful, must choose schools and districts that have the talent and willingness to use their resources enthusiastically and well. But the dilemma is that the schools that can best do that are probably already serving students well. Leadership, Barksdale said, is "the critical difference, something that I would write in stone. When we find a principal who is the true instructional leader of the school, who knows what's going on, who does commit to this and follows through, we see really good changes in the school, we see better instruction, and we see the reading scores go up," he said.

COMMUNITY ENGAGEMENT

Another approach foundations try is to stand back and encourage schools and districts to turn to their communities to identify ideas for improving education. In the 1970s and 1980s, Ford helped establish community funds across the nation. Annenberg more recently spent millions on the Public Engagement Network, which advocates for greater investment and citizen involvement in public education. The Lilly Endowment, the nation's second-richest foundation, with assets of about $11 billion, has long been a generous backer of higher education in the state of Indiana, expending nearly $1 billion between 1996 and 2004. The endowment also gave $414 million during that period to K–12 education in the state. Almost all of that money went to local education foundations or to Indiana counties to address local problems or needs, with few strings attached. The money was used for such services as AP classes in community centers, full-day kindergarten, help with homework, GED classes, and other needs.

The overall goal of the endowment is to increase college attendance among Indiana students, as is that of the Gates Foundation. But the endowment's strategy provides a stark contrast with that of Gates. "A lot of our grantmaking is to encourage people to get outside the schoolhouse doors and talk to businesspeople and professional people and government people in their own areas, and to take a tally of what other people think and how the schools could help the situation," said Gretchen Wolfram, a spokeswoman for the endowment.

"This is a very confusing area to know where you can make a difference and how you're going to know if you do," Wolfram said. "That's one of the reasons we said, OK schools, where do you think $50,000 or $2 million can make a difference? Knowing that this is not going to be forever."

SCHOOL CHOICE

During the late 1990s and in the early 2000s, many of the nation's foundations became major supporters of school choice. Foundations helped fund the creation of charter schools, financed private scholarships, promoted publicly funded vouchers, paid for lawyers to argue pro-choice cases, and supported research and evaluations of choice programs.

Promoting choice is one of the key strategies of the Gates Foundation, Broad backs nine separate pro-choice initiatives, the Pisces Foundation backs KIPP, and Annenberg gave more than $10 million to underwrite an architecturally daring building for the Accelerated School, a highly successful charter school south of downtown Los Angeles. Financier Theodore J. Forstmann gave $50 million of his own money to start the Children's Scholarship Fund, which subsidizes private school tuition for low-income students. In 2001, according to the Foundation Center, the fund was the ninth-largest recipient of charitable donations in the area of K–12 education, and in 2002 it was the top recipient.[15] Forstmann and John Walton, one of the heirs of the Wal-Mart fortune, helped raise another $70 million for scholarships from donors that included Broad, former Hollywood super agent Michael Ovitz, and supermarket mogul Ronald W. Burkle. In 2004, charter schools received the largest share of charitable grants given by foundations in the area of K–12 education. The Walton Family Foundation has been the single most generous backer of school choice in the United States, followed by Gates.

"Our theory is that competition in a high enough degree will eventually create competitive pressures to encourage the existing systems to really try and compete," said Buddy Philpott, the foundation's executive director. As it tries to create competition for school districts, the Walton Foundation also searches for opportunities to help school districts working hard to improve. "If we see a district in an area where we are actively funding charter schools and choice that is really willing to step up to the plate and say, 'We want to get these students back,' we'd be willing to fund that," Philpott said. One district where the foundation had made an investment of that type was in San Diego. "Unfortunately, what happens with a lot of these things, some of the status quo doesn't like all those changes and so the leadership was forced out," he said, referring to the roily political situation there.

Philpott said both strategies are necessary. "I think when there's a combination of philanthropy and business that comes together to really shake things up and challenge the status quo, I think that's the only way things are really going to happen," he said.

CAN PHILANTHROPY MAKE A DIFFERENCE?

What does all of this effort and money add up to?

In 1972, the Ford Foundation published a remarkably frank critique of its own education reform efforts during the 1960s. Called "A Foundation Goes to School" and written by Ed Meade, Ford's longtime education program officer, the report observed that the projects the foundation supported "underestimated the complexity of improving schools" and did not fully account for the difficulty of working with unions, community leaders, parents, and the effect of broader social conditions.[16] Meade wrote that "despite remarkable individual efforts, generally the projects did not firmly establish innovations in practice or produce widespread improvement in the quality of educational programs."

Many involved in education philanthropy believed Meade's observation still held true 30 years later. Janice Petrovich of Ford said foundations should look to grantees to tell them how to proceed. "We best not cook things up too rigidly. We are better funders when we react to people bringing us ideas rather than saying what needs to be done. The most successful funding comes from figuring out how to support innovative people and new ideas rather than for us to be the innovator."

Funders may want to change the world. But "the lesson," Hewlett's Smith said, "is you don't need to be all things. Don't be grandiose. Work on specific issues. Broad comes in and works on leadership and trains school boards. Gates comes in and works with districts closely on setting up small schools." Foundations, he said, should help districts "create a vision if they want to have a vision. But they shouldn't try to lay on them some system or the responsibility for doing this mega-reform. There has to be ownership and it can't rest with the foundation."

The challenge for foundations is not to create the perfect initiative that will work precisely as planned—what Ted Lobman, formerly of the Stuart Foundation, called a "home run"—in terms of its effect. The challenge is to use a variety of strategies—investment, capacity-building, the creation of competition, parallel structures that challenge the status quo—to help the schools and districts themselves do a better job.

Alan Bersin, the superintendent in San Diego for seven years, said that during his tenure he saw great progress in the way foundations work with school districts. When he began, the district was receiving about $1.7 million a year in outside money from foundations, including the National Science Foundation. Early in his tenure, the funders pressured him to cooperate more with the local teachers union, which battled Bersin from the start, on issues related to teaching and curriculum. The funders soon were gone, for a variety of reasons. But Bersin said the point was clear: "The process was what was important. We had to be collaborative. The 'children's agenda,'" he said, took a back seat. By 2001, a different group of foundations, with an approach that was more focused on outcomes for students, had gotten involved. The district was receiving $40 million from foundations that included Hewlett, Gates, Broad, Walton, Carnegie, and The Atlantic Philanthropies. Each supported the district in a different way but did not dictate that Bersin and his team change their direction. Reporting requirements were less onerous. "They were much more agenda driven," Bersin said.

The idea of a foundation identifying a narrow focus and working solely in that area probably makes it easier to measure the impact of an investment. But it may contribute to fractured reform unless foundations adopt the kind of pragmatism that Bersin described in San Diego. Money is always seductive, especially when it does not have to go for such basic needs as paying teachers and keeping the lights on. It's easy to understand why districts seek out foundation grants and accept whatever money comes their way. But there can be a cost of doing so.

Tom Payzant, the veteran superintendent who heads up the schools in Boston, said large school districts get funding from national foundations, the charitable arms of local corporations, and community funds, as well as a variety of government grants. He said during his tenure he worked hard to persuade local and national funders to align their efforts and to try to avoid contributing to what he calls "project-itis," the term he uses for a series of ad hoc projects that make funders feel good but have little impact on students.

"It's been very hard for educators to stand up and say, 'I don't want the money unless it's aligned with what we're doing,' without being snooty about it," he said.

Lowell Milken said that one way to judge the work of foundations is whether the district is willing to invest its own resources in the effort and also whether other foundations and businesses are contributing. "Is the district willing to adjust its budget, and if it proves to meet its goals will it take on the whole cost? All those issues are critical to us in looking at how we should proceed," he said.

But foundations and philanthropists, particularly those who are new to the world of education, want to see measurable results for students. Vander Ark of the Gates Foundation said he recognizes that it will take as long as seven or eight years to determine whether more students are graduating from college as a result of the Gates funding. But the high school conversions the foundation is supporting should, he said, show results almost immediately in terms of improved attendance, less violence, and better teaching. The point is that more goes into the bottom line than simply higher test scores. Foundations need to be sophisticated about what they demand in terms of results and they need to be sensitive to when progress is being made, even if test scores aren't shooting up like a rocket.

There are certainly discouraging stories that can be told about the impact of philanthropy on K–12 education. Between 1998 and 2004, the J. A. and Kathryn Albertson Foundation gave $245 million to improve education in Idaho. In 1998, the foundation spent $28 million on 11,000 computers and 700 printers and trained about 3,000 teachers how to use them. Those computers were soon obsolete. The foundation also spent $37 million on a computer-based early reading program called Waterford and on another called Accelerated Reader. Schools did not keep the computers up, and books that were part of the Waterford program were given away to students and could not be replaced. Many teachers refused to take the training they needed to take full advantage of the Accelerated Reader program until the foundation threatened to take the program away. Although a rigorous evaluation showed that Waterford and Accelerated Reader both made a difference, they now are gone from the schools because the school districts did not see fit to take over the support.

"As we look back over the past few years, I think we've done some good things," said Thomas J. Wilford, the foundation's chief executive officer. "But our biggest problem is the sustainability of what we've done. That's a really tough thing. Schools focus on teachers' salaries and classroom size and everything else gets done only if they have the money, and so most reforms are not sustainable." In the future, he said, "there's not going to be any more just dumping money on people. We're going to ask, what are you going to do for your part? You can't have the reading program unless you agree to fund your part up front. There's always other places to go with your money, so if one person doesn't like the kind of agreement you want to make, you just go somewhere else."

Tom Vander Ark said that philanthropy had a long way to go before it could achieve the grand goals of donors for improving education and the lives of graduates. "You could ask, 'why is that?' There's a lot of reasons. . . . We probably don't take as much risk as we should, given that K–12 education is not making the sort of advances it needs to make. . . . Most of us act in proprietary ways. We don't share what we're learning and we don't work collaboratively. We each have to do our own thing and put our own name on it, and I think that reduces the collective impact of the field." Finally, he said, foundations, even foundations with the resources of a Bill Gates at their disposal, have relatively little financial power in comparison to the size of total education spending. "Ultimately, it comes down to how we spend our public investment on education so that 20 years from now, if we haven't helped to infuse justice and efficiency into the public delivery system of education in this country, we will have failed badly. In the long run, what we're shooting for is a public delivery system that works for the least advantaged kids in our society."

Despite all of that, it is reasonable to be optimistic. Rather than conclude that philanthropy cannot make a difference or that the public schools are beyond salvaging, some of the nation's wealthiest citizens have decided that public education deserves not only their concern but their dollars as well, injecting new energy and dollars into the sector. At the same time, they realized that private dollars will always be dwarfed by public dollars, and so they began finding ways to work with school district leaders, legislators, and others to make sure successful innovations are spread more broadly. The amount of private money spent on K–12 education will surely rise. Foundations are working together much more than in the past. Foundations not only invested in the existing system, they also took risks and set up parallel organizations to try to leverage the potential of competition. They began funding more evaluations, paying more attention to the results. They espoused the value of transparency and seemed more forthcoming about the strengths and weaknesses of their projects. In other words, they were not simply supporting what schools have always done in the past. They were pushing the education system, writ large, in new directions that may either pay off directly or at least may inspire systems to learn from the lessons. Nor are foundations today functioning exactly as foundations did in the past. Individual philanthropies and philanthropists are closely monitoring their impact and trying to get better results. They also, crucially, are keeping the issue of equity alive at a time when American society seems to be turning its back.

CHAPTER 2

Buckets into the Sea

Why Philanthropy Isn't Changing Schools, and How It Could

Jay P. Greene

Philanthropic giving to K–12 education has the potential to spark widespread reform that could improve education for millions of students. Unfortunately, most educational philanthropy is currently carried out in a way that is very unlikely to have this kind of wide-reaching effect. Philanthropists simply don't have enough resources to reshape the education system on their own; all their giving put together amounts to only a tiny fraction of total education spending, so their dollars alone can't make a significant difference. In order to make a real difference, philanthropists must support programs that redirect how future public education dollars are spent.

Trying to reshape education with private philanthropy is like trying to reshape the ocean with buckets of water. Unloading buckets into the sea won't raise the water level, won't change the ebb and flow of the tides, and won't purify the salt water. The reason is simple: There's just too much water in the ocean and not enough water in the buckets. Philanthropic efforts to reform education simply by pouring private dollars into the ocean of K–12 spending are doomed to failure for the same reason. Even high-profile philanthropic efforts that may seem very large are simply too small to significantly raise the level of resources available to schools, change the ebb and flow of incentives that hinder progress, or purify dysfunctional systems. Philanthropic spending is just too tiny compared to the enormous size of public education expenditures for the buckets-into-the-ocean strategy to be effective.

But reforming education through philanthropy is not hopeless. It just can't be done through the force of private dollars alone. The only realistic strategy for reform by philanthropists is to leverage their private giving by attempting to redirect how future public expenditures are used. To extend our nautical metaphor, if philanthropists want to reshape the ocean, they need to put down the buckets and start building dykes, channels, and desalinization plants.

There are a number of ways in which philanthropists can reasonably hope to alter future public expenditures. They can support research and advocacy efforts that inform education policy debates; they can create new types of public schools or administrative structures through which public dollars will flow; and they can develop alternative professional associations and credentials that have the potential of altering the political activities of educators or government regulations affecting who can become an educator. These "higher-leverage" activities use relatively small private efforts to attempt to redirect very large public efforts.

But all too often, philanthropic organizations support "lower-leverage" activities that have little hope of redirecting public expenditures. Providing training to educators, offering them pedagogical or curricular innovations, or just giving schools additional resources or equipment is unlikely to change how future public expenditures are used. Giving schools things, techniques, or ideas does little more than subsidize activities that schools could have undertaken on their own anyway, especially since public resources for acquiring things, techniques, and ideas swamp those that philanthropists can offer. And if schools are not genuinely interested in the training, curriculum, or equipment that is offered to them, they are generally free to ignore those gifts and do whatever they want with public resources. Without altering the incentives or structures of public education, philanthropic efforts are like trying to reshape the ocean without dykes or channels—the water will all just run back into the sea.

Philanthropists might be content with having an effect in a particular place, on a particular set of students, and along a particular dimension. Even the relatively modest sums involved in philanthropic giving to K–12 education, when used in lower-leverage ways, can achieve limited goals. This kind of limited goal can be very worthy of philanthropy, and giving to limited causes is laudable. But if philanthropists aspire to improve public education more broadly, they cannot do so through the force of their private giving alone. Their private dollars have to be leveraged by redirecting future public expenditures. Unfortunately, only a fraction of the already relatively small amount of philanthropic contributions to K–12 education is being used in a higher-leverage way.

HOW DO WE KNOW THE SCOPE OF PHILANTHROPIC ACTIVITY?

It is impossible to know precisely how much philanthropic giving to K–12 education there is. Nonprofit organizations only face limited disclosure requirements when it comes to the purposes of their expenditures. They have to list all recipients and amounts of their grants, but they do not have to describe exactly how those dollars will be used or who the ultimate beneficiaries really are. For example, a charitable organization might give money to a second charitable organization, and it may not be clear which of the second organization's many activities were supported with those funds. Was a major gift to a university designed to support an education research project or to build a new physics lab? Without more detail than is required by public filings, it is very hard to tell which gifts are intended to support K–12 education.

Many large foundations have helped reduce the ambiguity surrounding the purposes of their grants by collaborating to create the Foundation Center, which collects and tracks information on nonprofit activities. Unfortunately, the Foundation Center largely depends on participating organizations to categorize their own expenditures. Because the categories are overlapping and ambiguous, and because foundations are not consistent in how they classify their grants with this system, the Foundation Center's data on how much philanthropy goes to "education" are imprecise. And the Foundation Center's data are not helpful for the purpose of distinguishing between higher-leverage and lower-leverage giving, since they do not classify giving within K–12 education finely enough.

There is also some ambiguity in defining what exactly constitutes philanthropic support of K–12 education. Is support of afterschool programs part of supporting elementary and secondary schools? How about mentoring programs? Or literacy programs for parents? In this study, none of these are classified as giving to K–12 education. Although a reasonable person could define the category differently, in this study only expenditures that directly concern school activities (those that take place in a school, during the regular school day) are counted as part of K–12 giving. Note that programs can "directly concern" school activities without themselves being school activities. For example, a study evaluating the effectiveness of an in-school reading program or an organization that sends people into schools to talk about drug abuse would directly concern school activities (the reading program, the drug abuse talks), even though the study and the organization themselves are not school activities.

Just because there is ambiguity and imprecision involved in tracking K–12 philanthropy does not mean that we cannot venture to make reasonable estimates about its scope and the activities that it funds. It is important that the best not be the enemy of the good. This study attempts to develop reasonable estimates of total philanthropic giving to K–12 education, and to classify that giving into several categories.

In this study I employ two broad approaches to produce those estimates. First, I examine the public filings of 30 foundations identified by the Foundation Center as the largest donors to elementary and secondary education.[1] Sifting through every expenditure listed in their 2002[2] public filings (IRS Form 990), I was able to calculate each organization's total contributions to K–12 education and to put those donations into categories for analysis.[3] Because the 990 forms are generally only available as PDFs, whose text could not be copied and pasted into other programs, coding all expenditures of the 30 largest foundations required manually assessing and entering thousands of grants.

Of course, my identification and classification of contributions is subject to errors and ambiguity, just as the Foundation Center's tally is. But at least my errors and subjective interpretations will be relatively consistent across foundations, while the Foundation Center's tally is vulnerable to inconsistent classification by the foundations themselves. A consistent examination of expenditures should produce a more reliable overall estimate of philanthropic efforts in elementary and secondary education.

The second approach I use to estimate philanthropic activity in K–12 education is to conduct a survey of the 100 largest school districts by student population, asking them for information on philanthropic activity. I received responses from 41 of those 100 districts. In total, the 41 districts contained 4.3 million students, roughly 41 percent of the 10.6 million students in the 100 largest districts and roughly 9 percent of the 48 million students in public schools nationwide. District officials were asked to provide information on their receipt of philanthropic donations in the most recent academic year for which records were available. Dividing the total reported donations received in those districts by their enrollment allows me to produce an estimated amount of philanthropy per pupil. Assuming that the responses from 41 of the 100 largest school districts are nationally representative, it is then possible to extrapolate that per-pupil amount to all students, producing an estimate of philanthropy received by the public K–12 system nationwide.

To be sure, these approaches only help us triangulate the true scope of K–12 philanthropic activity. Nonetheless, even imprecise estimates will give us a snapshot of the amount and type of charitable giving to elementary and secondary education more revealing than has previously existed. The precision of our estimates can be improved over time with additional expertise and information. But no matter how much that precision improves, we are very unlikely to learn anything that changes the two basic findings of this study: The total amount of philanthropic giving to K–12 education is tiny compared to public expenditures, and only a small fraction of those charitable dollars are being given in a way that is likely to alter future public expenditures.

HOW MANY PRIVATE DOLLARS ARE DONATED TO SUPPORT K–12?

As of 2002, public elementary and secondary schools in the United States were spending approximately $427 billion each year. The U.S. Department of Education's *Digest of Education Statistics* puts per-pupil spending at $8,922 during the 2001–02 academic year, the most recent year for which information is reported.[4] The *Digest* also reports that there were 47,917,774 students enrolled in public elementary and secondary schools during the fall of 2002, also the most recent information available.[5] Since per-pupil spending steadily increases each year, it is safe to say that those nearly 48 million students had at least $427 billion spent for their education that year.

How large is the private contribution to K–12 education? Philanthropic giving to support elementary and secondary public education is probably about $1.5 billion per year and almost certainly does not exceed $2 billion. While this is a large amount of money, it represents only about one-third of one percent of all education expenditures. It amounts to little more than a couple of buckets in the ocean of K–12 spending.

This $1.5 billion estimate is derived in part from an examination of public filings by the largest foundations involved in supporting elementary and secondary education (see Table 1). The largest 30 education donors, as identified by the Foundation Center, gave a total of almost $650 million to support K–12 education, according to my analysis of their 990 IRS forms for 2002.[6] More than one-third of that amount came from just one source: the Bill & Melinda Gates Foundation. There were only seven other foundations that gave more than $20 million in that year. Fewer than half of the largest 30 donors spent as much as $10 million during 2002 in support of K–12 education.

It is important to note that my calculations of spending by these organizations are different from the Foundation Center's calculations—sometimes dramatically so. The Center puts the Gates Foundation's contributions at about $124 million, only half of the figure I estimate. To take another example, the Center reports that the Paul G. Allen Charitable Foundation gave more than $10 million, while I find its contributions to be less than half a million dollars. These discrepancies are explained in part by the ambiguous and inconsistent classification of donations by foundations participating in the Foundation Center's system, and by the Foundation Center's reliance on foundations' announcements of grant amounts rather than on public filings of actual expenditures.

While these discrepancies regarding contributions by individual foundations are sometimes quite large, it is useful to step back and compare my calculation of total giving by these large foundations to the number that the Foundation Center reports. I calculate that these 30 foundations gave a total of $649 million to K–12 education in 2002, while the Foundation Center reports their total giving as about $669 million. Differences in our methods may produce some very different figures for individual foundations, but the overall picture is consistent.

If the Foundation Center's overall figures are accurate, then total giving to K–12 education is well below $1.5 billion. The Foundation Center reports that the largest 100 foundations gave a total of $739 million in support of elementary and secondary education in 2001.[7] Giving by smaller foundations diminishes rapidly as one goes down the list. The next 907 foundations in size after the 100 largest gave a total of about $474 million in 2001, less than two-thirds what the 100 largest gave. In all, the largest 1,007 foundations examined by the Foundation Center gave a little more than $1.2 billion to support K–12 education in 2001. While even smaller foundations and individual donations may add to that total, it is hard to imagine that philanthropic giving toward elementary and secondary education exceeded $1.3 billion, given the diminishing contributions from smaller organizations.

It is also important to note that these figures include contributions to private elementary and secondary education. In my analysis of the largest 30 foundations, about 13 percent of their expenditures were devoted to private education. If that is representative of all charitable activity, then it is likely that less than $1.2 billion was given to support *public* K–12 education from all private sources.

An estimate of about $1.2 billion in philanthropic support for public K–12 education is consistent with the results of my survey of the largest school districts. Those districts reported having received $115.2 million in donations during the most recent academic year. Since the responding districts contained about 4.3 million students, that works out to about $27 per pupil. If

TABLE 1   Comparison of Public and Philanthropic Spending on K–12 Education

	Total	Per Pupil
Public Spending	$427,522,379,628	$8,922
Spending by the 30 Largest Foundations	$649,203,841	$14
as a percentage of public spending	0.15%	0.15%
Public Spending	$427,522,379,628	$8,922
Philanthropic Donations Reported by Public Schools	$1,275,091,966	$27
Other Philanthropic Donations for K–12 Education	$272,850,161	$6
Total Philanthropic Spending	$1,547,942,127	$32
as a percentage of public spending	0.36%	0.36%

we generalize this rate of philanthropic support to the nearly 48 million students in public schools, we arrive at a total of close to $1.3 billion.

But this figure only includes donations received by public schools. Some philanthropic activity, particularly from large foundations, is designed to support K–12 public education without going directly to those schools. Examples of this kind of giving include research and advocacy, professional development, and curriculum design. From my analysis of the donations from the 30 largest foundations, I estimate that as much as $273 million of their contributions in support of K–12 education might not have been reported by public school districts. Since smaller foundations, and especially individuals, are much less likely to support public schools in ways other than giving to the schools themselves, it is unlikely that much more than this $273 million figure is being donated to indirectly support public education. Adding that indirect support to the almost $1.3 billion that went directly to public elementary and secondary schools, we arrive at a total estimate of a little more than $1.5 billion in philanthropic support for K–12 public education from all private sources.

There is good reason, however, to suspect that this estimate is a little high. The largest school districts included in the survey are more likely to attract philanthropic dollars, especially from large donors, than smaller school districts. So, extrapolating the per-pupil rate from those large districts to all public school students would likely overstate total contributions received by public schools. The bias potentially introduced by generalizing from large school districts could explain why I estimate total philanthropic support at around $1.5 billion, while the Foundation Center's figure is around $1.2 billion (once I subtract private school donations and add an estimate of small contributions). Another possible explanation is that my survey is based on more recent information, and private giving is likely increasing over time along with public expenditures.

Whatever the precise figure, it is clear that total philanthropic support for public elementary and secondary schools is somewhere around $1.5 billion per year. Given that total public spending on K–12 public education is around $427 billion per year, the private contribution to this effort is about one-third of one percent.

WHY PEOPLE MIGHT THINK PRIVATE CONTRIBUTIONS ARE LARGER

It is understandable that people involved in education philanthropy might be fooled into thinking that they would able to transform public education through the sheer force of their private dollars. Grants in the millions or tens of millions of dollars feel like a large amount of money, even to the wealthiest people. That's because they really *are* a large amount of money. And people able to give millions of dollars to education may be accustomed to seeing enormous accomplishments resulting from their investments of large sums of money.

While wealthy people and large foundations may think they know what really significant riches look like, they haven't seen anything until they grasp the kind of money associated with public education. A system that spends more than $427 billion every year dwarfs the wealth of even the richest individuals, corporations, and foundations. To put the scale of spending on public education in perspective, if you liquidated the entire net worth of all 400 individuals on *Forbes'* list of the richest Americans and donated 100 percent of the proceeds to public education, it would barely cover two years of public school spending.[8] You could donate the entire assets of the 100 largest foundations and not even pay for half a year of public education.[9] Or you could sell entire large companies, such as Microsoft or Wal-Mart, and the resulting money would barely pay for half a year of public education. The wealth that the richest Americans, the largest foundations, and the biggest corporations have taken decades or generations to accumulate is expended every year by public schools.

Businesspeople accustomed to transforming an entire industry by acquiring another company for several billion dollars may not appreciate how little influence their seemingly large donations might have over public school behavior. Similarly, foundation officials accustomed to grant applicants being

responsive to the foundation's wishes may not expect public schools accepting foundation dollars to disregard the foundation's operational guidance.
But public schools are insulated from the influence of philanthropists precisely because those schools have access to much more public money than
the philanthropists can offer.

People might also be inclined to overstate the potential influence of the
sheer force of philanthropic dollars because they may be led to believe that
charitable giving to K–12 education is significantly larger than it really is.
In part, this overstatement of philanthropic dollars to support elementary
and secondary education is attributable to foundations' normal practice of
announcing the total contribution involved in multiyear grants. A $10 mil-
lion gift over five years feels a lot bigger than a grant of $2 million per year.
People more regularly hear the larger number and thus are more likely to
think that education philanthropy is bigger than it really is.

This overstatement is exacerbated by claims to and by the media about
how large education philanthropy is. For example, the *New York Times*
recently ran a piece that suggested that public schools raise almost $9 billion
in donations each year.[10] Following the subtitle, "Those Bake Sales Add Up,
to $9 Billion or So," the piece observes that federal statistics showed that of
the $373 billion in revenue reported by public schools in 1999–2000, "nearly
$9 billion of that came from nongovernmental sources." The problem with
this claim is that the $9 billion figure cited comes from an "other" category
that includes all nongovernment revenue, not just charitable donations.
Schools own property that they sometimes rent to businesses or community organizations. Schools charge fees and tuition for a variety of services,
including afterschool, summer school, and adult educational programs. Philanthropic giving is captured in this "other" category, but it is only a fraction
of other revenue.

The *Times* may have believed their $9 billion figure was credible because
the National PTA claimed that their members' contributions alone amounted
to more than $10 billion. The PTA produced this estimate for the *New York
Times* based on "an informal survey of about 100 of its member organizations." In particular, they claim that PTAs at "the poorest 25 percent of
schools surveyed typically contributed $13 to $68 a student, while the [PTAs
at the] wealthiest 25 percent of schools surveyed typically donated $192 to
$279." These numbers are simply not credible. First, my survey of school dis-
tricts finds that districts report receiving about $27 per student in charitable
donations from all sources, not just the PTA. In addition, the federal statistics
cited in the same *Times* article put total nongovernmental revenue at $9 bil-
lion, less than the $10 billion that the National PTA claims that it alone con-

tributes. Unfortunately, there is a tendency among some charitable organizations to inflate their roles. This puffery may have the unintended effect of misleading people into thinking that private philanthropy can make a bigger difference simply by the force of its dollars than it really can.

Public schools spend more each year than the entire gross domestic product of every country in the world except for the 16 wealthiest nations.[11] But while public schools are rich, it is also important to note that public schools address very serious needs. Public schools spend so much money in part because they have a lot of things they are supposed to do for a large number of people. Similarly, most people do not think of Russia as a rich country. It does produce $433 billion in goods and services every year, about the same as what U.S. public schools spend. But with that $433 billion, Russia has 145 million people to feed, house, clothe, and educate (not to mention paying for everything else people like to do, such as go to the movies, buy cars, etc.). U.S. public schools have to use their $427 billion each year to educate and sometimes feed the 48 million students in their charge. Great responsibilities require great wealth.

The point here is not whether public schools have more than enough money to do their job well. The point is that private contributions are just too small to make much of a difference, even if public schools are lacking in money compared to their responsibilities. Philanthropic donations can only cover a very small amount of public school activity. While most people would not regard Russia as rich, they would also tend to agree that offering the country a mere $1.5 billion (or even $9 billion) in aid would be very unlikely to change Russian policy in any meaningful way. It's just too little relative to all of the resources Russia already has at its disposal, even if Russia also has enormous needs to satisfy.

HOW CAN PHILANTHROPY MAKE A DIFFERENCE?

By now it should be clear that philanthropy has little chance of reforming the public education system through the sheer force of private dollars. Philanthropists need a strategy to leverage their private giving to redirect future public expenditures. On some level, everyone seriously involved in education philanthropy knows this is true. At least rhetorically, every large foundation and major philanthropist has, or aspires to adopt, a leverage strategy for their giving.

The problem is that most education philanthropy is not actually guided by a feasible strategy to redirect future public expenditures, even when the philanthropists say that's what they want. It is all too tempting to forget how little leverage one's dollars have over the school system. It is even easier to forget this when one believes that schools badly need money, a perception that is reinforced by claims from schools and others about how much they need additional funding. If you focus on how schools lack resources, it is hard to resist the leap to the belief that your dollars will make a big difference.

But, as we have already shown, private dollars by themselves cannot make much of a difference in reforming the public education system. Private dollars can only have a substantial effect on public education if those dollars alter how future public dollars will be spent. The question then becomes, how can private philanthropy reasonably hope to have sufficient leverage to redirect future public spending?

While any answer to this question is certain to spark debate and controversy, I believe it is clear that certain types of giving are higher-leverage in that they have a better chance of changing public spending. In particular, those higher-leverage strategies can alter future public spending by supporting research and advocacy efforts that inform education policy debates; by creating new types of public schools or administrative structures through which public dollars will flow; or by developing alternative professional associations and credentials that have the potential to alter the political activities of educators or government regulations affecting who can become an educator. These are not the only ways education philanthropy can make a substantial difference, but I think they encompass more promising strategies for reforming the public education system.

In identifying more promising strategies for making a difference in public education with private dollars, I am not making any claims about the desirability of the content of any particular reform. In this study at least I am attempting to be agnostic about whether we need smaller schools, smaller classes, greater emphasis on basics, more phonics, less phonics, restructured incentives, etc. My point is that whatever reform philanthropists favor, they have little chance of spreading it widely unless they adopt higher-leverage strategies.

Lower-Leverage Grants

Most philanthropy in education, however, does not support these higher-leverage activities. Instead, the majority of charitable dollars in K–12 education go to activities that have relatively little chance of redirecting future public spending. These "lower-leverage" types of giving usually provide money for materials or ideas that the public schools could have bought with their own dollars, or for materials and ideas that the public schools could disregard if they wished. If we agree that private philanthropy cannot give schools enough money to make a substantial difference, then meaningful reform has to focus on things that money can't buy—or at least on things that schools could not have bought and cannot disregard.

According to my coding of grants made by the 30 largest foundations involved in K–12 philanthropy, the bulk of giving is directed toward these lower-leverage activities. About 61 percent of their charitable contributions related to primary and secondary schools had little chance of redirecting future public expenditures (see Tables 2 and 3). Since expenditures by the Bill & Melinda Gates Foundation constitute more than a third of all donations from these 30 largest foundations, it is also useful to look at the giving of the median large foundation to reduce the influence Gates has over the results. The median foundation among the top 30 givers devotes about 79 percent of its donations to activities that have little chance of redirecting future public expenditures. The lion's share of the already relatively modest sum given to K–12 education is unlikely to produce substantial reform of public education.

It is useful to examine the logic behind donations of professional development to schools to illustrate the limitations of lower-leverage grants. Professional development of teachers and administrators constituted the largest single category of giving I identified. About $135 million of the $649 million spent by the 30 largest education foundations, or about 21 percent, went to staff training. Some of that professional development may have promoted effective classroom practice, and some of that development may have supported less-effective methods and fads. But whatever the merits of this professional development, it is hard to see how these efforts could substantially reform K–12 education. Because schools have a lot more resources than private philanthropists, they also have a lot more money for professional development if they want to purchase it. If donors give money to schools for a particular type of professional development, then they are just subsidizing something that the schools could have bought on their own. This is especially true when one remembers how much more money schools have than donors. And if schools would not have used their superior resources to buy this staff training in the absence of foundation money, this means that they did not really want it, so donating it to them is likely to have little effect. They can receive the training and ignore it. Or they can provide additional professional development that contradicts the training that was donated.

Supporters of donating to professional development might suggest that it is important to provide schools with training because they are particularly lacking resources in this one area. Schools may have money, but most of it is already spoken for. On this argument, giving schools the right professional development fills this critical gap in their resources, letting them get better use out of everything else they do spend money on.

But even if it were true that schools have no money to spare for key professional development, donating that training to them does not solve the fundamental problem. Presumably, staff will continue to need training in the future, so the benefit fades unless philanthropists make an unlimited commitment to continue providing training. And if schools really have no money to spare for important professional development, the benefit of donating that training would be limited only to the schools that received the donation, since other schools would be unable to buy it on their own. So this kind of philanthropy only benefits a few schools, and only as long as those schools continue to receive philanthropic funding.

It might be more realistic to assume that schools do have money for what philanthropists consider important professional development, but are unwilling or unable to purchase it. Schools might not have chosen to purchase it because they do not really want it or do not consider it a priority. If that is the case, then donating training that they do not really want or do not consider a priority will make little difference over the long run. Schools are always free to ignore or reverse the training that they receive.

Or schools might be unable to purchase key professional development because there are political or institutional barriers to allocating funds in that way. Perhaps collective bargaining agreements restrict the availability of funds for key professional training or the coalition governing the schools is opposed to spending money on certain types of training. If these or other impediments exist, then donating professional development to schools does nothing to address the fundamental barriers to reform. These barriers will block schools that do not receive philanthropic donations from adopting the desired professional development, and even at schools that do receive donations, these barriers will block it from being continued after the donations cease.

Helping children, even a limited number of children, is a worthy and laudable goal of philanthropy. If the professional development provided by philanthropists significantly helps improve student outcomes in the limited number of schools that receive the training for the limited time they receive it, that's good. But if philanthropists want to reform the education system more broadly, they are very unlikely to do so by donating professional development to schools.

The same logic applies to the other lower-leverage categories of expenditures. The next biggest category of lower-leverage expenditures by the 30

TABLE 2   K–12 Education Giving by the 30 Largest Educational Donor Foundations, in Dollars

Foundation	Small Public Schools	Higher-Leverage	
		Research and Advocacy	Charter Schools
Bill & Melinda Gates Foundation	$83,788,670	$13,464,188	$2,908,398
Walton Family Foundation	$0	$10,778,528	$27,495,939
Annenberg Foundation	$0	$9,126,302	$0
Carnegie Corporation of New York	$0	$5,190,336	$28,967
Lilly Endowment	$0	$100,000	$0
New York Community Trust	$0	$3,562,793	$873,250
Ford Foundation	$0	$3,663,800	$0
W.K. Kellogg Foundation	$0	$5,097,600	$24,259
William and Flora Hewlett Foundation	$0	$5,686,450	$23,000
Oberkotter Foundation	$0	$0	$0
MBNA Foundation	$0	$398,800	$631,329
Danforth Foundation	$0	$401,516	$0
Pew Charitable Trusts	$0	$7,365,340	$0
Goizueta Foundation	$0	$0	$0
Robert R. McCormick Tribune Foundation	$0	$1,555,127	$71,000
Community Foundation of Texas	$0	$40,000	$2,250
Lucent Technologies Foundation	$0	$442,910	$333,334
Robertson Foundation	$0	$1,000,000	$100,000
Longwood Foundation	$0	$250,000	$50,000
Ewing Marion Kauffman Foundation	$0	$1,210,120	$0
Houston Endowment	$0	$188,000	$100,000
J.A. and Kathryn Albertson Foundation	$0	$0	$100,000
Charles Stewart Mott Foundation	$0	$2,203,117	$40,000
Howard Heinz Endowment	$0	$677,500	$0
William Penn Foundation	$0	$2,738,756	$0
James Irvine Foundation	$0	$1,941,500	$0
Sierra Foundation	$0	$0	$0
Bank of America Foundation	$0	$635,432	$30,740
Hiawatha Education Fund	$0	$0	$2,000
Paul G. Allen Charitable Foundation	$0	$75,000	$0
Total	$83,788,670	$77,793,115	$32,814,466

	Higher-Leverage				
Vouchers	Public Early College Schools	Other Special Public Schools	National Board Certification	Vocational & Alternative Public Schools	Alternative Professional Association
$0	$8,877,812	$1,054,838	$1,024,583	$0	$220,000
$29,113,780	$10,000	$220,000	$0	$0	$100,000
$0	$0	$0	$0	$0	$0
$0	$937,500	$0	$0	$0	$0
$0	$0	$4,997,680	$0	$0	$0
$1,529,800	$0	$1,799,515	$0	$13,300	$0
$0	$0	$0	$0	$0	$0
$0	$1,500,000	$0	$0	$0	$0
$0	$0	$0	$10,000	$0	$0
$0	$0	$0	$0	$0	$0
$60,000	$0	$79,295	$0	$384,033	$0
$0	$0	$0	$0	$0	$0
$0	$0	$0	$875,000	$350,000	$0
$0	$0	$0	$0	$0	$0
$212,000	$0	$0	$0	$250,000	$0
$5,000	$0	$0	$0	$0	$0
$0	$0	$733,177	$0	$0	$0
$1,512,000	$0	$48,350	$0	$0	$0
$0	$0	$0	$0	$0	$0
$0	$0	$50,000	$0	$0	$0
$0	$0	$5,000	$0	$0	$0
$0	$0	$0	$0	$83,000	$0
$0	$0	$100,150	$0	$0	$0
$0	$40,000	$0	$0	$0	$0
$0	$0	$0	$0	$0	$0
$1,000	$0	$0	$0	$0	$0
$0	$0	$0	$0	$0	$0
$0	$0	$0	$0	$0	$0
$0	$0	$0	$0	$0	$0
$0	$0	$0	$0	$0	$0
$32,433,580	$11,365,312	$9,088,005	$1,909,583	$1,080,333	$320,000

TABLE 2   K–12 Education Giving in Dollars (continued)

Foundation	Lower-Leverage			
	Public School Professional Development	Private School Grants	Public School Grants (General Purpose)	Public School Grants (Special Purpose)
Bill & Melinda Gates Foundation	$99,870,258	$5,980,742	$4,175,849	$7,527,134
Walton Family Foundation	$583,000	$4,808,400	$3,578,767	$5,000
Annenberg Foundation	$407,000	$4,612,500	$18,947,217	$5,721,706
Carnegie Corporation of New York	$2,705,860	$0	$15,680,451	$301,100
Lilly Endowment	$996,100	$15,080,000	$0	$0
New York Community Trust	$4,317,570	$6,052,269	$682,474	$141,720
Ford Foundation	$5,605,000	$0	$6,740,000	$3,430,000
W.K. Kellogg Foundation	$1,089,056	$165,000	$3,758,500	$236,000
William and Flora Hewlett Foundation	$861,700	$0	$10,806,667	$841,000
Oberkotter Foundation	$0	$0	$0	$0
MBNA Foundation	$24,500	$4,671,582	$856,159	$6,353,875
Danforth Foundation	$375,000	$13,500,000	$1,204,482	$0
Pew Charitable Trusts	$2,694,300	$120,000	$943,000	$2,579,077
Goizueta Foundation	$3,800,000	$5,981,746	$4,000	$0
Robert R. McCormick Tribune Foundation	$350,500	$1,714,000	$250,000	$969,500
Community Foundation of Texas	$5,000	$5,961,225	$1,250,015	$0
Lucent Technologies Foundation	$2,468,617	$0	$0	$3,450,756
Robertson Foundation	$0	$3,543,000	$0	$1,000,000
Longwood Foundation	$0	$6,300,000	$0	$0
Ewing Marion Kauffman Foundation	$2,277,332	$57,997	$2,034,234	$283,922
Houston Endowment	$3,539,500	$317,450	$50,000	$576,000
J.A. and Kathryn Albertson Foundation	$168,638	$290,000	$3,774,490	$765,531
Charles Stewart Mott Foundation	$978,559	$25,275	$572,750	$705,461
Howard Heinz Endowment	$900,000	$0	$0	$1,199,800
William Penn Foundation	$165,000	$0	$275,000	$765,700
James Irvine Foundation	$5,000	$35,000	$320,000	$220,500
Sierra Foundation	$0	$2,500,000	$0	$0
Bank of America Foundation	$551,000	$0	$558,420	$185,613
Hiawatha Education Fund	$0	$1,129,885	$12,260	$0
Paul G. Allen Charitable Foundation	$0	$140,000	$0	$50,000
Total	$134,738,489	$82,986,071	$76,474,735	$37,309,395

	Lower-Leverage						
Public School Curriculum	Disability Focus	Technology in Public Schools	Other	Total	Higher-Leverage	Lower-Leverage
$1,917,598	$0	$15,053,064	$0	$245,863,134	$111,338,489	$134,524,645
$75,465	$590,000	$0	$122,900	$77,481,779	$67,718,247	$9,763,532
$1,088,200	$0	$200,000	$0	$40,102,925	$9,126,302	$30,976,623
$663,092	$0	$0	$0	$25,507,306	$6,156,803	$19,350,503
$0	$1,909,565	$0	$0	$23,083,345	$5,097,680	$17,985,665
$789,550	$790,900	$0	$189,615	$20,742,756	$7,778,658	$12,964,098
$989,500	$0	$50,000	$0	$20,478,300	$3,663,800	$16,814,500
$8,389,475	$0	$0	$0	$20,259,890	$6,621,859	$13,638,031
$587,000	$0	$160,000	$0	$18,975,817	$5,719,450	$13,256,367
$0	$17,881,044	$0	$0	$17,881,044	$0	$17,881,044
$633,274	$1,605,338	$0	$0	$15,698,185	$1,553,457	$14,144,728
$0	$0	$0	$0	$15,480,998	$401,516	$15,079,482
$59,000	$65,000	$0	$0	$15,050,717	$8,590,340	$6,460,377
$1,987,352	$1,625,770	$0	$0	$13,398,868	$0	$13,398,868
$2,908,500	$53,000	$0	$0	$8,333,627	$2,088,127	$6,245,500
$153,900	$303,450	$0	$105,518	$7,826,358	$47,250	$7,779,108
$0	$0	$0	$0	$7,428,794	$1,509,421	$5,919,373
$116,000	$0	$0	$0	$7,319,350	$2,660,350	$4,659,000
$250,000	$50,000	$0	$0	$6,900,000	$300,000	$6,600,000
$915,458	$0	$0	$0	$6,829,062	$1,260,120	$5,568,942
$1,365,000	$594,479	$0	$0	$6,735,429	$293,000	$6,442,429
$712,185	$0	$0	$0	$5,893,844	$183,000	$5,710,844
$80,000	$0	$0	$7,300	$4,712,612	$2,343,267	$2,369,345
$1,280,870	$0	$50,000	$0	$4,148,170	$717,500	$3,430,670
$68,475	$0	$0	$0	$4,012,931	$2,738,756	$1,274,175
$421,000	$1,000	$0	$5,000	$2,950,000	$1,942,500	$1,007,500
$0	$0	$0	$0	$2,500,000	$0	$2,500,000
$69,500	$5,000	$0	$13,750	$2,049,455	$666,172	$1,383,283
$0	$0	$0	$0	$1,144,145	$2,000	$1,142,145
$135,000	$15,000	$0	$0	$415,000	$75,000	$340,000
$25,655,393	$25,189,546	$15,513,064	$444,083	$649,203,841	$250,593,064	$398,610,777

TABLE 3   K–12 Education Giving by the 30 Largest Educational Donor Foundations, in Percentages

Foundation	Small Public Schools	Higher-Leverage Research and Advocacy	Charter Schools
Bill & Melinda Gates Foundation	34%	5%	1%
Walton Family Foundation	0%	14%	35%
Annenberg Foundation	0%	23%	0%
Carnegie Corporation of New York	0%	20%	0%
Lilly Endowment	0%	0%	0%
New York Community Trust	0%	17%	4%
Ford Foundation	0%	18%	0%
W.K. Kellogg Foundation	0%	25%	0%
William and Flora Hewlett Foundation	0%	30%	0%
Oberkotter Foundation	0%	0%	0%
MBNA Foundation	0%	3%	4%
Danforth Foundation	0%	3%	0%
Pew Charitable Trusts	0%	49%	0%
Goizueta Foundation	0%	0%	0%
Robert R. McCormick Tribune Foundation	0%	19%	1%
Community Foundation of Texas	0%	1%	0%
Lucent Technologies Foundation	0%	6%	4%
Robertson Foundation	0%	14%	1%
Longwood Foundation	0%	4%	1%
Ewing Marion Kauffman Foundation	0%	18%	0%
Houston Endowment	0%	3%	1%
J.A. and Kathryn Albertson Foundation	0%	0%	2%
Charles Stewart Mott Foundation	0%	47%	1%
Howard Heinz Endowment	0%	16%	0%
William Penn Foundation	0%	68%	0%
James Irvine Foundation	0%	66%	0%
Sierra Foundation	0%	0%	0%
Bank of America Foundation	0%	31%	1%
Hiawatha Education Fund	0%	0%	0%
Paul G. Allen Charitable Foundation	0%	18%	0%
Total	13%	12%	5%

	Higher-Leverage				
Vouchers	Public Early College Schools	Other Special Public Schools	National Board Certification	Vocational & Alternative Public Schools	Alternative Professional Association
0%	4%	0%	0%	0%	0%
38%	0%	0%	0%	0%	0%
0%	0%	0%	0%	0%	0%
0%	4%	0%	0%	0%	0%
0%	0%	22%	0%	0%	0%
7%	0%	9%	0%	0%	0%
0%	0%	0%	0%	0%	0%
0%	7%	0%	0%	0%	0%
0%	0%	0%	0%	0%	0%
0%	0%	0%	0%	0%	0%
0%	0%	1%	0%	2%	0%
0%	0%	0%	0%	0%	0%
0%	0%	0%	6%	2%	0%
0%	0%	0%	0%	0%	0%
3%	0%	0%	0%	3%	0%
0%	0%	0%	0%	0%	0%
0%	0%	10%	0%	0%	0%
21%	0%	1%	0%	0%	0%
0%	0%	0%	0%	0%	0%
0%	0%	1%	0%	0%	0%
0%	0%	0%	0%	0%	0%
0%	0%	0%	0%	1%	0%
0%	0%	2%	0%	0%	0%
0%	1%	0%	0%	0%	0%
0%	0%	0%	0%	0%	0%
0%	0%	0%	0%	0%	0%
0%	0%	0%	0%	0%	0%
0%	0%	0%	0%	0%	0%
0%	0%	0%	0%	0%	0%
0%	0%	0%	0%	0%	0%
5%	2%	1%	0%	0%	0%

TABLE 3   K–12 Education Giving in Percentages (continued)

Foundation	Lower-Leverage			
	Public School Professional Development	Private School Grants	Public School Grants (General Purpose)	Public School Grants (Special Purpose)
Bill & Melinda Gates Foundation	41%	2%	2%	3%
Walton Family Foundation	1%	6%	5%	0%
Annenberg Foundation	1%	12%	47%	14%
Carnegie Corporation of New York	11%	0%	61%	1%
Lilly Endowment	4%	65%	0%	0%
New York Community Trust	21%	29%	3%	1%
Ford Foundation	27%	0%	33%	17%
W.K. Kellogg Foundation	5%	1%	19%	1%
William and Flora Hewlett Foundation	5%	0%	57%	4%
Oberkotter Foundation	0%	0%	0%	0%
MBNA Foundation	0%	30%	5%	40%
Danforth Foundation	2%	87%	8%	0%
Pew Charitable Trusts	18%	1%	6%	17%
Goizueta Foundation	28%	45%	0%	0%
Robert R. McCormick Tribune Foundation	4%	21%	3%	12%
Community Foundation of Texas	0%	76%	16%	0%
Lucent Technologies Foundation	33%	0%	0%	46%
Robertson Foundation	0%	48%	0%	14%
Longwood Foundation	0%	91%	0%	0%
Ewing Marion Kauffman Foundation	33%	1%	30%	4%
Houston Endowment	53%	5%	1%	9%
J.A. and Kathryn Albertson Foundation	3%	5%	64%	13%
Charles Stewart Mott Foundation	21%	1%	12%	15%
Howard Heinz Endowment	22%	0%	0%	29%
William Penn Foundation	4%	0%	7%	19%
James Irvine Foundation	0%	1%	11%	7%
Sierra Foundation	0%	100%	0%	0%
Bank of America Foundation	27%	0%	27%	9%
Hiawatha Education Fund	0%	99%	1%	0%
Paul G. Allen Charitable Foundation	0%	34%	0%	12%
Total	21%	13%	12%	6%

	Lower-Leverage						
Public School Curriculum	Disability Focus	Technology in Public Schools	Other	Total	Higher Leverage	Lower Leverage
1%	0%	6%	0%	100%	45%	55%
0%	1%	0%	0%	100%	87%	13%
3%	0%	0%	0%	100%	23%	77%
3%	0%	0%	0%	100%	24%	76%
0%	8%	0%	0%	100%	22%	78%
4%	4%	0%	1%	100%	38%	62%
5%	0%	0%	0%	100%	18%	82%
41%	0%	0%	0%	100%	33%	67%
3%	0%	1%	0%	100%	30%	70%
0%	100%	0%	0%	100%	0%	100%
4%	10%	0%	0%	100%	10%	90%
0%	0%	0%	0%	100%	3%	97%
0%	0%	0%	0%	100%	57%	43%
15%	12%	0%	0%	100%	0%	100%
35%	1%	0%	0%	100%	25%	75%
2%	4%	0%	1%	100%	1%	99%
0%	0%	0%	0%	100%	20%	80%
2%	0%	0%	0%	100%	36%	64%
4%	1%	0%	0%	100%	4%	96%
13%	0%	0%	0%	100%	18%	82%
20%	9%	0%	0%	100%	4%	96%
12%	0%	0%	0%	100%	3%	97%
2%	0%	0%	0%	100%	50%	50%
31%	0%	1%	0%	100%	17%	83%
2%	0%	0%	0%	100%	68%	32%
14%	0%	0%	0%	100%	66%	34%
0%	0%	0%	0%	100%	0%	100%
3%	0%	0%	1%	100%	33%	67%
0%	0%	0%	0%	100%	0%	100%
33%	4%	0%	0%	100%	18%	82%
					Mean Percentage	
4%	4%	2%	0%	100%	39%	61%

largest education foundations is donations to private schools. About $83 million of the $649 million (13%) donated by the largest foundations in 2002 went to support private elementary and secondary schools. Those donations may help students at those particular private schools, but it is not clear how they can have an effect on the public school system. Giving money to private schools does not redirect how public schools will spend their money in the future.

General-purpose grants to public schools comprise the next largest category of lower-leverage donations by large foundations, amounting to about $76 million, or 12 percent of the $649 million in total expenditures. Grants were coded as "general purpose" if the money went to support activities in public schools and the description of the purpose was vague, along the lines of "helping to improve the quality of education." Of course, it is possible that behind this vague description lay a detailed plan for leveraging private dollars into systemic reform, but these grants probably consist largely of adding money to public school coffers. As we have already seen, adding private dollars to public spending on schools is not a promising strategy for large-scale school reform.

Special-purpose grants to public schools are the next biggest category of lower-leverage donations by large foundations, amounting to $37 million, or 6 percent of all expenditures in 2002. Special-purpose grants are a close cousin of general-purpose grants. They differ in that their descriptions specify a particular project for which the money will be used, and that project is not captured by any other category. Money given to schools to build a new playground or to fund a dropout-prevention program would fall under special-purpose grants. Again, these may be very fine programs that help the students that participate in them, but they are very unlikely to lead to significant reform of the public school system. Just as with professional development, giving schools programs or goods does not address the fundamental barriers to their purchasing those things with public funds. The benefits are likely to be limited to the participating schools, and even at those schools they will fade after private support ceases.

Donations to provide public schools with curricula constituted $26 million, or 4 percent of giving by large foundations. This category includes not only traditional academic curricula like reading instruction programs, but also other kinds of in-class content, such as guest speakers and activity programs. As with other lower-leverage activities, one has to ask why schools were not purchasing this curricular content with their own funds. If they had no funds to spare, then how does giving foundation-sponsored training to a small number of schools solve that problem at other schools or in the future at all schools? If they didn't believe it was desirable or a priority, how does giving it to them make them want it or change their priorities, let alone changing the desires and priorities at other schools? If there was political or institutional resistance to buying it, how does giving it to them erase that opposition? Donors of curriculum must either be content with helping a limited number of students or be forgetting how small their efforts are relative to all public spending.

Donations to assist in the education of disabled students, including grants to both public and private schools, totaled about $25 million, or 4 percent of total giving by large foundations. Grants for educating disabled students were placed in this category even if they also fit the criteria for other categories, such as providing professional development or curricula. These grants are very unlikely to have systemwide effects, for all the same reasons as those we have discussed so far: They do not overcome any of the fundamental barriers to larger-scale adoption of reform ideas.

The same holds true for donations to purchase classroom technology for schools, which added up to about $16 million, or 2 percent of large foundation expenditures. Whatever obstacles existed to public schools buying that technology remain in place at schools that did not receive the donation and will also remain at schools that did receive the donation after the private support ends.

Higher-Leverage Grants

While much of the money from large foundations is being donated in ways that are unlikely to produce broad reform in public schools, some of their donations are being made in higher-leverage ways that have a better chance of producing systemic change. The largest category of higher-leverage giving was to the creation of small public schools, constituting $84 million, or 13 percent of spending by large foundations (see Tables 2 and 3). Donations to create small schools have higher leverage because they create new administrative structures and institutions through which future public expenditures will flow. Making public schools smaller may or may not be a desirable reform. But if it is a desirable reform, donations to support it are likely to have effects beyond those that can be produced from the private giving alone. Once a small public school is created with private money, it will be supported far into the future by public operating dollars because of the per-pupil revenue generated by each public school student who attends the small school. Using private philanthropy to create new administrative structures through which future public dollars will flow is like building a channel through which the ocean will flow. Once you finish the private effort of digging, the ocean of public dollars will move on its own in this new direction.

Several other higher-leverage categories of donations involve creating new administrative structures. These include developing charter schools, early college high schools, vocational and alternative schools, or other special public schools (such as schools for the arts). Large foundations donated about $33 million, or 5 percent of their spending, to developing charter schools. Early college high schools attracted $11 million, or 2 percent of giving. Vocational and alternative schools received about $1 million, while other special public schools received about $9 million from the largest foundations.

While all of these types of donations have the advantage of redirecting future public spending, it is important to note that their effects may be limited to the schools that receive the donations. If there are barriers to creating small schools, early college schools, charter schools, vocational and alternative schools, or other kinds of special schools, then giving money to overcome those barriers in some locations will not necessarily solve the problem in other locations. Donations do not have to overcome all obstacles to systemwide reform in order to be classified as higher leverage. They just have to have a reasonable chance of leveraging their private money by redirecting some substantial amount of future public expenditures in a way that can produce more systemic change than could be produced by private dollars alone.

The other major higher-leverage tactic is to support research and advocacy. About $78 million, or 12 percent of giving by large foundations, goes to support research evaluating education programs and policies, or to advocacy efforts that seek to change educational policy either through direct lobbying or indirectly by changing public opinion. These efforts are higher leverage because they attempt to inform policymakers and practitioners about effective reforms so that those reforms can be adopted and funded with public dollars. While persuading policymakers and practitioners is a difficult endeavor, it is also likely to have the broadest impact. The benefit of persuading policymakers to adopt a particular reform is that the change can occur across many schools and for a very long time, all funded with public dollars.

Whatever reforms philanthropists believe are desirable can be promoted in a higher-leverage way by supporting research and advocacy. Even the education practices currently supported through lower-leverage giving could often be better promoted through research and advocacy. If philanthropists believe that a particular type of professional development or curriculum would significantly improve schools, they have a greater likelihood of achieving that reform across a larger number of schools and for a longer time if they support research on, and advocacy of, those innovations. Research on those reforms could help demonstrate that they actually are beneficial, and advocacy could help inform policymakers and practitioners of those potential benefits.

But pilot programs without research and advocacy have very little chance of affecting future public policies and spending. No matter how great the professional training, curriculum, or other program is, almost no one will learn about how great it is unless it is carefully studied and vigorously promoted. Philanthropists tend to invest far too much in pilot programs and far too little in research and advocacy on those programs. The research is important to find out whether the great idea behind the pilot program really is great, and the advocacy is important to make sure that policymakers are actually influenced by the research. Great ideas do not prove themselves and do not promote themselves; that requires research and advocacy.

Another large category in the higher-leverage group is support for privately sponsored voucher programs, which amounts to $32 million, or 5 percent of all giving by large foundations. In some ways these privately funded voucher programs resemble lower-leverage support for private schools in that they directly assist students who attend private schools; the benefits are limited to those students and last only as long as the scholarships continue. But in important respects, private voucher programs have higher-leverage features that similar grants in other categories don't. Donors not only fund the programs to expand the choices of low-income students, but also to facilitate research evaluating and publicizing the potential benefits of expanding school choice. These programs were also designed to publicize and cultivate demand for choice among low-income parents, which has an important advocacy dimension. Grants to provide financial aid to students at one particular private school were not included in this category because such grants have no higher-leverage dimension. These grants were included in the lower-leverage category of donations to private schools.

Donations given to national board certification and alternative professional associations are also included in the higher-leverage group. However, together they only amount to about $2 million in grants, or less than 1 percent of spending by large foundations. These types of grants are counted as higher leverage because they offer the potential of altering the political role of educators. National board certification may open the door to a new professional class of educators who might then be more effective in advocating for certain types of reforms, such as merit pay or higher standards for all teachers. Alternative professional associations may change the political role of teachers unions, which may be a barrier to certain types of reforms.

While only a minority of grant dollars from large foundations are given to higher-leverage activities, it is likely that among smaller donors, the proportion of giving for higher-leverage activities is even lower. Almost all donations by individuals, from the bake sale at the local public school to constructing a new building at the local private school, is lower-leverage giving. Individuals are not redirecting future public spending with these donations. Most small foundations are also unlikely to be giving in higher-leverage ways. Without significant professional staffing, smaller foundations may have a harder time planning and implementing a higher-leverage strategy. Instead, smaller foundations probably tend to provide direct support for institutions and causes that are personally connected to board members and founders. On the other hand, there are some notable small foundations that have adopted higher-leverage strategies for their charity precisely because they appreciate how limited their funds are and wish to get a lot more bang for their buck.

Given that the median large foundation gives about 21 percent of its spending to higher-leverage activities, it is probably reasonable to estimate that no more than 20 percent of all education charity could be classified as higher leverage. If there is a total of about $1.5 billion in education philanthropy, total higher-leverage giving is probably no more than $300 million each year. Since large foundations gave approximately $251 million in higher-leverage grants in 2002, additional higher-leverage giving from smaller donors probably amounts to no more than $50 million.

CONCLUSION

We have seen that most current education philanthropy is just dumping buckets of water into the ocean of public school spending, consisting of approximately $1.5 billion in private dollars compared to public expenditures of around $427 billion. Only a fraction of private educational charity is being given in a way that is likely to have much of an effect on the public school system as a whole. Only about $300 million is donated to higher-leverage activities that are designed to redirect future public expenditures.

While that $1.2 billion in lower-leverage philanthropy could bring significant benefits to some students, we have to recognize that those benefits are likely to apply to a limited number of students in a limited number of places and only last for a limited amount of time. Even these limited benefits are important and worthy of charitable efforts. We should remember the Talmudic proverb about how saving one life is like saving the whole world. But many philanthropists hope that their giving will have a significant effect on the public education system as a whole, not just on individual lives.

Why, then, does such a small share of philanthropic giving go to support higher-leverage activities that have a better chance of achieving systemwide reform? This is true in part because it is hard to appreciate how small private efforts are relative to public spending. When people give what feels to them like a lot of money, and when they have the best of intentions for improving education, they just can't easily imagine how their efforts wouldn't lead to significant reform of public education.

But the surprisingly small share of philanthropic dollars devoted to higher-leverage activities may have a deeper explanation. An unstated but seductive theory draws people toward lower-leverage philanthropy. The theory is that public education would significantly improve if only it were provided with examples of good reforms. Policymakers and practitioners face no real barriers, the thinking goes, they just lack good ideas for reforms. Provide those good examples, and policymakers and practitioners will find them and adopt them on their own. It is as if public schools were gardens with perfect soil, sunlight, and moisture just waiting for philanthropists to toss their seeds to sprout systemwide reform.

But the garden this theory imagines would have to be the Garden of Eden to produce this kind of desired change. We would have to ignore all of the self-interest, organizational inefficiency, and political conflict that stand in the way of widespread adoption of any reform, good or bad. Because of self-interest, policymakers and practitioners might not spend their energy searching for effective reforms, preferring instead to reduce their work by waiting for others to bring effective reforms to their attention through research and advocacy. Even then, self-interest might blind policymakers or practitioners to an effective reform if it contradicted their interests. Because of organizational inefficiency, schools are not perfect at identifying and adopting effective reforms. And because of partisan conflict, our democratically governed public schools might shun effective reforms for partisan advantage.

While this garden theory holds sway over education philanthropy, few would apply it to reforming Russia. With $1.5 billion to reform a country that produces around $430 billion in goods and services, we would be keenly aware of the self-interest, organizational inefficiencies, and political barriers to the imitation of effective pilot reform projects. When trying to influence Russia, we would devote most of our private resources to addressing those barriers to meaningful reform. But when it comes to primary and secondary education, we somehow want to return to the Garden and wish away these obstacles rather than address them.

It is important to note that these barriers also impede higher-leverage strategies for reform. But at least higher-leverage strategies acknowledge barriers to reform and directly address them. If self-interested laziness hinders policymakers and practitioners from learning of effective reforms, higher-leverage approaches like supporting research and advocacy help overcome this barrier by bringing the information to people's attention. If organizational inefficiency hinders the creation of small schools, then the higher-leverage approach of building new administrative structures helps overcome that barrier. If partisan resistance to effective reforms is fueled by narrow interest groups representing teachers, supporting the creation of new professional associations could change the partisan calculus.

We should be under no illusion that higher-leverage strategies are certain to overcome these barriers and produce meaningful reform, but they have a better chance of succeeding than wishing away the obstacles. We should also be aware that some reform ideas will prove not to be effective, and these ideas ought not to be imitated throughout the primary and secondary education system. After all, different philanthropists back mutually inconsistent reform ideas, so at least some of them must be wrong. But if one hopes to produce systemwide change, there is little alternative to backing what one believes to be effective reforms and then engaging in higher-leverage grant-making to advance those reforms.

CHAPTER 3

The "Best Uses" of Philanthropy for Reform

Leslie Lenkowsky

During the past decade, no area—other than religion—has received more support from American philanthropy than education. In 2004, for example, nearly one of every seven dollars given to charity—$33.84 billion—went to an educational institution, compared to the roughly one in twelve that wound up in either health or human services agencies. Foundations were even more likely to direct their money toward schooling than individual donors were, with the thousand grantmakers included in the Foundation Center's sample sending nearly one-quarter of their grants to it.[1]

Generous as these sums are, they are just a small portion of what Americans annually spend on education, as Jay Greene points out in his chapter. Schools still obtain most of their revenues from tax dollars and tuition payments from (or on behalf of) students. Moreover, although the share going to elementary and secondary education has been growing during the past decade, perhaps as much as three-quarters of the gifts to education go to colleges and universities.

Even so, philanthropic support has played an important role in the development of precollegiate education in the United States. From colonial times to the present, donors have sought to shape schools in light of their concerns about the character of American society, the demands of its economy, and the upbringing of its children. While the least successful efforts have long since been forgotten, the traces of those that did have influence—for better or worse—can still be seen in the nation's schools today.

Moreover, private philanthropy's role in elementary and secondary education seems to be growing. In little more than a decade, several thousand charter and private schools have been created, most receiving partial or even substantial assistance from individual donors, corporations, and foundations. Public schools in many districts have also established supporting organizations to raise philanthropic funds to pay for a variety of educational programs and facilities. New and sizable privately financed scholarship programs have been set up as well to enable needy students to enroll in nonpublic schools. Reflecting these developments, a survey of large foundations by the Foundation Center showed that giving to elementary and secondary education in 2003 for the first time exceeded the amount given to higher education.[2]

This chapter looks at the record of giving to precollegiate education, not just to uncover the roots of practices that are now widely accepted, but also to identify the strategies donors and reformers have used to affect schooling—and what they suggest about the "best uses" of philanthropy.[3] Although much has changed about American education since colonial times, the question facing philanthropists and those seeking their support is still the same: how to employ private resources to further their vision of the public interest, which presumably in this area of activity means better-educated students. The answers, though, have varied considerably, depending on the source of gifts, the role of government, and, especially, donors' and educators' ideas about what is right or wrong with existing schools.

Some donors have concentrated their efforts on establishing new schools or transforming how the existing ones operated. Others have focused on raising the skills of instructors or fostering new methods of teaching. Still others have sought to promote improved curricula or measures of accomplishment, such as standardized tests.

More than a few philanthropists have concentrated on fixing the communities in which schools exist, believing that the relationship between the two is critical for learning. And others have addressed their efforts directly to the needs of students, such as by trying to improve their readiness for school or providing scholarships for private schools.

The lines between these strategies have not always been distinct, nor has interest in each been limited to a particular historical era. Differences among donors—between small, local foundations and large, national ones, for example—have also influenced what they tried. Also of importance is that what "improving education" means has varied among donors and reformers at different times in history.

However, to generalize, earlier philanthropists—then chiefly individual patrons and religious bodies—mostly concentrated on establishing schools, providing scholarships, and training teachers. But as government became the principal source of support for education, private givers shifted their efforts. From the latter part of the 19th century onward, with their resources increasing and new philanthropic institutions, such as foundations, being formed, donors became bolder in their goals, pursuing ambitious changes in how schools functioned, what they taught, and who controlled them. A number of important legacies resulted, but trying to affect the organizationally and politically complex world of education often proved to be no simple matter. Partly as a result, while not abandoning efforts for more comprehensive changes, more donors are now again embracing the older strategy of concentrating on particular schools or school districts (and students) as the "best uses" for philanthropy in precollegiate education.

The following survey of milestones in private support for schooling illustrates this progression. In view of the scope and variety of both American education and philanthropy, it cannot aspire to be a complete account. Those looking for exceptions or omissions will undoubtedly find them. Moreover, it necessarily relies heavily on the research and judgments of historians and others who have chronicled the development of schooling in the United States, or who have examined the programs of major foundations, such as Carnegie and Ford. But for those philanthropists or reformers who want to learn from what earlier generations of donors have done, this overview should at least provide a useful starting point and some relevant lessons.

CREATING BETTER SCHOOLS

Not surprisingly, supporting new schools was an early preoccupation of American philanthropists. This was not just because the new colonies needed places to educate the young and lacked the governmental structure to pay for them. John Winthrop, Cotton Mather, Benjamin Franklin, and William Penn, "the real founders of American philanthropy" (in Robert Bremner's judgment),[4] saw schools as critical for establishing a new society and for transmitting a common culture, one rooted in the Western intellectual and religious heritage. Therefore, supporting schools was important not only educationally but also morally and socially, as it remains for many donors today, notwithstanding the fact that most schools are now publicly financed.

Depending largely on the part of the country in which they were located, a mixture of gifts and tax revenues sustained the earliest schools. In Philadelphia, for example, the Friends Public School (later called the William Penn Charter School) was established in 1689. Although it was described as a public school in its founding document, it was, in fact, a private one supported by the Quakers.[5]

Corporate philanthropy also played a role. In New Amsterdam (today New York City), the West India Company began operating schools in the 1640s to attract settlers. "School books, paper, slates, and other supplies were furnished by the Company. New Amsterdam's magistrates provided the school site, which was usually in the schoolmaster's home or a public house in the community."[6] Setting a pattern that continues to this day, those whose children attended the schools—the local colonists—frequently disagreed, Lawrence Cremin observes, with those who ran them—the directors of the company in Amsterdam.[7]

Bequests were used to establish schools as well. Cremin cites the example of a 1635 bequest by Benjamin Syms of 200 acres of land and the produce from eight cows to support the Syms Free School in Elizabeth City Parish, Virginia.[8] Another sizable bequest came several years later from Dr. Thomas Eaton to underwrite the Thomas Eaton School, also in Elizabeth City Parish.

In New England, philanthropy was somewhat less important. Within the first decade of settlement there, writes Cremin, at least seven of the 22 towns of Massachusetts had experimented with public action for the provision of schooling, ranging from court orders to establish schools to setting aside money for educational uses.[9] Although based on the British public grammar school model, the model for schooling adopted in New England was one often initiated and supported by local officials, rather than religious ones (as was common in England).

Still, philanthropy continued to figure prominently in New England school-building efforts. In his influential 1710 work, *Bonifacius: Essays to Do Good*, clergyman Cotton Mather urged his fellow Puritans to support schools and colleges on the grounds that "the endowing of these, or maintaining of them, is, at once, to do good unto many."[10] Judging from the large bequests made to establish several of the New England grammar schools, more than a few of his wealthy followers heeded his advice.

Colonial religious societies also tried building schools outside their own communities. In 1701, the Society for the Propagation of the Gospel in Foreign Parts established the first schools for slaves in the South. Cremin writes that this Episcopalian group, supported by the Church of England, possessed "purpose and structure that were unprecedented, combining as they did imperial evangelism with philanthropic benevolence and the power of a royal charter with the force of private initiative."[11] Donations to the society and fees charged to students who could afford to pay sustained the schools.[12]

Philanthropic interest in creating schools for black students intensified after the Civil War. Although religious groups set up many, their efforts were eventually overshadowed by secular foundations, starting with the establishment of the Peabody Education Fund in 1867 by a Massachusetts-born merchant living in London. It was soon joined by the most notable of all, the General Education Board (GEB), founded in 1902 by John D. Rockefeller with an initial endowment of $33 million. The GEB reflected a new style of philanthropy, not only because of its immense resources and clear focus, but also because it enlisted "energetic officers—men who were both creative and well connected with business and political leaders in North and South" to carry out its work.[13] So influential and visible did it become that the GEB spawned a host of imitators, including the Jeanes Fund (1907), the Phelps-Stokes Fund (1911), and the Julius Rosenwald Fund (1917), which eventually comprised an "'interlocking directorate' of calculating altruism."[14]

These philanthropies not only sought to create schools but, increasingly, to work with state and local governments to improve education for black and white students in the South. The GEB, for example, underwrote teacher training, rural school agents, the development of state education departments, and a variety of studies, demonstrations, and conferences. Moreover, through endowment and building funds, as well as fellowships, it promoted the growth of postsecondary education that was heavily oriented toward vocational programs along the lines of the Hampton-Tuskegee model, which had been popularized by Booker T. Washington. At a time of minimal government spending on public services in the region (and especially on those benefiting blacks), the work of the GEB and its closely allied foundations tried—with more than a little success—to fill the gaps in Southern education, while also advancing the cause of racial equality.[15]

A largely unanticipated by-product of this funding turned out to have more influence on education than the grants themselves. In the late 1930s, Carnegie Corporation of New York sought to evaluate the efforts foundations had been making to improve Southern education and identify additional steps that could be taken to improve American race relations. Seeking a fresh perspective, it enlisted the European economist Gunnar Myrdal to lead the project. After several years of research, during which Carnegie officials worried that the study had grown too expansive, Myrdal produced *An American Dilemma: The Negro Problem and Modern Democracy*, a book that helped conceptualize the civil rights movement and was cited in *Brown v. Board of Edu-*

cation, the 1954 U.S. Supreme Court decision outlawing segregated schools. But, as Ellen Condliffe Lagemann has written, the report "seems by and large to have been ignored" by Carnegie Corporation, since it seemed to offer little of practical value for its grantmaking.[16]

In the North, where public support of education had become more extensive, school-building efforts took a different form: the development of separate institutions for Catholic children. Faced with a rising population of Irish immigrants in the middle and latter parts of the 19th century, officials in New York and elsewhere embarked on a campaign to create a "non-sectarian" atmosphere for education. But, as Diane Ravitch has pointed out, the schools turned out to be nonsectarian in name only. In reality, they embodied Protestant values that the new immigrants regarded as offensive, or worse.[17]

Led by religious leaders, such as New York's Bishop John Hughes, Catholics began to establish their own schools in response. At first, they hoped to finance these schools at least partly with tax dollars. In the 1840s, for example, the New York legislature considered a plan that would have decentralized the control of New York City's public schools and permitted a community to operate sectarian schools if it wanted to do so. However, when the bill was finally enacted in 1842, while it put the public schools under the control of ward commissioners, it denied funding to religious schools.[18]

Following these and other failed efforts to secure public funding for religious education, the Third Plenary Council of American bishops, meeting in Baltimore in 1884, decreed that all parishes should establish schools for their congregants. As a result, the number of parochial schools expanded rapidly (tripling, for example, in New England by the beginning of the 20th century).[19] Financed mostly by gifts (including the donated time of teaching priests and nuns), as well as by tuition payments from parents, they reached a peak enrollment of over 4.5 million children in the 1960s, a significant fraction of whom were not even Catholic. They have also served as a model for other religious groups seeking to provide moral and spiritual as well as academic and practical knowledge to the children of their members.

In 1925, the creation of these schools also led to a landmark Supreme Court decision, *Pierce v. Society of Sisters*, which found an Oregon law requiring compulsory attendance at public schools unconstitutional because it violated the Fourteenth Amendment.[20] The ruling in this case not only affirmed the right of Catholic parents to choose how to educate their offspring, but more generally provided a firm legal basis for philanthropic efforts to create new schools, notwithstanding the virtually universal availability of publicly financed ones.

Not all school-building efforts were driven by concerns for the needs of particular groups. In the Progressive Era, a number of philanthropists helped establish schools to test new approaches to education. Perhaps the most famous was the Laboratory School at the University of Chicago, started in 1896 by John Dewey and his wife Alice with support from the university, parents, foundations, and wealthy individuals. Dewey's ideas about using experience as part of education, concentrating on group work and cooperation, caught the attention of other educators, but as Ravitch points out, his experiment was only replicable in a small private school. It did not provide a model that could realistically be implemented in the public school system.[21]

A more influential experiment was the General Education Board's creation of the Lincoln School at Teachers College, Columbia University, in 1917. Thanks to the GEB's deep pockets (over $6 million in gifts, according to one estimate),[22] Lincoln was able to have a far-reaching effect on educational practice through publication and circulation of writings by its "teacher-practitioners." The school also helped develop the curriculum at Teachers College, thereby influencing the training of future teachers.[23]

Usually with support from individual benefactors, other educators influenced by Dewey and his child-centered approach established their own schools throughout the United States. Among the more notable were the Francis Parker School, founded in 1901 with financial assistance from Anita McCormick; the School of Organic Education established in Fairhope, Alabama, in 1907, by an organization of women in Greenwich, Connecticut; the Dalton School, launched by Helen Pankhurst in 1919 in New York with the financial backing principally of Mrs. W. Murray Crane; and the City and Country School, set up in Buffalo, New York by Caroline Pratt in 1912 with Lucy Sprague Mitchell as the primary benefactor. With the help of her cousin, Elizabeth Coolidge, Mitchell also began the Bureau of Educational Experiments in 1916, which pioneered the idea of the nursery school and eventually became the Bank Street College of Education.

Since the Progressive Era, philanthropic efforts to work within existing public schools have generally supplanted efforts to create new ones. However, the 1960s saw a brief resurgence of school-building activity, albeit for quite disparate reasons: avoidance of desegregation orders after the *Brown* decision, the demands placed on the public school facilities by the baby boomers, and the counter-cultural rebelliousness of the era. According to Ravitch, school critics who felt that the public schools were beyond fixing set out to form "parent-controlled, privately financed 'free schools.'"[24] These "alternative schools" were funded by individuals, foundations, and even businesses.

But lacking clear lines of authority and frequently split by disagreements over goals or methods, they typically had extremely abbreviated life spans, though their existence and the media attention given them occasionally led public schools to adopt some of their practices.

In addition, some philanthropists have tried creating new schools "from the inside out," as it were. These efforts have become known as systemic reforms: changes aimed at so thoroughly altering how schools operate that they amounted effectively to redesigning them. Among the earliest examples was Ronald Edmonds's "effective schools" movement, which sought to identify the features of high-performing schools in inner-city neighborhoods and establish a process for widespread adoption of them. With a mixture of public and private support, the National Center for Effective Schools Research and Development was established in 1987 to coordinate these efforts.

Though differing in the scope and substance of what they tried to do, other organizations engaged in systemic reform included the Coalition for Essential Schools (led by Theodore Sizer) and the New American Schools Development Corporation (the brainchild of former Xerox CEO David Kearns). Foundations (such as Ford, Carnegie, Lilly, and MacArthur) and businesses (notably RJR Nabisco, Procter & Gamble, and IBM) invested heavily in these initiatives. So too did publishing magnate Walter Annenberg, whose $500 million grant to promote systemwide improvements in urban schools was, at the time it was made in 1993, the largest gift ever for a single purpose.

Not all donors were content to work from within. As the 1990s began, with gains in educational achievement seemingly hard to come by, both institutional and individual philanthropists began providing support for new schools. The Ford Motor Company, for example, financed the creation of the Henry Ford Academy of Arts and Sciences, which opened in the fall of 1997 in Dearborn, Michigan. Pfizer made an old factory in Brooklyn available for a privately run elementary school, bankrolled by a successful investor. Honeywell set up a special school for teenage mothers. The spread of charter school laws has offered additional opportunities for philanthropists, such as the Walton and Fisher families, to put their money into start-ups, rather than dealing solely with existing schools. The nation's largest foundation, the Bill & Melinda Gates Foundation, has already committed over $1 billion to create new high schools in communities throughout the United States.

Although Catholic schools labored to keep up financially, a new generation of religious schools also began to appear. Often nondenominational Christian in outlook, they reflected dissatisfaction among parents, with not just the academic quality but also the moral environment of the public schools.[25] Smaller foundations, businesses, and individual donors provided the initial backing, with tuition fees (and volunteer time) from parents comprising the sustaining support.

Compared to donations for projects in (or directed at) public education, this upsurge in funding for new private or charter schools was of relatively small financial significance. (Indeed, according to a survey by the Council for Aid to Education, donors gave slightly less than $1 billion to a core group of independent schools in 1999, less than 5 percent of all gifts to education and probably no more than one-fifth of contributions for precollegiate schooling. Over half came from alumni and parents, most of which undoubtedly went to long-established institutions.)[26] But in view of the extensive efforts philanthropists had been making for close to a century to use private funds to improve public schools, the fact that a noticeable number of givers were purposefully directing their money elsewhere was a surprising development, if not a harbinger of widespread change in funding priorities.

CREATING BETTER TEACHERS

Philanthropic support for training teachers has always been closely associated with gifts for creating schools. Indeed, more than a few of the nation's oldest universities owe their origins to benefactors who wanted to ensure that those providing instruction (or ministering to congregations) possessed not just practical knowledge, but also the right moral and spiritual grounding. But as government took on greater responsibility for training and certifying teachers, philanthropists became increasingly frustrated with the education of educators and looked for alternative ways of developing better teachers (and administrators).

Early in American history, anyone with a college degree could, and often did, become a teacher. However, largely through the efforts of 19th-century philanthropists, the idea of establishing specialized schools—"normal schools"[27]—for training teachers began to take hold. In 1826, for example, Stephen van Rensselaer opened an institute in Troy, New York, for preparing science teachers, offering free tuition to those who agreed to teach for at least one year.[28] A decade later, a wealthy member of the Massachusetts Board of Education offered to donate $10,000 to create a school for teachers if the legislature would match the funds.[29] This pattern was followed elsewhere with the result that, through the 1890s, more than half of the teacher-training institutions were essentially private.[30]

Closely related was the effort, also inspired by 19th-century philanthropic groups, to identify teaching as a profession. In 1830, for example, the American Institute of Instruction, a membership organization, was formed in Boston and began to liken education to a science, requiring careful preparation of the individual teacher.[31] As the number of teachers grew, calls for the development of professional standards arose, and by the 1850s, many states were enacting certification laws.[32]

Philanthropists responded by underwriting programs that brought teacher education into the university curriculum. One of the most successful efforts began in 1880, with support from Grace Dodge, the daughter of William E. Dodge, one of New York's wealthiest merchants and an activist in the Children's Aid Society and other community groups. Originally established as the Kitchen Garden Association to teach household management to slum dwellers, the program soon changed into the Industrial Education Association, and in 1887, with Nicholas Murray Butler at the helm, it grew into the New York College for the Training of Teachers, the forerunner of Teachers College at Columbia University. By 1900, Cremin reports, one-quarter of higher education institutions were offering formal professional work in education for their students.[33]

At first, the burden of obtaining the skills necessary for certification was placed on the teachers themselves. In the years following the Civil War, private donors, such as the Peabody Fund, which was active in the South, also helped out by providing scholarships for educators to attend normal schools.[34] But eventually, publicly supported normal schools became the main vehicle for teacher education.

These schools focused on classroom techniques rather than on the subjects instructors were expected to teach. In 1920, the Carnegie Foundation for the Advancement of Teaching endorsed this approach. In a report entitled "The Professional Preparation of Teachers for American Public Schools," which grew out of a study of normal schools in Missouri, Carnegie called for a "professionalized" curriculum for teachers (as opposed to a thorough grounding in the liberal arts).[35] Nearly two decades later, the General Education Board granted $1.1 million to the American Council on Education to create a Commission on Teacher Education. After studying the quality of teacher preparation and in-service training, the commission recommended expanding the normal school curriculum to four years rather than the customary two—further widening the gap between the education of teachers and others enrolled in higher education.[36]

The vocational approach to preparing teachers came under fire as part of a post–World War II reevaluation of American education. Studies, often supported by foundations or nonprofit groups, argued that the teachers' colleges had gained too much control over school curricula and were "miseducating" future instructors, thereby increasing the chances that children would receive an inadequate education in primary and secondary school.[37]

Perhaps the most influential of these critics was Arthur Bestor, a University of Illinois historian who authored *Educational Wastelands* in 1953. Disparaging the work of his university colleagues in formulating the curriculum for "life adjustment-education," he called instead for teachers to get a firm grounding in the liberal arts and sciences.[38] Bestor also proposed eliminating special schools for teachers and raising teacher-certification requirements.

Bestor was not content simply to publish his views, but also tried to enlist nonprofit groups to put them into effect. In 1952, for example, he proposed that the American Historical Association foster "sound intellectual training in the public schools," but his plan for a "Permanent Commission on Secondary Education" was rejected by its governing council.[39] Four years later, however, with support from foundations and wealthy individuals, he and Mortimer Smith created the Council for Basic Education, an organization to promote reform of teacher education and raise curricular standards.

Also joining the chorus of critics was the Ford Foundation, which not long after the end of the World War II had become the nation's largest and most influential grantmaker. Through its Fund for the Advancement of Education, it committed, in the 1950s, a large amount of its resources to changing teacher-training and teacher-certification requirements. Among its initial programs was the creation of a Committee on Faculty Fellowships, which provided study grants to teachers to enable them to improve their knowledge of the liberal arts. The fund also supported a program, begun by James Conant when he was president of Harvard, that allowed liberal arts students interested in teaching careers to obtain a master of arts in teaching degree and qualify as classroom instructors.

In 1951, under the direction of Abraham Flexner, another fund program in Arkansas questioned the requirements for certification and suggested instead that a broad liberal arts education combined with a teaching internship should be enough. However, as with other fund efforts, this idea was resisted by professional teachers organizations and had no lasting impact.

Even so, professional development for teachers continued to attract philanthropic support. In the 1980s, *A Nation at Risk* emphasized the need for more training (and increased salaries) for teachers to make their positions "competitive, market-sensitive, and performance-based."[40] Shortly afterward, Carnegie Corporation sponsored a Task Force on Teaching as a Profession that produced the report *A Nation Prepared: Teachers for the 21st Century*, and eventually led to the establishment of the National Board of Professional

Standards, one of several efforts to develop new ways of accrediting class-room instructors.[41]

Foundations and corporations have also been instrumental in setting up in-service training programs, especially in science and math, as well as establishing awards for innovative teaching, such as the Milken Educator Awards, sponsored by the Milken Family Foundation. In addition, philanthropists have contributed to the development of programs that provide alternative pathways to careers in education, such as Teach For America, which recruits, trains, and places liberal arts graduates without standard teaching credentials in schools—typically rural or inner city—that have difficulty obtaining instructors.

Valuable as such programs may be, their overall impact on American education is probably small. By far the bulk of teachers receive their training in teachers colleges, those institutions descended from the efforts of earlier philanthropists, rather than in liberal arts or sciences courses. And largely because of the success of the idea of teaching as a "profession" (and its embodiment in certification rules and union contracts), using instructors who do not meet standard qualifications—or who want to teach in especially creative ways—is difficult, even for nonpublic schools. (A critical issue in debates over charter school legislation, for example, is the amount of leeway the new schools should be allowed in selecting faculty members.) Yet, with enrollments in elementary and secondary education growing, teacher shortages looming, and a new generation of philanthropists appearing that claims to be skeptical of professional pretensions, the quest for finding new ways of creating better teachers and administrators seems certain to continue.

CREATING BETTER CURRICULA

Along with building schools and training teachers, early philanthropists also gave support to developing new teaching methods and courses of study. As government funding came to dominate the day-to-day finances of American education, this kind of underwriting became even more popular among donors. Funding curricular changes seemed to offer a way of having a sizable impact for a relatively modest investment of money, since a successful innovation might be adopted by schools throughout the country. However, while some philanthropic efforts have indeed had that kind of influence, whether or not they have had much success in improving education is questionable.

In 1809, for example, with enrollments growing, the New York Free School Society, a charitable group that also received state funds, popularized a method of instruction known as the Lancaster system.[42] It incorporated teaching methods that aimed to do for the classroom what new machinery was doing for textiles. The Lancaster system, Ravitch has written, "was not only analogous to an industrial machine, it was a machine, the school machine. Each part of the machine has a role to perform, which was spelled out in minute detail in manuals."[43] Using it, the Free School Society was able to inexpensively increase the number of children in its schools from 1,000 in 1817 to 12,000 by 1834, but the result was large classes and rigid instruction.[44]

Another curricular innovation introduced shortly afterward, the kindergarten, was meant to be a response to the growing number of children from immigrant backgrounds. Based on German educator Friedrich Froebel's experiments in early education that emphasized the "cultivation" of young children in a much less-structured manner than had been standard in the United States, it aimed to bring out "the divine spirit" in them and promote social harmony. (This was also the goal of the version developed by William McClure in Robert Owen's New Harmony experiment of the 1820s, which was meant to overcome social-class differences rooted in child-rearing practices.) Two private education reformers, Carl Schurz and Elizabeth Peabody (who was Horace Mann's sister-in-law), introduced Froebel's idea to the United States in the 1860s and 1870s. But throughout the 19th century, kindergartens remained private and primarily served wealthy families.[45]

Perhaps the most important, long-lasting, and controversial curricular reform influenced by philanthropists was the development of standardized testing. It arose from the desire of Progressive Era reformers to make schools more efficient, as compulsory attendance laws and waves of new immigrants were swelling their enrollments. New "scientific management" techniques, such as Taylorism (after its most determined proponent, Frederick Taylor) and the "Gary plan" (a version of the "platoon" school), seemed part of the answer and were promoted by nonprofit groups. But, professional organizations and others also turned to more radical ideas.

In 1918, a committee of the National Education Association issued a report entitled the *Cardinal Principles of Secondary Education*. In contrast to another report by the so-called Committee of Ten just 25 years earlier, which called for establishing standards for college admission and an academic curriculum devoid of a tracking system, this one endorsed the idea of high schools offering a variety of different curricula and tracks for students, depending on their abilities. But how were schools to make such decisions "efficiently" and fairly?

Philanthropists responded to this question by helping to develop ways to identify and sort students for the various tracks that were contemplated.

The Carnegie Foundation for the Advancement of Teaching—one of several endowments created by Andrew Carnegie—led the effort.[46] In 1928 it launched a ten-year project called the Pennsylvania study, which gave standardized tests to students who had taken the same classes. The results demonstrated that their ability and knowledge varied greatly. To decrease "waste in education,"[47] the research suggested, schools would be well-advised not to assign students according to the work they had already completed, but rather to use testing as a way of setting standards and measuring students against them.

Carnegie followed up by supporting additional efforts to develop standardized testing. In 1930, it formed a committee, under the direction of the College Entrance Examination Board, to produce an exam that measured aptitude for higher education (rather than assess levels of achievement). It was chaired by Carl Brigham, who had been instrumental in developing the intelligence test administered to soldiers in World War I, the forerunner of the Scholastic Aptitude Test. In 1948, after the College Board had tested and refined the exam, Carnegie endowed a new nonprofit, the Educational Testing Service, to administer it.[48]

Testing continued to interest philanthropists in the 1950s and 1960s, not least because they thought it would give them (and their allies in the universities) the ability to influence what went on in the public schools. Among the most notable efforts was the backing for the Kenyon Plan by the Ford Foundation's Fund for the Advancement of Education. In 1955 it became the Advanced Placement Program of the College Board, which encourages high schools to offer college-level courses for their most able students.[49] Another was the creation of the National Merit Scholarship Program, the result of collaboration between Ford and Carnegie, which also sought to encourage schools to become more rigorous in their academic programs.[50]

Donors did not overlook those students who were unlikely to go to college. In 1944, the Educational Policies Commission (formed a decade earlier by a grant from the General Education Board) called upon schools to pay attention to vocational efficiency, civic competence, and personal development as well. Based on the expectation that only "15 to 20 percent of the nation's youth" would attend college, it recommended "courses in homemaking, mental hygiene, and 'the world at work'" for the rest.[51]

Eventually, former Harvard president James Conant brought together these two perspectives on what schools should teach into what turned out to be the most influential vision for the future of American education to come out of the philanthropic world. In 1953, following a two-year, $350,000 study financed by Carnegie Corporation, he published *The American High School Today*, a report that became a nationwide best-seller.[52] Conant advocated the development of the "comprehensive" high school, which would provide an academic education for all students but use ability grouping to identify those who needed either more challenging or remedial classes.

By combining "progressive" methods with academic ends, Gilbert Sewall would later write, the Conant report created a design that quickly became the norm for precollegiate education. It led to the creation of new high schools with a plethora of offerings for their large numbers of students, as well as the consolidation of many smaller ones.[53] But at the same time, critics such as Arthur Bestor and Mortimer Smith worried that in the pursuit of comprehensiveness, schools might give short shrift to educational quality, especially for the most gifted students.

At least some foundations apparently shared this concern. In 1952, Carnegie Corporation supported the formation of the Committee on School Mathematics, headed by Max Beberman of the University of Illinois. The group (which was one of several with similar goals) brought together faculty from the liberal arts, education, and mathematics to devise a new approach to teaching high school mathematics—the so-called new math—that would cultivate higher levels of comprehension and thinking skills in students. Its efforts were eventually picked up by the National Science Foundation and had a substantial impact on high school curricula.

Similar groups were established to develop, test, and distribute improved curricula for the sciences. In 1956, the Physical Science Study Committee, led by MIT physicist Jerold Zacharias, began with an initial $303,000 grant from the National Science Foundation, but soon received $750,000 more from the Ford and Alfred P. Sloan foundations.[54] A new nonprofit, the Education Development Center, was created shortly afterward to test the new curricula and operate summer training institutes for high school physics teachers (which were chiefly supported by the National Science Foundation).

As a way of improving the quality of education, philanthropists also began to experiment with new technologies. Television looked like the most promising, not just for reaching large numbers of communities, but also for providing a solution to the teacher shortages that the baby boom had helped produce. From 1953 to 1958, Ford's Fund for the Advancement of Education made grants totaling $5.6 million to support educational television projects in schools, colleges, and universities.[55] One was the Midwest Program of Airborne Television Instruction, which sent an airplane circling over Purdue University in Indiana to transmit educational programs to as many as five million school children. Technical problems limited the usefulness of this experiment, but other grants laid the groundwork in several states for educational television stations, broadcasting material for classroom use.

Another initiative drew on research by Benjamin Bloom and others about the importance of early childhood development for children in low-income families. With support from Carnegie and Ford, the Children's Television Workshop was born in 1967 and two years later launched its flagship program, *Sesame Street*.[56] The program's success in reaching needy youngsters, Joel Spring reports, was not entirely due to the omnipresence of television; its sponsors also went to great lengths to publicize it through clubs, door-to-door visits, and the distribution of announcements via libraries and other community organizations, as well as to create partnerships with inner-city social service programs.[57] Yet even with all this effort (and a good deal of critical acclaim), *Sesame Street* appears to have had more success in preparing regular viewers for entering school than in having a lasting impact on their academic performance.[58]

Achieving gains in schooling also proved difficult for other notable philanthropic efforts. In the 1960s, the Ford Foundation invested $30 million on the Comprehensive School Improvement Program, which aimed to help schools utilize the high-powered curricula developed in the 1950s and 1960s and establish closer links between schools and universities. However, a 1972 evaluation of the program concluded that its impact was minor, principally because of the complexities of making changes in public schools and the difficulties outsiders faced in imposing their ideas from the top down. At best, the program seemed to add a bit more professionalism to teacher development.[59]

In 1983, the U.S. Department of Education's *A Nation at Risk* report tallied up the consequences of curricular innovation since Conant's influential report. The broadening of the school's mission (further stretched by 1960s efforts to use education to promote social equality) had indeed led to a loss of focus on student academic accomplishments. Whatever else they had done, privately funded efforts to create better curricula had not managed to offset that—and some might even have made matters worse. American education should return to "the basics," the report said, including four years of English, three of mathematics, three of science, three of social studies, a half-year of computer science, and two of a foreign language for the college-bound,[60] a recommendation the Committee of Ten would undoubtedly have found congenial.

A number of donors have taken this advice to heart. In recent years, IBM, RJR Nabisco, and other corporations (as well as some foundations) have devoted a large portion of their resources to promoting higher academic standards for education. E. D. Hirsch's Core Knowledge curriculum is one of several new ideas about what schools should teach that emphasize the basics; at least initially, philanthropic funding (though often, not much of it) made them possible. Efforts to develop specialized "schools within schools" (such as science and math academies) or to adopt phonics-based methods of teaching reading have also attracted private donors, as well as public support.

Because American philanthropy is nothing if not diverse in its interests, curricular innovations continue to take a variety of forms. Concerned about the potential for violence in the nation's schools, some donors have underwritten conflict-resolution programs geared for teenagers. Others have fostered the development of middle schools in place of the more traditional junior high school, believing they are better suited to the educational and social needs of adolescents. Still others have supported challenges to the use of standardized tests on the grounds that they discriminate against children from minority groups or with disabilities. And led by the most influential contemporary philanthropist, Microsoft founder Bill Gates, many grantmakers are putting their money—often in copious amounts—on the latest technological fixes: the computer, the Internet, and distance learning.

Changing what schools teach or the methods they use seems like an obvious and potentially high-impact way of using private dollars. But if the history of philanthropy in education offers any lessons at all, it is that attempts to create better curricula face numerous difficulties in the complex world of American schools—and may easily wind up producing unintended consequences. Today's bold innovation may be tomorrow's explanation for educational failure.

CREATING BETTER COMMUNITIES

From colonial times, schools and the communities they serve have been expected to have a close and reciprocal relationship. Educating children properly was deemed essential for building the "city on a hill" (to use John Winthrop's famous expression). But communities that had the right kinds of values were also thought necessary to produce the right kinds of schools. Consequently, in their strategies to improve education, philanthropists have devoted attention to what went on outside the walls of the schools, as well as inside them. What they have focused on, however, has changed a great deal throughout American history.

At first, funders concentrated on promoting high moral standards, which were thought to be necessary for both a good school and a good community.

Thus, it was not uncommon for the 19th-century benevolent societies, most of which were linked to religious groups, such as the Evangelical Society of Philadelphia and the Boston Society for Moral and Religious Instruction of the Poor, to be concerned about education, too. "These various organizations," Bremner writes, "collected and dispersed funds for distributing Bibles and religious tracts, for promoting foreign and home missions, for advancing the cause of temperance, Sabbath observance and the Sunday-school movement."[61] Many became early backers of more public funding for education so that they could devote more time to religious and moral teaching in their Sunday schools, and leave instruction in reading, writing, and other subjects to educators.[62]

Another privately led effort built around the relationship between schools and communities was the "common school" movement, led by Horace Mann in the early 1800s. It stressed the idea that "raising the general level of culture through more and better schools was the only sure way of accomplishing a thoroughgoing reform of society."[63] In his attempt to gain the support of the wealthy (whose children attended private academies), Mann emphasized that the moral education provided by schools was "the cheapest means of self-protection and insurance" they could find.[64]

The theme of public education as an agent of moral and social redemption was perhaps the most fundamental assumption underlying the common school movement.[65] However, it quickly became clear that this would have to be accomplished in large part through nonsectarian instruction. In New York City, for example, an 1820 ordinance denied public funding for schools set up by religious societies.[66] The influx of Irish Catholic immigrants led to more controversy over moral and religious education in the schools, which was eventually resolved by the creation of a separate educational system that could embody its own values in instruction, a precedent adopted by subsequent groups.

But if public schools were thus limited in one way of strengthening communities, philanthropists soon sought new ways. By the end of the 19th century, many had concluded that children could not learn if they were hungry, impoverished, or forced into work at an early age. Consequently, what they needed was not just moral instruction, but also more food, better housing, and improved health care. Private foundations and nonprofit associations encouraged this idea by publicizing the poor social conditions, high delinquency rates, and child-labor abuses that were keeping young people from succeeding in school.

Foremost among these was the Russell Sage Foundation. Founded in 1907 by Margaret Olivia Sage, it sponsored research, fostered the professionalization of social work, and served as a "think tank for the charity organization movement."[67] The foundation also pioneered the development of school surveys; launched educational organizations operating outside of school, such as the Playground and Recreation Association of America, which was founded in 1906; and promoted a variety of public health measures.[68] Perhaps its most important accomplishment, however, was underwriting the White House Conference on Children in 1909, which gave birth to the Children's Bureau in the U.S. Department of Labor, a major force for developing public policies affecting the welfare of young people.[69]

Philanthropists also took other paths aimed at building better communities. Starting in 1886, Andrew Carnegie began his ambitious attempt to create public libraries throughout the United States. By the time he was done, he had been successful in over 1,400 communities, opening up opportunities for schoolchildren to educate themselves, as he had done.[70]

Another important philanthropic initiative was the development of the mental hygiene movement. Under the leadership of the Commonwealth Fund, which was established by the Harkness family in 1918, a series of efforts was undertaken, ostensibly to address child psychiatric problems that might lead to juvenile delinquency. Their real agenda, however, was broader and sought to have educators "accept responsibility for the whole child." This, William Cutler has written, they willingly did, moving schools toward becoming social service agencies.[71]

As part of this transformation, a new position, the "visiting teacher" or school social worker, was created. Introduced to the United States in 1906, it was promoted by settlement houses and women's clubs as a means of identifying and remedying social problems that were hurting a child's schoolwork. The Commonwealth Fund provided support for special training programs, such as one at the New York School of Social Work.

The visiting teacher was not the only idea for addressing community problems that linked settlement houses with schools. In the 1890s, the Henry Street Settlement in New York started the first public school nursing program and the first program for the care of handicapped children. In 1901, from one of her housekeeping centers at the settlement house, Mabel Hyde Kittredge began serving lunches for children whose mothers worked. A local principal asked her to bring her operation into the schools, and by 1919 the New York City Board of Education had taken over the program. Elsewhere, the Los Angeles Settlement helped introduce "domestic science" into the public schools, the Chicago Settlement began a school for deaf children, and the Roadside Settlement in Des Moines, Iowa, opened a night school for immigrants.[72]

As schools began to take on responsibility for the whole child, building bridges to parents became more important as well. In 1897, with support from Phoebe Apperson Hearst, the National Congress of Mothers was established. Its purpose, said founder Alice Birney, was to bring "maternal wisdom" into education. By the late 1920s, the organization's successor, the National Congress of Parents and Teachers, had over 8.8 million members and was instrumental in setting up local parent-teacher associations (PTAs), as well as in fostering a parent education movement.

Especially in the aftermath of the 1954 Supreme Court case *Brown v. Board of Education*, which held that segregated schools were inherently unequal, philanthropists devoted increasing attention to racial issues in education. Much of the legal work that followed that decision was paid for by contributions to groups such as the NAACP Legal Defense Fund. Grants aimed at ending housing discrimination often had a secondary purpose of improving opportunities for black children to attend racially mixed schools. Court-ordered busing or other methods of integration were also frequently accompanied by philanthropic support for teacher training, community meetings, and various services aimed at building better racial relationships.

Perhaps the most ambitious attempts to build better communities were undertaken by the Ford Foundation. In 1960, it established the Great Cities School Project to work in communities that were deemed "culturally disadvantaged." The program involved putting resources into the schools to transform them into multiservice agencies, providing job training, preschool care, adult education, remedial reading, afterschool activities, and other enrichment programs. Notwithstanding opposition from teachers, school administrators, and city residents, Ford invested over $30 million in the effort. Nonetheless, although the program may have influenced some Great Society initiatives, it failed to produce meaningful results, suggesting that schools were not particularly well-suited to promoting community change.[73]

Even more controversial was a second Ford program to promote community control of the schools. By changing how educational decisions were made, schools were expected to become more attuned to the needs and aspirations of parents and students. But after a brief period in which Ford helped create experimental school districts and support community activist groups, the effort was abandoned. Instead of bridging the gap between parents and their children's schools, the program had wound up widening it. Instead of improving education, it had led to teacher strikes and community unrest that took years to subside.[74]

This record has not kept philanthropists from continuing to search for ways of increasing achievement by fixing the social conditions that are supposedly holding students back. The Annie E. Casey Foundation, for example, embarked on a comprehensive neighborhood development effort in the 1980s called New Futures, only to obtain results similar to what Ford obtained from its Great Cities project. Some donors have also underwritten challenges to school revenue formulas that supposedly allow more resources to go to wealthier communities than poorer ones, while others, such as the Lilly Endowment, have tried to foster community-oriented giving, including for the purpose of improving public education. And unlike the 19th century, when education was used to assimilate immigrants into a common culture, today's philanthropists have often sought, as the nation's population has grown more diverse, to adapt the public schools to the languages and cultures of the new arrivals, on the theory that this kind of multiculturalism would be good for children.

Unfortunately, there is not much evidence that this theory (or any of the newer community-oriented strategies) is correct. Starting with *Equality of Educational Opportunity*, the landmark research by sociologist James Coleman for the U.S. Office of Education in 1966, researchers have found that the factors that make the most difference for school achievement are those related to children's parents and friends, not the social or economic circumstances in which they live. To be sure, students who lack enough food, suffer serious illnesses, or live in hovels without adequate lighting or ventilation (or attend school with those who do) are apt to have trouble learning. But fortunately, those are not the conditions most American children have to endure. As a result, even if philanthropists really could do more to create better communities, the educational benefits would be slim.

CREATING BETTER CHILDREN

Many donors have long accepted the limits of social reform as a way of improving schools. As an alternative, they have focused on increasing the ability of children, regardless of their circumstances, to obtain an education. Some have helped establish "free schools" and provided scholarships for "pious young men" motivated to better themselves.[75] Others have underwritten a variety of activities aimed at enhancing the readiness of students (and their parents) to learn. Both inside and outside of schools, philanthropists have also backed efforts to instill habits and values conducive to education. Because of their paternalistic overtones, these child-centered efforts have sometimes been controversial, but they seem to be enjoying renewed popularity among philanthropists today.

Historically, scholarships have been the most common means by which donors have provided direct assistance to children. But with the advent of publicly funded schools in the early 19th century, such support became less important for elementary and secondary schools than for higher education. Still, for independent and religious private schools, funds for students with academic promise or financial need continued to be created. Donors also underwrote "free" or partially subsidized schools for particular types of children, such as orphans, the principal concern of two of the most notable American philanthropists, Stephen Girard and Milton H. Hershey, and children with disabilities, who received attention from, among others, Thomas Hopkins Gallaudet, Samuel Gridley Howe, and Thomas H. Perkins (the wealthiest man in New England at the time of his death in 1854, whose gifts helped establish a renowned school for the blind).

Such gifts were often designed not only to enable children to go to schools they might not otherwise be able to afford, but also to induce them to be better students. A recent example of this approach, which has received considerable attention, is the work of the "I Have a Dream" Foundation. Founded in 1981 by the New York businessman Eugene M. Lang, the foundation provides a vehicle for donors to offer sixth-grade students the incentive of scholarships for college or vocational education, if they finish high school. The program also offers year-round tutoring, cultural enrichment activities, and mentoring to the children, who come from low-income communities. So far, over 180 "I Have a Dream" projects have been established in 64 cities, with more than 13,500 children involved.[76]

Gifts for scholarships have also been used to stimulate greater parental involvement in education. Starting in 1991, when Indianapolis businessman J. Patrick Rooney established the Educational CHOICE Charitable Trust, individual philanthropists and corporations have established funds in dozens of cities to provide partial assistance for elementary and secondary students whose parents desired to enroll them in private schools. (The largest, the Children's Scholarship Fund, created by investment banker Ted Forstmann and John Walton, of the Wal-Mart family, has raised enough money to underwrite 67,000 scholarships in 40 cities.[77]) By giving low-income parents the opportunity to choose the schools their children attend, these scholarships, the underwriters assumed, would help motivate them (and their offspring) to be more committed to schooling (and motivate the schools, in turn, to be more accountable to them).

Philanthropists have also looked to child psychologists for help in creating better students. Six years after it was created in 1918 by John D. Rockefeller in memory of his wife, the Laura Spelman Rockefeller Memorial helped establish the Institute of Child Welfare Research at Teachers College, Columbia University, to study child-rearing practices. It would soon be joined by a foundation-created professional group, the Federation for Child Study (later renamed the Child Study Association of America).[78] The foundation also supported efforts to incorporate child development into the curricula of women's colleges and the launching of a periodical, *Parents' Magazine*, which repackaged the latest wisdom of child psychologists into instructions ordinary parents could understand and apply.

These initiatives were among the earliest of what has become a long string of preschool and lower-school programs relying on child-rearing research, including Head Start, which, though primarily government funded, often operates through private, nonprofit groups that receive at least partial support from philanthropists. One of the most heralded recent efforts is the School Development Program, started in 1968 by James Comer at the Yale Child Study Center with support from the Ford and Carnegie foundations. A psychiatrist by training, Comer believed that inner-city children received insufficient developmental support in their homes and communities. By restructuring how schools operated (including their relationships with parents), his program sought to overcome the developmental gaps that hindered student learning.[79] Over 500 schools in 20 states have now adopted Comer's methods.

Another well-known effort, supported by foundations and corporations, along with government agencies, is the Perry Preschool Project in Ypsilanti, Michigan. Sponsored by the High/Scope Educational Research Foundation, it provided a "high-quality preschool program" to 123 low-income African American children in the early 1960s and followed their progress thereafter. Compared to a control group, participants in the project were more likely to graduate from high school, stay married longer, earn higher incomes, and have their own homes, and were less likely to get in trouble with the law.[80] Although only a small number of children were involved, the results of the project seemed to buttress the case for focusing on creating better children as the route to better schooling.

For some philanthropists, however, even child-development programs have not appeared to be enough. In 1854, for example, a New York missionary named Charles Loring Brace, founder of the Children's Aid Society, organized an effort to take destitute children from their homes and resettle them in the West. Although it was criticized by Catholics as an attempt to convert their young into Protestants (and by Westerners for sending unruly youth to their communities), its sponsors persisted for nearly 40 years, establishing foster care as an alternative to institutionalization for improving the prospects—educational and otherwise—of children.[81]

Other "child-saving" programs have used somewhat less controversial methods. The first decade of the 20th century saw the formation of a variety of voluntary associations for young people, including the Boy Scouts and Campfire Girls, Big Brothers/Big Sisters, the 4-H Clubs, and Boys Clubs.[82] More recent examples are City Year and other community service programs, which try to combat student apathy and sense of helplessness by enlisting young people in highly structured, local improvement groups. Though organized outside (but often in close contact with) schools, all of them have aimed at creating new ways of building character and imparting skills useful for education, as well as for other aspects of life. In addition, all have relied on gifts of money and time from donors and members to begin and sustain themselves.

Philanthropists have also been interested in helping young people overcome particular problems they face. The widespread incidence of teenage pregnancy, for example, has led to the formation of groups such as the Best Friends Foundation, set up in 1987 by the wife of former secretary of education William J. Bennett. With funding entirely from private supporters, it aims to help adolescent girls stay in school by teaching them to abstain from sex, drugs, and alcohol. Drug use, delinquency, drunk driving, smoking, and other activities harmful to the health of children and teenagers have spurred the creation of similar organizations.

Tutoring and mentoring directed at overcoming educational or personal problems have been popular among donors as well. An especially notable example was created in the wake of a national summit on "volunteering" in 1997, when a number of foundations and corporations helped establish America's Promise: The Alliance for Youth. Initially chaired by General Colin L. Powell, the organization sought to mobilize businesses and other groups to make "commitments" to fulfill "five promises" to young people: ongoing relationships with caring adults, safe places with structured activities during nonschool hours, a healthy start and future, marketable skills through effective education, and opportunities to give back through community service. Within three years, over 500 national companies and nonprofits had signed up, most of which donated employee volunteer time, as well as money and in-kind gifts.[83]

How much of a lasting impact such efforts will have on education is difficult to say. Although research indicates that small, well-designed programs to create better children, such as the Perry Preschool Project (or Big Brothers/

Big Sisters), can produce significant, long-term gains, their ability to increase in scope to reach large numbers of young people without losing their effectiveness has yet to be demonstrated. Nor have all of these efforts been well designed. Not long ago, for example, a number of donors underwrote programs to bolster the "self-esteem" of schoolchildren, especially those from the inner city. While the students generally wound up feeling better about themselves, their academic performance showed little if any improvement.

In any case, philanthropic efforts to create better children face a formidable challenger: parents. Unless they are taken away from their mothers and fathers (a practice that both child development specialists and child protection advocates frown upon much more than they did in Charles Loring Brace's day), young people are bound to spend far more time with their families than they do in school or in mentoring activities. Whatever benefits child-centered programs might have, they can—and almost surely have been—offset by changes in how much parents are "contributing" to the educations of their own sons and daughters.

THE BEST USES OF PHILANTHROPY IN EDUCATION

If there is one lesson philanthropists should have learned from their efforts it is that improving education is not easy. Parents and peers (not to mention popular culture) influence what children are capable of learning. And public funding for schooling far exceeds and outweighs what private donors can contribute. (Hard as it is to imagine, less than a century ago Carnegie Corporation spent more on education than the federal government did!) Furthermore, the decentralization of American schools works against efforts to make comprehensive changes. So do differences of opinion about the sorts of changes that would be desirable.

Nonetheless, philanthropy has left its mark in ways that donors and reformers interested in improving education today would do well to ponder. Providing support for schools—whether for particular groups, such as religious or racial minorities, or to test innovative methods—has repeatedly proven its usefulness. Notwithstanding the dominance of normal schools in their training, philanthropic efforts to foster greater subject-matter knowledge among teachers, as well as more flexible ways of certifying them, have helped raise the professional standards of educators. Likewise, despite controversies that have occasionally swirled around them, the role donors played in developing standardized tests and accelerated course offerings, such as those of the Advanced Placement program, has pushed American education toward higher expectations for students.

If philanthropic attempts to turn schools into social service agencies or community centers have had few educationally valuable results, donor support for local amenities, such as libraries, and for educational television appears to have been more productive. And well-designed scholarship programs, child-development efforts, and extracurricular activities have led to gains as well (though numerous poorly designed ones have also received backing from grantmakers).

Not surprisingly, perhaps, successful educational philanthropy has much in common with successful philanthropy in other fields.

First, the efforts of effective grantmakers are reasonably focused and long term. In education, they have started schools, developed methods of testing, created television shows, or funded merit-oriented scholarships for children. None of these were small undertakings, nor were they unambitious. But they were of a scale that enabled philanthropists to know what they were trying to accomplish and underwrite them long enough to see results. By contrast, efforts to change school systems, reconstruct communities, or change how parents raise their children were not only impossibly heroic, if not impossibly vague, in their goals, but also depended on overcoming a complex array of customs, institutions, and interests. Moreover, they required a sizable and well-nigh unlimited commitment of resources that would inevitably be hard to sustain for the period of time necessary to produce any visible impact.

Other successful philanthropists have displayed the same kind of focus. For example, in 1988, in response to concerns about a rapidly spreading, poorly understood, and often fatal disease, the Aaron Diamond Foundation convened a group of philanthropists to discuss underwriting research aimed at uncovering its causes and developing cures. The following year, together with the New York City Department of Health, the foundation established a laboratory and recruited a prominent microbiologist from the University of California, Los Angeles, Dr. David D. Ho, to lead it. Remaining faithful to its original purpose, the laboratory is often credited with having played a key role in identifying the biological origins of HIV/AIDS, as well as the "drug cocktails" now used to treat it.

The lesson: Often the most effective and influential philanthropy is the most simple, direct, and persistent.

A second characteristic of successful philanthropy is that its methods are often unconventional. In education, creating schools for African Americans in the South (or Catholics in the North), establishing libraries throughout the United States, and giving inner-city parents opportunities to enroll their children in private schools were not steps public officials (or even most donors) at the time were likely to take. Yet, they proved to be educationally sound ideas. On the other hand, grantmakers who directed their support toward the kinds of activities that were well within the mainstream of professional thinking, such as child-development programs or reforming schools from within, often had less to show for their efforts.

This is true as well in other fields. In 1944, The Rockefeller Foundation, with the cooperation of the Mexican government, created the Cooperative Wheat Research and Production Program. Directed by Dr. Norman Borlaug, the program's aim was to develop new strains of wheat and other food staples that could survive in difficult climates and better withstand insects and other agricultural predators. By breaking new ground in the use of fertilizers, crop-planting techniques, irrigation, and the development of hybrids, the project dramatically improved farm production in Mexico, and later, in India, Pakistan, and other countries that had experienced regular famines. Ironically, its methods, regarded as advanced and beneficial at the time they were being tried, are today viewed as retrogressive and harmful by both economic development advocates and their philanthropic supporters.[84]

The great advantage of private philanthropy is that it can try approaches that are original, unorthodox, and even unpopular. Because of the overwhelming influence of government and practitioners in American education, as well as in other fields, philanthropy is often most useful when it fosters innovations that would be hard pressed to receive public backing.

Finally, successful donors understand that philanthropy is more than a matter of techniques and methods. It also involves having a compelling social or moral vision. In education, the most effective grantmakers were motivated by purposes such as transmitting religious and cultural values or expanding opportunities for children from disadvantaged backgrounds at least as much as by a desire to foster more rigorous training for teachers, more demanding curricula for students, or more choices for parents. By contrast, those donors who viewed schools narrowly as agencies for delivering educational, social, and health services or whose vision for schools was limited (e.g., as an instrument of community power) have found themselves unable to build the kind of lasting support for their efforts necessary for success.

This struggle to build support has affected donors in other arenas of public policy. For example, after welfare dependency became a major concern in the 1960s, Ford, Rockefeller, Annie E. Casey, and many other liberal foundations launched major initiatives to assist single mothers and to promote changes in income maintenance programs. But while their efforts wound up supporting important projects that tested some of the methods under consideration to reduce dependency, their work was, at best, "modestly involved" in the debate that led up to the enactment of a major welfare reform bill in 1996.

"Looking back," write Mark Greenberg and Michael C. Laracy, "the 'left out' funders and their grantees may not have been confident they had much to say." Greenberg and Laracy add, "They didn't want to defend an indefensible status quo, but didn't have a shared vision or organizing themes to offer as a replacement."[85] Much of what they had championed turned out to be unresponsive to what concerned public officials—and Americans generally—thought about welfare policy.

In short, though pilot programs and demonstration projects may be necessary, they are never enough. At the heart of good philanthropy in education, welfare, and elsewhere lies not just an understanding of good practice, but also an image of the "good society" that grantmakers hope to foster.

Ultimately, a grant can only be as successful as the grantee allows it to be. The lessons drawn from the history of philanthropy in education apply not just to donors, but to recipients as well. Projects that are ambitious yet focused, willing to try unconventional methods, and rooted in a clear and convincing educational vision stand a better chance of having an impact on American schools than those that are not. The critical question is whether such projects are more likely to be funded too, or if philanthropists will find grand gestures, using repeatedly tried methods, in pursuit of slender goals more to their liking.

As a new generation of donors comes of age, many of whose fortunes spring from the information industry, the likelihood that education will recede as a preoccupation of philanthropy seems small. However, that will be of little consequence if these donors have not schooled themselves in how best to use the vast resources they are expected to have at their disposal and apply what they learn in practice.

CHAPTER 4

How Program Officers at Education Philanthropies View Education

Tom Loveless

This chapter examines the educational views of program officers at education philanthropies. It is based on the results of a survey conducted in 2005 which was inspired by a 1997 survey of education professors conducted by Public Agenda. Published as *Different Drummers: How Teachers of Teachers View Education*, the findings revealed that "professors of education have a distinct, perhaps even singular prescription for what good teachers should do—one that differs markedly from that of most parents and taxpayers."[1] Education professors were found to value process over content and learning how to learn over mastering basic skills. They did not favor memorization, rewards and punishments for good behavior, basic skills, or tough discipline. The report concluded, "While the public's priorities are discipline, basic skills, and good behavior in the classroom, teachers of teachers severely downplay such goals."[2] Indeed, the professors seemed well aware that they held views contrary to the general public. More than three-fourths, 79 percent, agreed with the statement, "The general public has outmoded and mistaken beliefs about what good teaching means."[3]

WHY SURVEY PHILANTHROPIES?

The record of philanthropic foundations in promoting education reform is known more for its failures than its successes. In fairness, the reputation does not come from a systematic evaluation of a large number of grants over an extended period of time, nor from a meta-analysis of individual evaluations, but from a few very large and very famous cases. The last half of the 20th century is bracketed by two such examples. The Ford Foundation launched a major initiative targeting K–12 education in the 1950s. In the 1960s and early 1970s, one component, known as the Comprehensive School Improvement Program, supported what is known today as systemic reform—seeking fundamental changes in governance, curriculum, staffing, and teacher training in communities across the country. Remarkably ambitious, the program was based on the conviction that in order to change schools, everything must be changed. By the early 1970s, however, Ford had concluded, in the words of one program officer, that "generally the projects did not firmly establish innovations in practice or produce widespread improvement in the quality of educational programs."[4]

The Annenberg Challenge grant of $500 million in 1993 was, at the time, the largest single gift to public education in history. The money funded a multipronged school reform effort: challenge grants in nine urban districts (eventually expanding to 14 localities), a rural schools initiative, programs to support arts education, and an endowed national school reform institute at Brown University. Twelve years later, most accounts describe the results as disappointing. A 1999 report commissioned by the Challenge concluded that the award "left small yet encouraging footprints," an accomplishment the Fordham Foundation called "less than staggering."[5] A 2002 series in the *Chronicle of Philanthropy* described the results as "mixed."[6] Frederick M. Hess quotes Michael Casserly, executive director of the Council of the Great City Schools, as saying that the lesson from Annenberg is "don't do that again."[7]

The experiences of the Ford and Annenberg projects, spanning the past several decades, have contributed to the impression that philanthropies are ineffectual in promoting school reform. Several explanations have been offered, including faulty theories of change, the undermining of reform by the social environment of schools, and a dearth of ongoing, unbiased feedback to foundations on program effectiveness. Some explanations are contradictory. Foundations have been accused of being too timid in seeking fundamental change and yet too ambitious in seeking systemic change; too reliant on the status quo and yet too willing to rely on outside experts to change local practices.[8]

These explanations are all about implementation. Missing from them is a consideration of what is being implemented, of the content of reform initiatives or the philosophical premises on which they rest. What are the problems with education that philanthropic reforms are attempting to change? And what are the proposed solutions? Content is not divorced from implementation. One would hope that a bad idea does not survive even if guided by a wonderful theory of institutional change. Unpopular school reforms, especially if they alienate teachers, parents, taxpayers, and other key stakeholders in education, will undoubtedly be difficult to implement in any lasting way.[9]

This brings us to surveying education professors and foundation program officers. In the Public Agenda study, education professors' ideas were found to fall mainly in the camp of progressive education, a philosophy or worldview of schooling that has held sway in academia since the dawn of the 20th century. Central tenets of progressive education include a reverence for student-centered learning, a preference for active learning and instruction involving hands-on materials over didactic forms of teaching, and the conviction that expecting students to learn such traditional material as the rules of spelling, grammar, and punctuation is largely irrelevant to good teaching.

Educational progressivism has both passionate defenders and fierce critics. Contemporary progressive thinkers, such as Alfie Kohn, argue that schools are too focused on factual knowledge broken down into small, often meaningless bits of information.[10] Howard Gardner's "multiple intelligences" are now foundational to progressives' conviction that traditional school subjects only draw on a small portion of human thought and creativity, the logical-mathematical and linguistic, ignoring at least six other "intelligences" (e.g., musical intelligence, body-kinesthetic intelligence).[11] Along a similar line of thought, followers of "constructivism" subscribe to the notion that new knowledge is constructed on a base of previous knowledge, which students learn best when they actively construct new concepts on a "scaffold" of what they already know. The key tenets of progressivism are individualization over whole-class instruction, child-centered learning over didactic instruction by a teacher, active learning over book learning or learning while passively listening to lectures, and motivating learners by tailoring the curriculum to student interests, not to an external standard imposed by authorities.

Critics of educational progressivism, E. D. Hirsch being the best known in recent years, argue that progressive beliefs are unsubstantiated by scientific evidence. Idealistic about learning, based on romantic notions of childhood, cut off from the self-checking regimens of traditional academic disciplines, and isolated in education schools, educational progressivism, Hirsch argues, has hardened into dogma, a "thought world" that permeates the scholarship of educationists.[12] The historical record of how progressive programs play out in schools and classrooms is certainly discouraging. Diane Ravitch's *Left Back: A Century of Failed School Reforms* could just as appropriately have been subtitled, "A Century of Failed Progressive Reforms." For indeed, the book was about just that—how in decade after decade in the 20th century progressive reform movements sprang forth, at first full of hope and enthusiasm, then crashing to earth in frustration and failure. But progressivism's impact on policy is not consigned to history; it lives on in many contemporary reforms. Elements of educational progressivism can be found today in whole-language reading instruction, contemporary math reform, numerous programs promoting "critical thinking" and "higher-order thinking skills," instructional reforms that cast teachers as coaches and facilitators instead of instructors who impart knowledge to children, portfolios and other nonstandard measures of student assessment, constructivist approaches to pedagogy, and the small schools movement.

The perennial disappointment of educational progressives is at least partially attributable to their failure to win over parents, teachers, and the general public. Another fascinating study by Public Agenda found high school students hostile to the progressive cause.[13] The views of education professors place them outside mainstream opinion on American school reform. What about education philanthropies? Have program officers, like education professors, adopted a worldview that is in opposition to the beliefs of ordinary Americans? If so, that would constitute a reasonable hypothesis for foundations' disappointing track record on school reform. The Ford and Annenberg initiatives are solidly—and famously—in the progressive tradition. Among the innovations that Ford money supported were open classrooms, team teaching, and interdisciplinary curricula—mainstays of progressive education.[14] Annenberg supported the development and dissemination of student-centered, hands-on learning materials. Two heroes of contemporary progressive education, Ted Sizer and Deborah Meier, played key roles in the formative years of the Annenberg Challenge. Sizer served as the founding director of the Annenberg Institute for School Reform, and Meier was instrumental in putting together the coalition of education groups that became the New York Networks for School Renewal, the sponsor of the Annenberg Challenge in New York City.[15]

Program officers are the primary contact point between foundations and grantseekers. They represent a foundation's mission and beliefs in a concrete way. A survey of their views will help answer the question of whether foundations operate within the mainstream of public opinion on education or whether, like education professors, they march to the beat of a different drummer.

METHODS

The survey of program officers was conducted from January to March in 2005. Surveys were mailed in three waves, with postcard reminders approximately one week after the mailings in waves one and two. A total of 240 surveys were mailed to foundations that are active in K–12 grantmaking. Responses were received from 128 program officers, each at a different foundation, a response rate of 53.3 percent.

Survey questions were drawn from previous Public Agenda studies, and the wording of questions was unaltered. Topics such as vouchers, charter schools, and other forms of school choice were not included. Like all mail surveys, self-selection may introduce bias if respondents differ markedly from nonrespondents on their educational views. The 53 percent response rate reduces but does not eliminate the potential that selection bias has affected the results. Program officers who are most passionate in their opinions may have been more likely to answer the survey, but whether this tipped the results and rendered specific responses unrepresentative is unknown. One aspect of the survey lessens the possibility of systematic ideological bias. Some questions ask respondents to react to statements expressing a point of view. These statements were well balanced, meaning that a question with a bias toward a particular point of view is mirrored by another question on the survey expressing the opposite point of view.

Public Agenda interviewed education professors by telephone. Are results from a mail survey comparable? The research literature on how different survey methods affect results is small and atheoretical. Cui describes the key differences between mail and telephone surveys:

1. Order effects are less likely to occur in mail surveys than telephone surveys (Bishop et al., 1988). In other words, which questions are asked first appears to influence respondents more during telephone surveys than mail surveys.
2. Telephone respondents tend to select more extreme answers than mail respondents when vaguely quantified scale categories are used. Mail respondents tend to distribute themselves across the full scale (Hochstim, 1967; Mangione et al., 1982; Walker & Restuccia, 1984).
3. Mail surveys are more reliable than telephone and face-to-face interview surveys (DeLeeuw, 1992).[16]

Phone and mail surveys probably have trade-offs that wash out with samples of the sizes examined here (the sample size of education professors was 900). The second point above—that more extreme responses are produced on phone surveys and answers are distributed more evenly across the scale on mail surveys—may be germane to interpreting the responses in Table 3. Readers will be cautioned when those results are discussed.

SURVEY RESULTS

We first asked respondents to supply some background information. Program officers report that they have worked an average of 6.6 years at their current foundation. About one in five (22.8%) has an education degree. Four out of ten (40.4%) have no teaching or administrative experience. About one-fourth of the program officers have school administrative experience, and they served an average of 11.3 years, a significant tour of duty. More than half (56%) of the officers have teaching experience, and they taught for an average of six years. The overwhelming majority of former teachers (80%) taught in public schools. Let's now turn to the survey questions.

Questions are discussed below in the same order as presented in the survey. Questions are grouped into five categories: teachers, classroom activities, perceptions of the nation's public schools, school reform, and the problems of local public schools. For the first three categories, I will compare program officers' responses to those of education professors. In the last two categories, the officers' responses will be compared to those of parents, K–12 teachers, and the general public. Unless otherwise noted, differences that are singled out for discussion are statistically significant, using the significance tests detailed below each table.

Teachers

The first group of questions addresses teaching. Although soliciting opinions on the qualities teacher-training programs should impart to their students, the real significance of the questions is in revealing what respondents consider to be the characteristics of good teachers. Table 1 reports the percentage of respondents describing a particular characteristic as "absolutely essential." Program officers and education professors rank the attributes of good teachers quite similarly. Any differences are in emphasis. Look at the top three characteristics. Approximately three-fourths of both program officers (78%) and education professors (72%) believe "teachers who will have high expectations of all their students" are absolutely essential. A clear majority of program officers also believe it is absolutely essential that teachers promote active learning by students (72%) and that teachers be lifelong learners themselves (66%). Education professors embrace these goals even more emphati-

TABLE 1   Teachers

Teacher education programs can impart different qualities to their students. Which qualities do you think are most essential and which are least essential? Please use a 1-to-5 scale, where 1 means least essential and 5 means it is absolutely essential to impart.

	Percentage responding "absolutely essential"	
	Program Officers	Education Professors
Teachers who will have high expectations of all their students	78	72
Teachers committed to teaching kids to be active learners who know how to learn	72**	82
Teachers who are themselves lifelong learners and constantly updating their skills	66***	84
Teachers who are deeply knowledgeable about the content of the specific subjects they will be teaching	47*	57
Teachers prepared to teach in schools with limited resources and where many kids come to class not ready to learn	45	45
Teachers trained in pragmatic issues of running a classroom such as managing time and preparing lesson plans	27**	41
Teachers who are well versed in theories of child development and learning	27***	46
Teachers who maintain discipline and order in the classroom	18***	37
Teachers who expect students to be neat, on time, and polite	14	12
Teachers who stress correct spelling, grammar, and punctuation	12	19

Note: * p < 0.05, ** p < 0.01, *** p < 0.001 (test for equal proportions).

Source: Data for foundation officers were collected by the author for this study. Data for education professors are from Steve Farkas and Jean Johnson, *Different Drummers* (New York: Public Agenda, 1997).

cally, with 82 percent believing that students should be active learners and 84 percent believing that teachers should constantly update their skills.

The content knowledge of teachers is valued more by education professors than by program officers. A majority of education professors (57%) believe it absolutely essential that teachers are "deeply knowledgeable about the content of the specific subjects they will be teaching." Less than half of program officers (47%) grant content knowledge such importance. State laws on teacher certification hold schools of education responsible for producing teachers knowledgeable in content, which may explain the education professors' responses. But it does not explain the lukewarm response of program officers to the notion that teachers must thoroughly know the subjects that they teach.

Program officers are also less likely than education school professors to see the importance of teachers who are trained in pragmatic issues of running a classroom (27%, vs. 41% of education professors who consider this absolutely essential), teachers who are well versed in theories of child development (27%, vs. 46% of education professors), or teachers who maintain discipline and order in the classroom (18% vs. 37%). It is important to note that both program officers and education professors give the lowest priority to characteristics related to teachers enforcing rules. Only 14 percent of program officers deem it absolutely essential for teachers to expect students to be neat, on time, and polite, and only 12 percent believe stressing spelling, grammar, and punctuation is absolutely essential.

In sum, education professors value characteristics in teachers that they have a hand in developing in teacher-training programs—an active learning approach to instruction, the constant updating of skills, knowledge of content, a grasp of child development theories, and classroom management. Program officers join education professors in valuing teachers with high expectations for all children, teachers who promote active learning, and teachers who are lifelong learners themselves. They are not as keen, however, on classroom management skills or deep content knowledge. And, in a pattern that will be reinforced by data still to be examined, program officers do not place great importance on teachers who maintain classroom discipline and control, teachers who expect students to be neat, punctual, and polite, or teachers who stress such basic skills as spelling, grammar, and punctuation.

Classroom Activities

The next table examines classrooms (see Table 2). Respondents were asked whether they would like to see more, less, or about the same amount of several learning activities. Again, there are differences in emphasis, but the relative ranking of priorities is similar between program officers and education professors. About 78 percent of education professors would like to see portfolios and other authentic assessments used more, compared to 68 percent of program officers.

Four activities that are considered mainstays of traditional classrooms are shunned by both program officers and professors of education—homogeneous grouping, memorization, prizes for good behavior, and multiple-choice exams. Opposing these practices are hallmarks of modern progressive education. Of the program officers surveyed, those who say they want

TABLE 2   Classroom Activities

Thinking about the typical K–12 classroom, would you like to see more, less, or about the same of the following learning tools?

	Percentage responding "more"	
	Program Officers	Education Professors
Portfolios and other authentic assessments	68*	78
Mixed ability grouping	49	50
Computer programs that enable kids to practice skills on their own	45***	69
Homework assignments	21***	41
Penalties for students who break the rules	19**	37
Homogeneous grouping	16	15
Memorization	11	14
Prizes to reward good behavior in the classroom	11	13
Multiple-choice exams	4	2

Note: * $p < 0.05$, ** $p < 0.01$, *** $p < 0.001$ (test for equal proportions).

Source: Data for foundation officers were collected by the author for this study. Data for education professors are from Steve Farkas and Jean Johnson, *Different Drummers* (New York: Public Agenda, 1997).

to see fewer of these activities in classrooms are three to four times the number who want more. Only 16 percent support more homogeneous grouping, while 53 percent want less (the figures for those wanting less of an activity are not shown in the table). Only about one in ten (11%) program officers support more memorization, with 57 percent wanting less.

Eleven percent would like to see more prizes to reward good behavior, compared to 49 percent who would like to see fewer. A paltry 4 percent of program officers support the use of more multiple-choice exams, swamped by the 70 percent who would like to see fewer.

Interesting differences between the two groups of respondents appear in the middle of the table. Program officers are less enthusiastic than education professors about computer programs that enable kids to practice skills on their own. It is impossible to say whether it is computers, practicing skills, or students working on their own that dampens enthusiasm for this idea. Only 45 percent of officers endorse the activity, compared to 69 percent of education professors. And program officers are more hostile to homework and penalties for students who break the rules. Among program officers, only 21 percent want to see more homework assignments (vs. 41% for education professors). Only 19 percent want to see more penalties for students who break the rules, compared to 37 percent of education professors. In other words, education professors are about twice as likely as program officers to endorse more homework and penalties for students who break rules. Program officers have a difficult time supporting classroom practices that can be construed as arduous (homework) or punitive toward students (discipline).

Perceptions of the Nation's Public Schools

Unlike the previous tables, substantial differences emerge between program officers and education professors in Table 3. The survey asked respondents to evaluate several common perceptions about the nation's schools. Included are both negative and positive assertions that might be encountered in a newspaper editorial, at a cocktail party, or in discussions with neighbors or colleagues at work. Table 3 shows the percentage of respondents saying a particular statement is "very close" or "somewhat close" to one's own point of view. The striking thing about the education professors' responses is that only one statement—the last one in the table, which asks about urban schools—elicits less than 50 percent support. It appears education professors consider themselves on the front line in debates about public schooling, and when hearing opinions—whether positive or negative—they react strongly to them. Program officers are more ambivalent in their responses. Please note, however, as discussed above, the stronger opinions of education professors could also be an artifact of being collected by a phone survey. The differences may not be as significant as the data presented here suggest, although most of the differences are so large that tempering the education professors' responses—or strengthening the responses of program officers on the Likert scale—would make very little difference.[17]

Many of the statements in Table 3 defend public schools' performance and characterize popular criticisms as unwarranted. In general, program officers are not as sympathetic to these defensive statements as education professors. Program officers exhibit independence from arguments put forth by what is often referred to as the "public school lobby." Almost two-thirds of program officers (65%) support the accusatory statement that "more often than not, teacher tenure is an obstacle to improving schools," the only item on which the percentage of program officers in agreement exceeds that of education professors (52%). A solid majority of program officers, 64 percent, believe

TABLE 3   Perceptions of the Nation's Schools

Here are some perceptions about the nation's public schools. How close does each come to your own view: very close, somewhat close, not too close, or not close at all?

	Percentage responding "very close" or "somewhat close"	
	Program Officers	Education Professors
Public education is the nation's most critical democratic institution and should be protected at all costs.	92	95
The general public has outmoded and mistaken beliefs about what good teaching means.	74	79
Too many school systems are top heavy with bureaucracy and administration.	70	77
More often than not, teacher tenure is an obstacle to improving schools.	65**	52
The schools are expected to deal with too many social problems.	64***	85
Academic standards in today's schools are too low and kids are not expected to learn enough.	63***	78
Even when the schools get more money, it often does not get close to the classrooms.	60***	78
The schools should pay very careful attention to what business wants from high school graduates.	59***	75
Considering the differences in the children they teach, private schools don't do a better job than the public ones.	48***	67
Too many kids get passed on to the next grade when they should be held back.	46**	61
Many of the criticisms of the public schools come from right-wing groups who want to undermine public education.	46	54
Much of the decline in public confidence in public schools is a result of negative press coverage.	37***	65
One of the most effective ways to improve schools is to give them a lot more money.	30***	54
Most of the problems facing schools today are confined to urban school systems.	11**	22

Note: * $p < 0.05$, ** $p < 0.01$, *** $p < 0.001$ (test for equal proportions).

Source: Data for foundation officers were collected by the author for this study. Data for education professors are from Steve Farkas and Jean Johnson, *Different Drummers* (New York: Public Agenda, 1997).

schools are expected to deal with too many social problems, but among education professors the figure is a whopping 85 percent. Attributing the decline of public confidence in public schools to negative press coverage is only supported by 37 percent of program officers, but 65 percent of education professors hold this belief. About half (48%) of program officers agree that "considering the differences in the children they teach, private schools don't do a better job than the public ones." That is significantly less than the two-thirds (67%) of education professors who doubt that private schools really do a better job. Interestingly, since they are in the business of giving money, the wisdom of giving schools "a lot more money" as a means of improvement is only supported by 30 percent of program officers. More than half, 54 percent, of education professors believe a lot more money would improve schools.

One response stands out for echoing a pattern noted above, that program officers do not like to see anything resembling punitive action taken with students. Fewer than half of program officers (46%) endorse the view that "too many kids get passed on to the next grade when they should be held back." Such ambivalence toward holding kids back is not shared by education professors, with 61 percent of them endorsing this statement critical of social promotion. Another position places program officers shoulder to shoulder with education professors in wanting to change traditional views of teaching. About three-fourths of program officers (74%) and 79 percent of education professors believe "the general public has outmoded and mistaken beliefs about what good teaching means." Both program officers and education professors see themselves as reformers who are not supported by the general public.

School Reform

Table 4 covers questions on school reform. Respondents were asked to rate various proposals for changing how schools teach on a 1-to-5 scale, with 5 meaning the change would improve academic achievement a great deal and 1 meaning it would not improve academic achievement at all. In addition to education professors, K–12 teachers and the general public have answered the same questions, and the responses of these groups are tabled so that they may be compared with the responses of program officers.

Program officers are frequent outliers in their views on school reform. To fully appreciate this point, for a moment only consider the data on the three other groups—education professors, K–12 teachers, and the general public.

TABLE 4   School Reform

Here are some ideas for changing the way public schools teach. For each, please indicate if you think it would improve kids' academic achievement. Please use a 1-to-5 scale, where 1 means it would not improve academic achievement at all and 5 means it would improve academic achievement a great deal.

	Percentage responding "4" or "5"			
	Program Officers	Education Professors	K–12 Teachers	General Public
Setting up very clear guidelines on what kids should learn and teachers should teach in every major subject so the kids and the teachers will know what to aim for.	76	71	80	82
Not allowing kids to graduate from high school unless they clearly demonstrate they can write and speak English well.	62**	76	83	88
Emphasizing such work habits as being on time, dependable, and disciplined.	49***	78	93	88
Replacing multiple-choice tests with essay tests to measure what kids learn.	44**	60	47	54
Raising the standards of promotion from grade school to junior high and only letting kids move ahead when they pass a test showing they have reached those standards.	34**	49	62	70
Mixing fast learners and slow learners in the same class so that slower kids learn from faster kids.	33***	54	40	34
Permanently removing from school grounds kids who are caught with drugs or with weapons.	32***	66	84	76
Taking persistent troublemakers out of class so that teachers can concentrate on the kids who want to learn.	30***	66	88	73
Adapting how schools teach to the background of students, such as using street language to teach inner-city kids.	23	18	15	20

Note: * $p < 0.05$, ** $p < 0.01$, *** $p < 0.001$ (test for equal proportions).

Source: Data for foundation officers were collected by author for this study. Data for education professors, K–12 teachers, and the general public are from Steve Farkas and Jean Johnson, *Different Drummers* (New York: Public Agenda, 1997).

Education professors are frequently the outlier group, the least enthusiastic about ideas that parents and teachers overwhelmingly support—for example, permanently removing from school kids caught with drugs or weapons—and the most enthusiastic about ideas the public and teachers do not support—for example, mixing fast and slow learners in heterogeneously grouped classes. Indeed, as noted in this chapter's introduction, that is precisely why Public Agenda named the report presenting the survey results on education professors *Different Drummers*.

Program officers appear even more different than the different drummers in the education professoriat, diverging sharply from the general public's views on how to improve schools. On only three of the ten reforms presented in Table 4 are program officers' views close to those of the general public—expressing mild support for replacing multiple-choice tests with essay exams, skepticism about mixing fast and slow learners in the same classroom, and opposition to adapting how schools teach to the background of students, such as using street language to teach inner-city kids.

Program officers stand alone in either not supporting or tepidly supporting five proposals that garner the backing of at least 70 percent of the general public. The five issues deal with student accountability, basic skills, and discipline. Sixty-two percent of program officers believe kids should not be allowed to graduate from high school unless they can clearly write and speak English. Although a convincing level of support, it falls significantly short of the support the idea receives from education professors (76%), K–12 teachers (83%), and the general public (88%). About half of program officers (49%) believe emphasizing such work habits as being on time, dependable, and disciplined would improve academic achievement. This is far below the level of support registered by education professors (78%). The stunning contrast is with K–12 teachers (93%) and the general public (88%), who are nearly unanimous in believing that student achievement benefits from better work habits.

Only about one-third (34%) of program officers support requiring students to pass a test as a condition of promotion from grade school to junior high, short of the support of education professors (49%). Teachers and the public give even stronger support to the idea (62% and 70%, respectively).

As has been indicated by other survey items, program officers are reluctant to endorse proposals for tightening student discipline. The gaps are enormous between program officers on the one hand, and education professors, K–12 teachers, and the general public on the other. Only 32 percent of program officers want to see students who are caught with drugs or weapons permanently removed from school, an idea that enjoys the broad support of education professors (66%), K–12 teachers (84%), and the general public (76%). Only 30 percent of program officers think "taking persistent trouble-makers out of class so that teachers can concentrate on the kids who want to learn" would be a good idea, with education professors (66%), K–12 teachers (88%), and the general public (73%) strongly favoring such tough measures.

Local School Problems

Table 5 asks program officers to evaluate their own local schools. It has long been noted that poll respondents offer different perspectives on local and national education performance. The Phi Delta Kappan/Gallup poll, for example, has consistently uncovered an "I'm OK, you're not" phenomenon. Americans think their local schools are perfectly fine, while simultaneously believing that the nation's schools are going to hell in a handbasket. For the questions in Table 5, program officers were asked to gauge the seriousness of several problems in their local schools. The percentage answering "very serious" or "somewhat serious" is tabled. Data from four additional groups of respondents that Public Agenda has surveyed in the past using the same set of questions are also tabled—the general public, white parents, African American parents, and traditional Christian parents.

Three things stand out in Table 5. First, one conclusion drawn from earlier data must be tempered. Three-quarters (75%) of program officers believe that "schools are not getting enough money to do a good job" and about two-thirds (66%) hold that "classes are too crowded." The public supports such arguments but not as strongly as the program officers. A little more than half of the general public (58%) believes schools are not getting enough money, and exactly half (50%) believe classes are too crowded. Education foundations are located predominantly in large cities, so if program officers are using urban schools as their "own community's local schools," their responses may reflect problems particularly acute among urban schools. Recall from Table 3 that program officers were significantly less sympathetic than education professors to the claim that "one of the most effective ways to improve schools is to give them a lot more money." The officers do not reject the claim altogether, however. Their own community's schools, the program officers believe, would benefit from getting more money.

The second headline from Table 5 is that program officers do not recognize student discipline or deficiencies in basic skills and work habits as severe problems. Complaints about "too much drugs and violence in schools" and "teachers who are more interested in being popular than in requiring respect and discipline" are more likely to be voiced by parents and the general pub-

TABLE 5   Local School Problems

Please tell me how serious a problem each is in your own community's public schools.

	Percentage responding "very serious" or "somewhat serious"				
	Program Officers	General Public	White Parents	African American Parents	Traditional Christian Parents
Schools are not getting enough money to do a good job.	75***	58	67	77	69
Kids are not taught enough math, science, and computers.	71***	52	46	66	56
Academic standards are too low and kids are not expected to learn enough.	71*	61	49	70	57
Classes are too crowded.	66***	50	55	63	54
There's too much drugs and violence in schools.	61**	72	58	80	66
Schools are not clear and specific enough about what they want kids to learn.	51	47	43	56	45
There is not enough emphasis on the basics such as reading, writing, and math.	42***	60	52	61	56
Schools don't teach kids good work habits such as being on time to class and completing assignments.	41*	52	36	47	37
Classes and textbooks stereotype minorities and women.	31	30	24	53	30
Too many teachers are more concerned with making kids feel good about themselves than with how much they learn.	30	37	32	39	38
Too many teachers are more interested in being popular than in requiring respect and discipline.	17***	41	35	43	38
Schools fail to teach religious values.	6***	47	51	65	70
Schools are too graphic and explicit when teaching sex education.	5***	24	19	27	30

Note: * p < 0.05, ** p < 0.01, *** p < 0.001 (test for equal proportions).

Source: Data for foundation officers were collected by author for this study. Data for education professors are from Steve Farkas and Jean Johnson, *Different Drummers* (New York: Public Agenda, 1997). Data for the general public and parents are from Jean Johnson and John Immerwahr, *First Things First: What Americans Expect from Public Schools* (New York: Public Agenda, 1994).

lic than by program officers. Drugs and violence are seen as serious problems by 61 percent of program officers, short of the 72 percent figure for the general public. Only 17 percent of program officers see permissive teachers who seek popularity as a serious problem. Among the public, the figure is 41 percent. The statement that "there is not enough emphasis on the basics such as reading, writing, and math" finds agreement with only 42 percent of program officers, compared to 60 percent of the general public. The charge that "schools don't teach kids good work habits such as being on time to class and completing assignments" is supported by 41 percent of program officers versus 52 percent of the public. These data add details to a pattern consistent across the survey. Program officers not only doubt that cracking down on discipline or emphasizing basic skills and good work habits will improve schools, but they also do not agree with the general public that these are urgent problems.

The third headline is that program officers diverge sharply with the public on the importance of teaching values. Only 6 percent of program officers see it as a serious problem that "schools fail to teach religious values." But the general public is far more concerned, with nearly half (47%) saying that the failure to teach religious values is a serious problem. Among black parents the concern rises to 65 percent, and among traditional Christian parents to 70 percent. Nor are program officers worried about schools teaching sex education that is "too graphic and explicit." Only 5 percent judge that a serious problem, compared to 24 percent of the general public.

Let's sum up. Program officers disagree with the general public, parents, and K–12 teachers on the most serious problems facing schools and the best way of addressing them. Three issues stand out—discipline, basic skills, and student accountability. Program officers appear humanistic on questions regarding discipline—critics may call it permissive—skeptical that poor student behavior is a pressing problem and wary of stricter treatment of students who break rules. On basic skills, program officers stand decisively in the progressive education tradition, believing that basic skills should not receive great emphasis in the classroom. In fairness, the program officers are not anti-intellectual. They support high expectations for students, more learning in academic subjects, and clear standards. But support plummets for any learning activity that hints at "basic skills," such as requiring students to memorize material or to learn the rules of punctuation and spelling. Education professors join program officers in standing apart from the public, parents, and K–12 teachers on these issues. But in most cases, the views of education professors are closer to the general public than those of program officers.

Let's now dig deeper into the data to examine one factor that may influence the views of program officers.

THE INFLUENCE OF TEACHING EXPERIENCE ON PROGRAM OFFICERS' VIEWS

As noted above, about 56 percent of program officers have experience as classroom teachers—44 percent do not. Table 6 compares the views of these two groups. With all responses on the survey items arrayed on Likert scales, I grouped items addressing the same topic into clusters, then computed the sum of each program officer's responses (some scales were reversed to make the direction of opinion consistent). The cluster sums by themselves are meaningless, but they do allow for a comparison of the teachers' and nonteachers' mean responses. Any difference that does appear can be significance tested (i.e., generate a p-value) to compute the probability of the differences occurring by chance alone if in fact the two groups' means are equal.

Table 6 displays the means of the clusters by topic, along with the items making up each cluster. Recall that program officers are generally wary of proposals to strengthen school discipline. They are not monolithic in that response, however. Program officers with teaching experience are much more likely to support stronger discipline in the schools than program officers without teaching experience (p < .001). Program officers with teaching experience are also significantly more likely to support an emphasis on basic skills and good work habits (p < .01). Also note that they are more likely to support policies holding students accountable for learning, although this last cluster barely misses the threshold of p < .05 for statistical significance (p = .06) and thus is not included in the table.

The former teachers support stronger discipline on all five survey items. On four of the items, the differences are statistically significant. The teachers and nonteachers exhibit significant differences on permanently removing kids from school grounds if they are caught with weapons or drugs (p < .01) and on taking persistent troublemakers out of class (p < .01). The former teachers are also more likely to see teachers who favor popularity over respect and discipline as a serious problem in local schools (p < .05) and to believe that maintaining discipline and order in the classroom are attributes of good teaching (p < .05). Program officers who do not have teaching experience are less likely to support policies promoting stronger discipline, less likely to see classroom control as a crucial characteristic of good teaching, and less likely to see discipline and order as prominent problems of local schools.

TABLE 6   Topic Clusters

Survey items clustered by topic area, responses of program officers with and without teaching experience.

Cluster or Item	Teaching Experience Mean	No Experience Mean	p-Value t-Test, between Group Means
Discipline Cluster (5 items)	14.5	12.4	0.0005
Permanently removing from school grounds kids who are caught with drugs or with weapons	3.23	2.57	0.0052
Taking persistent troublemakers out of class so that teachers can concentrate on the kids who want to learn	3.20	2.60	0.0077
Too many teachers are more interested in being popular than in requiring respect and discipline	2.07	1.72	0.0118
Teachers who maintain discipline and order in the classroom	3.95	3.58	0.0148
Penalties for students who break the rules	2.09	1.96	0.2634
Basic Skills and Work Habits Cluster (5 items)	13.6	12.0	0.0094
Emphasizing such work habits as being on time, dependable, and disciplined	3.85	3.25	0.008
There is not enough emphasis on the basics such as reading, writing, and math	2.57	2.11	0.0117
Homework assignments	2.14	1.98	0.1827
Memorization	1.59	1.43	0.2311
Teachers who stress correct spelling, grammar, and punctuation	3.50	3.29	0.2679

Program officers with teaching experience are more likely than officers without teaching experience to support an emphasis on basic skills. On two of the five basic skills items, the differences are statistically significant. Program officers with teaching experience are more likely to believe emphasizing such work habits as being on time, dependable, and disciplined will boost academic achievement (p < .01). They are also more likely to say that there is not enough emphasis on the basics such as reading, writing, and math (p < .05). Although the differences do not reach statistical significance, program officers with teaching experience also view homework, memorization, and correct spelling, grammar, and punctuation more favorably than program officers who have never taught.

SUMMARY AND CONCLUSION

Whether progressivism is good or bad for American education lies beyond the scope of this chapter. Its merits have been debated for over 100 years, and the debate continues today. The survey data above show that education professors and program officers at foundations active in K–12 education have taken the same side in the debate—they support key tenets of progressive education. It is not a foregone conclusion that the side they have taken is the right one for improving American schools. The jury is still out, in terms of conclusive scientific evidence, on much of the progressive agenda. This is politically noteworthy because progressivism comprises core beliefs that are unpopular with parents, teachers, students, and the general public—hence the title of Public Agenda's report on the education school professoriat, *Different Drummers*. Indeed, program officers appear to hold a worldview that is similar to that of the education professoriat and, in many respects, one that is even more different from mainstream public opinion than that of the different drummers examined in the Public Agenda study.

Program officers agree with the public that teachers should have high expectations for all students. Both want clear standards established saying what kids should learn and teachers should teach. Program officers are leery, however, of consequences for students who fall short of standards. Program officers favor socially promoting failing students in grade school over holding them back, a position opposed by K–12 teachers and the general public. The public believes that there is not enough emphasis on basic skills and wants schools to stress such work habits as being on time, dependable, and disciplined. Program officers see neither student behavior nor basic skills as urgent problems. They do not want schools to focus more attention on the basics. They do not want to see tougher sanctions on students who break rules, do not support permanently removing kids who are caught with weapons or drugs, and do not favor taking persistent troublemakers out of class.

In *Different Drummers* the authors declare, "Ordinary Americans, along with teachers of students, have made their essential expectations of public education abundantly clear: safe orderly schools that graduate students who master basic skills, develop good work habits, and learn such values as honesty and respect."[18] These are not the top priorities of program officers.

What should be made of the discrepancy? Foundations have the most to gain by examining the survey data here. They should be concerned because their legitimacy and status rest on advancing the public good. Unless foundations take it upon themselves to change the public's view of what constitutes good public schooling—a challenge that they are probably ill-suited to tackle—their future efforts at school reform are destined to be uphill battles. Education reforms that have parents, teachers, students, and the general public as allies have a chance of succeeding. Reforms that have them as enemies are doomed.

With that in mind, I offer four constructive suggestions on how foundations can use these findings. Admittedly, the recommendations are speculative, but they flow naturally from the foregoing data and analysis. I begin with the assumption that foundations will want to move their organizations closer to mainstream opinion on education. How can they do that?

First, when hiring program officers, give preference to those with teaching experience. Teaching has a way of softening even the most strident ideologue. The pragmatic demands of the classroom take precedence over abstract ideals, as kids' and parents' needs and interests must be met. Having experienced teachers work with grantholders in the field also enhances foundations' credibility with practitioners. But this will not completely move foundations into the mainstream. The former teachers in the survey are five to eight points closer to the public in answering questions on discipline and basic skills, but that only takes a small chunk out of the gap. More will need to be done.

Second, hire a staff with balanced views. Deborah Wadsworth, writing about the findings in *Different Drummer*, remarks that "the disconnect between what the professors want and what most parents, teachers, and students say they need is often staggering. It seems ironic that so many of those who profess to believe that 'the real endeavor' is about questioning and learning how to learn are seemingly entrapped in a mind-set that is unquestioning in its conviction of its own rightness."[19] Foundations, too, can become cloistered places that suffer from self-affirming "groupthink." Ideological diversity and intellectual openness can help prevent that from occurring.

Third, appoint an outside review committee comprised of parents, teachers, taxpayers, and the general public to annually give feedback on your grant portfolio. Bring in disinterested outsiders who will be willing to tell you when you have gone off the track.

Fourth, tie evaluations to outcomes that matter to the public. The public wants schools that are safe, orderly, and teach students good work habits and the basics—reading, math, history, and science. Foundations that fund projects demonstrating effectiveness in attaining these goals will move to the center of the national effort to improve American schooling. Those that do not will be relegated to the margins of that effort.

Approaches to Reform

CHAPTER 5

Philanthropy and Urban School District Reform

Lessons from Charlotte, Houston, and San Diego

Lynn Jenkins and Donald R. McAdams

Much has been said in recent years about the disappointing results of philanthropic investment in K–12 education reform. This chapter is not a broad assessment of philanthropy's accomplishments or shortcomings in this arena, however. It is simply a circumscribed examination of the role and impact of philanthropy in three urban school districts: Charlotte-Mecklenburg Schools (CMS), Houston Independent School District (HISD), and San Diego City Schools (SDCS). Its focus is the period beginning in 1994–95, soon after Ambassador Walter Annenberg made his magnificent gift to public education in the United States, and ending a decade later, in 2003–04.

Why these three districts? They are among a handful of urban school systems across the country that have embarked on far-reaching reform initiatives based on fairly clear theories of action for change. Over the past decade, they have tackled the challenges of raising student achievement and eliminating the achievement gap in different ways, with very different leadership, and within dramatically different community and political contexts.

Has private giving helped these districts enact their theories of action and move farther down their chosen reform paths by lending sharper focus or coherence? Or, conversely, has it altered the districts' reform strategies and priorities, either distorting or subverting local efforts? How has the giving affected, and been affected by, the processes or politics of district reform?

To answer these questions, we surveyed leaders in the districts, asking them to tell us about the largest grants received over the decade, what these monies were intended to accomplish, and how results were evaluated. Finally, we asked them (and ourselves) the ultimate question: What has been the impact of the giving? Has philanthropy contributed to lasting systemic changes in these districts?

OVERVIEW OF THE THREE DISTRICTS

Size and Demographics

As Table 1 shows, the three districts in our study range in size and characteristics. In terms of total student enrollment, budget, and number of schools, HISD is the largest of the three. CMS is the smallest, but it is growing rapidly; its enrollment has risen approximately 16 percent since 2001–02.

Though once predominantly white, all three districts now serve disproportionately large percentages of low-income, English-learner, and racial/ethnic minority students. Houston has by far the most children eligible for free or reduced-price lunch. Both Houston and San Diego enroll a significant percentage of English learners. Charlotte has the highest percentage of white students, San Diego the highest percentage of Asian students.

Reform Efforts

Charlotte, Houston, and San Diego have all attracted national attention for their successes in recent years. But as noted earlier, these successes have been attained in different ways, with different leaders, and in very different circumstances. Before focusing on philanthropy's part in these reform efforts, it is useful to review the recent history of reform in each of these districts.

Charlotte

Dramatic changes began in CMS in 1996 when Eric Smith became superintendent, and they continue to the present—almost a full decade later. Smith was chosen by a board determined to focus on student achievement, measure performance, and equitably meet the needs of all children. From 1996 to the present, through numerous board elections, a working majority of the board has continuously embraced these core commitments.

Smith and the board refocused the district on four goals: increasing student achievement, providing safe and orderly schools, increasing community collaboration, and creating effective support networks. Superintendent Jim Pughsley, who moved up from the position of deputy to succeed Smith

TABLE 1   Characteristics of the Three Districts

	Charlotte	Houston	San Diego
Number of students (2004–05)	121,640	208,945	135,807
Student population trend	Increasing rapidly	Increasing slowly	Decreasing
Low-income*	42%	83%	56%
English learners	8%	27%	28%
Special education	11%	10%	11%
Race/Ethnicity			
White	40%	9%	26%
African American	43%	29%	15%
Hispanic	10%	59%	42%
Asian	4%	3%	16%
Annual budget	$890.3 million	$1.3 billion	$1.06 billion
Per-pupil expenditure	$7,311	$6,222	$7,805
Number of schools	148	302	180

*Eligible for free or reduced price lunch program

in 2002, continued to advance the district's reform agenda and added a fifth goal: ensuring equity across the schools. The two major tools used to achieve these goals were an emerging instructional management system and equitable distribution of resources.[1]

To measure progress and focus attention on the goals, the district put into place a "balanced scorecard" tracking system that set specific targets within each of the five goal areas and tracked progress toward attaining them. For 2004–05, for example, a target for the "attaining high academic achievement" goal is to reduce the dropout rate among all student groups. A target for the "ensuring community collaboration" goal is to increase the number of partnerships and volunteers engaged in specific activities to achieve other district goals.

Aggressive implementation of the reform strategy and accompanying gains in student performance in the early grades have earned Charlotte national acclaim. In 2004, CMS was a finalist for the Broad Prize for Excellence in Urban Education. Nevertheless, the district faces numerous challenges, including lack of progress in raising high school achievement, lingering tensions over desegregation, and extremely high rates of teacher turnover in high-needs schools. Currently, there is agitation in some suburban areas to break up the district, and business leaders have organized to examine fundamental structural and governance issues.

Houston

Major reform efforts in HISD began in 1990, when the school board, spurred by five new trustees (including this chapter's second author), drafted and committed itself to a *Declaration of Beliefs and Visions*. The document delineated a new educational structure focused on the relationship between teacher and student, decentralization, and shared decisionmaking, performance rather than compliance, and a common core of academic subjects for all students.

The theory of action embraced by the Houston school board has been referred to as "performance/empowerment." Its essence is that employees are held accountable for performance, and so they must also be empowered. Accordingly, "Participative management and employee involvement prevail, and as much power as possible is pushed out into schools and classrooms. Since students are accountable, parents, on their behalf, are also empowered. They are given public school choice and great influence in the schools they choose."[2] Two superintendents failed to embrace the HISD board's reform agenda. Finally, in 1994, the board chose one of their own, Rod Paige, to lead the district. Paige fully understood and fully supported the vision; as much as anyone, in fact, he had helped create it. And he was intent on enacting it, regardless of the obstacles that might lie in the way.

Under the leadership of the new superintendent and a working majority of the board—and in later years, strong backing from the local business community—the district entered a lengthy period of systemic change: accountability, decentralization, business outsourcing, weighted student funding, and, later, managed instruction. Improvements in student achievement outpaced the state, and the achievement gap narrowed. By the late 1990s, HISD was also attracting national attention, and in 2002 it won the first Broad Prize.

Throughout this period, though marred by fierce controversy and some periods of instability, the board remained committed to its *Beliefs and Visions* document. In 2001, with a clarifying addendum, the trustees reaffirmed the document. When Paige departed to become secretary of education, he was succeeded by long-term HISD teacher and administrator Kaye Stripling, who continued on the same reform path, though perhaps with less energy.

In 2005 she was replaced by another HISD insider, Abe Saavedra. In recent years, however, there has been much turnover on the HISD board, and it is not clear where the new board and superintendent wish to take the district.[3]

San Diego

In education circles, the term "blueprint" has become synonymous with the reform plan launched in SDCS by nontraditional superintendent Alan Bersin and veteran educator Tony Alvarado. Officially approved in March 2000 by a slender 3–2 school board majority, the *Blueprint for Student Success in a Standards-Based System* made closing the achievement gap the district's highest priority. According to a review conducted by the American Institutes for Research, the vision was to "focus all district activities on strengthening the educational core: teaching and learning in the classroom."

The *Blueprint* focused on instructional leadership of principals, professional development for teachers, monitoring and accountability procedures to identify low-performing schools and students, new structures to enhance parent communication and involvement, new literacy and math frameworks and materials, and increased time and intensity of instruction for low-performing schools and students.[4] While the theory of action in San Diego was clearly top-down implementation of a comprehensive instructional management system, in 2004 Bersin and board leaders began to consider how to make the transition from managed instruction to more empowerment, balanced with accountability for high-performing schools.[5]

From the beginning, implementation of the *Blueprint* was contentious. The teachers union fought Bersin's reform agenda every step of the way. So did two of the district's five school board members, and it was only with a narrow 3–2 majority, sustained through two election cycles, that Bersin was able to keep moving forward through controversy after controversy. The district began to reap significant performance gains in elementary school performance, and there were signs that the *Blueprint* was winning increasing acceptance by teachers. But the future of San Diego's reforms is in doubt. The November 2004 board elections returned a 4–1 board opposed to the *Blueprint*, and the new board moved swiftly to obtain Bersin's agreement to an early expiration of his contract.

RESEARCH METHOD

To explore philanthropy's role in Charlotte, Houston, and San Diego, we designed a three-stage data collection and research process, summarized below. (A full list of the survey questions is provided in the Appendix.)

- *Stage 1:* Following preliminary phone calls to introduce the study and obtain contact information, we administered a two-page survey of district staff via e-mail. The survey requested information about gift and grant money received by the district from all private sources over the 10-year period from 1994–95 through 2003–04.[6] Respondents were asked to identify the largest sources of giving to the district during the 10-year period, including the purpose and terms of the gift or grant. Respondents were also asked for specific information about local foundations dedicated to supporting the school district and other local nonprofit organizations that provide gifts or grants to schools within the district.
- *Stage 2:* A structured telephone interview was conducted with district and local leaders to collect in-depth information about the largest grants and gifts received during the 10-year study period. The survey asked respondents to provide details about the grant/gift (e.g., terms, purpose, origin of idea); the relationship between the purpose of the grant/gift and the district's reform agenda (e.g., impetus, connection to other reform efforts in the district, focus on incremental improvements vs. fundamental change); and the evaluation process and results (e.g., methods and findings of interim and final evaluations, evidence of long-term impact, lessons learned, unanticipated consequences, and level of satisfaction with results).
- *Stage 3:* We reviewed proposals, evaluation reports, news archives, research literature, and other documents pertaining to the intent, design, implementation, and results of the reform activities supported by the major grants/gifts identified in Stages 1 and 2. In addition, we collected information about the work of local organizations (such as local education funds, or LEFs) external to the school district but active in local school reform.

Before discussing the findings of our research, it is important to make a caveat. When we began, we expected the task of collecting information about philanthropic giving in these districts to be straightforward. These expectations were quickly dashed. In each district, different people (and in some cases, different organizations) were responsible for different grant projects, and no one seemed to have a grasp of the whole. Preparing a coherent account of this topic was therefore less like telling a story and more like assembling a puzzle from widely scattered pieces.

We discovered that other researchers seeking to quantify philanthropic involvement in public education have been similarly thwarted. As one put it, "Extant systems for capturing information in both the education and philanthropy sectors render imperfect data. The picture is further complicated by the proliferation of local education foundations and other organizations that raise, manage, and distribute funds on behalf of schools and districts."[7]

This lack of coherent information is significant. If the districts we studied are not systematically evaluating, overseeing, and coordinating the various philanthropy-funded efforts occurring within their boundaries, then who is ensuring that all of the parts of the system are working smoothly together to move the district in a single direction? The answer appears to be "nobody." This permissive approach may be advantageous in terms of maximizing the flow of private dollars, but it greatly increases the risk that the district's reform momentum will be slowed, if not diverted, and that district staff will be pulled in many competing directions.

We acknowledge that the limits of the available data and the confined scope of our research leave many questions on the table. Gauging philanthropy's impact on urban school reform, even within particular districts, is an extremely complex undertaking. Nevertheless, we believe our small study succeeded in its goal of capturing the philanthropic experiences of these three districts, illuminating some of the key tensions and conflicts that have arisen, and conveying lessons with broader relevance.

FINDINGS

Charlotte

Like their counterparts in the other two districts, leaders in Charlotte were unable to provide precise figures on the total amount of philanthropic gift and grant money the district has received over the past decade. Information about specific philanthropic activities was accessible, albeit from separate sources. Again, this lack of information is revealing.

We concentrate below on three pools of funding dedicated to school reform in Charlotte: a large Ford Foundation grant, a newly formed CMS foundation, and a local education fund known as Charlotte Advocates for Education (CAE).

The Ford CERI Grant

The largest sum of private foundation money CMS received for the purpose of school reform during the study period was a series of grants totaling $1.05 million from the Ford Foundation under a project entitled the Collaborating for Educational Reform Initiative (CERI). This was not a case in which a district sought out funding to support its strategic intent. Rather, it was a case in which a foundation seized upon a reform idea and tried to find districts ripe for implementation.

The Ford Foundation developed the CERI program in the late 1990s out of frustration with the transitory results it was obtaining by funding "traditional" school reform efforts. According to this tradition, reform ideas originated inside the central office of an urban district and were moved forward by a visionary superintendent. This was fine while it lasted, but it usually didn't last long; when the superintendent moved on, as so often occurred, the reform effort perished.

Ford's experience with its Urban Partnership Program, as well as its conversations with other funders (such as Annenberg and Pew), had convinced the foundation that reform efforts required widespread community buy-in and support in order to survive the regular turnover of district leadership. The CERI grant program was built on this premise. As the Request for Proposals stated, "system-wide reform efforts require effective coalitions among organizations which are committed to systemic educational reform over an extended period of time and who project their efforts to the state level."[8] Ford staff were not alone in recognizing the importance of local collaboration. This was also one of the priorities identified by then-superintendent Smith, and it was clearly an urgent need in Charlotte. The district had endured a long, divisive battle over school desegregation, and it was not over. Fights between the district and the courts over student assignment continued to divide the community and divert attention from school reform. A grant designed to build a shared community vision for better schools would seem to be of very high value. The goals of the Ford Foundation and the needs of the district appeared to be closely related.

In their proposal to Ford, the Charlotte grantwriters described a host of ambitious plans, including expanded parent involvement and stronger links among organizations, all aimed at raising student achievement. Seven partners would participate in the initiative, including CMS, the local education fund, the Public School Forum of North Carolina, the North Carolina Education and Law Center, and several higher education institutions. According to the proposal, these partners would jointly explore promising activities and bring their recommendations to a new council of principals, which would then choose activities for implementation. The primary focus would be on the schools in West Mecklenburg, the district's poorest section.

Along with seven other sites across the county, Ford awarded CMS an initial planning grant of $150,000 in 1998, and successive implementation grants totaling $900,000 were awarded in subsequent years. Ford intended to continue funding projects for up to a decade—if sufficient progress was seen.

As with many grants, what actually happened in Charlotte bore little resemblance to the proposal. Table 2 summarizes information about the CERI grant as provided by district staff and external evaluators. As these responses and the following discussion show, the early aims of the grant quickly unraveled.

Soon after the grant was awarded, according to the RAND researchers who evaluated the project, the district began to exert top-down control over the project. Most decisions were made by the project director and regional superintendent rather than by the collaborative. As a result, the principals became disenfranchised, and several of the CERI partners disengaged. Furthermore, the grant seemed to be paying for "business as usual." Instead of being channeled to new school reform models, as intended, most of the grant money was being used to pay for teacher professional development via existing programs.

Faced with disappointing results, unhappy partners, and mounting pressure from Ford, CMS and its partners restructured the CERI project in 2002. The two state-level partners left, and the local chamber of commerce stepped in to replace them. The leadership changed, and responsibility for managing the project was shifted from CMS to the local education fund. As one local leader wryly commented, "This was the result of an 'aha' midway into the initiative: If you really want to see dramatic reform, then having the project housed in the school system is not such a good idea."

Realizing that the original CERI collaborative had failed to reach the goals it had initially defined for itself, the reconfigured group narrowed its focus to a single problem plaguing the high-poverty schools in West Mecklenburg: teacher turnover. (The turnover rate was nearly 20 percent districtwide and approached 40 percent in some schools.) This shift in focus was consistent with new CMS central office initiatives focused on teacher recruitment and retention.

With this change in leadership and direction, CERI embarked on new projects to promote teacher mentoring and retention in partnership with the chamber. A pilot program known as Teacher Keepers, for example, sought to improve the working environment for teachers through better student discipline, teacher recruitment incentives, and expanded training for teachers and principals.

Did the restructuring enable the CERI partners to finally work together successfully and form the kind of collaborative that Ford had envisioned? The refocused initiative apparently did generate some productive exchanges of ideas. For example, local business partners took what they knew about managing large companies and applied this to schools. Executives from

Charlotte's corporations coached the principals in how to create a culture that would make teachers want to stay.

Yet evaluators found that, a year after the restructuring, the collaborative still lacked cohesion. The higher education partners still did not feel deeply involved. Commitment from principals was minimal, and parents seemed barely engaged. The evaluators concluded, "Members were still struggling in spring 2003 with how to pull the collaborative together. They had planned for neither how to proceed as a collaborative, how to develop a policy agenda, nor how to sustain the types of efforts they were backing."[9] The evaluators not only examined the collaborative's ability to define and pursue shared goals; they also sought to determine whether the project had had any measurable impact on improving students' academic performance—a core goal stated within the original RFP. While data from CMS show that test score increases for the West Mecklenburg schools have exceeded those for the district as a whole, the evaluators found little evidence that the CERI collaborative has contributed significantly to these gains. District initiatives such as providing additional funding to "Equity Plus" schools and placing math and literacy coordinators in low-performing schools may rightly claim credit for the progress observed.

It is therefore difficult to say, after more than six years of investment, whether the Ford CERI grant has had any lasting impact either on building productive, sustainable collaborations or on raising student achievement in the Charlotte-Mecklenburg district. Margaret Carnes, director of the local education fund, put it aptly: "It's been a great learning experience for everybody. The problem is, the project was not created so that we could measure well what happened."[10]

This observation returns us to the issue of evaluation. The Ford Foundation insisted upon a rigorous, independent analysis of its efforts by the RAND Corporation, which ended up painting an often unflattering portrait of the foundation's investment, particular with respect to Charlotte's implementation. This type of evaluation may be painful for a funder to read, but there is no doubt that it provides the kind of hard, clear information needed to improve programs and increase the probability of success in future investments.

It is also worth noting that CMS does not appear to have engaged in any systematic evaluation of the CERI grant. As we observed earlier, there is little incentive for CMS, or any district, for that matter, to evaluate the results of its philanthropic gifts. To do so would force a choice between conducting a rigorous evaluation (which might reveal a project's shortcomings and thus curtail the flow of philanthropic dollars) or a less rigorous evaluation (which might gloss over the shortcomings and fail to inform necessary program-

TABLE 2   Summary of Ford CERI Grant, Charlotte-Mecklenburg

Survey Items	Responses*
Amount and terms of grant/gift	$1.05 million, 1998–2003
Initiated by funder or district?	Funder
Goal of grant: incremental change or structural/systemic change?	Structural/systemic change. The idea was to reduce systemic barriers to reform by strengthening local collaboration. This was Ford's philosophy.
How was the grant evaluated? What data were collected and examined?	RAND conducted formative evaluations starting in 1999. The evaluations looked at student performance data and conducted surveys/interviews of staff and others involved in the collaborative.
What did the evaluations show?**	Little progress was made in developing organizational linkages. Lack of shared vision. Policy changes were planned, but there was insufficient support to sustain them.
Did the grant have a long-term impact?	No evidence of this.
Lessons learned?	How important it is to involve key stakeholders within the organization, and how difficult it is to get them to work together. While challenging, this determines the life of a project beyond the funding.

*Responses were provided by district staff and local leaders interviewed during the study. As such, they reflect only the views of the interviewee(s) and may not reflect the opinions of other district staff or of the authors.

**The answer to this question was obtained from the RAND evaluation of the CERI program.

matic improvements). Better to continue receiving, and not ask whether the investments are adding value, than to ask too many questions and place a precious funding stream in jeopardy.

One might argue that a school district has no obligation to assess a project that is entirely funded by philanthropy and requires no local tax dollars; that the school system should simply be grateful for the gift and allow the funder to evaluate the results. But this is a straw argument. District leaders do, of course, bear responsibility for all of the district's resources and programs, no matter who is funding them. Without rigorous evaluation and oversight on the district's part, who is to say that a private donation is doing no harm? Who can say that it is not diverting staff's attention from other, more worthy programs and initiatives that *are* funded by taxpayers? We argue that school districts should, in fact, play a far more proactive role in evaluating their private donations, judging each one thoroughly and critically for what it might add to (or subtract from) the district's overall reform strategy. The failure to do so invites confusion of purpose—a great enemy of progress.

The Charlotte-Mecklenburg Public Schools Foundation

The second pool of private funding dedicated to school reform in Charlotte-Mecklenburg comes not from a single source but from the many local businesses and major corporations with headquarters in Charlotte. Local businesses had long supported public education, but the district until recently lacked a single point of entry for business involvement—a fact that rankled the local chamber of commerce. Central office had no clear mechanisms for coordinating fundraising or targeting funds to priority schools and programs.

The impetus to change came two years ago when county commissioners urged Superintendent Pughsley to seek alternative streams of funding to meet the district's growing budget demands. The superintendent, supported by a board majority, decided to create a nonprofit foundation within the school district. Launched in the spring of 2004, the foundation is managed by CMS's Office of Strategic Partnerships.

Director Debbie Antshel described the CMS foundation as playing the role of a matchmaker "connecting business strengths and school needs."[11] Corporate financial support and management assistance is now cultivated for specific district projects and priorities, such as teacher recruitment and retention, leadership development for principals, and other needs submitted by individual schools. For example, executives from Wachovia Bank advised the district on how to create its balanced scorecard. The business community has also been working with CMS leaders to address the serious teacher recruitment and retention problems noted earlier.

While the new CMS foundation has raised little money thus far, a major fundraising campaign is planned for fall 2005. The first contribution to the foundation was a $50,000 grant from the BellSouth Foundation, targeted to "teacher mentoring programs which are known to have a direct impact on student achievement."[12] Joined with the CERI grant, this gift was aligned with the district's priority on improving teacher recruitment and retention.

It remains to be seen whether the CMS foundation will substantially help the district to solve its most intractable problems, like improving high schools and getting the best teachers into the neediest classrooms. More resources, carefully targeted, will undoubtedly help. Creative approaches, strong leadership, and community support may be even more critical.

Charlotte Advocates for Education

Charlotte Advocates for Education (CAE), the local education fund, has a staff of just three and a budget of less than $1 million. But despite its small size, the nonprofit has a significant voice in the local dialogue about school improvement. CAE and its LEF counterparts elsewhere across the country have been praised for providing "a constructive bridge" between the local community, business, and district leadership.[13] CAE focuses its efforts on educating the public and building local capacity for school reform. It conducts intensive public awareness campaigns to educate the community about school board candidates and educates candidates about their responsibilities as board members. It issues a weekly electronic newsletter to inform the community about relevant local, state, and national education news and produces guides explaining the school budget to the lay public. It also manages a speaker's bureau.

This was not always its role. When it was formed in the early 1990s, CAE's purpose was to cultivate funding from corporations and regrant them in small amounts to individual schools and projects. But by the late 1990s, staff members were reexamining their accomplishments and finding them wanting. As director Margaret Carnes put it, "Our work had earned a lot of happy faces in the schools, but it was having little or no impact. Our budget was small, so we knew we would never be able to provide adequate resources to achieve significant change. We felt that we were enabling inadequacy."

The LEF decided to transform itself from a resource provider to a research and advocacy organization. "There was, and continues to be, a strong need for an independent, nonpartisan entity in the community to assess school performance and stimulate conversations about how to achieve change," says Carnes. These conversations are more important now than ever. The desegregation battles have left a residue of bitterness and distrust among different factions in the community. The district has also grown larger and more diverse, and the attention of Charlotte's corporate leaders is increasingly focused nationally and internationally rather than locally. As a result, adds Carnes, the district is facing greater challenges and must engage stakeholders in working together to address them.

Summary

Viewed as a whole, these findings suggest to us that the philanthropic funding CMS has received has not diverted it from its primary goals. In fact, private monies are increasingly being channeled to address equity problems and teacher turnover—two core priorities defined by the superintendent and board. But if private giving is helping CMS enact its theory of action and move farther down its chosen reform path, the results are surely not what they could be. Ongoing fractures in the community stemming from desegregation and student assignment appear to have largely derailed the best intentions of the Ford CERI initiative, even though it was largely harmonious with the district's theory of action.

Charlotte's experience with this philanthropic effort highlights the extent to which local context trumps philanthropy. This is hardly news. Years of experience and reams of thwarted efforts have clearly shown the extent to which divisions in a community can complicate the work of philanthropists investing in urban district reform. Funders (and district leaders, too) would be well-advised to pay close attention to the local context, particularly the roles and interests of various stakeholders.

The question is, how can district leaders and philanthropists together foster the broad support and civic capacity that enables good reform ideas to be sustained over a long period of time? Houston's experience, explored in the following section, provides one possible answer to this question.

Houston

Three philanthropic efforts dedicated to school reform stand out in Houston. Two nonprofits external to the district have led major reform initiatives: the Houston A+ Challenge and Project GRAD. There are also significant private funds provided directly to HISD to support a wide variety of reform activities, programs, and scholarships.

The Houston A+ Challenge

This public-private partnership originated in 1996 when a group of local business leaders, supported by The Brown Foundation and the Houston Endowment, established a coalition with local educators to initiate and sustain systemic reform in the local public schools. Fueled by an Annenberg Challenge grant of $20 million and an additional $40 million in matching funds from Houston foundations, the newly formed Houston Annenberg Challenge (later renamed The Houston A+ Challenge) directs "the largest sum of money ever dedicated to public school reform in the greater Houston area."[14]

Working closely with HISD, the local business sector, and other community partners, The Houston A+ Challenge launched a campaign to generate and sustain whole-school reform in HISD and other Houston-area districts. The work proceeded in two phases. During the first phase, Houston A+ provided direct funding to 88 schools in six school districts. Activities focused on three core "imperatives":

1. Teacher learning—in particular, transforming teacher professional development
2. School isolation—specifically, fostering communication and engagement within schools and between schools and their surrounding communities

3. Size—creating small, personalized learning environments to meet the needs of every student and ensure that no student "slips between the cracks." In a second phase, which began in 2000, Houston A+ sought to influence other forces that were shaping the public school system. Among the efforts pursued were a revamped teacher-preparation program developed in collaboration with four local postsecondary institutions, an academy to train principals in distributed leadership, summer institutes for teachers and principals, an initiative to place K–5 math specialists in classrooms (in conjunction with ExxonMobil and HISD), projects aimed at restructuring high schools, and the creation of "professional learning communities" involving teachers and administrators.

Table 3 summarizes the work of Houston A+ under Phases I and II, which extended from 1997 through 2002. At the end of this period, Houston A+ was awarded another $20 million from Annenberg and $10 million from The Brown Foundation to continue its work for five more years. In addition, the Carnegie Corporation and the Bill & Melinda Gates Foundation awarded Houston A+ $12 million to embark on a new "Houston Schools for a New Society" initiative. These efforts extend beyond the time parameters of our study.

Has the Annenberg Challenge/Houston A+ had any measurable impact in Houston? The official evaluations, conducted by professors Pedro Reyes and Joy Phillips of the University of Texas at Austin, have been highly positive. But a closer scrutiny of the achievement data raises some questions, too. For example, in summarizing trends in performance on the Texas Learning Index[15] from 1998 to 2002, the evaluation report indicates that Beacon middle schools (reform-ripe schools receiving high levels of Annenberg funding) "continue to outperform other funded schools and HISD middle schools in reading and mathematics achievement." This is true. What the report does not say, but what its graphs show, is that middle school math scores increased by only four points at the Beacon schools from 1998 to 2002 (from 82 to 86 on a 100-point scale), while performance at HISD schools overall rose by 10 points (from 74 to 85). In other grades and other subject areas, the gains made by the Annenberg schools were often no greater than those for district schools overall.

Furthermore, the evaluators' surveys showed that many teachers in the Annenberg-funded schools did not perceive that the Challenge activities had been very effective in bringing about reforms. And the teacher turnover rate of 12 to 13 percent at the funded schools remains unacceptably high.[16]

Despite these ongoing challenges, Houston A+ executive director Michelle Pola has no doubt that the Challenge has had a highly positive impact on school reform in Houston. She points to the district's flourishing local partnerships and its strong emphasis on accountability, peer review, and collaboration as evidence of lasting systemic changes that the Annenberg project has advanced. "The Challenge has changed the culture and the dialogue in the city around public school reform," Pola observes. It has also put Houston on the national map, attracting recognition to its reforms, encouraging the replication of the district's successes elsewhere, and inspiring additional private giving to support urban school reform.

A thorough evaluation of The Houston A+ Challenge's accomplishments lies beyond the scope of this study. We do note, however, the contrast between Pola's and the evaluators' positive assessment of the grants' impact in Houston and the less glowing evaluations given to the Annenberg program nationally. Has Houston A+ succeeded where other Annenberg efforts have failed? If it has, perhaps it is because of its theory of action. The project is grounded in the belief that "those who work closely with children and know them best should decide on changes needed for the school." Furthermore, "community support is essential for sustaining school reform."[17]

These statements are consistent with the HISD board's "performance/empowerment" theory of action, described earlier. Thus, even though the enormous Annenberg gift was directed by an external entity rather than from within the district, it does not appear to have distorted or diverted HISD's reform agenda. Rather, The Houston A+ Challenge seems to have supplemented and extended the district's already strong commitment to decentralization and school and teacher empowerment, with accountability for results.

Will the Annenberg Challenge have a lasting impact in Houston? This will be the ultimate test of Houston A+'s success. As one observer has remarked, "Success isn't simply a question of whether test scores go up or whether other donors step forward, although these are important goals. . . . Success turns on whether enough new knowledge is generated about large-scale urban reform to inform other funders and policymakers."[18] Time will tell.

Project GRAD

Another Houston nonprofit, Project GRAD, has also played a significant role in Houston school reform, though in an entirely different way. Project GRAD (Graduation Really Achieves Dreams) has a singular focus: ensuring that at least 80 percent of students in the city's lowest-performing schools graduate from high school and at least 50 percent of those graduates enter and complete college. Its larger purpose, as Holly Holland, the historian of Project GRAD, put it, "is to change the culture of urban education from passive

TABLE 3   Summary of Annenberg Phase I and II Grant, Houston

Survey Items	Responses*
Amount and terms of grant/gift	$60 million, 1997–2002
Initiated by funder(s) or district?	Funders (originated by The Brown Foundation and the Houston Endowment)
Goal of grant: incremental change or structural/ systemic change?	Structural/systemic transformation. The goal was to build capacity for whole-school change.
How was grant evaluated? What data were collected and examined?	Interim and final evaluations were based on student performance data, reflection sheets, portfolios, site visits, and observations, which were scored using detailed rubrics. Accountability was built into projects from the beginning; schools knew how they would be evaluated (e.g., peer reviews).
What did the evaluations show?	Performance gains were observed in many of the project's "Beacon" and "Lamplighter" (focus) schools. There was also evidence of improvements in culture: for example, more professional networking and collaboration within the district, a sharper focus on accountability, and more widespread use of peer review.
Did the grant have a long-term impact?	Definitely. The project created momentum around school reform, brought different stakeholders together, and changed the district culture. School staff and district leaders now use terminology learned from Houston A+, speaking of the "cycle of inquiry" and "theories of action."
Lessons learned?	This effort began with the district and the business community at the table together. Accountability was part of the culture in Houston. This created the right conditions for success.

*Responses were provided by district staff and local leaders interviewed during the study. As such, they reflect only the views of the interviewee(s) and may not reflect the opinions of other district staff or of the authors.

acceptance of failure to the expectation that academic success will follow every student who receives the right preparation in school."[19] The project's history is by now widely known. In 1988, Tenneco chairman and CEO Jim Ketelsen decided to initiate a four-year college scholarship program in Houston's lowest-performing secondary school, Davis High. Within a few years, the number of Davis graduates who were graduating and continuing on to college had more than quadrupled. But Ketelsen was dissatisfied: This was still far below his goal. Furthermore, college admissions test scores had failed to rise, and the school's high dropout rate had not budged. Ketelsen realized that to have a real impact, it would be necessary to reach students long before they entered 9th grade.

Ketelsen and his associates decided to make their unit of reform the feeder pattern: Davis High School and all of the elementary and middle schools feeding into it.[20] (The project is now preparing to extend its focus further still, to higher education, to ensure that its students not only enroll in college, but continue on to complete their degrees.) Ketelsen and colleagues identified curricula and programs found to increase basic skills, improve student behavior, and reduce the risk of dropping out of school. These core components—the Success for All reading program, MOVE IT Math, a classroom management program, social services, parental involvement, and the high school program—begin in kindergarten and continue on up through graduation.

With its successes in the Davis feeder pattern bearing fruit, Project GRAD expanded to serve other highly disadvantaged feeder patterns in HISD. Today it serves five feeder patterns, which together encompass 71 schools, nearly 50,000 students, and more than 3,000 teachers. Ninety-eight percent of the students Project GRAD serves in Houston are poor and at risk.

Over the ten years of our study period, Project GRAD's revenues, like its enrollment, grew steadily. Starting with less than $200,000 in annual revenue during the early 1990s, its annual budget now exceeds $16 million. And revenues no longer come primarily from local philanthropy. Only about one-quarter of Project GRAD's revenues now come from private donations; more than half are in the form of federal grants, and 19 percent are from HISD. For the 2003–04 fiscal year, this amounted to just over $3 million.[21]

Project GRAD has countless fans. Former president George Bush has praised the organization for "closing the achievement gap" and urged individuals and organizations involved in school reform to "follow their example." HISD superintendent Abe Saavedra has said that the district's partnership with Project GRAD generates "incredible achievements for both our students and our teachers."[22] And author Holly Holland has called Project GRAD "the major catalyst for improvements in the Houston schools it serves, giving hope to impoverished students who thought college was out of their reach, bringing better consistency to schools accustomed to chaos, and improving professional development for many educators."[23]

The evidence used to support these laudatory claims is impressive indeed. In the feeder patterns where Project GRAD has been implemented, test scores have climbed, graduation rates have increased, AP and honors-level course enrollment have risen, disciplinary referrals have dropped, and teenage pregnancy rates have declined. These and other indicators of success have been documented in a series of evaluations conducted by Kwame Opuni of the

University of St. Thomas in Houston. These research efforts, which began in 1994 and are funded by the University of Houston, are designed to assess the project's impact and obtain formative information for refining its various components.

While Project GRAD's successes deserve to be celebrated, it is also important to point out that the project cannot claim credit for all of the gains seen in the city's schools. HISD launched many initiatives over the same period of time, such as aligning the curriculum with the state's academic standards, which led to student achievement gains districtwide. The evaluations that have been performed to date make it hard to disentangle Project GRAD's achievements from those of the district as a whole.

Though it is painful to criticize a project that is doing much good, it is also important to acknowledge what is said by Project GRAD's critics. Some have questioned the program's accomplishments, arguing that programs like AVID have achieved better results. Others have challenged GRAD's choice of reading and math curricula. MOVE IT Math, for example, has been disparaged for lacking a solid research base, and Success for All is often criticized as being too prescriptive and rigid. When some HISD schools wanted to replace Success for All with a different reading program (RITE, developed by the Rodeo Institute for Teacher Excellence) that they believed was more effective, Project GRAD resisted. Though its leaders have allowed some local adaptations and refinements, they believe that continuity and adherence to the program's core components are essential to maintaining program quality.

This returns us once again to the recurring theme of evaluation. Uri Treisman, director of the Dana Center at the University of Texas at Austin, has argued that Project GRAD needs to be subjected to a more rigorous evaluation by unaffiliated researchers than has heretofore been conducted. "I have sympathy for the challenge of working in some of the cities they've chosen to work in," says Treisman. "That's a big plus they've taken these on . . . [but] that doesn't mean they're doing it effectively."[24]

Project GRAD is now, in fact, undergoing an independent five-year evaluation by MDRC designed to provide detailed information about the project's impact in Houston and four other expansion sites across the country.[25] This research will permit careful scrutiny of the extent to which the program is contributing to observed changes in a variety of key outcomes.

But Treisman's comments raise a larger point, too: the importance of distinguishing between good intentions and good work. Many philanthropists have the best of intentions, as the title of this volume suggests. And much of this work deserves acclaim, for noble effort if not for results. But in the end, it is the results that matter. Should each component of a program be rigorously evaluated on a regular basis by unaffiliated parties with no incentive to conceal potentially unflattering results? Clearly, yes. Are school districts obligated to use this information to assess the "value added" by each program in a clear-eyed, objective manner? Certainly. In this era of accountability, every dollar a district spends must be scrutinized. And every single reform effort must be viewed in light of the whole.

Philanthropic Giving to HISD

Last, we turn to philanthropic giving cultivated and controlled by the Houston school district itself. Business involvement in the city's public schools can be traced back to the late 1970s, when the "adopt-a-school" model was in vogue both locally and nationally. "HISD made it clear from that point on," reflects assistant superintendent Carol Hoey, "that they wanted partnerships with the business community—that they needed their help to improve the schools."[26] Both monetary and in-kind contributions to HISD have grown steadily ever since. By the mid-1990s, annual contributions by area businesses exceeded $8 million annually, and today it is estimated the private giving well surpasses $16 million per year. These funds are increasingly being channeled through the HISD Foundation, which, after an abortive start in the early 1990s, has become an active, effective conduit for HISD fundraising. The district uses these funds to support a broad assortment of initiatives, ranging from scholarships, science programs, and fine arts initiatives to teacher professional development.

Like Debbie Antshel of CMS's foundation, those who head the HISD Foundation view their role as matching schools' needs with business partners' strengths and interests. Says Hoey, "Over time, schools have developed strong relationships with individual corporations. These companies know exactly what the dollars are being used for, and they can see their impact."

One of the largest donations to HISD in recent years was a $2.4 million gift by local companies to support the development and implementation of a schoolwide character education program. (Though the original gift predated our study period, the money was expended throughout the decade and, in fact, lasted until quite recently.) The project was the vision of a local business leader, Transco CEO Jack Bowen, who was troubled by the lack of moral integrity among his employees. Bowen approached then-HISD superintendent Joan Raymond and told her he was willing to raise the money for a character-education program in the schools if she was willing to implement it. Raymond and the board gave their unanimous support, Bowen raised the funds, and the project was launched.

HISD staff, led by project director Dot Woodfin, researched character education programs around the country, developed an extensive curriculum,
and implemented it throughout the school system through extensive training and dissemination activities. Fifteen years later, the project continues
to run strong. Evaluations indicate that the project has been successful in
reducing problem behavior (though the research methodology may not meet
the highest standards of social science research), but clearly many challenges
remain in this domain. Nevertheless, to date more than 28,000 staff have
been trained, the program is strongly supported by teachers and parents, and
educators from all over the country have come to study and try to replicate
the Houston program.[27] Did the initial leadership by Jack Bowen and the $2.4
million gift by Houston's business leaders to support character education in
the public schools help HISD carry out its theory of action for change? Probably not. Did it succeed in having a positive impact in the district? Certainly.
Impact, in other words, can be measured on many levels. Philanthropy may
benefit a district even when it is not tied to the district's theory of action and
does not even focus on student achievement.

Summary

This exploration of philanthropy's role in Houston's school reform efforts
only begins to scratch the surface. Still, the findings clearly indicate that private giving has helped the district enact its theory of action. Funding has
been targeted on an array of district priorities, including but not limited to
professional development. This work has been expedited by the unity of purpose among Houston's leaders, and by sustained leadership from the superintendent and board. Within this supportive context, the district has been
able to continue developing the same reform strategy over a sustained period
of time. As we see in the following section, San Diego also managed to pursue its reforms over a relatively long time. But the path it pursued and the
challenges it faced bore little resemblance to those in either Charlotte or
Houston.

San Diego

Philanthropy in San Diego looks quite different from that in Charlotte and
Houston. For one thing, there are few corporate headquarters in the city, so
large corporate gifts and grants to the public schools are less common. The
district's Partnerships in Education program solicits financial, human, and
in-kind donations of goods and services from the local business community,
mostly for human resources enrichment. While no significant local philan-

thropic funds appear to have been garnered to support implementation of the *Blueprint for Student Success in a Standards-Based System,* superintendent Alan Bersin was extremely successful in attracting national philanthropic support for the district's reforms.

Foundation Support for the Blueprint

The primary intent of the reform plan developed by Bersin and Anthony Alvarado was to significantly improve student achievement in literacy and mathematics in San Diego's public schools, narrow the achievement gap, and end social promotion. To achieve these goals, the district pursued a variety of prevention strategies designed for all students, intervention programs for struggling students, and retention programs for students who failed to meet performance criteria on districtwide reading and math assessments.[28]

Bersin realized these strategies would require substantially increased resources for professional development and chronically low-performing schools. They would be extremely human-resource intensive. Even after a significant reallocation of district resources to support teaching and learning, there were insufficient resources in the system to achieve the changes he and Alvarado intended. As chief academic officer Mary Hopper later commented, the core work of the *Blueprint* never would have happened without an infusion of private money.[29]

Accordingly, Bersin initiated conversations with several foundations, and in 2001, these efforts were rewarded with a series of grants totaling $22.5 million from the Hewlett, Gates, Carnegie, and Broad foundations and The Atlantic Philanthropies. These monies were used to fund a variety of activities, including professional development, peer coaches, and math and literacy initiatives.[30] A summary of these philanthropic investments in the San Diego reforms is provided in Table 4.

It is worth noting that the divisions on the school board extended even to the issue of accepting these funds. Two of the board members opposed to Bersin and the *Blueprint* refused to vote in favor of accepting private money to support core elements of the district's reform plan. Others in the district also disapproved, says Hopper, of the huge influx of private funds. The local teachers union was adamantly opposed to the reform initiatives—and particularly the manner in which they were imposed, without substantial teacher input—and did not welcome resources to support Bersin and Alvarado's agenda.

The impact of the Bersin-Alvarado reforms on student achievement in SDCS in the early grades is widely acknowledged. Between 1999 and 2004, the percentage of San Diego elementary schools scoring at the top category of the state's Academic Performance Index (API) rose by more than one-third,

Table 4   Summary of the Blueprint Grants, San Diego

Survey Items	Responses*
Amount and terms of grants/gifts	$22 million, 2001–06
Initiated by funder or district?	District (superintendent)
Goal of grant: incremental change or structural/ systemic change?	Structural/systemic change. The goal was to reorient all district functions to support the relationship between teacher and student.
How was the grant evaluated? What data were collected and examined?	Interim and final evaluations. At the beginning, monthly reports were provided to the funders. These include information about implementation as well as results (e.g., student achievement data).
What did the evaluations show?	Gains in student achievement in the early grades. Many of the *Blueprint* objectives were achieved, but there is still much work to be done.
Did the grant have a long-term impact?	Yes. The instructional focus is now deeply ingrained.
Lessons learned?	Once you jump-start reforms, how do you maintain momentum? How do you sustain the reforms after the private funding ends?

*Responses were provided by district staff interviewed during the study. As such, they reflect only the views of the interviewee(s) and may not reflect the opinions of other district staff or of the authors.

and all but one school climbed out of the bottom category. The district also succeeded in narrowing the achievement gap between minority and majority students. But growth in literacy appears to have come at the expense of progress in math, and achievement at the middle and high school levels remained flat.[31]

To the extent that SDCS has improved, the grants have certainly contributed to this achievement. Yet few would claim that the *Blueprint* has been as successful as it could or should have been, even with the remarkable infusion of private funding that Bersin secured. Why? Rick Hess, among others, has pointed out that Bersin and Alvarado gave so much attention to training for principals and faculty that they failed to focus sufficiently on infrastructure and curricula. Even after seven years of "diligent work," Hess observes, "by 2004 the district still had not promulgated a coherent curriculum for reading and English. Consequently, while teachers were using the prescribed methods, there was too little attention to the quality of content."[32] The lack of a well-defined curriculum would appear to explain the district's failure to achieve progress at the middle school and high school levels, where instruction is more content-laden.

What ultimately derailed the district's reform momentum, though, was a lack of broad public understanding and support. There is little evidence that the business community rallied around the superintendent and his reform strategy or that the public and the teachers were united behind the district's reform agenda. To the contrary: Broad stakeholder support was clearly needed to ensure the long-term success of the *Blueprint*, yet the centralized, managed instruction model of improvement that Bersin and Alvarado had chosen was, by design, ill-suited to build it.

As Hess has observed, "If the legacy of [Bersin's] seven-year run is in doubt, the San Diego experience illustrates, above all, that even the boldest attempts to overhaul urban schooling are today undermined by the same institutional and organizational failings that they are intended to address."[33] Bersin's departure and the new makeup of the school board, combined with recent budget shortfalls that have necessitated cuts in some core elements of the reform agenda, has already slowed the district's reform momentum—and may eventually change its direction altogether. Will the philanthropic funding for San Diego's reforms continue? The foundation grants were made contingent on stable leadership, and with Bersin's early departure, funding could be terminated. The future of the SDCS reforms, and the grants that have helped make them possible, remains to be seen.

The Lack of a Local Education Fund

It seems noteworthy that San Diego, unlike Charlotte and Houston, lacks an LEF. Instead, there are hundreds of individual school foundations in San Diego that collect and disperse their own funds, exacerbating resource disparities between schools serving advantaged and disadvantaged students.

Though it may seem odd to tell the story of something that never came to be, the story of why San Diego has no LEF is revealing. In 2001, the Public Education Network (PEN) received a small grant from the Edna McConnell Clark Foundation to explore the creation of a San Diego LEF. Through an effort known as the San Diego Dialogue, many different stakeholders in the community came together to discuss the idea. Business leaders, university people, community representatives, and parents took part in the discussions. There was much interest, participants recall, in creating a forum for the community to partner with the district around school reform issues.

"People were deeply concerned about school reform," recalls Beth Dilley of PEN, who was involved in the effort. "They wanted the community to be engaged in reform." But, as she remembers, it became clear to the participants that Bersin saw no value in having an independent, outside organization dedicated to school reform. "This was a reform agenda that was tightly controlled by the school system," says Dilley. In the end, the effort to create an LEF died.

Is this significant? The lack of local stakeholder input in SDCS's reform efforts may have enabled the Bersin-Alvarado reforms to move forward quickly. But in the end, the lack of community support seems to have undermined the initiatives. In the context of the political battles already underway and much history we do not know, could the people of San Diego have created an effective LEF? We do not know, but the question of how to appropriately involve the community is clearly a crucial one that district leaders and philanthropists alike have to consider when embarking on a reform path.

Summary

What do we learn from San Diego? Probably the most significant lesson here is that the *Blueprint* reforms would likely never have occurred (at least to the extent that they did) without substantial external funding. As was the case in Charlotte, however, local conditions in San Diego ultimately thwarted philanthropy's best intentions. A divided school board and community, and a contentious relationship between the district and the teachers union, eventually undermined the Bersin reforms, despite abundant philanthropic support. The message is clear: Philanthropy alone cannot save urban school reform. Broader stakeholder support along with stability in district leadership are also vital.

LESSONS LEARNED

It is clear in these difficult fiscal times that urban school districts urgently need philanthropic support in order to meet the twin challenges of raising student achievement and closing the achievement gap. Still, philanthropy can never provide enough money to educate America's urban children—nor should it. Educating America's children is the responsibility of American taxpayers. Properly funding urban districts is the responsibility of elected officials.

Philanthropy as a percentage of district budgets will always be almost immaterial. Though the three districts in our study were unable to provide accurate estimates of the total amount of philanthropic money they had received over the past decade, even the highest figures they provided represent just a small share of these districts' operating budgets. Still, we believe that philanthropy has had an impact in these districts. One writer has likened this to a small rudder turning a large ship. "Shrewdly invested," Christine Campbell opined, "comparatively small amounts of foundation money can leverage major movement."[34]

For all the reams of private money poured into urban schools over the years, however, the results have been largely disappointing. Many funders who were once deeply invested in the field have since given up and put their money elsewhere, like preschool education, where the promise of positive returns seems greater and the challenges seem less daunting. Why have philanthropic investments in urban schools fallen so far short of what they might be? Why are stories of positive impact the rare exception rather than the rule?

There are many reasons, as touched on in this chapter. But we believe that one of the primary reasons has to do with "the vision thing." Few school districts possess a clear theory of action for change. Without this, the school system is left to sway in the political winds and be tugged to and fro by multiple, often competing goals. Private dollars poured into such a system might have a positive impact and achieve stunning results, but the likelihood of this happening is very low.

We believe that every school district can, and indeed must, set forth a clear and compelling theory of action for change, much like the three districts highlighted in our study. Once this road map has been drawn, the district can leverage every dollar it gets to pursue its priorities. Philanthropic dollars are especially valuable because they can be invested in activities that have no political constituency but are high priorities for reform leaders, and also in long pay-out investments like research and leadership training. School districts with clear theories of action and the promise of stable leadership are high-impact opportunities for philanthropists.

Sadly, these conditions are rare. Where they do not exist, philanthropists would be wise to wait for political action to change conditions on the ground before investing in specific districts. There is still plenty that can be done with philanthropic dollars to fund research, education, leadership training, and the dissemination of information to inform policymakers and shape public opinion. But direct district investments are likely to be wasted.

Where district leaders do have a clear theory of action, however, or even an implicit one that can be clarified, where leadership appears to be stable, and especially where broad stakeholder buy-in exists, then investments at the margin to leverage change can be indispensable. All three of the districts we studied had a theory of action. Philanthropy was at least loosely aligned with this theory of action. There was also stable leadership, with long superintendencies (and, in some cases, relatively limited board turnover), which enabled philanthropic dollars to be continuously applied to the same district priorities over time.

In all three cases, philanthropy made a difference. Whether or not this impact will endure seems to hinge more than anything else on broad stakeholder ownership. It is clear that in San Diego ownership was too narrow—perhaps inevitably so, perhaps not, but too narrow nonetheless. For all that was accomplished, it may be that the philanthropic investments in San Diego will not provide long-term returns. In Charlotte, likewise, a community still divided over pupil assignment—the visible remnant of segregation/desegregation—has yet to prove that it can pull together over the long haul. Only in Houston does the board's theory of action seem to have become the district's and the city's theory of action. Houston A+, Project GRAD, and numerous other major partnerships coexist in a district that has embraced empowerment balanced with accountability for performance. Stakeholdership seems to be broad and deep, even as current leadership appears to be uncertain.

We agree with those who say that more money alone cannot save urban districts. What can save them are communities willing to pull together to support strong, courageous leaders with clear and effective theories of action. Philanthropy can do much to help create these conditions. And where these conditions exist, philanthropy can add the vital margin of focus and resources required for success. Even where these conditions do not fully exist—because they never do—philanthropy must continue to take calculated risks. One can never know just what the return will be, and the stakes are too high to do nothing.

APPENDIX

Survey Contents

Stage 1—A two-page survey, submitted to district staff via e-mail, explained the purpose of the study and requested information about the following:

- The total dollar amount of gift and grant money received by the district from all private sources (i.e., community, local, national, and corporate foundations, and corporations) over the 10-year period from 1994–95 through 2003–04.[35]
- The largest sources of giving to the district during this 10-year period, including the purpose of the gift or grant, the total dollar amount, and the year(s) for which it was given.
- Other avenues of giving to the district; specifically, the survey asked whether the district had a local foundation that is dedicated solely to supporting the school district, and whether there were any other local nonprofit organizations that provide gifts or grants to schools within the district.

Stage 2—A structured interview conducted with district and local leaders asked a series of questions about the largest grants and gifts received over the study period. (Follow-up questions were used to probe more deeply when this seemed fruitful.)

Section A: Details about the grant/gift
- What were the terms of the grant/gift?
- What was its purpose?
- Who initiated the idea for the grant/gift, the district or the funder?
- Why do you think your district received this grant/gift? Who, or what factors, were influential?

Section B: Relationship between grant/gift and district's reform agenda
- What was the impetus for the grant/gift? Did it solve a problem or fill an unmet need?
- Was this grant/gift an isolated project, or was it connected to other reform efforts in your district?
- In your opinion, was this grant/gift intended to make improvements or modifications to your existing school system or to fundamentally change the way your system operates?
- Do you think the program or activities being supported by this grant/gift would have happened even if the grant/gift had not been received? Or was the funding essential?

Section C: Evaluation of the grant/gift's impact
- How was this grant/gift evaluated? Interim evaluations? Final evaluations?
- What data were collected and examined as part of the evaluation?
- What kinds of measures were used to determine the grant/gift's impact?
- What did the evaluation show?
- To what extent do you think the grant/gift achieved its objectives?
- Did this grant/gift have any long-term impact? If so, what was it?
- If there is a lesson to be learned from this grant/gift, what is it?
- Were there any unanticipated consequences or outcomes of this grant/gift? If so, what were they?
- Do you think that the program(s)/activities provided for by this grant/gift could be replicated in other school districts?
- Do you think that district staff were generally satisfied or dissatisfied with the results of this grant/gift? Funders?

CHAPTER 6

Philanthropy and Labor Market Reform

Jane Hannaway and Kendra Bischoff

INTRODUCTION

Philanthropy has played a number of important roles in American society for well over a century. Philanthropic efforts, for example, have supplemented government services that are inadequate for some given need; they have complemented government services through forming public-private partnerships; and they have played a pace-setting role attempting to prod the government to behave differently.[1] We focus here on the pace-setting role: efforts by philanthropies to influence public policy, specifically education policies. This influence has generally resulted from key philanthropic support for experimentation and innovation. Indeed, the involvement of philanthropy is becoming recognized as one of the distinguishing characteristics of the American education scene. On a recent U.S./U.K. exchange on education policy and practice, a member of the prime minister's strategy unit commented, "The number-one thing that the United Kingdom can learn from the United States is experimentation . . . and the vibrancy of the third sector."[2] Given concern about the performance of the U.S. education system— both its performance relative to other industrialized countries and its performance for particular student subgroups—any efforts designed to stimulate the system in new productive ways merit serious attention.

This chapter examines the role that philanthropy has played in recent years in structural reform in American education. Perhaps the best-known structural reforms are those involving school choice and competition, and these are dealt with elsewhere in this volume. The analysis in this chapter

157

focuses on another major aspect of the system's structure—the structure of the labor market. We look at two major reform initiatives—the National Board for Professional Teaching Standards (NBPTS), an effort to recognize and reward superior teaching of experienced K–12 educators, and Teach For America (TFA), a program designed to attract new, quality entries into the profession. Our purpose here is not to evaluate the effectiveness of these programs, say, in terms of their contribution to student achievement, though there is encouraging evidence for both programs that we discuss later. Rather, it is to tell their stories as philanthropically supported initiatives and the ways they have successfully maneuvered within the complex structure of the American education system. They have not only facilitated and informed policy debates, but have also introduced new ways of maneuvering within the traditional teacher labor market.

We focus on labor market reforms for two reasons. First, while parents, teachers, and school administrators have long been aware of the significant role that teachers play,[3] research is now clearly showing that teachers are the most important in-school factor affecting student achievement.[4] It is also clear that there is large variation in effectiveness from teacher to teacher. Teacher effects are large enough that having good teachers for a number of years in a row could overcome much of the gap between lower- and higher-income families.[5] So reforms intended to identify, attract, retain, recognize, or reward quality teachers—as NBPTS and TFA do—should be at the top of any education reform agenda.

Second, education in the United States is structurally complex, characterized by interlocking, but relatively independent, institutions, which combine to make reform difficult, perhaps especially labor market reforms. It is thus insightful to see how these two innovative programs found their place in the system.

TEACHERS, TEACHER QUALITY, AND ACADEMIC ACHIEVEMENT

Emerging evidence confirms that teachers matter; indeed, as noted earlier, it points to teachers as the number-one school contributor to student achievement. These findings uphold the early results of the Coleman Report (1966), as well as parents' longstanding claim that individual teachers make a difference. This body of evidence also underscores cause for concern, because standard indicators of teacher quality signal the existence of a significant educational problem. The number of teachers with relatively low academic skills is high,[6] and a significant number of teachers have neither a major nor a minor in the subject area that they teach.[7] In schools serving high-poverty children, teachers are more likely not only to lack state certification,[8] but also to be less qualified along other dimensions.[9]

Demand for high quality teaching has developed at the same time as widespread awareness of the shortcomings of the current teacher population. The educational accountability movement, and significantly the No Child Left Behind (NCLB) legislation, has increased pressure on performance in the classroom. The legislation further requires that states employ only teachers who are "highly qualified" by the end of the 2005–06 school year.

Part of the problem facing states and school systems seeking to respond to NCLB's call for highly qualified teachers is that there is no consensus on the aspects of teacher quality that produce consistent gains in student learning.[10] For example, reviews by Eric Hanushek[11] have concluded that there is no strong evidence that teacher education and experience matter for student achievement, while a meta-analysis by Greenwald et al.[12] showed the same variables do relate to student achievement. Others have concluded that experience matters, but that the marginal effect of early years of experience, say up to five years, is much larger than that for later years. Indeed, the contribution of experience may plateau after three to five years.[13]

A growing body of literature is examining specific characteristics of teachers in order to better understand the interface between teacher quality and student achievement. Probably the most agreement centers on the teacher's own academic proficiency or abilities, measured, for example, by the selectivity of the college the teacher attended or test performance.[14]

Heavily debated are the merits of different types of teacher preparation and the relative focus on content knowledge and pedagogical techniques. Content knowledge has been linked to student learning by some studies, but the effect varies by subject. For example, teachers with degrees or reasonable training in a subject appear to be successful teaching that subject, but the effect may be limited to teaching advanced math and science courses.[15] Others have found that subject-specific courses in pedagogy, such as courses in undergraduate mathematics education, contribute more to student learning than content courses in undergraduate mathematics.[16] Still additional studies have not found a relationship between an education degree, presumably a course of study focused heavily on pedagogy, and student learning.[17] In general, a lack of good information about the actual content of teacher-education courses limits our understanding of the relationship between preparatory programs and student achievement. Despite the limitation, teacher-preparation programs play a pivotal role in determining the caliber and characteristics of the teacher workforce because they feed into state certification requirements and thereby screen the teaching profession's pool of potential hires.

In summary, we know that teachers make an important difference. We also know that their academic abilities, their preparation in the subject they teach, and at least some modest amount of experience matter. But with few exceptions, the standard indicators of quality, for example, an advanced degree, do not appear to be strongly or consistently predictive of teacher effectiveness, and the filters or state certification standards for new hires do not seem to be based on solid, evidence-based criteria. But that's not the end of the story.

In a sense, things get worse. High-quality teachers appear to be inequitably distributed between urban and suburban schools (with fewer in urban schools),[18] and teachers who move (to a different school or out of the profession) are more likely to be the more qualified teachers.[19] Moreover, the churning is highest among the schools serving high-poverty students.[20] So, schools serving the most challenging students are most likely to have weaker and less experienced teachers. And while there is evidence that teachers' job choices are sensitive to wage differentials,[21] salary policies for teachers are not designed to alleviate this inequitable distribution.[22]

Clearly there is a case for some reform in the structure of the labor market in education.

INSTITUTIONAL RIGIDITIES

The above discussion begs the question, Why hasn't the structure of the labor market in education adapted to take into account what we know about teacher quality and its importance for student performance, especially for the performance of students from low-income families?

Part of the explanation is no doubt that education in the United States is institutionally complex, characterized by a high degree of decentralization and overlapping responsibilities. States have constitutional authority for education and delegate much of that authority to the 15,000 school districts in the country. Teachers, while required to some degree to meet state certification requirements in order to be licensed, are hired by school districts, where compensation decisions are made, and many school districts delegate at least some hiring authority to the 100,000 schools in the country. Thus, policy, and certainly policy as implemented, is determined at many levels and with the involvement of multiple actors and agencies. The distribution of personnel authority in the United States is in sharp contrast to that in many other countries, where teachers are part of the national civil service and policies are more centralized. Changes in the United States require a coordinated effort across a number of jurisdictions and levels of responsibility.

Coupled with the decentralized and complex nature of the formal education system is the significant role that unions play, both through collective bargaining and political activity. This involvement further complicates policymaking. Unions act in ways that protect the interests of their members; that is their purpose. And they strive to ensure that all their members are treated equitably. As a consequence, teachers unions have traditionally supported state certification requirements based on clear and measurable criteria, such as degrees and coursework, that can be easily counted. And they have resisted attempts to differentiate teacher salaries on the basis of teacher effectiveness or teaching assignment. Instead, they generally support a uniform salary schedule. Thus, if states and districts attempted labor market reforms that affected the criteria by which teachers are certified and the base for compensation, they would likely run into resistance from teachers unions.[23]

Below we focus on two philanthropically supported initiatives—the National Board for Professional Teaching Standards and Teach For America—that have been able to institute changes in the structure of the teacher labor market. The changes they established are ones that the system itself would not have been likely to generate on its own, for the reasons given above. The genesis, mission, and strategies of these two initiatives differ, but each has managed to make significant inroads in the structure of the education labor market. They clearly do not solve all the issues associated with the structure of the labor market in education, but they are forging new paths, and each has succeeded in the face of tremendous odds. Moreover, these reforms have served as catalysts for innovative thinking—many new reforms, such as the NewSchools Venture Fund, the New Teacher Project, and the American Board for Certification of Teacher Excellence to name a few, have been inspired by the success of these two organizations. Most importantly for the discussion in this volume, we attempt to show that the inception of NBPTS and TFA would not have taken place without philanthropic support, even though they provide critical benefits for the system.

THE NATIONAL BOARD FOR PROFESSIONAL TEACHING STANDARDS

The National Board for Professional Teaching Standards was launched in 1986 with support from Carnegie Corporation of New York. It was not the first time that Carnegie had ventured into education labor market issues. In 1917, a grant from Carnegie started TIAA-CREF, now one of the largest retirement systems in the world, to provide security for individuals in nonprofit education and research organizations and to lift labor mobility constraints through pension portability.

Funding for NBPTS was an outgrowth of the Carnegie Report, *A Nation Prepared: Teachers for the 21st Century*,[24] which was published in 1986 and written by an impressive and diverse task force, including businessmen, academics, governors, state education commissioners, and the heads of both teachers unions—the AFT and the NEA.[25] The report was striking for its time. It was written on the heels of *A Nation at Risk* and made the case that "without a (teaching) profession possessed of high skills, capabilities, and aspirations, any reforms will be short lived,"[26] a claim that is hard to dispute. It then specifically recommended, among other things: the creation of NBPTS, "to establish high standards for what teachers need to know and should be able to do, and to certify teachers who meet that standard"; to restructure schools, "freeing them to meet state and local goals for children while holding them accountable for student progress"; to "restructure the teaching force, and introduce a new category of Lead Teachers . . ."; and to "relate incentives for teachers to school-wide student performance."[27] Setting high standards, differentiating the teaching staff, promoting school autonomy, and instituting performance-based incentives for teachers were radical ideas at the time; indeed, they still are. While the research base identifying the nature of teaching inadequacies was not as strong 20 years ago as it is today, the dimensions of the situation were well understood by these observers of the education establishment.

Both teachers union heads—Futrell of the NEA and Shanker of the AFT—signed the task force report, but Futrell did so with deep skepticism. She wrote, "I have deep reservations about some of the report's conclusions and recommendations. . . . The report gives the impression that teachers are not doing their jobs. . . . I am concerned about the potential for abuse in the Lead Teacher concept . . . (which) suggests that some teachers are more equal than others."[28] Shanker was more enthusiastic: "This report deserves full support. It promises to turn teaching into a full profession, make major structural changes in schools, and take giant steps in the improvement of learning."[29]

Given its ambitious goals, the existing structure of the education system, the likely resistance from some of the major players in education, and the lack of a research base for defining and identifying quality teachers, the odds of success for NBPTS were seemingly low at its inception. Indeed, it had significant hurdles to clear—on both the supply and demand sides. The organization had no certification process, nor was there an existing research basis

FIGURE 1   NBPTS Board Composition 2004

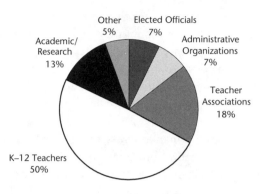

Source: NBPTS Annual Reports

for assessment. In addition, it was unclear why teachers would opt for this special certification, given the prevalence of the single salary schedule. Most observers probably saw NBPTS as a "reform du jour" that would soon fade from the landscape, despite the reality and seriousness of the problems it was trying to address. But it didn't happen that way.

Carnegie Corporation of New York provided an initial discretionary grant of $1 million to NBPTS in 1987; a 63-member board was established, and the first president, James A. Kelly, was hired.

Selecting the members of the board was the first major challenge. While AFT's Albert Shanker had called for the creation of a national board two years earlier at the National Press Club, AFT's then bitter rival, the NEA, was skeptical, perhaps to put it mildly. The composition of the board resulted from a political compromise that became incorporated into the organization's bylaws and established that a majority of the board were to be classroom teachers (see Figure 1). This compromise kept everyone at the table. All the major players were included, including representatives of administrator groups and the school boards. These groups were not known for working well together. According to one board member, the earliest meetings were the "hairiest." But the basic composition of the board has managed to hold until the present.[30] Like most boards, the composition represents the resources, in this case mainly the political resources, necessary for the NBPTS to survive and effect change. The board wisely limited its focus to teaching and teaching quality. This is an area where all could agree, at least conceptually. Issues associated with teacher salaries, for example, where agreement across groups was weaker, were never discussed.

The selection of Kelly as president was masterful and contrasts sharply with the discussion that follows about TFA. Kelly was seasoned, well connected, and skilled in terms of getting things done in the education establishment with philanthropic support. As a senior program officer at Ford, he largely orchestrated the school finance reform movement of the 1970s that resulted in significant litigation and remedies in states across the country, strategically buttressing the movement for decades by supporting the development of scholars of school finance across a number of disciplines. He knew everybody, and everybody knew him. Smart, quick-witted, and able to defuse tension with humor, he took on a complex research, management, and political reform task that few could have handled.

But observers claim that NBPTS probably would never have survived without the intensive and steady involvement of Governor James B. Hunt Jr. (D-NC), who served as chair of the board for ten years. He brought political acumen, experience with state policymaking, and extensive political connections to the service of NBPTS for more than its first decade.

NBPTS was not fast out of the gate. It was not until 1994 that the first national board certified teachers (NBCT) were certified. The board spent the first seven years doing research and development, with heavy emphasis on the development of assessments. This was a long time. Research, however, was necessary. NBPTS was not tweaking an established model, but trying to create a new paradigm. The board and president agreed that an up-front research and development investment would be well worthwhile. The important point for this volume is that Carnegie apparently agreed with this need and provided unrestricted annual grants of $1 million for 11 years, which sustained the organization while it laid its foundations. This relatively long-term unrestricted support is viewed by NBPTS as having been essential to getting off the ground. In addition, the Ford Foundation, The DeWitt Wallace-Reader's Digest Fund, the Lilly Endowment, The Pew Charitable Trusts, The Atlantic Philanthropies, as well as several corporations such as Xerox, IBM, DuPont, AT&T, and Chrysler, contributed significant sums of money in the early years.[31]

The board had two major tasks. The first was developing something credible to sell—national board certification (NBC). The second was developing a demand for obtaining certification. The research support worked on the supply side. Political support was needed on both the supply and demand sides. Many voices needed to be heard and managed.

Creating the Supply

The standards for the certificates needed to be established, along with credible means of assessing them. The task was difficult and complex, and there were acknowledged false starts. How many certificates should there be? How should the profession be divided up? One board member reported that at the time there were 1,700 separate state certifications for teachers across the country. The Lilly Endowment provided support for the development of the first two assessments' certifications. Federal support began under President George Bush and then increased greatly under President Clinton. Conceptually, the national board fit well with the standards-based reform programs of both presidents. The board received its first federal money in 1991 and was able to invest more seriously in research and development. All together, well over $100 million dollars of federal money, and an equivalent amount from foundations and corporate sources, was spent on research and development over 15 years. With increased support, the number of certificates quickly multiplied.[32] In 1993 there were only two certificates available, covering fewer than 5 percent of the teaching workforce; by 2000 there were 25 certificates covering over 95 percent of all teachers.[33] Probably not to be underestimated in securing federal funding was the close personal relationship between President Clinton and Governor Hunt, who chaired the NBPTS board. But, notably, NBPTS was never a partisan venture; from the outset it also received support from key Republicans, including governors Thomas Kean (R-NJ) and Tommy Thompson (R-WI), and Lamar Alexander, secretary of education under George Bush.

Creating the Demand

Board certification, of course, would only work if teachers sought certification. There had to be demand for it. Indeed, teachers had to be willing to pay for it in terms of both time and money. The process takes an estimated 300 to 400 hours and the current fee is $2,300. Why would teachers do it?

The board, of course, understood the demand side of the equation, and a task force that included Governor Hunt and Governor Terry Branstad (R-IA),[34] the heads of both teachers unions, and others was established to develop strategies. The intent of the board and its founders was always that fees associated with national board certification would be paid by or on behalf of teachers. The task force's thinking ended up centering on state salary incentives for teachers who received national board certification. The need to develop incentives put additional pressure on the establishment of the national board certificates. For equity reasons, many governors only felt comfortable establishing incentives if NBC was available to cover all or most teachers. Shortly after the first pilot assessments were concluded in 1993–94, Governor Hunt took the lead and offered a 4 percent salary increase to any NBC teacher in North Carolina. Not to be outdone, Governor George Voinovich (R-OH) quickly followed suit offering NBC teachers a $2,500 boost in salary. Today state incentives are available in every state in the country, and federal subsidies for the application costs are also available in all 50 states. Considerable local support from corporations and foundations is also available for application subsidies. The incentives for certification include monetary rewards—such as annual salary increases, salary percentage increases, and one-time stipends—as well as other benefits such as career ladder advancement opportunities, release time to complete the application, and license portability, which means a state will accept a relocated teacher's NBC in lieu of the state's licensing requirements. In addition, the heavy involvement of teachers on the board in the development and piloting of the certificates enhances the credibility of the certificates in the eyes of teachers.

Organizational Maturation

With its certification process now largely in place, NBPTS is certifying teachers at a fairly high rate. While in 1994 just 177 teachers received national board certification, over 8,000 were certified in 2004, and 20,000 more are in the pipeline this year. Over 40,000 teachers have been certified in the board's first decade. According to NBPTS staff, fewer than half of applicants receive certification.

The board is moving quickly toward becoming self-sustaining. Figure 2 shows the percentage of revenue from different sources between 1989 and 2002. Philanthropic or private support, originally the only sources of revenue for the board, was only 3 percent in 2002. The largest source of revenue (62%) is fees for service. Granted, this is subsidized by government and private support, but there is a business model in place and it appears to be working.

This is not the end of the story. NBPTS recognizes that it is at a new stage in its life cycle. The initial developmental stage is pretty much complete, but serious challenges remain.

One challenge is defining feasible long-term objectives for NBPTS. If the objective of the board is to have national board certification become the norm for teachers, as it is for many medical specialties, then there is a long way to go. Only about 1 percent of teachers are now certified. Becoming the norm is a very different objective from the objective of creating "lead teach-

FIGURE 2   NBPTS Sources of Revenue (%). 1989–2002 Challenges*

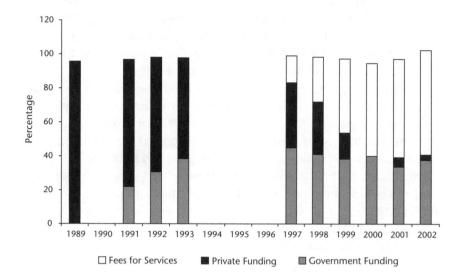

Source: 1997–2002: Private Funding = Direct Public Support + Indirect Public Support (IRS 990s); 1989–93: Private Funding = Unrestricted Grants + Restricted Grants (annual reports)

*1990, 1994–96 Missing Data

ers," as discussed in their "birth document," the 1986 Carnegie report. And it is unclear whether becoming the norm is either viable or desirable. The costs of board certification are high, both in terms of the application and the salary increases teachers receive, though perhaps no higher than the additional compensation teachers receive for obtaining advanced degrees. Moreover, NBC arguably may generate greater efficiency benefits in terms of retaining *quality* teachers in the classroom. As states face tighter fiscal constraints, limits on both the size of the salary incentive for NBC and the number of teachers who can receive it are increasing, though such cyclical pressure should probably be expected. In addition, while medical schools have high standards for admission, education programs are notoriously low. Board certification for all teachers may just not be feasible. It may also not be desirable. Not targeting the most proficient teachers might dilute any incentive effect to keep the best and the brightest in teaching. Concerns about board certified teachers teaching disproportionately in more affluent schools are also being raised.[35] Both of these issues have implications for targeting incentives, which states and NBPTS will have to consider strategically as NBPTS moves forward. The good news for NBPTS is that research is showing that the board certification does, indeed, signal higher teacher quality.[36] In a sense, NBPTS has done much of its job; it has developed a system that distinguishes high-quality teachers. The question now is will the system respond so that these high-quality teachers are allocated in ways that are equitable and that make most sense given the educational needs of students.

The second set of challenges for NBPTS includes management challenges. As any organization moves into an operational phase issues change, and they are changing for NBPTS. NBPTS staff report that customer relations, efficiency, sustainability, and keeping the system updated are becoming priorities, and research and development is taking more of a back seat.

In summary, NBPTS is a success story. With critical support from philanthropy at key junctures in the research-and-development period, the organization was able to survive and make a concept operationally viable. Without this support, it probably never would have happened. We return to this discussion in the last section of this chapter.

TEACH FOR AMERICA

The Teach For America story is in some ways similar to the NBPTS story, and in other ways it is very different.[37] Like NBPTS, TFA started with a simple idea, and also like NBPTS, it had to be developed out of whole cloth. But while NBPTS emanated from a national blue ribbon panel, was signed on to by just about every major education group in the country, and was headed by a seasoned president, the idea for TFA developed in the mind of Wendy Kopp, a Princeton undergraduate with no professional or political connections in education, during solo morning jogs before class. The idea became her senior thesis.

The Idea

Kopp's plan was simple. The problem was already defined; low-income school districts did not have enough teachers. Tapping a new labor source—new college graduates eager to give back to society through service—was her idea. Why couldn't needy schools take advantage of the growing desire to contribute to society that she observed among her many talented classmates? The more she got into her thesis, the more determined she became to create a national teacher corps. And the funding? She had confidence that the philanthropic sector, with its longstanding support for improving the education system, would help. Kopp was clearly naive. As she has written, "I didn't have the experience to see why it couldn't be done."

Teach For America, as it came to be known, took on a persistent and serious labor problem in American public schools—teacher shortages in low-income schools. It also posed a solution that ran counter to the education establishment thinking about teachers. The establishment wanted to elevate "teacher professionalism," primarily through requiring more training in traditional programs. Whether Kopp and her colleagues fully realized it at the time, they blatantly challenged this view. TFA implicitly claimed that, in spite of the fact that its recruits would have little pedagogical training or classroom experience, it could make a difference by providing intelligent, motivated, and enthusiastic young adults who by and large would try their very best to be effective teachers.

Although a simple, logical, and ultimately successful proposal, Kopp entered the game as a novice. In contrast to the masterfully planned NBPTS project, Kopp learned along the way that the education labor market is somewhat of a jungle, and Teach For America ran the gauntlet in its early years.

The Start

Immediately after graduating in May 1989, Kopp moved to New York City to begin the long, hard road to building a nonprofit from the ground up. During the first year, she single-handedly solicited funds from corporations and foundations, using Princeton as a conduit of funds until Teach For America became incorporated. Young and full of idealism, Kopp was not just trying to start another run-of-the-mill nonprofit; she was truly aiming to start a movement. In the fall of 1989, TFA's mission extended far into the future, but their financial plans did not. After assembling the first board of directors, which was made up of a group of education and service-oriented nonprofit entrepreneurs, the real foundations began to take shape as her small team of recent Ivy League graduates prepared to recruit, train, and place their first cohort of teachers.[38] Working out of office space that was donated by Morgan Stanley,[39] the nonprofit received early funding from Union Carbide,[40] Carnegie, McGraw Hill, and the Echoing Green Foundation, as well as valuable support for their recruiting efforts from Hertz and American Express.

Throughout the fall and winter of 1989, Kopp and her colleagues hammered out the details of whom they actually wanted to fill these teaching slots and how they were going to get enough applicants to reach a level of selectivity that they strived for. They targeted the 100 best colleges in the country and sent 12 recruiters on the road to muster up as much hype and enthusiasm for this new movement as possible. In the spring of 1990, Teach For America selected 500 of the 2,500 submitted applications and had agreements with six districts across the nation.[41] The districts were clearly taking a risk, but they needed bodies in the classroom and TFA provided at least that, and hopefully more.

The Troubles

Teach For America encountered many of the challenges that are common to emerging nonprofit organizations: sensible organizational structure, efficient allocation of resources, employee satisfaction, and of course the behemoth, adequate and stable funding. Throughout the early 1990s, Teach For America maintained a hand-to-mouth existence, consistently falling short of their annual budgets and having trouble securing funding due to their weak sustainability plan. Foundations did not want to throw their money into a black hole or get caught in long-term support. Although the application numbers continued to rise and the low acceptance rates were making the program prestigious, the program continued to struggle with management issues and financial instability.

To boot, TFA was dealt a blow when Linda Darling-Hammond, a leading national analyst of teaching, then Columbia professor, and former president of the American Educational Research Association, wrote a scathing review of the program in a 1994 issue of *Phi Delta Kappan*.[42] Darling-Hammond put her hefty professional weight on the side of teacher preparation as the vehicle for improving schools; TFA implicitly challenged this view. While Kopp was struggling to get TFA off the ground and trying to convince funders of its merits, she was thrown into the spotlight. Among other things, the article claimed that "TFA's shortcomings are serious, and they ultimately hurt many schools and the children in them" . . . and that "good intentions that fail to produce good teaching for African American and Latino children look like a thin veil for arrogance, condescension, and continuing neglect." Kopp was hailed by some as a hero, but as naive and injurious by others. It couldn't have helped with funders.

The funding and public relations crises led to the realization that in order to survive, TFA needed professional allies and diversified funding. It was too risky to depend on a few big funders, and the organization needed guides to help it maneuver the political currents in education. Hard decisions were made; solid management and business plans were the order of the day. Carnegie Corporation, which had donated $300,000 in 1990, hosted a meeting of previous TFA funders in 1995, giving Kopp a chance to convince them to continue funding her initiative at a time when many of the initial contributions were waning. Despite the support of a high-profile philanthropy and TFA's new survival strategies, the meeting left most of the funders uncertain—they wanted some assurance that TFA was viable before committing to any further contributions. Becoming more accustomed to the workings of the system, Kopp had an influential independent consultant, who had helped her before, contact the funders to confirm that TFA was stable and planning systematically for the future. TFA finished the year with a surplus.

Like NBPTS, TFA also received funding from the government, although in a very different form. In 1994, Teach For America received its first federal funding through the newly created Corporation for National and Community Service (Americorps). The following year, however, the government was reluctant to renew the grant without some changes, which served as another warning about the risks of a narrow funding base.[43] Just days before its summer institute was to begin, accompanied by much stress and some major compromises, TFA received an eleventh-hour grant renewal.

Today TFA remains a member of Americorps, which in addition to program funding gives their teachers benefits such as forbearance and interest payments on student loans. This type of federal support, however, is inherently unstable and sharply contrasts with the federal funding for NBPTS. NBPTS, stacked with members of the education A-list, successfully moved to insert itself at the intersection of politics and education and obtained legislated line item funding. Program officers make the decision whether or not to fund TFA each year, and in fact, it did not receive funding in 2003 due to government cutbacks.

The Success

In 1995, things began to look up for TFA in terms of embedding itself in the education landscape and solidifying its role in teacher labor market reform. Given the odds stacked against such reforms, the very fact that TFA lasted this long is an accomplishment. And in 1996 it began to hit its stride as it implemented a new and highly effective fundraising campaign that turned its attention to local and regional contributions. Three conditions suggest TFA is on its way to successfully institutionalizing itself.

TFA's financial standing 15 years after its inception is one important indicator of its success. Until 1993, its funding was heavily dependent on national corporations and foundations. In 1994, many of these funders, who view their task as stimulating change, not providing ongoing institutional support, declined to renew their grants, and TFA began to diversify its revenue sources and ultimately moved toward a more sustainable funding structure. The second half of the 1990s saw a steady and significant increase in funding from local and regional entities, indicating a shift toward a more distributed and stable model. In this way, TFA was able to tap into revenue sources that were more proximate to its sites and more aware of the benefits of its services. In fact, over 65 percent of its budget was funded by these sources in 2001, and this amount has remained around 60 percent ever since. Similarly, the percentage of resources from national groups has steadily declined and accounted for only 10 percent in 2001. If the size of a nonprofit's budget is any measure of success, TFA certainly has made its mark, operating with a $35 million budget in 2004 (see Figure 3).

A second powerful indication of success for TFA is its ability to steadily increase its supply of high-quality candidates. More and more college graduates from the very best institutions are seeking admission into the program. In 2005, TFA received 17,000 applications, including applications from 12 percent of the senior classes at Yale and Spelman and from 9 percent of the senior classes at Princeton and Harvard. Out of those 17,000, very few were accepted. In 2004, only 16 percent of the applicants were accepted, and 77 percent of those entered the program. While the absolute number of teachers placed has increased, the acceptance rate has always remained low, and the matriculation rate has remained high (see Figure 4). The demand for TFA has steadily increased over the years as well; serving just six sites in its first year, TFA now provides teachers in 22 areas for 66 districts.

And third, TFA has succeeded in garnering a diverse group of allies in the education system. In addition to its relationship with the government, it has also, by and large, served its districts well, forming a foundation of support at the ground level. TFA is a significant force in some regions, offering a substantial labor infusion. In Houston, for example, TFA teachers accounted for 8 percent of all new hires in 2001–02.[44] Gaining support and approval from their service sites is essential. Similar to teachers' support of NBPTS, principals' support of TFA has legitimized the program. In a study conducted for TFA by an independent research firm, 95 percent of principals reported that they would hire more TFA teachers if given the chance, and 72 percent rated TFA teachers as more effective than other beginning teachers.[45]

These trends exhibit not only the popularity of TFA among the nation's best college graduates, but also TFA's ability to select strong candidates. Eliminating some of the barriers to teaching has widened the pool of potential hires. Although there is still resistance to this expedited path, both among

FIGURE 3   TFA Revenues as Percentage of Fiscal Total

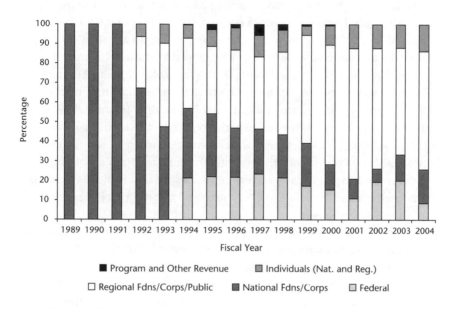

Source: TFA Financial Documents

FIGURE 4   TFA Acceptance and Matriculation Rates

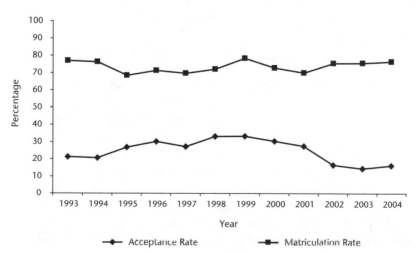

Source: TFA

some education analysts and school-level staff, research has provided some positive feedback. Most recently, Mathematica completed a random-assignment study in six Teach For America regions, concluding that students of TFA teachers had significantly higher math score gains than those of other novice teachers and, indeed, were performing as well as students of more experienced teachers. The study also points to the fact that while all TFA teachers had at least some student teaching experience, more than half of the novice control group had had no student teaching at all.[46] In short, TFA teachers had more, not less, classroom experience before their first year of teaching than the average new teacher. One common criticism of TFA is that most corps members do not stay in the teaching profession after completing their two-year commitment. In fact, according to a recent report by TFA, over one-third of their alumni remain K–12 teachers, and fully 62 percent are working full-time in education careers.[47]

These results are encouraging and raise some interesting points beyond the specifics of this organization. TFA supplies districts with a particular type of individual, one with positive personality characteristics and a superior academic record. The selection process is intense, involving transcripts, writing samples, essays, in-person interviews, and group exercises. If the existing literature is correct in saying that a teacher's own academic record is a good predictor of teacher quality, then perhaps these positive results should not be surprising. Ideally, an ample supply of experienced and thoroughly trained teachers would be available to fill the demand in poor and urban districts, but this is not the reality. The reality is that TFA appears to be filling a niche; it is filling a hole in the teacher labor market.

LESSONS AND CONCLUSIONS

This chapter has tried to show the important role that philanthropy has played in recent years in challenging traditional structures of the labor market in education and in testing new solutions to ingrained problems. We focused on two initiatives: the National Board for Professional Teaching Standards and Teach For America. Both were focused on the critical need in the country to attract, identify, and retain high-quality teachers for our schools. Both had their beginnings outside the system. Both were pretty much cut from whole cloth. Both have been able to find a place in the system. But almost everything else about these two initiatives was different.

The idea for the NBPTS emerged from a high-profile expert panel and was managed by seasoned actors in the politics of education. TFA was based on the idea of a naive undergraduate student. Without minimizing the hard work that went into generating financial support, NBPTS was able to tap into the major foundations and the federal government with credibility, since the players were well known and well connected. TFA had to prove itself again and again and to beg for every nickel. NBPTS was able to work with, some might say co-opt, the traditional education interest groups; TFA challenged the conventional wisdom head on.

Despite the differences, there are perhaps five common lessons to be learned about reform in education, at least reforms that venture into the structure of the education labor market. These lessons imply that philanthropy is not only helpful for reform; it may well be necessary.

First, initiatives aimed at reforming education labor markets are not likely to come from within the system. As we explained, the education system is a complex web of jurisdictions, agreements, traditions, and interests that involve state legislatures, state departments of education, local school districts, teacher-training institutions of higher education, local school districts, and teachers unions. Dismantling or reforming even a piece of the existing arrangement is exceedingly complex. This is not peculiar to education; any large complex system naturally resists change. Any substantive change affects too many parts, and complex systems respond with a type of benign resistance.

Second, labor market issues typically encompass both bread-and-butter issues and professional identity issues for hundreds and thousands of individuals. Therefore, any changes are likely to be not only difficult, but also highly charged. Thus resistance is not only to be expected; it may well be hostile. While the structure of NBPTS was able to contain disagreements within its structure by having all the players at the table, TFA initially got broadsided in public with no defenders in sight.

Third, by definition, reform means trying something new. There is bound to be a period of learning. So some period of incubation is important before any formal institutional fit is appropriately shaped. Both NBPTS and TFA spent considerable time and resources, sometimes with false starts, before they hit their stride.

Fourth, for any reform to be successful, attention has to be given to both the supply side (the development of the reform) and the demand side (the development of the fit of the solution in the system). NBPTS had to worry about the development of incentives; TFA had to sell itself to school districts. The demand side seldom just emerges for something new; it requires focused attention and effort.

Five, and this is related to lesson four above, if the reform fits a real need and a demand has developed, it will be able to survive largely on its own. Indeed, in the case of both NBPTS and TFA, once they were developed, their most stable and long-term sources of revenue were from local and regional sources close to where their services were delivered, an indication of meeting a market test.

CHAPTER 7

Choosing to Fund School Choice

Bryan C. Hassel and Amy Way

INTRODUCTION

Philanthropy in support of "school choice" made big headlines in 2004. In the space of five months, the "newspapers of record" in both the philanthropy and education industries ran extensive profiles of the Bill & Melinda Gates Foundation's philanthropic efforts, in both cases highlighting the foundation's massive level of support for the creation of new small high schools across the United States. A few months earlier, *USA Today*'s Money section featured the education philanthropy of John Walton and other Wal-Mart heirs, focused primarily on charter schools and vouchers.[1] The heavy involvement of these two donors in school choice causes is indeed headline worthy: according to the Foundation Center, the Gates and Walton foundations are, respectively, the first and second largest givers to elementary and secondary education in the United States, together making up more than 25 percent of K–12 grantmaking.[2]

These articles came on the heels of 15 years of rapid growth in school choice nationally. There has always been a considerable amount of school choice in the United States. Parents with the means to pay tuition or who have access to scholarships have long been able to send their children to private schools; parents with flexibility around where to live have long been able to choose schools by choosing their neighborhoods of residence. Families in some places have also long had limited access to choice options within the public system, such as magnet schools. What has been new in the last two decades is an effort to extend these options to more families (especially low-income families), and to do so in a way that is more independent of existing school districts. There are two broad categories of school choice programs that have emerged in this period:

- *Private school choice programs*, which seek to allow more children to attend private schools by subsidizing all or part of families' tuition with "vouchers," scholarships, or tax benefits. Three states and the District of Columbia now provide publicly funded scholarships for low-income children or children attending low-performing public schools, and six offer tax benefits related to private school tuition. The oldest and largest scholarship program is in Milwaukee, where a program enacted by the state legislature in 1990 has grown to serve some 14,000 students in 2003–04. In addition, more than 23,000 low-income children are receiving privately funded scholarships through the national Children's Scholarship Fund. Countless others are receiving scholarships from other sources for which there is no central catalog.
- *Public school choice programs*, which allow individuals and organizations to create new public schools of choice operated with some independence from traditional public school governance and policy. Forty states and the District of Columbia now have laws authorizing "charter schools," following Minnesota's pioneering law in 1991. Over 3,400 of these schools educate more than one million students nationwide. Numerous school districts are also creating schools of choice within their own jurisdictions, for example, by breaking up large high schools into multiple small high schools.

No one would dispute the fact that philanthropy has played a central role in these developments. But how extensive *is* choice-related philanthropy in the United States? How many foundations are involved, and at what level? What sort of choice-oriented activities are they supporting? Why are they putting the resources into school choice, given that a large percentage of American students still attend regular district schools? And how effective have their philanthropic strategies been to date?

This chapter aims to shed light on these questions in two major sections. The first section surveys the current landscape of philanthropic giving related to school choice. Drawing on a survey of the top 50 K–12 givers and an extensive analysis of their Internal Revenue Service filings, this section outlines the extent of philanthropy related to school choice, the types of school choice activities receiving funding, and differences among foundations in their school choice giving. The second section discusses important trends and patterns that have emerged in choice-related giving over time. Based on interviews with leading philanthropists and their representatives, our survey data, and a review of foundation websites and publications, this section analyzes the rationales philanthropists invoke for making grants in support of school choice, the types of institutions and activities they have come to support, the important role of political giving related to school choice, and the effectiveness of choice-oriented giving to date.

THE SCHOOL CHOICE PHILANTHROPY LANDSCAPE

Data and Methods

Our purpose was to evaluate the extent and nature of financial support for school choice by the top K–12 education donors in the United States. We began by identifying the top U.S. foundations donating money to elementary and secondary education. A list compiled by the Foundation Center ranks the top 50 organizations awarding grants for K–12 education in 2002. The Foundation Center is the nation's leading authority on U.S. philanthropic activity. It collects, organizes, and shares data on U.S. philanthropy, and conducts research to uncover trends in philanthropic giving.[3]

We proceeded to collect data on these 50 foundations using two methods. First, we obtained an Internal Revenue Service 990 or 990PF (for private foundations) form for each foundation, which detailed their grantmaking activity in 2002. We also surveyed them regarding their support of school choice-related activities.

IRS 990 Forms

Our primary method of data collection involved coding data from the IRS 990 forms. Every nonprofit organization with an income of more than $25,000 is required to file Form 990 annually with the Internal Revenue Service, which provides a range of financial information about the foundation's activity. Most importantly for our purposes, foundations must list all grants awarded in that year. To conduct an analysis of these lists, we built on work carried out by Jay Greene for his chapter in this volume. Greene assigned K–12 education grants made by the top 30 givers into 17 categories as follows: research and advocacy, charter schools, vouchers, small public schools, public early college schools, other special public schools, vocational and alternative public schools, national board certification, alternative professional association, public school professional development, general- and special-purpose public school grants, public school curriculum, disability focus, technology in public schools, private school grants, and other.

We identified seven of Greene's categories as related to school choice and combined them into five categories, as follows:

- small and alternative public schools[4]
- choice-related research[5]
- charter schools
- vouchers
- private school grants

For the remaining 20 of the top 50 foundations, we examined the organizations' lists of grants awarded in 2002 and determined which grants qualified as supporting elementary or secondary education. We then assigned relevant grants to the five choice-related categories listed above.

In our initial attempt to put together an annual grant report for each organization, we found the IRS 990 forms to be the most accessible and most complete source of information. Using this approach, however, carried certain important limitations. First, assigning grants to our five categories often required judgments based on inherently limited information. While every organization provided a list of grants for 2002, these lists varied in their degree of usefulness. Many foundations grouped all of their education grants together, while some only listed all grants in alphabetical order; some foundations provided a sentence or two describing the purpose of each grant; others only listed the name of the grantee. Due to the sheer number of grants, it was not possible to research every one to ascertain its specific function. When the purpose of a grant was not clear, we simply had to use our judgment and assign the grant to one reasonable category or another.

Second, the use of these five classifications raised the question of what exactly we mean by school choice. Our primary interest in this project was in philanthropic efforts to *expand the extent and quality of choices available to K–12 students in the United States.* Yet in many cases, it was difficult to ascertain whether particular grants had that purpose. "Private school grants," one of our five choice categories, is a good example of the challenge. A grant awarded to a private school often *does* reflect an effort to expand school choice. For example, some grants to private schools are intended to be used for scholarships for students who could not otherwise afford a private education. In other cases, grants are given to private schools because they are long-standing institutions traditionally supported by a foundation or its benefactors. Donations may be intended for landscaping or athletics and have nothing to do with supporting the social policy of expanding choice. Leaving out private school grants would not represent the numerous donations that are intended to give low-income families a choice among quality education options. But assuming that all private school grants are for the purpose of supporting choice would create a skewed interpretation as well. Since we were not able to determine which private school grants were intended to support our definition of school choice and which were not, we have presented two sets of results in the analysis that follows—one that includes the private school grants category and one that does not. "Small public schools" is also a questionable category. In principle, a school district could create small public schools or break up a large school into smaller schools without making the new institutions schools of choice.

Finally, these 990 forms do not capture all of the nation's choice-related grantmaking. Foundations whose overall K–12 grantmaking places them below the top 50 are not included, even if they may make large contributions to choice-related causes. For example, the Pisces Foundation, funded by Gap founders Don and Doris Fisher, and the Challenge Foundation in Florida are both significant backers of choice-related activity, yet not included. In addition, direct contributions by individual philanthropists to such causes as political campaigns of candidates who support choice are not recorded, since they do not (and cannot) run through these individual foundations. It is important to understand that the top 50 foundations, while a good indicator of overall trends, are not the whole story. There are many smaller foundations, as well as individual and corporate donors, whose contributions do have an impact.

Despite these limitations, the data presented below are the most comprehensive compilation to date of information about school choice-related philanthropy in the United States. As the information available about foundation grants improves, future researchers will be able to build on this work with more definitive analysis.

Results

Our first step in organizing the data from the 990 forms was to separate all K–12 education grants from noneducation grants. In total, these 50 foundations awarded $282,978,441 in choice-related grants in 2002—36 percent of their total $784,915,729 in K–12 grants. As discussed earlier, however, the inclusion of private school grants in this total probably overstates the amount of support that is actually supporting choice-based reform as it is more conventionally understood.

Therefore, we recalculated total giving to school choice by excluding private school grants and only including giving directed to charter schooling, small and alternative schools, school vouchers, and research. When calculated in this fashion, the total giving to choice-based reform falls sharply—to $176,576,491, or 23 percent of K–12 giving. These calculations are summarized in Figure 1.

This overall picture masks significant variation in the prevalence of school choice within the grantmaking portfolios of individual foundations. Therefore, we calculated the percentage of each foundation's education grant funding that went to choice-related activities. The results are presented throughout this chapter in two forms: calculations including private school grants, and those excluding them. It is imperative that the reader understand the complex nature of the data and interpret the calculations accordingly.

One useful way to examine the data is by grouping the foundations according to what percentage of their education giving went to school choice. With private school grants included, 24 of the top 50 foundations gave less than 20 percent of their total education grants in choice-related giving, while just six gave 80 percent or more. When private school grants were removed from our calculations, the results were much different. When calculated in that fashion, just seven of the 50 foundations gave 20 percent or more of their giving to choice-related causes, and none donated as much as 80 percent. The leading givers to choice, defined in this fashion, were The Walton Family Foundation (with 75% of non–private school K–12 giving to choice-related activities), The Annie E. Casey Foundation (54%), and the Bill & Melinda Gates Foundation (39%).

We can gain further insight by investigating how these foundations distributed their grants across different categories of school choice activity. Private school grants attracted 38 percent of money donated, while small and alternative public schools accounted for 34 percent of choice giving. Charter schools and vouchers made up 14 percent and 13 percent, respectively, while research in the area of school choice accounted for just 1 percent.

Another way to gauge foundation interest in the different topics is by taking a simple count of how many of the 50 organizations awarded at least some funding in each category. Private school grants were again the most popular cause by this metric, with 37 of the 50 foundations awarding such grants. Charter school grants, though they made up just 14 percent of total giving, received support from 34 of the 50 foundations. This suggests that many foundations are making very small gifts to charter schooling. A smaller number of foundations supported vouchers (16) and small public schools (14). Research on school choice was again last, funded by only seven organizations.

The data from all 50 of the top organizations paint one picture, but we must look closer in order to get an accurate idea of the amount of support the

FIGURE 1   Allocation of K–12 Grants by the Top 50 Education Donors, 2002

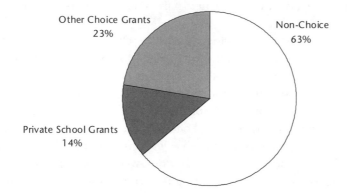

Other Choice Grants
23%

Non-Choice
63%

Private School Grants
14%

school choice movement is receiving from philanthropists. Looking back at the breakdown of data for all 50 organizations, it is evident that the top two organizations, the Bill & Melinda Gates Foundation and The Walton Family Foundation, are the primary supporters of choice activities. With combined choice-related giving of $164,321,491, these two foundations alone account for fully 58 percent of the education grants awarded in the area of school choice. When private school grants are excluded, these two funders account for fully 87 percent of choice-related funding.

These two funders often find themselves supporting the same initiatives, such as the Charter School Leadership Council, a national organization that advocates for the charter school movement. But their approaches are also distinctly different. Most of the Walton Foundation's giving flows to choice efforts that are outside of conventional school districts—including both independent charter schools and private school–based programs. Walton alone accounts for nearly 75 percent of charter and voucher funding. The Gates Foundation backs these kinds of choice initiatives as well, but it also provides a great deal of support for within-district efforts to create small schools, primarily by breaking up existing large high schools. While this funding generally flows to independent nonprofit "intermediaries" and support organizations rather than to districts, its aim is to back change within district schools. Gates alone accounts for 95 percent of small schools funding.

Since these two foundations' portfolios are so dominant in this sector, it is useful to reanalyze the data focusing only on the other 48 foundations (Figure 2). The exclusion of these top two donors changes the landscape drastically. The remaining 48 organizations contribute $118,656,950 to school choice, 26 percent of their total education grants in 2002. Of this giving, 81 percent falls under grants to private schools. Charter schools become only 8 percent of their choice donations, vouchers 6 percent, small public schools 4 percent, and research 1 percent.

Strikingly, the total amount of giving awarded to school choice aside from the direct support of private schooling is $23,044,142—or just 5 percent of all education grants in 2002 by these 48 foundations.

To obtain a more fine-grained view of how donors are allocating funds, we surveyed foundations about the school choice–related activities they supported. Participants were provided with 14 choices and a space to write in any activities that were not given as an option. Eleven organizations answered the question, and the most common activities were supporting charter schools, providing technical assistance and other services for choice schools, and expanding research about school choice. The least common activities were supporting magnet schools, funding scholarships for students to attend schools of their choice, supporting private schools directly, providing scholarship funds to allow students to attend specific private or parochial schools, sustaining charter school authorizing, and providing legal defense for school choice programs.

The low proportion of respondents reporting support for private schools runs directly counter to our findings from 990 data about the high levels of support for private school grants. Interestingly, it appears that respondents frequently do not regard their private school donations as school choice–related. For instance, staff at three different foundations indicated that they do not support school choice, even though each reported significant private school grants on their 990s. This suggests that they think of their private school donations as serving some other purpose than enhancing school choice.

At first glance, it appears that school choice–related activities make up a very significant portion of U.S. philanthropy, comprising over one-third of K–12 grantmaking in the year we analyzed. Yet this initial picture is misleading in two ways. First, the lion's share of choice-related grantmaking comes from just two funders—the Bill & Melinda Gates Foundation and The Walton Family Foundation—which together contributed nearly six of every ten philanthropic dollars flowing to school choice in 2002. Looking just at the other foundations lowers the percentage of choice-related giving from 36 percent to 26 percent. Secondly, and even more importantly, these 48 funders as a group are heavily focused on grants to private schools within their choice portfolios, with 81 percent of their choice dollars flowing to private schools. Only 5 percent of their overall K–12 funding was devoted to charter schools, vouchers, small public schools, and research on school choice.

FIGURE 2   Distribution of Choice Grants Excluding Donations from Gates and
Walton Foundations, 2002

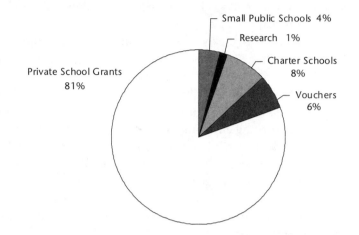

TRENDS AND PATTERNS IN SCHOOL CHOICE PHILANTHROPY

Though the data from foundations' IRS filings provides some information
about the quantity and focus of choice-related philanthropy, it tells us little
about funders' motivations and strategies or about the effectiveness of their
grantmaking. To examine these issues, we looked to a range of more quali-
tative sources and to our own survey of grantmakers. Our data collection
included interviews, public documents, existing research, and personal experience in this sector.

This section discusses several issues emerging from this research. First, we
explore the rationales funders provide for investing in school choice activities. Second, we discuss two hallmarks of school choice grantmaking strategies: building new institutions and investing in political advocacy. We conclude with a discussion of the effectiveness of school choice grantmaking to
date.

Rationales

Like the broader school choice "movement," school choice philanthropy has
attracted a set of strange bedfellows, spurred to support school choice by a
variety of motives. Of ten major foundations willing to respond to inquiries
about their motivation for supporting school choice, the majority endorsed
the rationale that "children have a wide array of needs." Otherwise, a vari-

ety of proffered rationales—"extending rights to less affluent parents is a civil rights issue"; "school choice injects competition into public education"; and "existing schools are too difficult to change"—all were endorsed by less than half of the foundations that responded.

Such examination makes it quickly apparent that there are multiple rationales for philanthropies that support school choice. To begin with, there is an *educational* rationale. As indicated by the high survey response rate to the idea that "children have a wide array of needs," many funders appear to be motivated by the idea that different children are likely to achieve their best results in different learning environments. A "one-size-fits-all" system is likely to serve some students well and others poorly. In theory, it would be possible for a system without choice to provide this kind of differentiated set of offerings, but many funders are skeptical that the current system is likely to do so. As the Kimsey Foundation's Lydia Miles Logan remarked at a Denver meeting of funders in 2004, "We still have the majority of students in [district] public schools. We don't want to forget what happens to them. But if there are new ways to reach those children, and affect hundreds of lives, and turn them around, . . . we should pay attention."[6] These funders tend to place more faith in parents, whom they consider in the best position to judge a particular child's learning needs and to act on that understanding.

This sort of thinking is what leads some funders into a second set of rationales, which have more to do with arguments about the circumstances under which "systems" are likely to work well (or not work well) for different children. Here, many funders express great frustration with the pace of change and improvement within existing public schools. They point to experiences like those of the Annenberg Foundation, which, in their interpretation, demonstrate that even huge investments in the existing system have failed to produce significant changes.[7] Rather than waiting for change to happen in established systems, these funders believe they can have an immediate impact on children by helping them take advantage of options outside of the existing system. As San Antonio philanthropist Jim Leininger states, "It helps kids right now, kids who need a way out. There has to be some immediate safety valve for the children presently underserved by the system."[8] Giving families a choice, plus creating new high-quality options, is a more promising strategy in these funders' eyes than continually pressing for changes in the way existing schools work.

Choice funders seem to differ, however, in just how thoroughly to "give up" on change efforts in existing systems. As shown in the quantitative analysis of grantmaking discussed above, almost all of the top funders that support choice-related activities also continue to make grants to change efforts within existing public systems as well. Funders also seem to differ in just how much "outside" the system one needs to go in order to offer meaningful choice. Charter schools, which remain "public" schools in important respects, have garnered wide philanthropic interest, with fully 33 of the top 50 foundations providing at least some support to them in 2002. For many funders with a history of supporting "public schools," backing public charter schools appears to be a more comfortable shift toward choice. Voucher programs, by contrast, only attracted the support of 16, though 36 funders supported private schools in other ways. But for some funders, only private programs provide the freedom from governmental constraint necessary to meet goals of choice. This divergence of funding strategies mirrors a similar diversion in the policy debate over school choice.

Whatever their stance on charter and private schools, many choice donors seem to believe that choice will ultimately lead to wider improvements in public education, not just for students who take advantage of new options, but for those who stay put in existing district schools as well. Summarizing his interviews with choice philanthropists, Brian Anderson asserts the primacy of this thinking: "The first thing they emphasized is that their goal is not just to improve the chances disadvantaged families have of finding good schools for their children, but also to improve all public schools by introducing competition into the existing monopolistic system."[9] John Walton, one of the principal leaders of The Walton Family Foundation, is quoted in the same publication: "The public schools are the repository of a tremendous amount of talent and infrastructure. What they lack is an environment that encourages excellence and sanctions failure. That's what choice provides."[10]

A final theme that emerges from funders' talk about reasons for supporting school choice is what they regard as a moral imperative to extend options, especially to low-income and otherwise disadvantaged children. Two quotes from The Philanthropy Roundtable's Donor's Guide are illustrative. William Oberndorf, an education donor and chairman of the Alliance for School Choice, put it this way: "It seems a great injustice to me that only certain members of society—determined primarily by their economic status—are able to choose schools of quality for their children, while others—primarily the urban poor—are forced to send their children to schools that all too frequently destine them to lives of failure."[11] Denver philanthropist Alex Cranberg echoed the sentiment: "It's been said that wealthy parents can ensure their children's education by sending them to the finest private schools. Middle-class parents can ensure their children's education by moving to neighborhoods where the better public schools exist. Parents in poor neighborhoods have no choice. We have to do something about that."[12] The "right" to choose one's child's school, in this argument, is one that needs to be extended much more broadly than it is now.

These three kinds of rationale respectively invoke the potential for immediate educational benefits for school choice participants, the possibility of system change through the creation of new institutions and influencing the old, and the moral imperative of offering a highly valued benefit to all. These are not mutually exclusive reasons, and certainly there are funders who espouse all of them. But they are different, and these differences can lead to divergence in how funders approach the work of supporting school choice. The two approaches pursued by the largest choice funders, the Gates and Walton Family foundations, make this potential divergence clear. In Greene's calculations, fully 94 percent of Gates's choice-related funding in 2002 went toward "public" choice: small public schools, alternative schools, charter schools, and the like. The remaining small slice, 6 percent, backs private schools, but directly rather than through voucher or scholarship programs. The Walton Family Foundation, by contrast, directed 46 percent of its grants to voucher programs and another 8 percent to private schools in that year. And within public choice, Walton invests solely in charter schools, while Gates also supports numerous within-district programs, such as the breakup of large district high schools into smaller ones. Though there is still quite a bit of overlap between these two funders (and numerous examples of organizations funded by both foundations), there is clearly also a great divergence in the mechanisms each prioritizes within the broad concept of school choice.

Strategies

One interesting aspect of school choice as an approach to stimulating educational improvement is that it focuses resources primarily outside of existing institutional structures rather than inside. Indeed, as noted above, impatience with the pace and nature of change within existing structures is precisely what has prompted many funders to make grants to choice-related activities. This outside focus yields a strategic necessity for school choice funders: developing new institutional structures in advancing their objectives. Though quite a bit of choice-related philanthropy goes to support preexisting private schools, much flows toward creating new institutions—new schools, new support organizations, and new political and advocacy organizations.

Figure 3 displays one map of this new institutional space. The map conceptualizes school choice grantmaking as pursuing two basic tracks, labeled

FIGURE 3   Map of Institution-Building by Choice Philanthropists, with Examples in Italics

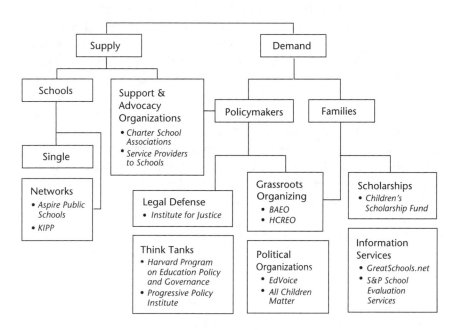

"Supply" and "Demand." On the supply side, philanthropists' strategy is to create high-quality new options for families and children. This strategy in turn has two branches. One is to provide direct support for the creation or expansion of schools. Many foundations have done so by supporting individual charter or private schools. For example, a primary way The Walton Family Foundation has backed the charter school movement is by providing grants to early-stage charter schools. Over 300 schools—more than 10 percent of all charter schools in existence at that time—had received $2.7 million from this program as of August 2003.[13] Walton has dispensed this funding through a variety of vehicles, including direct grants managed by the foundation itself and grants made through intermediaries such as charter school associations. The Challenge Foundation, though not among the top 50 overall K–12 donors, has directly supported 185 charter schools, giving over $18 million.[14]

But as funders have sought to achieve more scale on the supply side, they have increasingly focused in recent years on developing "networks" of schools—organizations seeking to operate or affiliate with numerous schools of choice all working under a single "brand" name. Notable examples include networks of independently operating schools like the Knowledge Is Power Program (KIPP); nonprofit "charter management organizations" (CMOs) such as Aspire Public Schools; for-profit school management organizations, such as Edison Schools; and private school networks like the Cristo Rey network of Catholic college preparatory schools. These networks operate differently from one another in terms of their geographic focus, degree of control exerted from the "central office," educational philosophy, and other parameters. What they have in common is an insistence that member schools meet certain criteria and maintain certain brand standards. Many funders hope these brand-name organizations will foster greater quality on average than stand-alone schools and achieve economies of scale in their operations.

The other strand within supply is providing funding for a host of "support organizations"—entities that do not operate schools themselves but provide important services that make it possible for new choice options to form and thrive. Some of these are general-purpose organizations providing a range of supports, such as the charter school associations and resource centers that have sprung up in every state with a charter school law. Others are more specialized, focusing on specific needs that new schools have, such as leadership development (e.g., Building Excellent Schools, New Leaders for New Schools), facilities financing, or real estate development (e.g., Civic Builders, a nonprofit real estate development firm). Still others specialize in specific target populations, such as the National Council of La Raza's (NCLR) Charter School Development Initiative (CSDI) focusing on Latino students. NCLR has provided funding for the start-up of some 30 new schools nationwide in places such as California, New Mexico, and New York, and CSDI has over 80 affiliated schools. Among the funders of NCLR's effort is the Bill & Melinda Gates Foundation, which has provided over $23 million for NCLR's new schools effort. As we discuss below, many of these organizations play an "advocacy" function as well as providing these sorts of technical services to schools and school networks.

The second track of institution-building is on the "demand" side. Demand has two dimensions in the school choice context. The first dimension is the more familiar one—reaching out to families who stand to benefit from expanded school choice options. Funders have backed the creation of three new kinds of institutions here. First, they have supported a range of organizations that seek to provide information to families about their options. One prominent example is GreatSchools.net, a Web-based provider of information on individual schools and a range of educational topics. Second, they have backed the creation of organizations aiming to organize parents at the grassroots level to demand more and better school choices. The Black Alliance for Educational Options (BAEO), for example, operates a national network of local chapters doing this work, which builds on the extraordinarily successful organizing work of BAEO founder Howard Fuller and his colleagues in Milwaukee. BAEO formed in 2000 to educate the public about parent choice initiatives and inform black families about their options. BAEO's website lists 15 chapters in cities across the country, with several more targeted for development. With significant start-up support from The Walton Family Foundation, BAEO has received backing from numerous foundations, including the Bader, Bradley, Annie E. Casey, Fleck, Kern, and Pumpkin foundations, and significant anonymous donations.

Finally, they have supported parent demand directly by building organizations that provide privately funded scholarships for low-income children to attend private schools. The largest of these is the Children's Scholarship Fund (CSF), founded in 1998 by Wal-Mart heir John Walton and Wall Street's Ted Forstmann. Over 1.25 million children have applied for scholarships from the organization, which average around $1,250. More than 23,000 students are currently using CSF scholarships in 38 communities around the country, including the nation's largest school districts: New York, Los Angeles, and Chicago.[15] In addition to providing a direct service to children, CSF and similar programs have arguably helped influence the policy debate about publicly funded school choice. If nothing else, they have demonstrated that there is a significant demand from low-income parents for school options. In the wake of these private programs, it is not plausible to argue that low-income parents are not interested in alternatives or are not alert enough to seek them out. In CSF-funded programs, low-income families contribute 50 percent or more of tuition payments, a further demonstration of commitment. As discussed further below, these private programs have also provided a basis for research on the outcomes of school choice, which has also been influential in policymaking and the courts. One chicken-and-egg dilemma for school choice advocates circa 1990 was that they could not muster any evidence to support their ideas in the political arena, but without policies enacting school choice, no research could proceed. Private programs helped resolve that dilemma.

Organizations that provide scholarships have proliferated in some states upon passage of state tax policies that provide tax credits for donations to these organizations. In Arizona, for example, taxpayers may claim a credit of up to $500 for cash contributions to nonprofit organizations that distribute scholarships or tuition grants to private schools, or up to $200 to public schools for extracurricular activities. In Florida, a 2001 law provides a tax credit to corporations that donate money to organizations that provide scholarships for low-income students to attend private schools or public schools outside their district of residence. Tax credits can amount to $88 million per fiscal year. In Pennsylvania, a 2001 law gives corporations a 75 percent tax credit for contributions to either scholarship organizations or "education improvement organizations," which make contributions to public schools for innovative programs. Up to $40 million in tax credits per year are possible, and all of the first year's credits were exhausted by September 2004. A state document lists 32 pages of organizations eligible to receive donations as scholarship organizations in Pennsylvania as of March 31, 2005.[16] The impact and scale of these young programs remain to be seen. For now, they are an interesting example of the use of public policy—in this case, tax policy—to stimulate philanthropic support for private school choice as well as public education.

The second dimension of demand-building—in addition to building parent demand—is that for school choice to expand, policymakers must create the space for it to do so by enacting or strengthening charter school laws, voucher programs, or other school choice initiatives. Without these kinds of policy changes, school choice is largely limited to families who can afford private schools or can manage a move to a part of town with good public schools. With these policy changes, donors can achieve the kind of "high-leverage" giving described by Jay Greene elsewhere in this volume, redirecting public funds into new options by having funds "follow" children as their families choose. These changes are typically fiercely resisted by organizations with a vested interest in the status quo, or with a vested interest in promoting other kinds of education reform that leave the "market structure" of schooling largely the same. These organizations include teacher organizations, which, by virtue of their enormous membership base, the propensity of their members to be active voters, and (in many states) their ability to raise large sums of money with dues, are formidable political players almost everywhere.

So a critical focus on school choice philanthropy has been stoking up "demand" among policymakers for expanded school choice. They have done so by funding the creation of new institutions in the categories shown in Figure 3. One type of institution, introduced above, is the set of general support and advocacy organizations that have emerged around charter schools and school choice. These have come to exist at all levels of geographic focus, from the municipal level (with organizations like New Visions for New Schools in New York and Milwaukee's Institute for the Transformation of Learning at Marquette University); to the state level (with a whole range of charter school associations and resource centers and statewide school choice coalitions); to the national level (e.g., Alliance for School Choice, Black Alliance for Educational Options, Center for Education Reform, Charter School Leadership Council, and others). One of the most sizeable is the California Charter Schools Association, whose website listed 30 staff members as of April 1, 2005.[17] An operation this large is capable of providing a range of member services (through four regional general managers on call to help charter schools and numerous relationships with insurance providers and other vendors) and conducting significant advocacy and public relations work.

Funders have also backed substantial *research* efforts related to school choice, often in newly created programs or units within established research institutions. Two prominent examples of such new units include Harvard's Program on Education Policy and Governance (PEPG), led by Paul E. Peterson; the Manhattan Institute's Education Research Office, led by Jay P. Greene; and a new Charter School Research Project based at the University of Washington's Center on Reinventing Public Education, led by Paul T. Hill. Funders, of course, have also supported ongoing school choice–related work in preexisting think tanks, such as the Heritage Foundation, American Enterprise Institute, Stanford's Hoover Institution, and the Progressive Policy Institute. Among the most prominent examples was funding that underwrote the research behind John Chubb and Terry Moe's 1990 book, *Politics, Markets, and America's Schools*, a volume that is widely credited as providing serious intellectual backing for school choice policymaking over the past 15 years. The book's acknowledgments list The Lynde and Harry Bradley Foundation and the John M. Olin Foundation among the funders of the research.[18]

The most prominent example has been the research issued from PEPG on various public and private voucher programs. Paul Peterson, William Howell, Jay Greene, and others have participated in these studies, which use randomized experimental designs to assess the effects of participation in voucher programs on a range of student outcomes, including achievement on standardized tests. Since there are typically fewer spaces available in voucher programs than there are candidates and lotteries are used to select students, such a design can compare those accepted and those rejected in the lottery. PEPG's research (and influential conferences) has been supported by many of the top choice-oriented funders, including the Walton Family, Bradley, Casey, Friedman, and Olin foundations, among others.

PEPG's influence can be seen in various ways. One is the fact that its papers were prominently cited in both the Rehnquist and O'Connor opinions in *Zelman v. Superintendent of Public Instruction of Ohio*, in which the U.S. Supreme Court upheld the constitutionality of Ohio's publicly funded scholarship program. Another is the range and level of media coverage of the program's work. PEPG's website lists a sampling of media mentions or op-ed publications of its research, including outlets such as the *Wall Street Journal*, *Education Week*, the *Washington Post, The Economist*, PBS, and ABC News.[19]

A third kind of institution is the growing number of political organizations devoted to school choice causes. These organizations differ from the "advocacy" organizations described above, which tend to operate within the regulatory limits of 501(c)(3) status and therefore focus on disseminating information, educating the public, and limited lobbying. These new political groups move beyond traditional 501(c)(3) activities and support more direct political activity on a number of fronts, including intensive lobbying, promoting voter initiatives, and providing donations to political campaigns. Typically, these are not eligible grantmaking activities for the foundations discussed so far in this report. For the most part, these activities are funded directly by individual philanthropists, not the foundations that often bear their names. For example, in a 2004 battle over Washington State's charter school referendum, Wal-Mart heir John Walton, Microsoft's Bill Gates, and Gap's Don Fisher each made $300,000 personal donations in support of enacting the charter law.[20] Organizations that fall into this category include the national All Children Matter, an organization that, among other activities, funds candidates who support school choice. Founded by former Amway president Richard DeVos, All Children Matter has been active in numerous state elections. For example, All Children Matter was the second largest independent contributor to Colorado campaigns in the 2004 elections, spending $1.2 million on mailings, phone banks, and radio and television ads backing candidates who supported vouchers.[21] The Alliance for School Choice, a national 501(c)(3), operates a 501(c)(4) affiliate called Advocates for School Choice. State level 501(c)(4) organizations such as California's EdVoice also fall into this category. EdVoice advocates for numerous education issues, among them charter schools, which EdVoice has been instrumental in defending and advancing. The group's advisory board is very broad based but includes a virtual who's who of choice-backing philanthropists, such as John Walton, Don Fisher, and Eli Broad.[22]

Other categories within this part of the map include legal defense efforts, formed when opponents of school choice programs have filed lawsuits challenging their constitutionality, and the grassroots organizations of parents mentioned in the discussion of family demand, which provide grassroots support for efforts to change state and national policy. Observers of Milwaukee, for example, have noted the importance of philanthropic support for this kind of grassroots backing for school choice.[23]

While some choice funders have supported particular pieces of this insti-tution-building agenda, some of the more influential choice-oriented phi-lanthropists have sought to promote the entire "map." One of the clearest examples of this broad-based strategy is Milwaukee's Lynde and Harry Brad-ley Foundation, which has been instrumental in Milwaukee's leading-edge school choice system (and beyond).[24] Bradley has invested tens of millions of dollars in choice-related activities, including support for:

- Partners Advancing Values in Education, initially a private school scholar-ship program that has shifted its focus over the years to become a charter school support organization;
- Milwaukee-area private schools, for the purpose of expanding their capac-ity to serve voucher-bearing low-income children;
- numerous research efforts, including Chubb and Moe's *Politics, Markets, and America's Schools*, Harvard's Program on Education Policy and Gover-nance, Marquette University's Institute for the Transformation of Learning, and numerous other pro-choice think tanks;
- the Institute for Justice, the Landmark Legal Foundation, and other entities for their defense of school choice programs in the courts;
- the Alliance for School Choice, one of the most prominent national pro–school choice advocacy organizations;
- Black Alliance for Educational Options;
- and many others.

It is difficult to overstate how influential the Bradley Foundation's efforts have been, both in Milwaukee and beyond. The Milwaukee experiment, the research conducted about it, and the ensuing legal battles have served to raise the national consciousness about school choice in a dramatic way. Pro-viding a consistent stream of philanthropic support across the entire map of institutions, the Bradley experience demonstrates the potential power of phi-lanthropy to advance an idea in policy and practice.

Creating new institutions, often from scratch, clearly opens up compel-ling opportunities for philanthropists. Rather than trying to wrench changes in existing organizations, which often resist them strongly, funders can oper-ate in "greenfield" sites where they have the chance to shape the mission and approaches their grantees take from the outset. This possibility invites a more hands-on form of philanthropy than many foundations tradition-ally have practiced, often referred to as "venture philanthropy."[25] Under this approach, funders may play an active role in launching new organizations, selecting their leadership, setting their vision, and participating as active board members involved in strategic management of the organization, much like venture capital funders do with firms in which they invest.

This approach can create controversy about the proper role of funders within a social "movement" or social sector, and school choice has been no exception. Within the charter school world, for example, charter-supporting funders have been very active in shaping the creation of the movement's support organizations in several states and nationally. One effort to form a National Charter School Alliance fell apart when the key expected funders, the Walton and Gates foundations, declined to provide the requested funding. A new organization, the Charter School Leadership Council, has since formed with a new governance structure and business plan that met with funders' approval.[26] In California, funders sought to bring about the merger of two prominent charter school support organizations. When talks broke down, the major charter-supporting funders threw their support behind one of the groups, which created the California Charter Schools Association and received large infusions of philanthropic funding.[27] As noted in the first section of this chapter, the great majority of funding for choice-related activity comes from a relatively small group of funders. Most top donors do not contribute much to school choice. As a result, the foundations that do make school choice a priority wield a great deal of influence regarding the kinds of organizations that form and the strategies they follow. While this concentration has enabled a strategic focus that would not be possible with a more far-flung group of funders, it raises tough questions about how healthy it is for a relatively small number of donors to shape the direction of school choice institutions so directly.

Effectiveness

Though individual foundations have evaluated specific aspects of their choice-related philanthropic strategies,[28] we are not aware of any wide-reaching effort to evaluate the overall impact of choice grantmaking. It is possible, however, to make some observations about how effective choice philanthropy has been over the past two decades.

At one level, this philanthropic activity has been extraordinarily effective. In 1985 there were no charter schools. Aside from some longstanding, publicly funded tuition-support programs in Maine and Vermont and a smattering of private scholarship programs, there were no significant "voucher" programs that enabled low-income young people to attend private schools. "School choice" for those without the means to afford private school (or to move to areas with the best public schools) primarily took the form of within-district magnet school programs whose intent was largely to induce voluntary desegregation or offer specialized instruction to students with particular interests or talents. There was no "school choice movement" to speak of, certainly not one with any capacity to influence policy or practice on a wide scale.

Twenty years later, the policy landscape has shifted dramatically. More than 40 states (including nearly all high-population states) have charter school laws on the books, with more than 3,000 charter schools now educating three-quarters of a million students nationally. Beginning with Milwaukee's pioneering voucher program enacted in 1990, states including Florida, Colorado, and Ohio and the District of Columbia have begun providing funding for low-income students and/or students in low-performing schools to attend private schools. Arizona, Florida, Illinois, Iowa, Minnesota, and Pennsylvania provide some kind of tax benefit related to private school tuition. All but four states have provisions in law mandating or allowing some kind of open enrollment between or within public school districts.[29] As stated above, the institutional landscape has shifted as well. Hundreds of nonprofit organizations now play a significant role in advocating for school choice, providing new options for children, helping schools that exist as options, and carrying out the other organizational tasks outlined in Figure 3.

Millions of families are now taking advantage of choice options. Between 1993 and 2003, the number of children attending schools other than their assigned district schools rose from 8.6 million to 12.5 million, a 45 percent increase during a time when the school-age population rose by just 4 percent. The greatest attendance increase occurred among children attending chosen public schools, up 57 percent to 7.4 million children.[30]

Of course, all of this activity cannot simply be chalked up to philanthropy. Numerous actors, from grassroots parent activists to corporate leaders, from policymakers to academics, have played critical roles in turning school choice from an idea into a very real policy or program in many parts of the country. At the same time, it would be difficult to deny the central role philanthropy has played in this set of trends. Donors have bankrolled the creation of the institutions that lie behind all of these developments, funded the research and information campaigns that have helped make the case for choice, and backed legislative initiatives that have led to policy change.

Questions about the effectiveness of choice philanthropy generally fall under the headings of "quality" and "scale." First, as the number of options has proliferated, to what extent have these new choices been "high quality" for the students enrolling in them? Charter school funders seem to agonize particularly over the apparent variable educational quality of the nation's charter schools. Second, there are concerns about scale. At present, choice options still make up a relatively small share of the educational "market." Choice options that are outside of traditional school districts (i.e., independent charter schools and private schools covered by substantial voucher programs) make up a smaller share still. Programs that include private schools are especially minuscule: only ten states even have voucher or tax-credit legislation on the books, and in those states the number of students attending subsidized private schools is relatively small. These numbers frustrate choice funders at two levels: They worry that they are not reaching all families that are in need of new and better options, and they doubt that, at its current scale, school choice can achieve the sort of systemic impact for which its proponents hope.

Are these challenges the inevitable growing pains of a still relatively young area of philanthropic work? Or are they barriers that will be difficult or impossible for choice funders to overcome? A great part of the answer may depend on whether the arithmetic outlined in the first part of this chapter changes. At the moment, a great deal of choice-related philanthropy is still in the form of grants to individual private schools. While some of these grants may serve to advance "school choice" in the sense discussed in this chapter, most of it arguably does not. Moving beyond the support of individual private schools requires foundations to engage in one of education policy's hottest controversies. Often, supporting wider school choice via charter schools or, even more so, vouchers, places foundations and philanthropists at odds with many of the leaders of their communities, both the educational system's leaders and the wider business and civic elite who see it as their duty to "support the public schools." Understandably, this position is uncomfortable for many potential choice philanthropists.

Outside of direct private school support, the better part of choice-related philanthropy is carried out by a relatively small number of philanthropic entities, especially the Gates and Walton Family foundations. Beyond this small cohort, support for school choice is thin. Tackling the challenges of quality and scale will likely require a much wider engagement of the philanthropic community in order to succeed. Whether such wider engagement happens or not will depend on donors' willingness—heretofore limited—to tread into the controversial waters of school choice policy and politics.

CHAPTER 8

Teaching Fishing or Giving Away Fish?

Grantmaking for Research, Policy, and Advocacy

Andrew J. Rotherham

It is no great secret that change in education is excruciatingly difficult. Historians David Tyack and Larry Cuban observe that through the decades, "little has changed in the ways that schools divide time and space, classify students, and allocate them to classrooms, splinter knowledge into 'subjects,' and award grades and credits as evidence of learning."[1] Many philanthropies interested in provoking change in K–12 education have observed this tendency firsthand, as their efforts have been rebuffed in one way or another.

This resistance to change is not, of course, always detrimental. Over time, schools have surely resisted bad ideas as well as good. Yet this resistance to change does create a problem for education foundations, most of which are seeking to drive (or prevent) changes in teaching and learning, the organization of schools, the delivery of education, or education policy.

However, most education grantmakers are neglecting the very process by which we make and codify change for a publicly provided service such as education—the political and policy process. They make relatively little investment in the area of public policy, research, and advocacy despite good examples of how these investments can change public policy and leverage broader changes than grantmaking alone. While a lack of attention to education policy is not the only reason that many philanthropic efforts in education have failed to cause lasting change or have fallen short of initial high hopes, this failure to engage in the policy process has at a minimum done nothing to mitigate the other challenges grantmakers face.

At the most basic level, change is a school-by-school and classroom-by-classroom game. Yet the policy and political contexts grantees operate in can help or hinder this process. For instance, a foundation seeking to foster the creation of charter schools or to expand public sector support for prekindergarten education programs must increase awareness of these issues among the key policy elites in a particular state or nationally. And if a grantmaker is seeking to institutionalize a specific change, research, policy, and advocacy are areas that simply cannot be ignored.

Moreover, education policymaking is highly politicized, ideological, and difficult. Powerful interest groups vie for control and vigorously resist any change that comes at the expense of their membership or prerogatives. For many foundations, the politically charged environment and the difficulty of enacting major change is a deterrent. Paul Hill, who directs the Center for Reinventing Public Education at the University of Washington and has worked on education policy issues for more than three decades, argues that most foundations "don't want to deal with the hard issues, and when they find that not dealing with the hard issues gets you nothing, they back away."[2] Yet backing away obviously has the same effect, namely, a lack of reform.

Overall, educational research faces a basic problem of marketplace incentives. In public education, the relentless pressure of the market does not spur research and development, as it does in the private sector. Unlike inefficient or ineffective private sector firms, the public schools cannot simply go out of business or be taken over by competitors. As a result, there is a lack of internal or external pressure for high-quality research and development work or the dissemination of such work.

Likewise, there is little pressure on policymakers to change public policies in a way that carries any burden for various constituencies with a stake in the current system. In fact, the political incentives are to do exactly the opposite. For custodians of public dollars and public responsibilities, information, analysis, and (perhaps most importantly given the thin empirical basis for most educational policy decisions) advocacy drive public policy decisions.

As a publicly provided service with labor costs consuming the majority of resources, education does not have the same amount of capital available for research as other sectors enjoy. In the private sector, companies are willing to invest a great deal in research and development because the returns on just a few advances or breakthroughs generally outweigh these costs. In education, the profit motive rarely exists outside a few specialized areas such as curricular and instructional models and add-on programs such as tutoring or assessments.

Meanwhile, in terms of research and development specifically, government does not fill the gap. Overall, the federal government makes relatively small investments in education research, and research at the state and local levels is almost nonexistent. The U.S. Department of Education's (DOE) research budget of $523 million for fiscal year 2005 represents less than 1 percent of total public spending on elementary and secondary education. According to figures from the American Academy for the Advancement of Science, the DOE spends less on research than most cabinet agencies. The DOE is spending just $66 million in 2005 to support the work of its regional education laboratories, which are intended to undertake research and assist states, school districts, and schools in translating research into policy and practice. There are concerns about the quality of some of the labs and their work, but they remain the federal government's front line for applied research. Yet, on an annual basis, several of the largest education foundations each give roughly as much or more to education activities than these labs receive from the DOE.

In this relatively arid environment, philanthropic interests can play an especially important role by filling the gap. When invested wisely, foundation giving can be a key leverage point for driving educational policy change. Estimates vary, but it is widely assumed that foundations funded efforts in K–12 education to the tune of approximately $1–1.5 billion in 2002, a relatively small portion of total national K–12 spending of $440 billion in 2003.[3] Yet as several compelling examples show, the strategic and targeted nature of such investments has the potential to change the national policy agenda and correspondingly shape educational practice.

WHY POLICY AND RESEARCH MATTER[4]

Although changes to American education are difficult to achieve, they are not impossible. David Tyack and Larry Cuban argue that durable reforms share several common characteristics. Reforms that endure and change schooling are typically:

- add-ons rather than fundamental changes in how schools operate;
- uncontroversial;
- backed by i nfluential constituencies interested in perpetuation of the reform; and
- required by law and able to be monitored.[5]

All of these traits are dependent to some extent, if not entirely, on public policy or advocacy. For instance, statutory changes are generally required in order to effect fundamental changes in how schools operate, and the degree of controversy a given reform stirs up often depends on the public awareness and advocacy campaigns launched for and against that reform. Research should inform this process by providing as firm an empirical footing as possible for various reform strategies.

Public policy and advocacy are especially important in the education sector because most changes represent "general interest reforms," meaning that their adoption carries broad benefits for the public but may impose particular costs and burdens on certain constituencies. For instance, a reading program proven through rigorous research to help low-income students might be beyond the budget of a school district, forcing an increase in property taxes if it is adopted. Yet while the entire community (and obviously the affected students) would ultimately benefit from such a program, in the short term it is local property taxpayers who would bear the cost, perhaps sparking local anti-tax activists to actively oppose the change. Similarly, if public charter schools expand in disadvantaged communities and provide a higher quality education than children in those communities were receiving, it carries a benefit for those children as well as for society as a whole. However, such a change would also entail a variety of costs for powerful actors in that community. The host school district might be forced to compete more vigorously for students, or even to lay off personnel if enrollment dropped substantially because parents chose charter schools. The local teachers union might see its power, or even membership, diminished if teachers in the new charter schools decided not to join the union. And a host of other actors—vendors, advocacy groups, and others with privileged places in the current system—might see their positions threatened. Moreover, these interests are organized and can be quickly mobilized to press their case with politicians and policymakers.

The political dynamic here is obvious: Organized interests bearing concentrated burdens often work against reforms that are in the broader public interest. And this dynamic is hardly unique to education. The same pressures and lack of counterpressures are why it is difficult, for instance, to reform inefficient agriculture subsidies or the tax code.[6] Unfortunately, too often the media, general public, and grantmakers consider the special interest politics of education to be exceptional rather than generally similar to other issue areas.

Moreover, it's a dynamic that plays out every day. While large-scale policy changes such as No Child Left Behind are often episodic, the day-to-day business of policymaking is constantly ongoing in formal and informal ways. At the state level, for instance, legislators meet with lobbyists and work on legislation, state education boards and various state-level policymaking commissions promulgate regulations, and state education departments make implementation and policy decisions. These actions often are individually minor, but collectively they exert enormous influence over the policies governing public education. For foundations seeking to drive broad changes in schooling, to ignore this process is to unilaterally disarm in the battle of ideas.

There are different theories about how issues move on and off the policy agenda and what, in fact, causes policy changes to occur. The most obvious of these is the basic notion of mobilizations and countermobilizations around various issues. In theory, as one group works its will at the expense of another, the aggrieved group will respond, and over time a rough parity or consensus will emerge. Yet in practice, and particularly in the short run, even a casual observer of education can see that policymaking is not simply a vigorous free-for-all between different ideas and viewpoints, with the most favored winning out.

Instead, in K–12 education, various institutional arrangements, from state education boards and other state policymaking organs to local school districts, create constraints and incentives that have an impact on policymaking. In addition, certain interests, such as the teachers unions, school districts, and colleges of education, enjoy access and privileged places in the policy debate, creating so-called "policy monopolies" that can exercise enormous sway over key decisionmaking processes and consequently the decisions themselves.

These monopolies are informal networks of key decisionmakers in and out of government that have the effect of reinforcing existing power structures and institutional arrangements and excluding alternative voices. Thus, while various interests in a given debate can appear to be in equilibrium, those interests that are actively seeking ways to change the policy agenda and are promoting new and disruptive policies are often disadvantaged actors in the education arena.[7] In other words, all voices in the educational debate do not enjoy parity of access to policymakers and key decisionmakers or equal opportunity to make their case.

The most powerful players in most educational debates are local, state, and national teachers unions. Through their membership and resources they hold enormous sway in the political process. The conventional view is that the education debate basically consists of conservative foundations battling with Democrats and the teachers unions over high-profile issues like school choice. In fact, the politics are much more complicated and do not break down cleanly along partisan lines, because not all of those seeking reform are on the political right.

For instance, many program officers at foundations that are generally considered to be left-leaning voice frustration with teachers union resistance to a host of potential reforms. Rebecca Rimel, president of The Pew Charitable Trusts—a foundation generally considered to be middle of the road or left-leaning—remarked at a recent forum on philanthropic investments in public policy, "With respect to the teachers unions, this is something on which the school reform groups we supported broke their pick. Our grantees tried to work collaboratively with the teachers union in Philadelphia, our home town, to move along the union leadership. To let them be, shall we say, more thoughtful, more open to experimentation, less hostile. We failed locally, and we failed in some of our national work. I do believe that frustrating our children's ability to learn as much as they can is a national sin."[8] Many grantmakers privately say that the attractiveness of investments in higher education and prekindergarten education owes much to the fact that teachers unions are not major players in these areas.

Of course, many interest groups aside from the teachers unions actively resist various changes. The result is a treacherous political landscape around most key issues that many observers agree dissuades some foundations from becoming involved in elementary and secondary education.

Because the education policy debate is so politicized, any position is at least implicitly, if not explicitly, a rebuke of another. Paul Hill notes that, for foundations, impartiality in the various debates is impossible. Foundations cannot "be policy neutral in the education wars. Philanthropic investments can either buttress the existing system or pressure it to change," he says.[9] Bruno Manno, senior associate for education at the Annie E. Casey Foundation and a former federal education official, says many foundations are afraid to tackle the contentious issues because "if you position yourself in some manner, shape, or form, no matter where you position yourself you're liable to be criticized by those who think you're politicizing the foundation by taking a position they don't agree with."[10] Likewise, Chester Finn, president of the Thomas B. Fordham Foundation, notes that there is a media and public relations angle to the issue as well, saying that foundations overall, especially corporate foundations, want to be on the "front page being praised, not on the editorial page being lambasted."[11] Understanding these various dynamics is essential to considering the role of foundations in educational policymaking. First, many of the reforms foundations are supporting could carry broad benefits but concentrate the ire of established interests. In addition, while some foundations focus on add-on programs and reforms that don't challenge the status quo, foundations that desire to engage in high-impact philanthropy are seeking to create durable reforms that fundamentally change schooling rather than merely augmenting today's educational arrangements. Finally, many of today's active foundations, and many grantmakers historically, support interests that do not enjoy privileged positions in the policy-making process. As a result, foundations seeking high-impact change simply cannot afford not to meet their opponents head on.

In the 1960s and 1970s, the Ford Foundation worked to build policy networks in order to aid those working to get the issue of school finance reform on the policy agenda. An analogous contemporary example is the work of The Walton Family Foundation and conservative foundations such as The Lynde and Harry Bradley Foundation to advance school choice as a national issue. Currently, the dominant policymaking monopolies in education remain, at best, lukewarm to school choice–oriented ideas, forcing choice proponents to aggressively seek ways to move their issue onto the agenda.

However, the degree of disadvantage varies, depending on the issues a foundation seeks to address. For example, the work that the Broad or Wallace foundations have undertaken on school governance and leadership is more mainstream than school choice in terms of its acceptance by elites in the education community. Yet at the same time, this work is not as much a part of the national and state policy agendas as such issues as teacher preparation, mainly due to the privileged position of the teachers unions. Thus, a foundation like Carnegie Corporation, which focuses a great deal of grantmaking on teacher quality, enjoys more access to privileged policy actors and acceptance by current policy monopolies, and creates even less controversy in its work.

THEORIES OF CHANGE AND RELATIVE INVESTMENTS

Regardless of how they think about research and policy, most foundations are guided by an explicit or implicit theory of change that shapes their strategic thinking. As the Annie E. Casey Foundation describes it, a theory of change simply refers to a blueprint of "important destinations and guides . . . to look for on the journey to ensure you are on the right pathway."[12] Essentially, a theory of change helps organize the activities of an organization toward reaching its goals.

Figure 1 shows the theory of change that guides the NewSchools Venture Fund (NSVF), a San Francisco–based grantmaker that supports social entrepreneurial efforts in education, such as nonprofit charter school management organizations, Teach For America, and New Leaders for New Schools. It is by no means representative in its content, activities, or goals, but is a good representation of the thought process and logic behind a theory of change.

Although the specific activities funded by NSVF are primarily direct programmatic activities, the near-term and ultimate goals of NSVF obviously interact with public policies. For instance, in states with restrictive charter school laws or caps on the number of charter schools, NSVF would be unable to make large-scale investments because of a lack of public charter schools. Likewise, depending on the regulatory and political climate in a particular state, capacity-building activities such as Teach For America or New Leaders for New Schools might be unable to establish a foothold if policies concerning teacher or administrative licensure restrict opportunities for people trained in these programs.

In these ways, NSVF is fairly typical of education grantmakers. Most of the activities foundations are supporting today interact with the various regulatory and policy arrangements in different states and with national education policies such as No Child Left Behind and the Individuals With Disabilities Education Act. This interaction is either indirect, as in the case of activities that provide funding for professional development or afterschool programs, or direct, as in the case of NewSchools, because a certain set of policy conditions are necessary for their grantmaking to be successful.

Yet despite the integral role that public policy plays in their work, most foundations are investing relatively little in research or policy work. The 30 largest foundations making grants in elementary and secondary education gave a total of $77 million to research, policy, and advocacy in 2002, a figure representing just 12 percent of their total giving. The average among the ten largest grantmakers is 15 percent, but only four of the top ten foundations are investing more than one dollar in five in policy and advocacy. Of course, for the largest foundations, even a relatively small percentage of their giving can still mean a substantial investment. For instance, in 2002, just 5 percent of the Bill & Melinda Gates Foundation's grantmaking went to policy and advocacy activities, but that still represented more than $13 million invested.[13] The relatively low priority foundations place on research and policy indicates that one obstacle to their goals is insufficient work to support and translate their programmatic goals into policy changes—especially when one considers the difficulty of changing the policies of states or large school divisions and the substantial resources that other actors in the debate—for instance the teachers unions—can bring to bear. Few foundations see their giving patterns changing substantially during the next several years.[14] Yet despite these giving patterns, some close observers of foundations see a growing interest in research and policy work. Bill Porter, executive director of Grantmakers for Education, reports that among his members there is an increasing awareness of the importance of investment in these issues. "What I hear from my mem-

FIGURE 1 NewSchools Theory of Change

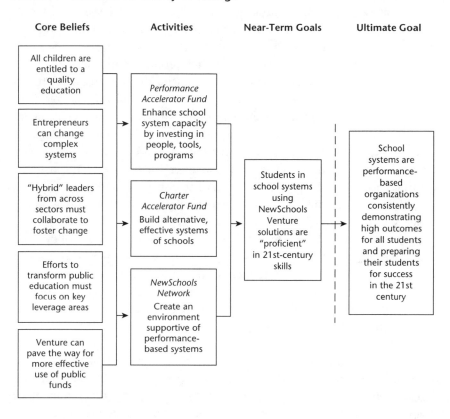

Source: NewSchools Venture Fund

bers is more interest in how to change policy. The problems are too large, the money too much, that unless you're focused on policy you can't change things very much," says Porter.[15] Likewise, Stephanie Saroki of The Philanthropy Roundtable says that her members are expressing a desire for better and more useful research and seem to recognize, more and more, how much research, policy, and advocacy matter in public policy debates. Saroki notes, however, that there is a frustration with the politicization of research and wariness about how it is used.[16]

Many foundation program officers echoed this latter concern and noted that in terms of returns on philanthropic investments, a well-designed study or analysis can be swamped by a lower quality but more media-savvy one. That's the nature of the education debate today. As Chester E. Finn, who has observed these issues inside and outside of government, notes, "education policymaking proceeds in an environment of astonishingly little knowledge about what works. Instead, things get battled out on the basis of interest, belief, and power but not on confident knowledge. We're in a primitive and politically dominated world."[17]

This fluid environment creates a distinct problem for grantmakers. As Peter Frumkin notes in this volume, sound grantmaking dictates that philanthropies work to minimize the risk that investments will not achieve their goals. However, such an approach is at odds with the variety of variables involved in the success of public policy, research, or advocacy work. A grantee's efforts can be nullified by political changes, public relations strategies, or even completely unrelated events that alter the policymaking agenda. Low tolerance for this sort of risk can serve to constrain donors to focus on safe but low-leverage investments and steer dollars away from public policy, advocacy, and research.

One program officer at a foundation that invests heavily in policy work argues that, to the contrary, the risk/reward ratio actually works in favor of making research and policy investments. "If you want zero risk you can fund a program that helps 100 children, and that's great. But if you can tolerate risk and think that there is a 40 percent chance you can help 100,000 children [through a policy-oriented grant], then that is a reasonable risk to take," this program officer argued.

However, in addition to the question of risk, this sort of giving runs against the grain of what attracts some individuals to grantmaking in the first place. Mike Kirst of Stanford University argues that many foundations would rather "invest in a school project where you can see it and feel it than in a policy study that may not get through some tortured political process."[18]

The understandable impulse among foundations to improve their own accountability by focusing their efforts on projects whose outcomes can be measured and evaluated also risks stifling broader progress. This impulse is not limited to philanthropy, but is part of a broader trend, with bipartisan support, that is sweeping education. As Frederick Hess points out, the emphasis on more rigorous research designs is a welcome change in education research. However, Hess notes that many proposed changes in governance, incentives, and management do not lend themselves to this sort of evaluation, nor are they supported by a rigorous body of research literature.[19] Similarly, as Leslie Lenkowsky demonstrates in this volume, work that does not fit these parameters can still end up catalyzing broad change. Lenkowsky cites Gunnar Myrdal's *An American Dilemma*, which was launched as a Carnegie Corporation project but later helped to inform the civil rights struggle.[20] Myrdal's work would not fit cleanly into metrics for grantmaking that required quantifiable and discernible results.

If one perceives today's educational challenges as mostly issues of teaching and learning, then today's giving patterns are more understandable. However, if one believes that American elementary and secondary education suffers from problems with its organizational, structural, and political arrangements, then the underinvestment in changing those circumstances surely hinders other reform efforts.

WHERE TO GIVE: TOP DOWN OR BOTTOM UP?

In addition to the constraints already discussed, the lack of investment in research and policy also stems from several practical and theoretical calculations by foundation personnel. First of all, like all observers of public life, foundations have different views about whether change is driven from the top by political elites, from the bottom by local activists and initiatives, or by some combination of the two. These different views about change manifest themselves in two ways. The first is an obvious tension between support for direct programs, such as opening charter schools or training teachers and administrators, and support for research and policy development activities.

For instance, The Walton Family Foundation's investments in school choice, while including some research and policy support components, focus on creating new independent schools and increasing choices for parents. In 2002, Walton invested just 14 percent of its grantmaking in advocacy and policy.[21] Essentially, the foundation is seeking to create compelling examples or "proof points" to influence the policy debate rather than engaging in the process more directly. Foundation personnel believe that this strategy offers a better chance of achieving their goals than, for instance, creating policy networks or other policy advocacy arrangements.[22] Likewise, the Pisces Foundation, known most prominently for its support for the Knowledge Is Power Program (KIPP), an intensive grade 5–8 charter school model, is using change at the bottom in order to drive change in the policy process. KIPP's Scott Hamilton, a veteran of policy jobs himself, has concerns about the quality and relevance of educational research and notes that "most people are looking for research to back up their point of view." Nonetheless, Hamilton sees changing policy as an essential long-term goal. Thus, while KIPP is focused on opening schools (there are now 38 KIPP schools around the country), they are doing so with an eye toward a deliberate research strategy. Hamilton says that KIPP has an overt goal of changing how people, including policymakers, think about what is possible in urban education. But "if we want to have [that effect]," says Hamilton, "we need to create schools that not only perform well but can be studied in a robust way." KIPP, Hamilton says, works to ensure that its schools can be rigorously studied with key variables isolated so that researchers can determine what aspects of the KIPP program, if any, are making a difference. The hope is that this information will subsequently inform and change policy.

While both Walton and KIPP are supporting many outstanding schools that are starting to have the broader effects they seek, the drawback of this approach is that the political and policy process does not stand still in the meantime. This creates a dual set of problems. First, in many cases grantees, here the schools, must operate in an unfavorable political or policy climate that increases the challenges they face. Second, while the political and policy debate continues, views and positions can harden and thus lessen the potential impact of such proof points down the road.

Conversely, some foundations focus overwhelmingly on change from the top. For instance, the Joyce, Pew, Spencer, and Smith Richardson foundations focus almost exclusively on policy and research work. These foundations believe that engaging in and informing the policy process ultimately leverages broader change than direct investments. For instance, in the past several years, Pew saw an opportunity in the emerging consensus around the importance of preK education. Recognizing that legislative and policy action were possible on this issue, Pew sought to enrich and advance the debate through its grantmaking and policy expertise.

In addition, many smaller foundations focus solely on top-down research and policy-driven change primarily for practical reasons, believing that with their limited resources they can have a greater impact by, in the words of one program officer, "finding points of leverage [in the policy process], because when you do make a difference it has a broader effect" than individual programs. One program officer at a foundation that focuses overwhelmingly on policy and research said, "Our small dollars are more likely to have an impact if they're used to change policy than support a particular program somewhere." This program officer likened this strategy to the adage about giving someone a fish to eat for a day versus teaching him how to fish so that he can eat for a lifetime.

To some extent, rather than just focusing on their aggregate investments, foundations can seek better coordination between those supporting direct programs and those supporting policy, advocacy, and research investments. Such communication and coordination is one goal of umbrella groups such as The Philanthropy Roundtable and Grantmakers for Education. However, there are limits to this strategy. Foundations have various points of view on different policy issues and are far from monolithic. For instance, while both Walton and Pew are working on reform, the specific initiatives and policies they support are quite different. In addition, the priorities of foundations change over time and with changes in leadership.

Finally, some foundations take a triage-like approach to thinking about these issues. Although The Broad Foundation invests in policy work as well as direct programs, Greg McGinity, policy director for Broad, argues that, for instance, if a school district "can't get good teachers and is hiring people two weeks after school starts," this creates such an immediate disadvantage that it essentially renders broader school improvement efforts impotent.[23] In other words, where extreme dysfunction exists, broader reforms are unlikely to have an impact, thus necessitating a more immediate strategy.

Foundation personnel complain that there are insufficient grantmaking opportunities for policy and research work. Most program officers, including some who are currently funding projects at colleges of education, expressed concern about the quality of these institutions and their ability to support change-oriented work. When discussing schools of education, most program officers echoed the familiar complaints about rigor, relevance, and the nimbleness to quickly address emerging programs and areas of need. This creates a serious constraint because a field's academic base is generally a source of research and new ideas.

Many foundation program officers also express concern about the think tank world and other nongovernmental outlets for research. There is a pervasive sense among program officers that the think tank world is generally ideological and produces work that is intended to confirm or support pre-existing positions. There is concern about these same problems in relation to the federal government's regional education laboratories and other quasi-public and university-affiliated policy organizations. There is also concern about the penetration and utilization of work from all of these outlets. One program officer said that the founder of his foundation has little patience for policy research, believing that most of it "sits on dusty bookshelves" rather than having an impact on the policymaking process.

However, some program officers argued that concerns about where to make grants reflected poorly on foundations, rather than potential grantees. One senior program officer said such concerns were "disingenuous and noncreative," while another argued that such a view was defeatist. "If you're smart and focused, with strategies and tactics," this officer said, "there is a reasonable chance, no guarantees, but a reasonable chance" to drive change using existing outlets.

Carnegie Corporation's Daniel Fallon argues that the relationship between foundations' grantmaking and the lack of high-quality research in education is in fact causal. "Educational research is weak, very weak, and we know this to be the case. Nobody needs to do a complicated analysis to show that," says Fallon. "One reason it's weak is that there have not been funding sources for high-quality research." Fallon points out that the federal government provides mostly narrowly tailored funds for research, and he describes the field of education research as a "target of opportunity." Fallon points out that there is much better research about math and science education than some other areas and that these have, not coincidentally, been a focal point of federal efforts.[24]

LEGAL AND POLITICAL CONSTRAINTS

Significant political and legal constraints also have an impact on the work of foundations, particularly as it relates to research and public policy. Since The Rockefeller Foundation was incorporated in 1910, there has been concern and debate about the concentration of wealth in foundations. With regard to research and policy work, this concern was perhaps most pronounced in the 1960s, as the Ford Foundation increasingly provided support for many New Frontiersmen leaving government in the wake of the Kennedy and Johnson administrations. This activity, along with Ford's growing influence and a disastrous Ford-sponsored school decentralization effort in New York City, sparked concern about the unchecked power of foundations. Along with an influential 1965 Treasury Department report on foundations, these issues led to foundation payout requirements and other regulations as part of the Tax Reform Act of 1969.[25] Under that law, foundations were required to pay out 6 percent of their assets annually, a requirement that was modified in 1976 to 5 percent. More important than the specifics of these and other regulations, the federal government had established a foothold to regulate foundation activity. Debates about disclosure, oversight, and regulations are still ongoing and a source of concern for many foundations.[26]

Foundations are also very limited in terms of their formal involvement in electoral or governmental politics. They can influence various policies only in very prescribed ways, such as publishing "white papers" on different issues. They may not participate in political campaigns, can only lobby state legislatures or Congress in special circumstances, and cannot give funds to other organizations specifically for these purposes, though they may support organizations that undertake these activities with funding from other sources.

However, while electoral and governmental politics are the most obvious forms of political participation, foundations can still influence the policy process by funding various research and dissemination efforts, supporting organizations that advocate specific policies, and helping to build policy networks around certain issues.

Yet many program officers express concern that even the perception of crossing the line, regardless of the actual legal limits, adds to the constraints they operate under. Some foundation personnel believe that these concerns unnecessarily limit potential grantmaking opportunities. Sue Urahn of The Pew Charitable Trusts, a foundation that invests almost entirely in policy and research work, argues, "Some foundations are so nervous about [crossing the line that] they don't come anywhere near the things that they can legally do."[27] Daniel Fallon of Carnegie Corporation agrees that "foundations can get timid" in the face of various political constraints.[28]

POLICY NETWORKS, ISSUE ADVOCACY, AGENDA SETTING, AND BUILDING CAPACITY

Despite real and perceived challenges, there are clear examples of where foundations have shaped and changed the policy agenda, and good models have followed. Foundations have successfully pursued four strategies for changing the policy agenda. First, foundations can help establish and catalyze policy networks; for example, formal or informal groups of key policy actors—academics, advocates, and policymakers—working together to address an issue. Second, foundations can engage in issue advocacy by supporting academics, advocates, and policymakers who are working to advance a particular policy solution. Third, foundations can actually help set the agenda through their ability to call attention to an issue and fund large-scale change. Some foundations can take an issue that is on the margins of the local, state, or national policy agenda and move it into the mainstream because of the resources they can focus on a particular issue or problem. Finally, as a fourth strategy, foundations can invest in creating the capacity for research and future research which is, for example, the primary educational undertaking of The Spencer Foundation.

Policy Networks

One strategy foundations have successfully employed to advance issues is to build policy networks and support policy entrepreneurs undertaking work on issues the particular foundation seeks to address. For instance, grantmaking by the Ford Foundation is generally credited with playing a key role in the creation of the policy networks that supported school finance litigation during the late 1960s and 1970s.[29] As part of its strategy, Ford identified two primary strands of work to support its goals. First, Ford sought "to support long-range efforts to build greater intellectual strength into the [school finance] reform movement." The foundation believed that "changing conditions in school finance have created a demand for a new breed of school finance expert. Governments, research organizations, and universities are searching for persons able to deal with the fiscal and political complexities of the subject." Second, the foundation sought to "assist in the development of national resource bases to aid the different reform activities."[30]

The policy network involved governmental and nongovernmental actors. Foundation support included direct assistance, such as supporting attorneys and expert witnesses, and indirect assistance, such as support for research, travel, and pubic awareness efforts. James Kelly, who helped spearhead the effort at Ford, says that while investing in scholarship and policy work was essential, a "parallel part was action-oriented grants, not just to build intellectual capacity and publication, but to quite openly assist groups that were challenging the structural inequities in education."[31]

Ford deliberately invested in a network, as opposed to a movement, meaning that investments were oriented toward the overall problem—inequity in school finance—rather than specific solutions or one Ford Foundation point of view.[32] For example, among many other grantees, Ford funded Jack Coons, the Berkeley law professor who sees school vouchers as a solution to financial inequities, as well as the American Association of School Administrators, which opposed vouchers. Grants went to leading academics at influential universities, including Berkeley, Chicago, Columbia, and Stanford, to produce basic research and policy analysis and development. The academic work was utilized by a network of advocacy groups, including national organizations and state-specific groups in states where school finance litigation was occurring or was likely to occur.[33]

Although the results of school finance cases were mixed and litigation continues in many states, many of the legal advocates, policy actors, and networks involved in finance litigation today trace their roots to the groundwork laid by Ford. In addition, as a result of Ford's efforts, the networks expanded and ultimately attracted additional philanthropic funding, as well as investments from government agencies such as the National Institute of Education, the precursor to today's U.S. Department of Education.[34] By strategically investing early seed money and catalyzing these efforts, Ford was able to leverage substantial additional legal and advocacy activity around an issue of priority to the foundation.

Today, perhaps the best example of the networking strategy is the work of The William and Flora Hewlett Foundation in California. In that state, Hewlett pursues a deliberate strategy of policy engagement. According to Hewlett's website:

> The Foundation's approach to K–12 school reform in California has three strands:
> 1. supporting research and policy analysis of the state's school finance and accountability systems as well as about the conditions of education broadly;
> 2. stimulating awareness and public engagement in school reform issues among Californians;
> 3. supporting innovative approaches to improving the quality of academic instruction in the state's demographically diverse public schools.[35]

Clearly echoing the earlier Ford Foundation strategy, Hewlett gives to a variety of organizations and scholars in California with an eye toward addressing these issues, but without championing singular solutions. Mike Smith, program director for Hewlett's education work, likens the strategy to a campaign. Not in the sense that it ends on a fixed date such as an election, he says, but rather because "you have to have the data, the research, the communications, the focus, goals . . . to campaign for hearts and minds" if you're seeking change in various public policies.[36]

Issue Advocacy

Foundations can also seize on one issue or proposed policy solution and promote it at the national or state level. For example, several foundations are deeply committed to the idea of school choice as a school improvement strategy. These foundations seek to address the problem of persistent low achievement by minority students. However, unlike the Ford Foundation's school finance effort, which supported a variety of solutions to a particular policy problem, these foundations are focusing on one solution—school choice. They are undertaking a deliberate grantmaking strategy, and the result has been an explosion of activity around school choice in the past 15 years.

Of course, the school choice issue is not new. To enhance its pedigree, many proponents like to trace the idea to the 18th-century pamphleteer Thomas Paine, although it was economist Milton Friedman who actually put the idea on the nation's policy agenda in his influential 1962 book, *Capitalism and Freedom*. Yet aside from a small federal initiative in the early 1970s and a few ill-fated ballot referendums, the school voucher issue had not gained much traction as a policy idea well into the 1980s.

To advance the idea, several foundations, in particular The Walton Family Foundation, The Lynde and Harry Bradley Foundation, and the John M. Olin Foundation funded (and are funding) a range of legal, political, and direct-action strategies designed to build support for private school vouchers. Their activities included funding advocacy groups, research, legal work, and actual programs.

As a legal matter, for private school choice to be a viable policy option, parochial schools must be permitted to accept public money for tuition. However, in two 1973 cases, *Committee for Public Education v. Nyquist* and *Sloan v. Lemon,* the U.S. Supreme Court ruled that direct aid to parochial schools is unconstitutional. A generation later, however, the Court's thinking about religion and schools had changed dramatically, due largely to a series of cases and legal arguments put forth by school choice advocates, many of whom received generous funding from foundations. In 2002, the Court found school vouchers constitutional in *Zelman, Superintendent of Public Instruction of Ohio v. Simmons-Harris*, providing the perfect illustration of how a deliberate legal strategy, in concert with changes in the Court's composition, can help change the contours of a policy debate.

Yet making vouchers constitutionally permissible did not embed them in public policy or the nation's political culture. Voucher proponents had to win politically as well. They did so by reframing the school choice debate to deemphasize Milton Friedman's focus on freedom and markets, instead emphasizing an equity-based argument focused on minority and low-income students. To bolster the latter formulation, they sought to develop a key "proof point" in the debate about vouchers by fighting for and funding actual school voucher programs that demonstrably improved educational outcomes for low-income youth.

The research that ultimately became the 1990 landmark book, *Politics, Markets, and America's Schools* by political scientists John E. Chubb and Terry M. Moe, was funded in part by the Bradley and Olin foundations. That book was as influential for what it said as for where it was published, the center-left Brookings Institution in Washington. The book became the organizing tome for a new generation of school choice advocates. "That book was a great help, in particular because of its association with Brookings," says Milton Friedman, the Nobel-laureate economist who has long championed school choice in the United States. Friedman says the book "started to break" the public perception that vouchers were just a conservative idea.[37]

In the wake of the publication of *Politics, Markets, and America's Schools,* Milwaukee, Wisconsin, became ground zero for the voucher debate. In 1990, the Wisconsin legislature, at the urging of then-governor Tommy Thompson, a Republican, and Representative Polly Williams, a Democrat, passed a pilot voucher program in Milwaukee. The program was immediately challenged in state court but found constitutional in 1991. It was subsequently expanded in 1995.

Prior to the program's passage, the Bradley Foundation had been making grants to the Landmark Legal Foundation, a pro–school choice legal advocacy group. So when the program was passed, and quickly challenged in court, proponents led by litigator Clint Bolick were prepared for the legal fight.[38] Moreover, because the program was small (only 341 students participated the first year) and precluded parochial schools from participating, the Bradley Foundation sought to demonstrate the need for more vouchers with an explicit aim of "sparking public debate." The foundation did so by supporting an existing community organization in running a much larger private scholarship program for 1,900 students.[39]

Joe Williams, who covered the development of the voucher program for the *Milwaukee-Journal Sentinel*, credits the comprehensive strategy that Bradley brought to Milwaukee for the success of the campaign there. Williams notes that in contrast to voucher foes who "parachuted" outside activists in for key events, Bradley cultivated a cadre of local activists and advocacy groups. Moreover, the foundation actively supported these activists. "You had the feeling that [local activists and supporters] could go to Bradley and get whatever they needed whenever they needed it," Williams says, noting that figures like Howard Fuller, a former superintendent of the Milwaukee Public Schools, had credibility in the community that outside figures did not.[40] Moreover, in supporting local advocacy, Bradley was willing to fund organizations that did not share its overall philosophy but did support the school choice effort. For instance, left-leaning groups in Milwaukee such as Transcenter for Youth and Homeboyz Interactive received support from Bradley. According to Joe Williams, "both groups were run by a great group of liberals, who were willing to take money from a 'conservative' foundation because they found they had overlapping missions of sorts."[41]

Debates still rage about whether students using vouchers in Milwaukee are learning any more than their peers in public schools. Yet these disputes are secondary to Milwaukee's political importance in the national school choice debate. In Milwaukee, voucher proponents had won a major victory. Milwaukee had a publicly funded voucher program that was championed by a Democratic mayor and some Democratic state legislators, and the program proved to be a potent symbol for school voucher supporters that only added to the political saliency of Chubb and Moe's analysis.

Using Milwaukee, and later Cleveland, Ohio, as examples, pro-voucher foundations funded a growing network of advocacy groups to work at the national and state levels to advance the school choice issue. For instance, national groups such as the Black Alliance for Educational Options, the American Education Reform Council, and the Center for Education Reform all received support for pro-voucher work from the network of foundations helping to build a broad pro-voucher infrastructure to engage in various policy debates. Moreover, much of this funding came in the form of general institutional support rather than project-specific funding. In his analysis of why liberal foundations and think tanks are losing the battle of political ideas today, Andrew Rich of the City College of New York notes that conservative foundations are much more likely to give general operating funding than liberal foundations. Such funding makes it much easier to build and sustain staff, projects, and priorities over time.[42]

National investments also changed the national playing field. Previously, voucher opponents such as teachers unions, school boards, and school administrators were able to fight, essentially full-time, against a loosely organized group of school choice advocates who generally also worked on other issues. Suddenly, because of the philanthropic support available for pro-voucher organizations, the debate was being fought on more even footing. This meant that while school choice proponents certainly did not enjoy privileged positions in the policy debate or access to key policymakers, they were at least able to get more attention for their issue in the media and public sphere and were able to churn out a steady stream of op-ed pieces, articles, and white papers to bolster their case. In fact, this network of advocacy groups may be why, paradoxically, voucher supporters have consistently failed in state referendums but had more success in legislative bodies.

Although vouchers remain controversial, the results of the school choice effort to date are noteworthy, considering the general difficulty of sparking change in K–12 education. The degree of change on this issue would have been almost impossible in the absence of sustained philanthropic support. The results demonstrate what strategic philanthropic investments can accomplish. Fifteen years ago there was one very small voucher program, in Milwaukee. Today, Ohio, Florida, Colorado, Utah, and Washington, D.C., also have passed some sort of publicly funded private school voucher program, and the issue is debated regularly and seriously in many more state legislatures.[43] In addition, the Supreme Court has given the green light to voucher programs that include parochial schools in a nonpreferential manner. This rapid progress is not happenstance, but the result of a deliberate grantmaking strategy undertaken by a few foundations committed to advancing the issue. Regardless of one's views about school choice, voucher proponents have shown the power of strategic philanthropy to change public policy.

Agenda-Setting

Although foundations hastened and shaped the process of policy changes in school finance and school vouchers, both issues were already to some extent on the policy agenda when foundations became engaged. However, foundations can, under some circumstances, quickly move issues from a marginal to a central position in the policy debate. By investing substantial resources into a particular issue area, foundations can call political attention to and set an agenda for a problem through direct grantmaking.

For instance, just a few years ago, the issue of high school reform and creating smaller learning communities was, at best, a marginal issue in terms of the policy agenda nationally and in most states, with only a small federal initiative addressing the issue. Today, by contrast, high school reform is the focus of a variety of national and state initiatives and a central issue in the national education policy dialogue. In the past year alone, President Bush proposed a national high school reform initiative, Virginia governor Mark Warner made high school reform the centerpiece of his agenda as chairman of the National Governors Association, and the Fourth National Education Summit focused on high school reform. Meanwhile, ongoing projects to increase rigor in the high school curriculum, such as the American Diploma Project, are underway.

How did this issue move from the margins to the mainstream in such a relatively short time? There was no major external stimulus in the way that, for example, the school shootings in West Paducah, Kentucky, and Columbine, Colorado, focused the nation's attention on school violence. Similarly, there was no blue-ribbon report like *A Nation at Risk* that galvanized policymakers and set the agenda.

Instead, the stimulus for the focus on high school reform came primarily from the philanthropic sector. For instance, the Bill & Melinda Gates Foundation is making major investments in high school reform, including more than $100 million for New York City's small high school initiative, more than $35 million to both Texas and Ohio, and almost $100 million to support a network of "early college high schools" in 25 states. In addition, numerous smaller grants to states and localities around the country are supporting various high school reform initiatives.

This emphasis is helping to set the nation's policy agenda. The Gates Foundation, the largest education grantmaker today, gave more than $124 million to educational activities in 2002 and has invested more than $1.2 billion since its inception.[44] It has had a rapid rise to prominence; in 1998 Gates was not even among the top 50 givers, according to the Foundation Center.[45] This much funding entering the system in such a short period of time, especially from a high-profile benefactor like Bill Gates, can demonstrably change the public agenda around an issue.

Although only the largest foundations can engage in national agenda-setting, smaller foundations can play the same role in more localized settings, as the Bradley Foundation did in Milwaukee by sponsoring actual vouchers for students, supporting activists, and sponsoring policy work to advance the cause of school vouchers there.

However, such agenda setting is controversial in both content and form. In the *Chronicle of Philanthropy*, Barbara Dudley, the former head of Greenpeace, attacked Gates, writing, "What offends is the fact that he gets to decide what the schools' priorities should be without having to churn his billions through a democratic process the way the rest of us churn our thousands." Dudley worries about the ability of Gates's largesse to trump local control in education.[46] In addition, efforts at agenda-setting on disputed issues are likely to engender even greater controversy. For instance, school choice is controversial, and both the Bradley Foundation and The Walton Family Foundation are widely criticized as unwanted interlopers by many educational organizations and activists for their focus on school choice. If Walton were investing its resources in a more mainstream issue, such as professional development for teachers, it is unlikely that its massive giving would provoke the same reaction.[47]

With the ability to set the agenda comes ownership of it. Just as the name Annenberg became synonymous with urban school reform after the Annenberg Challenge, Gates now owns high school reform. Some grantmakers say this perceived branding can deter other funders from entering a particular arena. Substantively, when major investments are being made, other grantmakers understandably wonder if their resources cannot be better invested elsewhere. Politically, grantmakers seeking public credit for investments are likely to eschew an area already seen as branded by another foundation.

Yet the perceived ownership can also be a positive force for change because it takes some of the perceived risk out of particular reforms. The public sector is by its nature risk averse, so change can become easier when a large out-side player is bearing some of the political and financial risk. The Gates Foun-dation's support for high school reform deflects some of the risk that local, state, and national politicians might otherwise feel on the issue.

In addition, by investing overwhelmingly in a sector and setting the agenda, a foundation can itself become a policy resource. The small high school initiatives sponsored by the Gates Foundation are calling attention to a variety of institutional constraints in education involving finance, choice, teacher quality, curriculum, and governance. As the foundation learns about these issues from grantees and brings policy expertise to bear on them, a sort of "reverse engineering" is taking place that helps inform the policy process. Ultimately, the foundation itself will be a repository for much of this pol-icy feedback and analysis about solutions to the challenges of high school reform.

Building Capacity

Foundations can also invest in building future capacity to address pol-icy and research problems. Just as foundations supporting New Leaders for New Schools or Teach For America are making a bet that these programs will train and support individuals who will later be change agents, founda-tions can support the development and training of future policymakers and researchers.

Currently, only one major foundation focuses substantial resources on supporting future researchers. The Spencer Foundation, based in Chicago, was founded in the late 1960s and began actively making grants in 1971. The foundation has made approximately $250 million in grants since then. In 2002–03, the foundation made $7.2 million in grants, making it the 32nd largest giver for foundations active in elementary and secondary education.[48] The foundation supports a robust and competitive fellowship program for "a new generation of scholars from a wide range of disciplines and professional fields to undertake research relevant to the improvement of education. These fellowships support individuals whose dissertations show potential for bring-ing fresh and constructive perspectives to the history, theory, or practice of formal or informal education anywhere in the world."[49]

Spencer is obviously hoping for a "downstream" effect by supporting up-and-coming academics who, it is hoped, will later make broader contribu-tions to education research and policymaking. In 2002–03, Spencer supported 87 fellowships. These included 30 Spencer Dissertation Fellows, 20 Amer-ican Educational Research Association/Pre-Dissertation Spencer Fellows, 34

TABLE 1   Fellowship Content, by Area

Pedagogy	40.2%*
Child Development	32.2
Culture	31.0
Race/Ethnicity	25.3
Subject-Based	16.1
Bio/Historical	14.9
International Education	14.9
Evaluation	12.6
Gender	8.0
Outcome-Based	8.0
Higher Education	6.9
Teacher Quality	5.7
Health-Related	4.6

*This would read that 40.2 percent of the fellowship proposals contain a pedagogical component.

Source: www.spencer.org

National Academy of Education/Post-Doctoral Spencer Fellows, and 3 Spencer Fellows at the Center for Advanced Study in the Behavioral Sciences.[50]

Table 1 shows the various areas of research that these fellows undertook. The percentages add up to more than 100 percent because many fellows' work dealt with multiple areas.

Obviously, there is a divergence between the emphases of many of the fellows and the issues dominating the policy agenda today, such as teaching, governance, and finance. In fact, Table 1 is an almost perfect inversion of the issues that are dominating the attention of state and national policymakers today. For instance, teacher quality and higher education are the focus of a great deal of attention from state and national policymakers, as are issues such as school governance and school choice, which are not represented in the table. Of course, this disconnection could be as much an indictment of the national policy agenda and the priorities of policymakers as it is of the type of work being funded. And research of course has aims other than informing the immediate work of state and national policymakers.

The nature of much of this inquiry also diverges with, for instance, the Bradley and Olin foundations' support for Chubb and Moe's *Politics, Markets, and America's Schools*, in the sense that many of these fields of inquiry are less likely to produce tangible ideas that policymakers can utilize immediately. The Chubb and Moe book, by contrast, laid out a stark indictment and offered policymakers a tangible and actionable solution: school choice.

To be sure, to some extent this disconnection has to do with the translation and accessibility of research for general audiences rather than the area of inquiry itself. Yet there is a more substantial divergence as well. One way to think about the difference is to consider research and policy work as "hard" or "soft." Both types of work can address important and relevant issues; however, hard research produces actionable work with tangible proposals, while soft research helps expand our understanding and thinking about various issues but has little impact on the day-to-day work of policymakers, who by the nature of their jobs must make decisions and take action even with incomplete or inconclusive information in a highly politicized environment.

There is no right or wrong answer about what kind of research aspiring scholars should be undertaking. However, different kinds of work and scholarship are more or less likely to be consumed by policymakers and to have an impact on state and national policy agendas. Foundations seeking to leverage high-impact results must think strategically about the kinds of work they seek to support.

CONCLUSION

Foundations invest relatively little in research, policy, and advocacy, choosing instead to invest most of their resources in various direct programs. In doing so, they fail to recognize both the importance of engaging in the public policy process and evidence that strategic grantmaking can change the policy debate and ultimately bring about broad changes in educational policy. Despite many promising practices and ideas, the actual habits and organization of schooling are deeply ingrained and buttressed by public policies. But it is precisely these ingrained habits that many of the most ambitious foundations are seeking to change. Because education is primarily a public sector undertaking, for educational changes to ultimately take hold, they must be codified in national, state, and local policies.

For their part, producers of research and policy also bear some responsibility. They must take seriously the legitimate concerns of foundation personnel about relevance, rigor, and penetration. Yet in the end, as Kim Smith, cofounder and CEO of the NewSchools Venture Fund, notes, educational change is ultimately a circle that either begins or ends with changes in public policy. "You can start with direct programs or start with R&D, but you have to close that circle one way or another," she says.[51] Highlighting the importance of advocacy as well as policy work, Carnegie's Daniel Fallon points out that the mechanism for disseminating change "has to be public policy; there is nothing else."[52] Failing to recognize this and engage in this process despite its challenges and uncertainties makes it likely that too much education grantmaking will continue to stimulate activity on the margins of the nation's policy agenda, rather than at the center of it.

APPENDIX

Interviews

- Anonymous Foundation Program Officer
- David Breneman, Dean, Curry School of Education, University of Virginia
- Gina Burkhardt, CEO and Executive Director, Learning Point Associates
- Daniel Fallon, Chair of Education Division, Carnegie Corporation of New York
- Chester E. Finn, Jr., President, Thomas B. Fordham Foundation
- Scott Hamilton, President of the Pisces Foundation/CEO of KIPP Foundation
- Paul Hill, Professor of Public Affairs, University of Washington and Director, Center for Reinventing Public Education
- James A. Kelly, Founding President, National Board for Professional Teaching Standards
- Ed Kirby, Senior Program Officer, Charter School Initiative, The Walton Family Foundation
- Jim Kohlmoos, President, National Education Knowledge Industry Association
- Michael Kirst, Professor of Education and Business Administration, Stanford University
- Cathy Lund, Senior Program Officer, Charter School Initiative, The Walton Family Foundation
- Bruno Manno, Senior Associate for Education System and Service Reform, The Annie E. Casey Foundation
- Gregory McGinity, Director of Policy, The Broad Foundation
- William Porter, Executive Director, Grantmakers for Education
- Stefanie Sanford, Senior Policy Officer, Bill & Melinda Gates Foundation
- Stephanie Saroki, Director, K–12 Education Programs, The Philanthropy Roundtable
- Mary Anne Schmitt, Vice President for External Relations and Public Policy, American Institutes for Research, and President, New American Schools
- Robert Slavin, Director of the Center for Data Driven Reform in Education, Johns Hopkins University
- Kim Smith, Cofounder and CEO, NewSchools Venture Fund
- Marshall (Mike) Smith, Program Director, Education, The William and Flora Hewlett Foundation
- Sue Urahn, Director of the Education Program and Other Policy Initiatives, The Pew Charitable Trusts
- Joe Williams, *New York Daily News*
- Constance Yowell, Program Officer, the John D. and Catherine T. MacArthur Foundation

The Voices
of Experience

CHAPTER 9

Lessons Learned from the Inside

Wendy Hassett and Dan Katzir

The Broad Foundation is a start-up education foundation created in 1999 by one of America's new breed of education venture philanthropists, business-man Eli Broad. In 2004, The Broad Foundation marked its five-year anni-versary of grantmaking in K–12 public education. From the beginning we sought to be different—in our mission, in our willingness to take risks, and in our philosophical insistence on entrepreneurship, innovation, and results. We wanted to be far more than an organization that simply writes checks to good causes, instead modeling ourselves on the venture capital firms that seed, grow, and sustain new business ideas. Such firms seek out talent and ideas, support their ventures with both human and financial capital, and require a return on their investments. In our case, the "return" is measured by the impact our investments have on student achievement and on closing achievement gaps among income and ethnic groups.

This chapter draws on the experiences of The Broad Foundation's first five years. We cover six major lessons we have learned so far and look ahead to potential challenges. As a new entrant in the field of K–12 education phi-lanthropy, we have experienced great success, as well as some missteps and failure. We explain what The Broad Foundation does and lessons we have learned in the course of our efforts. We also provide some illumination on how to ensure that foundation donations to K–12 are thoughtfully given and sensibly spent. We hope our experience will be useful to educators, policy-makers, and other philanthropists.

ABOUT THE BROADS

Eli Broad was the founding chairman and chief executive officer of two Fortune 500 companies—Kaufman and Broad (now KB Home) and SunAmerica, Inc. (now AIG Retirement Services). For more than 30 years, he and his wife Edythe have been active philanthropists in the worlds of art (through The Broad Art Foundation), higher education, medical and scientific research, and civic life in Los Angeles (through The Eli and Edythe L. Broad Foundation). In 1999, the Broads, becoming increasingly concerned about the quality of elementary and secondary public education in America, founded their third philanthropic enterprise, The Broad Foundation, with an exclusive focus on K–12 urban public education.

The foundation's mission is to dramatically improve urban public education through better governance, management, labor relations, and competition. Our approach emanates from our core belief that every child can learn at high levels, that achievement gaps can be eliminated, and that a high-quality K–12 education is critical to the future success of our democracy and economy. In our day-to-day work, we emphasize a commitment to results, high standards, extraordinary talent, and fiscal responsibility.

Educated in public schools in Michigan, the Broads believe that nothing is more important to the nation's future than a determined, long-term commitment to improve K–12 public education. Eli Broad was a CEO at age 22. The son of Lithuanian immigrants, he comes from a union family. He is an active Democrat, but also a great pragmatist. He has built two very large, complex, and successful organizations from the ground up and is not afraid of failure. He believes that education is the key civil rights and economic issue of our time, and that the long-term growth of our economy and the success of our democracy are dependent on ensuring that America has a highly skilled, well-educated workforce. Indeed, if we fail to give every child the education and skills necessary to meet the demands of our new knowledge-based economy, we will deprive our country of the workforce it needs. And if we fail to close the achievement gaps among children of different ethnicities and family backgrounds, we risk stratifying our nation even further into "haves" and "have-nots." Like most living donors, Eli Broad's "DNA" is inextricably woven into the fiber of our foundation. Not surprisingly, The Broad Foundation's beliefs and core values closely mirror those of our founder.

The Broads are among a group of highly successful business leaders who have made significant commitments to improving K–12 education during the past decade. Although they differ by degrees in focus, these leaders tend to share an interest in applying business principles to the education sector and trying to improve the system through competition and the replication of innovation. Donors such as Donald and Doris Fisher (founders of the KIPP and Pisces foundations), John Doerr (of the NewSchools Venture Fund), Bill and Melinda Gates, and John Walton all have slightly different ideas of how their philanthropy can contribute to improving K–12 education. This group of new philanthropists works closely together in many areas and parts ways in others. But all have focused agendas for change, all are risktakers, and all have national reach and scope.

LAUNCHING A K–12 PHILANTHROPY

From his involvement in various sectors, including business, medicine, and art, Eli Broad recognizes that there are no silver bullets when it comes to improving large, complex public or private entities. In education, effective teachers, quality instruction in reading and math, school safety, and parental involvement are all important. Deciding what specific area of urban education the foundation would focus its resources on was a critical step in the foundation's evolution.

When launching the foundation, Eli Broad held a number of specific beliefs about how his family's philanthropy could be leveraged to have the greatest impact, but he engaged nevertheless in a systematic effort to reach out and listen to others to confirm, alter, or inform his opinions. In the first few months before creating his foundation, Broad sought out leading opinionmakers to discuss K–12 public education and met with nontraditional school superintendents like Joseph Olchefske in Seattle, Alan Bersin in San Diego, and then–Houston superintendent Rod Paige to gain their perspective on urban education reform.

To help him build the foundation, Broad insisted on finding staff members with a commitment to innovative thinking and an instinctual aversion to excuses or nay-saying. He did not turn to longtime leaders in the education or philanthropic sectors. Instead, he looked for talent regardless of sector expertise—an approach that would later become a central tenet of the foundation's overall investment strategy. Turning to his local connections in higher education and civic life, Broad found Sibyll Carnochan Catalan, an education policy analyst who had worked for New York congresswoman Nita M. Lowy and holds a PhD in education policy from the University of California, Los Angeles, and Dan Katzir, a Harvard MBA with a background in corporate management consulting who previously had worked for Bain & Company, Teach For America, and Sylvan Learning Systems.

THE BROAD FOUNDATION'S THEORY OF ACTION

As noted above, The Broad Foundation's mission is to dramatically improve urban public education through better governance, management, labor relations, and competition. We focus on urban public education because the need in the nation's cities is especially great. One of every four children in America is educated in a central city school district, yet the schools in these districts are currently among the most troubled in the nation.

We focus on the school district as the unit of change because we believe that a strong and competent governing body, combined with a talented CEO and senior management team, can turn our public school systems from lackluster bureaucracies into high-performing enterprises. Historically, education philanthropy has made significant contributions to individual schools. As a result, we can identify many success stories, such as urban schools serving low-income and minority populations that achieve at high levels. Laboratory schools, magnet schools, "alternative" schools, and charter schools are all examples of such efforts and have provided many lessons about effective practices from which other schools can learn.

Unfortunately, education philanthropy has not had much success in taking these model schools and scaling them to systemwide proportions. The Broad Foundation, therefore, invests at the school district level with the belief that bold, innovative, large-scale systemic change can transform the K–12 system for all students. We believe that the maximum leverage point is to invest in school systems or in systems of charter schools. Being clear about our "unit of change" helps focus our resources and decisions on the opportunities that we believe will have the most impact.

We focus on the system's leadership: its board of directors (school board members), senior management (superintendents and central office staff), labor force (teachers union leaders), frontline managers (principals), and city, state, and federal policy leaders (i.e., mayors, governors, state legislators, and members of Congress). We invest in school system leaders because we believe these individuals have the political and positional power to lead bold, innovative, large-scale district change.

While the majority of our investments focus on improving and reinventing the current system, we also believe in healthy competition for K–12 education. Competition among our nation's great private and public universities raises the bar of excellence for postsecondary education. Similarly, we believe that investing in high-quality charter schools and other forms of parental choice will accelerate excellence and innovation inside America's public schools.

The foundation's assets grew from $100 million at its inception to $545 million in December 2004 as a result of additional contributions from the Broads. After having just two employees for its first two years, the foundation has grown to 17 full-time staff members. Staff members include the managing director, chief operating officer, five program directors, a program analyst, policy director, evaluation director, public affairs director, grants manager, and five administrative support staff. In 2004, the foundation received 344 grant requests, of which 42, or 12 percent, received funding. In the first five years, grant commitments ranged from a $250 one-time donation to a $20 million multiyear, 50-state initiative. Our median commitment in 2004 was $846,100. By December 2004, we had committed $142 million in grants and had disbursed $77 million, or 54 percent of that amount. In 2004 alone, the foundation gave away $30 million.

WHO WE FUND

The majority of the investments we have made in our first five years has been in people. The foundation's "brand" is most closely associated with our efforts to recruit, select, train, and support school and district leaders. Many of our national flagship initiatives (The Broad Superintendents Academy, The Broad Residency, The Broad Institute for School Boards) focus on developing the next generation of leadership talent for our nation's urban school systems.

Newer to the grant portfolio has been our work in systems and tools. As Broad-trained or Broad-funded leaders enter more school districts, they are asking for our support in developing systems, tools, and processes to help transform their districts from dysfunctional bureaucracies into high-performing enterprises. The systems and tools portion of the grant portfolio aims to support district leaders in building institutional capacity for success. To date, we have targeted our investments in three areas that are most closely connected to our people strategy: organizational design/transformation, reinventing the human resource function in the central office, and labor relations. In labor, we have focused on new models of collective bargaining and union contracts, encouraging policies and practices that enable districts to place the most effective educators in the neediest schools, and supporting unions and districts with plans to use incentive-based, professional compensation.

In addition to investing in people/leadership and systems/tools, we aim to influence the policy and operating environment so that our investments can flourish. We currently invest in limited ways in research, knowledge-sharing, and public policy, but believe that these areas of our portfolio will grow over time.

Below are a few examples of our grants in each of our focus areas to illustrate the types of programs and organizations we fund.

Governance

Our largest investment in governance has been our national flagship venture, The Broad Institute for School Boards. Since 2002, The Broad Institute has provided a week-long summer induction program for more than 80 newly appointed and elected school board members from 25 districts. Our partner in The Broad Institute is Don McAdams and his nonprofit organization, the Center for the Reform of School Systems (CRSS). The Broad Institute induction training focuses new school board trustees on using their power and influence to develop a policy agenda in the service of improving student achievement and closing achievement gaps. In 2004, the institute invited its alumni back for a "graduate course" at the Alumni Institute.

In 2005, together with CRSS, we launched Reform Governance in Action, a two-year training and executive coaching initiative in four cities: Charlotte-Mecklenburg, North Carolina; Christina (Wilmington), Delaware; Denver, Colorado; and Duval County (Jacksonville), Florida. Using The Broad Institute and Alumni Institute curriculum as a springboard, entire school boards and the superintendents from these four cities are working toward improving their board meetings, constituent service protocol, management oversight, and district reform strategy. Each board is also developing one or more policies aligned with their district reform strategy which is aimed at improving student achievement and closing achievement gaps.

Executive Management Talent

The Broad Superintendents Academy, founded in 2001, recruits and prepares the nation's most talented senior executives from the business, military, nonprofit, government, and education sectors to become the next generation of large urban school system CEOs. Two-thirds of academy graduates are currently serving as superintendents or cabinet-level executives in school systems across the country. Nineteen are serving as superintendents in cities such as Charleston, South Carolina; Christina (Wilmington), Delaware; Cobb County (Atlanta), Georgia; Fort Wayne, Indiana; Fort Worth, Texas; Houston, Texas; Minneapolis, Minnesota; Montgomery, Alabama; Oakland, California; and Paterson, New Jersey.

The Broad Residency in Urban Education, founded in 2003, recruits, trains, and places emerging private and public sector leaders with an MBA, JD, or masters in public policy into key central office management positions. In just three years, more than 1,000 candidates have applied for 55 residency placements in 17 districts and seven charter management organizations.

Central Office Systems

We invest in districts that aim to reinvent their human resources departments as part of their core strategy to improve operational effectiveness. Given that 80 percent or more of a district's budget is dedicated to people, improving the performance of human resources departments is a critical lever in transforming urban school systems. We see opportunities for integration with our labor relations efforts, where forward-thinking districts and unions might have common ground to dramatically change how school systems execute their human resources function while improving employee working conditions. For example, The Broad Foundation is currently investing in New York City's effort to improve its management of human capital. This initiative includes implementing a new organizational model for the human resources function, rethinking the teacher hiring and transfer process, and examining how to better use professional development spending so that it has the greatest possible impact on teacher effectiveness and student performance.

Aspiring Principals

We have invested in three districts (San Diego in 2001, Boston in 2003, Philadelphia in 2004) and one national program (New Leaders for New Schools) to attract and develop new talent to the principalship. These programs share the following core elements: 1) highly selective recruitment of excellent teachers with demonstrated leadership skills; 2) an in-school "residency" where fellows take on leadership responsibilities with the guidance of an experienced mentor principal; and 3) coursework focusing on instructional leadership that combines theory with practical application.

Labor Relations

The foundation seeks opportunities to work with those teachers unions that consider excellence in teaching and increasing student achievement to be paramount. In 2002, we made a capstone investment in Denver's pay-for-performance pilot (ProComp), and in 2004 made a follow-on grant to support a critical phase of information sharing and communication just prior to the teacher vote on ProComp, which helped yield a 59 percent margin for the proposal by the Denver Classroom Teachers Association.

Competition

We seek to expand the number of high-quality charter schools that operate in the nation's largest urban districts. To date we have concentrated our efforts on nonprofit charter management organizations that operate multiple charter school campuses in California, largely through our investment in the NewSchools Venture Fund. We have supported Green Dot Public Schools and Aspire Public Schools through the NewSchools Venture Fund. In addition, we provided funding for KIPP and the Alliance College-Ready charter schools in Los Angeles. These five charter management organizations currently serve more than 7,500 students.

THE BROAD FOUNDATION APPROACH TO GRANTMAKING

Grants can be differentiated across a number of variables: how and to whom grant funds are distributed, the level of staff engagement on a grant project, characteristics of the grantee partner(s), and the stage at which the foundation becomes involved with a project.

Direct vs. Indirect Grants

Many foundations will not make grants directly to school districts. Instead, they use intermediary organizations as conduits for grant funding and implementation. Strong and able intermediaries provide technical assistance, fundraising capacity, project leadership, civic involvement, and financial responsibility.

By contrast, we fund districts directly. Our "leadership first" strategy requires us to research and commit to a district's leadership before we approve any district grant. We are investing as much in the leaders (of the school board, district management, labor union, or charter management organization) and their entire strategic reform effort as we are in the individual grant project. In doing so, we hold the district directly accountable for results. Even if the district should choose to partner with an external entity for expertise and assistance, such as a local university or public education fund, the district is still directly responsible and accountable to The Broad Foundation for the work and results of the grant.

Some districts have expressed frustration with philanthropists who essentially cause them to adopt strategies and initiatives that are outside the scope of their own reform efforts in exchange for much-needed financial resources. In these cases, externally funded programs can distract from the core priorities of the district. We believe that private dollars have a far greater impact when invested in a district that has a clearly defined theory of action and when those dollars support essential initiatives that are wholly aligned with the district's core strategies for reform.

Indeed, it is this alignment that enables us to require that districts have their own financial "skin in the game." For district programs to have an impact, meaning, and rigor, we believe they must be "owned" by school-district managers. We believe that ownership includes having a serious financial stake in the operations and outcomes of any initiative. Typically, we require districts to cover one-third or more of a project's funding requirement through internal district budget reallocations, with another one-third matched by local or other national funders. Our foundation covers the final third.

An example of this type of funding arrangement occurred in Boston, where the foundation recently helped to fund the district's School Leadership Institute. In an effort to create a principal recruitment and training program for aspiring principals, the district combined its own resources and a federal School Leadership Grant to match our multiyear investment.

While this type of funding requirement theoretically may deter districts from applying for funding from The Broad Foundation, this has not been our experience. In most instances, districts are more than willing to put resources behind a priority initiative as long as the initiative is essential to its theory of action for reform. This often means shifting funds from another area of the district's budget or augmenting existing funds earmarked for similar work.

Gift Grants vs. Investment Grants

The Broad Foundation defines its giving in two ways—"gift grants" and "investment grants." Gift grants can be considered traditional charitable giving. Typically, these are donations given to an organization with few, if any, strings attached. Gift grants enable us to provide general operating support to worthwhile organizations, give small donations to programs that are connected but not central to our mission, and experiment with new ideas. Gift grants currently account for 3 percent of our total investment portfolio.

Investment grants, by contrast, are far more hands-on, require a high level of engagement from foundation staff, and have measurable benchmarks for the grantee to achieve. The disbursement of additional funding is always contingent on meeting preset performance benchmarks. Investment grants represent 97 percent of our grants. At this time, we categorize our investments in four ways: flagship investments, national investments, district investments, and multisite investments. Categorizing grants in this way helps us think about the most appropriate mix of investments for the foundation's portfolio and the most appropriate structure for an individual grant.

Flagship Grants

Flagship grants are branded with the Broad name and are incubated inside the foundation and then codeveloped and implemented with the help of a trusted national external partner. Flagships are by far our most high-involvement, high-touch investments.

The Broad Prize for Urban Education is one example of a flagship grant. The creation of the prize sprung from Eli Broad's belief that some urban districts were making great progress, but that the public was generally unaware of their success. In 1999, few organizations were dedicated to honoring and showcasing urban district success (with the Council of the Great City Schools being one notable exception). The $1 million annual Broad Prize, founded in 2002, is now the largest award in American education.

The Broad Prize honors districts that demonstrate the greatest overall improvement in student achievement while also closing achievement gaps across ethnic and income groups. Each year, the National Center for Educational Accountability collects and analyzes student achievement and demographic data on all of the eligible Broad Prize districts. This data is presented to a review board composed of national education leaders. The review board selects five finalist districts, which then undergo further review and site visits from teams of educational researchers and practitioners. Results are shared with the selection jury, composed of nationally prominent individuals from business and industry, government, and public service. The selection jury reviews the statistical data and on-site reports for each district and chooses one district as the winner of The Broad Prize for Urban Education. The winning district receives $500,000 for scholarships for graduating seniors to attend college or other postsecondary training. Each of the four additional finalist districts receives $125,000 for scholarships. All five districts participate in a year-long, foundation-funded process to share their best educational practices with other school districts throughout the nation.

As with any venture created from scratch, there are variables and challenges one cannot anticipate at the outset. Looking back, we were not prepared for how difficult it would be to collect and synthesize the education performance data needed for this project. Education data, particularly in 2001 when we first began the prize process, are far from complete, systemic, or comparable across multiple states. There is no single test. States have their own standards. Different grades are tested. Different academic subjects are tested, and which students are included (and exempt) in annual testing is a matter of ongoing debate. Today, the state of education data is becoming far more coherent and complete, but this unforeseen challenge has heightened the foundation's focus on increasing the availability of objective, transparent K–12 data. We hope that our work with the Prize and other follow-on national data investments encourages others to think about the importance of quality education data and serves as a catalyst for improvement. We are particularly pleased with our most recent investment in www.schoolmatters. com, now considered the nation's most comprehensive K–12 education data website.

Flagships are meant to be "leave-a-legacy" investments. Like Carnegie Corporation's spin-off venture, The Carnegie Foundation for the Advancement of Teaching, we see the flagships as a way to deeply influence the K–12 landscape in ways that a traditional investment—even a high-engagement philanthropy investment—can't match.

National Grants

National grants are directed toward organizations that are often working in multiple urban school districts. For example, the foundation is a supporter of New Leaders for New Schools, whose mission is to attract, prepare, and support a new generation of outstanding principals for urban public schools. New Leaders for New Schools currently operates in New York City, Chicago, Washington, D.C., Memphis, Oakland, and Baltimore. Since accountability follows the funding, the foundation holds the national organization accountable for meeting performance benchmarks. New Leaders for New Schools in turn uses these benchmarks to track performance at both the national and district levels.

Over the last four years, the foundation has made three separate grant commitments to New Leaders for New Schools, totaling nearly $9 million. Our giving has been structured to meet the needs of this evolving organization. Initially, the foundation, along with the NewSchools Venture Fund and New Profit, Inc., provided incubation, or start-up, funding to help the three founding entrepreneurs move from a paper business plan to a fully operating organization. Our second grant to New Leaders for New Schools was a challenge grant that allowed the organization to use the Broad name to seek out and secure matching funds from other local and national funders. Most recently, we provided additional funds to help sustain the local and national operations of the organization. Over time, our dollar investment has increased significantly, but our share of the organization's overall funding has grown smaller.

District Grants

District grants are those investments in which grant funds are given directly to the school district for a districtwide initiative aligned with the school system's theory of action for reform. All district grant opportunities are screened across five major dimensions: 1) the leadership of the school board, superintendent, and labor leaders; 2) the theory of action of reform; 3) the quality and potential impact of the specific grant project; 4) the district's commitment to securing the financial, managerial, and operational resources required for the success of the project; and 5) up-front agreement regarding performance benchmarks, including specific targets to outperform historical and control group student achievement growth metrics.

Multisite Grants

A multisite grant is one in which there is a looser locus of control than a district or national grant. In this case, many sites are involved in the grant effort, and the grant requires a significant investment of time and commitment on behalf of the site participants. The foundation's investment in the Teacher Union Reform Network (TURN) is an example. TURN is a national education network of 30 local teachers unions from the National Education Association and the American Federation of Teachers. TURN aims to unite progressive urban teachers union leaders in restructuring their organizations to become more effective partners in improving teaching and learning. The foundation supports TURN's efforts to rethink traditional positions and encourage the implementation of new approaches to labor-management relations.

Multisite grants are often more fluid and inherently allow for less grantor control. This factor requires the foundation to perform significant due diligence on the intermediary organization facilitating the project. Since the intermediary organization is often taking on the role we would typically play with a single-site grantee, we work hard to find partners who share our values and approach.

Multisite grants are also more "time bound" in that they are made for a specific period of time and are not renewable, as national and district grants are. With our grant to New Leaders for New Schools, we are investing in both the long-term sustainability and growth of the organization as well as the program itself, whereas the TURN grant has a specific project timeframe (three years) with a looser confederation of participants funded for a specific project purpose.

Program-Driven vs. Research-Driven

Foundations and their founders all share a common desire to promote improvement. But there are differing views on the types of activities that will have the greatest impact. Some foundations seek to drive change through the funding of research and knowledge dissemination. These foundations aim to discover, document, and promote promising and proven practices and policies.

The Broad Foundation, on the other hand, has generally adopted a more program-driven approach. Our value as a venture fund and as a venture partner is in assisting organizations with excellent program design and implementation. It is one of the unique contributions we feel we provide to the sector. This strategy allows us to closely monitor our programs and become more intimately involved in their operations (i.e., recruitment, selection, curriculum development, training, and overall operational quality). Moreover, this strategy allows us to drive change and see progress more quickly. That said, our program-driven investments have an impact on our own work in the areas of research, policy, and evaluation, and are themselves shaped by research findings. For example, we recently provided funding to the New Teacher Project to gather best practices on principal recruitment, selection, and hiring practices that will enable the foundation to improve the effectiveness of our investments in principal leadership.

Seed Investor vs. Later-Stage Investor

Foundations often choose to support organizations in particular phases of growth. The NewSchools Venture Fund, for example, dedicates itself to supporting selected ventures led by promising education entrepreneurs in their early years. New Profit, Inc., focuses on providing funding for existing, proven nonprofits to help them grow to scale. Many foundations will not support a grantee for more than a specified number of years, regardless of where the organization is in terms of its growth cycle.

The Broad Foundation has chosen not to limit itself in this fashion. We have provided seed funding to the National Institute for School Leadership, a national principal-training program modeled after the War College leadership development programs; early-stage funding to Aspire Public Schools, a non-profit charter management organization based in California; growth capital to Standard & Poor's School Evaluation Services, the creator of schoolmatters. com, a Web-based national education data service that provides in-depth student achievement and financial information and analysis about public schools; and later-stage support to KIPP, a national charter management organization. We do not limit the number of years we will support any one organization. We have sought to maximize our flexibility to fund great ideas, great people, and great programs in our core funding areas.

This approach has its benefits and challenges. By being open to organizations at all stages of development, we feel free to invest in the best ideas and can be responsive to organizational performance issues as they arise. At the same time, increased flexibility requires us to analyze every proposal on its merits and does not allow us to limit the volume of opportunities we consider based on an established set of criteria. In addition, we need to constantly monitor organizations we are currently funding to consider whether to re-fund them in the future. Finally, our lack of strict guidelines in this area can, at times, add up to less clarity for potential grantees trying to decipher whether they are eligible for funding.

LESSONS LEARNED

Lesson #1: Be clear on your approach to investing.

At The Broad Foundation, we do not regard our grantmaking as charity work. Instead, we think of our work as making investments in areas in which we expect a healthy return. We believe that our investments will yield the greatest return when foundation staff members are actively and deeply engaged in the scouting, development, implementation, and evaluation of grant initiatives. This perspective entails becoming active investors, not passive check writers. Our grantmaking process is not an impersonal, disengaged set of rote steps, checklists, and payment processing. Instead, we emphasize intense relationship development and hands-on program management with our grantees.

Before a grant concept is considered or developed, The Broad Foundation staff engages in a high degree of due diligence known as scouting. This process can be prompted externally by a grant request from a district or internally by staff members interested in soliciting a proposal from a promising district with strong leadership. Program staff members travel to the district to familiarize themselves with district leadership, the union, and the community as a whole. We attempt to gain a deep understanding of the district's strategic priorities and the relationships among the school board, senior management, labor, charter schools, and civic leaders. The scouting analysis reveals whether conditions are right for an investment. Indicators of a promising investment environment include a strong and capable superintendent; a collaborative, functioning board; a solid working relationship between management and the local teachers union; and a supportive local business and philanthropic community. Factors that would stand in the way of an investment include a district without stable leadership or without a sitting superintendent; a reform strategy that is not clear or compelling; contentious union relations; and turmoil among management, the board, and the union.

If the up-front analysis of the scouting phase is positive, the program staff and district move on to the development phase. The grant development phase is a highly collaborative process in which the grant applicant and the foundation program director subject all ideas to a rigorous analytic review. Foundation staff members scrutinize the grantee's capacity to undertake the described work, set forth the grant's goals and benchmarks, determine the grant's fit within the foundation's overall strategic goals, and estimate the cost of the initiative. During the development phase, detailed line-item budgets, operational plans, and implementation timelines undergo stringent review and often lead to numerous rounds of questioning and revision. This process has remained fairly consistent over time. It borrows heavily from the private sector, where reviewing business plans, unit cost, and the potential to achieve scale is commonplace.

Grantees are often appreciative of the thoroughness of our process and our hands-on approach. In some cases, however, grantees are initially startled by the level of engagement of our program staff and view our questioning as invasive. Many have not experienced this type of working relationship with other funders. However, we have found that in the long run, grantees value the collaborative nature of our process.

If a proposal is approved for funding, the grant moves into the implementation and evaluation phase. During this phase of the work, we hold ourselves to the same standards as the grantee for the success of the grant's implementation and outcomes and often act as consultants, offering guidance and taking on other duties outside the realm of the specific parameters of the grant. Examples of this type of work include assisting districts or national nonprofit organizations in finding qualified candidates for senior leadership positions; offering feedback on related but different grant proposals written for submission to other funders; and offering strategic counsel (from foundation staff, former superintendents, or other outside consultants) on the organization's overall strategic plan, organizational structure, budget, or communications efforts. For our largest national investments, such as New Leaders for New Schools, we take a seat on the board of directors. For district grants, we actively participate in whatever executive advisory structure the district establishes for the project. This type of participation requires frequent visits to the district to meet with district and community leaders, as well as the grant project team. During the implementation and evaluation phase, we expend considerable effort and resources monitoring and supporting the grantees' executive leadership, overall and unit cost spending, and program quality.

Our grant agreements also require the grantee to meet certain evaluative benchmarks and deliverables. Our funding is often parceled out in several payments during the term of the grant, and every installment is contingent on, or triggered by, the grantee achieving these benchmarks. For a grant to train principals, the following program benchmarks are typical:

- *Recruitment and Selectivity Targets:* To aim for an increasingly diverse, high-quality cohort of aspiring school leaders (Target: x% minority; y% male; z% rated 90 or higher out of 100 on a predetermined quality selection rubric).
- *Placement Rates:* To increase the percentage of trainees who actually take on school leader roles (Target: 1.5x the district's historical average).
- *Successful Performance:* To increase school performance as measured by intermediary metrics such as attendance and increased academic rigor in the school, and by student achievement measures such as reducing performance gaps and raising the academic performance of students in the lowest quartile (Target: Outperforming the district's historical average and control groups 80% of the time).

We have found that the provision of consultative, supportive resources combined with clear and measurable performance and accountability metrics works for us. We are clear with grantees that our hands-on approach during the scouting and development phase remains as intense during the implementation and evaluation phase. Our success as a foundation is tied to their success, and this clarity of approach helps to build stronger and longer-lasting grantee-foundation partnerships.

Lesson #2: Failure is an option.

As with any investment portfolio, the performance of individual investments will be mixed. Some will be winners, others moderate successes, and others will fail. We believe that an investment portfolio truly on the edge of discov-

ery and innovation will inevitably have grants that fail to reach their antici-
pated objectives. Recognizing that failure *is* an option and figuring out how
to appropriately "slim" our portfolio has been a key learning area for us.

For example, since school system leadership is critical to our mission, we
have included a CEO "poison pill" clause in the terms of our grants. Namely,
when a district superintendent leaves (or is fired), we put that district's grant
on "pause" to determine whether the investment is still a strategic priority for the new leader and whether he or she will continue to invest the district's financial and human capital in making the project a success. We have
learned that when we put our financial stake on hold, we need to dramatically increase our human capital stake. This often entails intensifying consultative and management support from the foundation staff in order to help
get the project back on track.

In addition to CEO transition contingencies, if performance benchmarks
are missed by the grantee during the term of the grant, we may also put
a grant on hold, restructure the timing of our payments, reduce our total
investment, or disinvest entirely. For example, when one grantee missed its
recruitment targets by a significant margin, our analysis showed that the
additional assets intended to bulk up national recruiting had not been fully
deployed. We worked with the grantee to execute this portion of their business plan the following year, and extended our grant payments over a longer
period to reflect the new organizational growth objectives.

In the rare case that a grant is just not producing the desired outcome or
is being mismanaged in such a way that the foundation staff feels it is impossible to get back on track, the foundation will disinvest entirely in the grant.
When a grant is ended early, we struggle not only with the loss of potential
impact, but also with the knowledge that the education sector as a whole
has a history of ideas that come and go. Philanthropies have, at times, been
a part of this tendency in education to move from one appealing idea to the
next. We are careful to avoid such swings in strategy, and we do not make
decisions to disinvest lightly.

Lesson #3: Be open to broadening your scope, but don't dilute your focus.

The Broad Foundation's original focus was on training superintendents and
school board members. Based on our early research and conversations in
1999, Eli Broad felt that there were few training providers that focused on
urban education challenges and even fewer that looked beyond the K–12 sector itself for best practices in large-scale organizational management and gov-

ernance. We were asked by the Broads to research and consider funding promising or proven programs already in existence, and to consider developing new programs to address the quality of school system leaders and trustees.

Prior to making our first grant, we engaged in a nine-month "listening-and-learning" tour across the country, meeting with leaders and entrepreneurs in both the education and the philanthropy worlds. We also held a number of strategic advisory retreats, engaging K–12 practitioners, university leaders, elected officials, and other philanthropists in discussions around our mission and focus.

These meetings caused us to broaden and deepen the scope of our programs. At an early retreat, superintendents told us that recruiting and training principals was critical to the success of district-level reform initiatives. Sensing their urgency, we began researching the suggestion. After a great deal of due diligence, the decision was made to add principal training to the foundation's grantmaking portfolio. Today, the upgrading of the pipeline to the principalship is one of our largest funding areas. The decision to expand the scope of the portfolio to include working with principals was a departure from our initial thinking, but it was directly connected to our mission of improving the management of urban school systems.

Since then, additional areas of need have emerged that are directly connected to the success of our grantmaking. The decision to expand into these areas has been carefully weighed to ensure that we are not diluting or diverging from our original focus. For instance, in late 2003, while our investments to recruit, train, and support school system leaders were progressing successfully, it had become apparent that even the most adept leader would be hindered by a weak, inefficient central office. Improving the performance of central office functions, while not included in our original scope, became an area that we could not ignore. Today, the foundation is aggressively pursuing opportunities to leverage private sector management techniques to reinvent the district central office as a whole, including its functions and culture, and to drive improvements in central office costs and delivery. For example, the foundation supports the Long Beach Unified School District's efforts to use the Baldrige quality system to improve the effectiveness and efficiency of its central office operations. Long Beach is beginning to see exceptional results in those departments that have embraced the Baldrige approach. Results of the Baldrige program include cost savings due to decreases in payroll errors and significant increases in customer satisfaction with departmental services to schools.

Foundations should be open to broadening their scope while being careful not to dilute their initial intentions. Foundations that ping-pong from one five- or ten-year strategic focus to the next do a disservice to effective programs and organizations seeking to have a broader and deeper impact on the communities they serve. Foundations, of course, should have the option to shift gears and disinvest as they see fit, but it is equally important for education philanthropists to choose a strategic focus and stick with it.

Lesson #4: Be willing to face inherent tension in grantmaking strategies.

Our foundation's theory of action often entails pursuing seemingly opposing strategies. Addressing and reconciling these inherent tensions has been an important factor in The Broad Foundation's development.

Inside the Belly of the Beast vs. Charters and Competition

Our foundation is committed to the belief that school districts can and should become high-performing organizations. The majority of our investments focus on the people (executive talent), systems, tools, and policies necessary to enable urban districts to achieve excellence. For real change to occur, we believe we must focus our efforts on reforming the existing school system. At the same time, we fund charter management organizations that manage public schools but are themselves outside the current system. How do we reconcile this inherent diffusion of interest?

We believe that our long-term investment success (and the success of American urban education) rests in the intersection of the district and the charter school. For public school districts to become high-performing organizations in the future, we believe they must be infused with new models of innovation and experimentation. We aim to use our resources to aid charter schools with the hope that school districts will find ways to integrate charters, choice, and competition into their current framework, rather than seeing charter schools as a threat to the current system. For instance, the district of the future may rely on charter management organizations as partners enlisted to tackle the district's lowest performing schools. We believe that both traditional district structures and charter management organizations have tremendous potential to positively impact K–12 education, and we therefore actively support both systems.

Supporting Elected Boards of Trustees vs. Mayoral Control

The Broad Foundation makes significant investments every year to induct, train, and support elected school board trustees. Our investments focus on enabling these school board members to develop strategies for systemic reform centered on improving student performance. At the same time, we see urban school systems across the country benefiting greatly from having a more centralized governing structure through mayoral control or some form of an appointed board. How do we reconcile investing in two opposing governance structures?

Our work in governance has shown us that different communities require different structural solutions to reach excellence in performance. In Houston in the early 1990s, for example, the dynamic elected board that included Rod Paige and Don McAdams set the path for improving student achievement in a district faced with mounting challenges. Conversely, cities under mayoral control are making significant progress in raising student achievement and narrowing achievement gaps. We see great promise in big-city mayors (and governors too) taking charge of highly dysfunctional and chronically underperforming urban school systems.

Other successful (and increasingly economically competitive) nations have a single national education system. The United States has nearly 15,000 public school systems. This fragmented governance structure may be impeding our nation's ability to provide an excellent public school education to every single child. The success of urban school systems is inextricably connected to the success of our cities, and therefore we have been supportive of districts such as Boston, Chicago, Cleveland, New York City, and Philadelphia, which have moved to an appointed board and mayoral control. We believe that effective governance is not restricted to a single governance structure, and we plan to continue to make investments to support both elected and appointed boards in the future.

Training Educators vs. Nontraditionals

The foundation actively recruits and trains noneducators to assume leadership managerial positions in large urban school districts. At the same time, as noted above, we target a large number of our investments to support traditional education leaders. How do we reconcile our efforts to work with educators already in the system with our goal of recruiting and promoting nontraditional executives to leadership roles?

We believe that K–12 urban public education deserves the best leadership talent America has to offer, regardless of sector or prior executive-level experience. Noneducators capable of transforming a school district into a high-performing enterprise should not be prohibited from entering the field. We believe that an infusion of new leadership from outside the overly bureaucratic mainstream will bring marked improvement to our children's skill levels and education. We have been inspired by successful nontraditional superintendents such as Alan Bersin in San Diego, John Fryer in Jacksonville, the late General John Stanford in Seattle, Paul Vallas in Chicago and now in Philadelphia, Roy Romer in Los Angeles, and, more recently, Joel Klein in New York City.

We also believe that there is tremendous talent inside districts already. We have been inspired and impressed by Tom Payzant in Boston, Carl Cohn in Long Beach, Laura Schwalm in Garden Grove, John Simpson in Norfolk, Beverly Hall in Atlanta, and Barbara Byrd Bennett in Cleveland. These school district CEOs are what we term "beacon" superintendents. And we aim to add to their ranks. Public education should draw executive talent from all sectors—from K–12 education, certainly, but also from business, government, nonprofit, higher education, and the military.

Facing Existing Tensions in the Grant Portfolio

We believe it is important for foundations to be aware of potentially conflicting or seemingly opposing funding strategies. As a newer entrant into the philanthropic community, we have spent a great deal of time, both internally and with external advisors, examining these areas of possible conflict within our grant portfolio. For instance, at a recent foundation strategic advisory retreat, we presented these perceived funding conflicts to a group of superintendents, board members, and policymakers. There was widespread consensus among the group that we should proceed with our current approach and not allow potential conflicts to derail our efforts.

Lesson #5: Find ways to make program evaluation meaningful.

Like other foundations, we rely on program evaluation to inform our investment decisions. Our "Terms of Grant" document contains detailed information on expected milestones. These milestones clarify the program outcomes we expect from grantees. When key performance benchmarks are met or exceeded, we may expand or deepen our relationship with the grantee. Conversely, when key performance benchmarks are missed, grants can be put on "pause" or ended. We also use evaluation to determine the impact of a category of grants (e.g., principal-training or central office investments). This higher level of evaluation helps us assess which areas of the foundation's portfolio are having the greatest overall impact on improving student achievement and/or the operational efficiency of public school districts.

Evaluating the success of our grants, however, has been a difficult task for a variety of reasons. A significant challenge in evaluating the foundation's grants lies in the nature of the investments we make and the desired out-

**EXAMPLE 1   Example for Elementary Literacy Results: Broad Foundation–
Funded Principal-Training Program**

Elementary Literacy	vs. own school (3 yr. history)	vs. other newly placed principals	vs. schools w/ similar demo-graphics	vs. district as a whole
Overall improvement				
Reduction in income gap				
Reduction in ethnic gaps				
Movement from bottom quartile				
Other (i.e., safety, attendance, graduation rates)				

comes of those investments. The foundation's success is measured by how effectively our grantees achieve their goals, which ultimately should have a positive impact on student academic performance.

For many of our grants, however, the link between the initiatives we fund and student achievement gains is not a clear one-to-one connection. There are many steps in between. A primary example of this is our investment in improving board governance. We firmly believe that a focused, reform-minded school board can create policies and an environment that will have a positive impact on student achievement, but the causal relationship is difficult to demonstrate. In fact, we have found few evaluative instruments that will enable us to evaluate many of our systems-level investments in ways that clearly tie back to student performance.

This problem is even evident with respect to our investments in principal training. While many researchers are interested in exploring principal leadership, few examine the actual effect the principal has on student achievement. Past studies have focused on the principal's effect on school climate, teacher attitude, parent participation, etc. At the foundation, we focus on the principal's direct effect on instructional quality and student achievement results and consider those as theoretical success factors in evaluating investments and grantee performance. Example 1 demonstrates the student achievement "evaluation matrix" that we use for all principal-training investments.

Some incoming grant proposals do not include money for evaluation. We now add and earmark dollars for evaluation to every investment grant we make. Most proposals do not clearly delineate program outcomes in specific, measurable ways. We now include an exhibit in our Terms of Grants that not only specifies performance metrics, but states numeric targets for each metric. Many of the organizations and districts we have encountered are reluctant to tie grant performance to student outcomes. After four years of struggling with this issue, we now have conversations with prospective grantees in the early stages of our grant development process regarding protocols, procedures, reports, and uses of student outcomes data.

Example 2 shows a 2004 end-of-year evaluation report created by the foundation. This customizable template is now shared with grantees at the very beginning of a grant to communicate exactly how our foundation will assess the results of the grant upon completion.

Lesson #6: Communications support is vital to ensuring that effective practices travel.

We envision the impact of our investments extending beyond the individual grantee, and that having a deeper impact depends heavily on effective communications efforts. Unfortunately, models of excellence rarely travel well in K–12 education. Somehow, every other industry in America has learned how to beg, borrow, replicate, and mimic good ideas. In education we hear instead, "That would never work *here*," and a litany of reasons why practices proven effective elsewhere cannot or should not be locally adopted.

As philanthropists, we must do more to demonstrate replicability and success, and we must insist on seeing that ideas, successes, and failures are effectively shared with the field. One critical area we have identified is the need to provide strategic communications support to some urban school districts. We work hand in hand with grantees, helping them draft press releases that are news focused to increase their media value, as well as compiling press lists to ensure that key local, regional, and trade reporters receive important announcements. On broader issues, such as a change in district leadership or widespread reform efforts, we offer the services of experts to coach districts and craft communications strategies. Media training, proactive communications practices such as the cultivation of supportive third-parties, and solid preemptive relationship-building with reporters are among the areas where we can bring value to district reform initiatives. Just as in every other industry, the effectiveness of both internal and external communications is the key to the successful implementation of change initiatives.

In addition to our own internal communications efforts, we have invested in organizations that disseminate best practices to the K–12 community. In particular, the foundation is supporting Edvance, a new nonprofit organization formed by the American Productivity and Quality Center in order to

EXAMPLE 2 End-of-Year Evaluation Report, 2004

Grantee	Principal Leadership Academy					
Category	Management / Principals					
Program description	The Broad Foundation is supporting this urban district's partnership with a local university to provide training for aspiring principals. The grant challenges traditional preparation programs by advocating a "medical residency model" for administrative credentialing that blends focused coursework with on-site apprenticeships and by drawing on the best faculty in both education and management from universities throughout the city. Of the academy's 53 graduates, 24 are now principals and 18 are site administrators. Schools led by academy graduates outperformed the district and other schools led by new principals in improving overall proficiency in literacy and raising the performance of low-performing students.					
Term of Grant	Duration	I: 8/99–5/01	II: 6/01–10/01	III: 11/01–8/04	IV: 9/04–8/07	TOTAL
	Commitment	$325K	$200K	$4.2M	$2.7M	Up to $7.4 M
TBF Disbursed	Grants I–IV: $5,351,563 (72%)					

Goals for Grant	Goals Achieved	Outcomes (by Cohort trained)						
Recruitment								
Recruit high-quality, diverse class of aspiring principals	◕		Coh I Actual	Coh 2 Actual	Coh 3 Actual	Coh 4 Actual	Coh 5 Actual	TOTAL
		Apps	82	54	48	67	55	306
		Fellows	11	14	14	14	15	68
		% Selected	13	26	29	21	27	22
		% Minority	54	36	14	29	47	35
>10% of vice principals and principals recruited from outside of the district	◕						2002–03	2003–04
		Externally Recruited VPs					11	2
		Total VP Vacancies (% externally recruited)					No Data	27 (7%)
		Externally Recruited Principals					3	5
		Total Principal Vacancies (% externally recruited)					44 (7%)	47 (11%)
Placement								
80% placed as principals or site administrators upon graduation	◕		Coh I Actual	Coh 2 Actual	Coh 3 Actual	Coh 4 Actual	TOTAL	
		Principal	4	6	6	2	18	
		Site Administrator	5	7	7	9	28	
		Total Fellows	11	14	14	14	53	
		%	81	93	93	79	87	

60% of graduates placed as prin-cipals within two years after graduation	◕		Coh I Actual	Coh 2 Actual	Coh 3 Actual	Coh 4 Actual	TOTAL
		Principal	8	10	6	–	24
		Total	11	14	14	–	39
		%	73	71	43	–	62

Retention		
80% remain in district five years after appointed to site leadership position	●	Cohort I: 89% (8 of 9) remain in district after 4 years Cohort II: 86% (12 of 14) remain in district after 3 years Cohort III: 93% (13 of 14) remain in district after 2 years

Outcomes		
Improvement on state proficiency tests by schools led by program graduates after two years is higher than • Performance of schools led by other new principals • District average • Performance of same school before placement	◑	• Second-year elementary principals who completed the program outperformed other new principals and the district average in improving overall student performance in reading and math and in decreasing gaps between income and ethnic groups. • First-year elementary principals have not yet gained traction—their schools have seen mixed to poor results vs. comparison groups. • Second-year middle school principals have had mixed performance versus the district average and historic trends in increasing overall proficiency and reducing income and ethnic gaps.

Evaluation Summary

Summary	Recruitment and Selection	◕
	Placement	◕
	Retention	●
	Student Outcomes	◑

Report	The academy is in its fifth year and has produced a cadre of 53 graduates who are experts in carrying out the district's instructional program. Sixty-two percent of graduates have earned positions as principals within two years of graduation, fulfilling its promise as a high-quality pipeline to address the principal shortage. Elementary schools led by graduates for two years are outpacing schools led by other new principals in both literacy and math.

○	No progress
◔	Limited progress achieved
◑	Moderate progress achieved
◕	Considerable progress achieved
●	Goal achieved

leverage its best practices, benchmarking, and knowledge-sharing expertise in the education arena. Edvance is working with a select group of teachers union/district teams that have initiated differentiated compensation reforms. The project is designed to enable these "promising practice" teams to share their innovations, experiences, and implementation strategies with other district and union leaders who are interested in developing similar reforms.

Beyond program grantmaking, education philanthropies are in a good position to share best practices and lessons learned with the public. By relying on our own dynamic in-house communications director and capable external partners, we have been able to further leverage our investments.

CONCLUSION

When Eli and Edythe Broad founded The Broad Foundation in 1999, Eli Broad said, "It is easy to give money away, but infinitely harder to be an investor-philanthropist. As difficult as it was to make my family's fortune, it is equally as hard to use it to make a difference."

Those words have proven true over and over again during the first five years of the foundation. We are profoundly humbled by the enormity of the work upon which we have embarked and the complexity of the challenges presented by K–12 urban education. We are grateful to the many education philanthropists who have gone before us, such as the Carnegie, Ford, and Annenberg foundations, and for the work of the new generation of donors contributing millions of dollars to improve educational opportunities for our country's most valuable resource—children.

We are pursuing our vision of K–12 educational excellence with focus and vigor. At the same time, we learn new lessons every day and try to incorporate these lessons into our grantmaking and our relationships with grantees and partners. The Broad Foundation, like other education ventures, is a work in progress. We look forward to continuing our journey; to having a dramatic impact (and some inevitable failures); and to sharing our work, approach, and results with the education and philanthropy community for decades to come.

CHAPTER 10

The International Dimension

Stephen P. Heyneman

Private foundations donated about $3 billion to activities outside the United States in 2000, with about $2.5 billion (80%) of that amount given by U.S.-based foundations. Fourteen percent, or about $300 million, of U.S. international funding was given to educational activities. The portion of philanthropic activities allocated to education by foreign foundations is not clear, in part because the definition of a foundation differs from one country to another. However, by some estimates, philanthropy is a far larger and more visible phenomenon outside the United States, for two reasons. First, governmental development assistance (foreign aid) is really philanthropy. Foreign aid is based on voluntary contributions of donor democracies and is often dedicated to educational and humanitarian purposes, which are roughly analogous to the domestic operations of philanthropic organizations. Second, in those parts of the world with very low incomes, this philanthropy can account for as much as 30 percent of gross domestic product (GDP), thus placing the philanthropists—whether or not they like or admit it—in a position of considerable power.

This chapter reviews definitions of philanthropy and estimates the size of both private—foundation and nongovernmental organization (NGO)—and governmental philanthropic activity outside of the United States. It provides estimates of general and educational philanthropic assistance and then raises several issues and dilemmas.

Among the most important lessons has to be that, as a competitor for philanthropic resources, education is fighting a losing battle. Of the total private philanthropy from the United States, only 14 percent is allocated to education, and of that amount, only 13 percent is allocated to K–12 education. In spite of numerous lofty goals of "basic education for all" to which all nations subscribe, education has accounted for only about 10 percent of the total assistance from public agencies across the industrial democracies. Why has education failed to be a significant priority?[1] And why has the mismatch between the rhetoric and the reality not been a topic of more debate?

A subsequent issue concerns the interactions between donor and recipient. If a project is created on the basis of a grant, as opposed to a loan, how does one know if its content and policy reforms are truly in demand? What is the proper relationship between staff of a philanthropic donor agency and potential recipients? To what extent does being in a position of deciding over resources imply a position of virtue? Who exactly should be responsible for the policies being supported? And who should be held accountable when those policies or supporting projects fail?

What is the public's right to know in terms of information or effectiveness? Even in the case of private foundations, such as the Soros or Ford foundations, to what extent does the public have a right to have access to an unbiased source for project effectiveness? Lastly, is private philanthropy a sign of entrepreneurial enterprise or of inadequate intervention and failed public responsibility?

QUESTIONS OF DEFINITION

There are about 57,000 foundations in the United States, and they account for more than 80 percent of private philanthropic giving worldwide.[2] American foundations are preeminent for three major reasons: 1) the U.S. economy is the world's largest; 2) charitable giving in the United States is encouraged by the tax code, which makes donations exempt from federal and state taxation; and 3) the relatively low marginal income tax rates in the United States (about 40% for high-income individuals, compared with 60% in some European nations) facilitate the accumulation of personal wealth. Consequently, American foundations tend to be larger and much older than foreign foundations. U.S. foundations have become so prevalent that it is common for Americans to mistakenly assume that the term "foundation" transfers across international borders and that philanthropy on behalf of foundations is a common enterprise.

Outside the country, the term *foundation* may apply to membership associations, corporations, and government-subsidized enterprises, and it may imply either private or public ownership. Foundations outside the United States may also be associated with functions that are not necessarily charitable, such as political lobbying, research, and fundraising for private and public purposes.

Legislation enabling individuals and corporations to reduce their tax burdens through charitable giving is not as common or as generous in other nations. Moreover, foreign foundations are often taxed on income received.[3]

Organizations with structures and functions similar to private foundations in the United States certainly exist abroad. But other nations also allow the government to establish public "foundations." In Germany, for instance, foundations founded by political parties and receiving public revenues are among the larger development assistance foundations. These include the Konrad-Adenauer-, Hanns-Seidel-, and Rosa-Luxemburg-Stiftungen.[4] In Switzerland, a foundation can be a fund in which families invest their corporate pensions for their own benefit. A British foundation drawing on commercial philanthropy may be illegal in France, and commercial profitmaking foundations operating in Norway would be illegal in Britain.[5]

Thus, the first challenge in analyzing the goals and extent of educational philanthropy abroad is to decide which organizations can be considered philanthropic and whether these are known as "foundations" or by some other term. This chapter follows the Organization for Economic Cooperation and Development (OECD),[6] which defines a foundation as an organization that:

- Is nongovernmental
- Is nonprofit
- Possesses a principal fund of its own
- Is managed by its own directors and/or trustees
- Promotes social, charitable, religious, educational, or other activities that serve the pubic good[7]

Throughout Europe, there are about 357,000 organizations that refer to themselves as foundations, but only 84,000 might be classified as nonprofit and nongovernmental in purpose.[8] About 56 percent of these foundations are located in Sweden and Denmark. Britain, Germany, and Switzerland account for another 19 percent of the foundations in Europe.[9] The majority of European foundations, as opposed to their American counterparts, have a large number of employees, which enables them to directly manage and implement their own projects, instead of making grants to others who implement projects on their behalf.[10] The American system of philanthropy, in which taxes are reduced for those who make philanthropic contributions, is becoming more common in Europe. For instance, a majority of the European foundations were established in the last two decades and were stimulated by changes in taxation legislation governing nonprofits. About a third of the foundations in Europe have projects in the field of education, while 25 percent have projects in social services and 17 percent in health care.[11]

Philanthropy in Asia is not as developed as it is in Europe. Japan treats NGOs and other nonprofit organizations as informal branches of public agencies. In Bangladesh and New Zealand, the government does not permit tax exemptions for donations to nonprofit organizations. Businesses in these two nations are given no reduction in taxes for charitable donations. Though three-quarters of the Australian population reports giving to charity, Australian foundations generate only 7 percent of their revenues from fundraising, while 37 percent comes from government sources and 47 percent comes from fees for service.[12] In Japan, foundations supported by large firms such as Toyota and Mitsubishi seem to mirror the Ford Foundation in intentions but not in philanthropic action. For example, Japanese foundations are more likely to be founded by the corporation itself than with the personal resources of a wealthy industrialist. In addition, the relatively high rates of taxation in Japan keep foundations' resources relatively small. A smaller after-tax income produces less inclination to donate. Also, Japanese foundations tend to concentrate on projects that cause little controversy (e.g., cultural preservation and seed crop development).

Philanthropy Organized through Religious Organizations

In both Europe and North America, religious organizations remain a common conduit for education and other activities and are financed by both public and private sources. The United States is the only industrial democracy in which public schools are not owned and managed by religious organizations.[13] Public schools managed by religious organizations are also common throughout Latin America, Africa, South Asia, and East Asia. For the most part, these schools are affiliated with Christian churches, but in the Middle East, North Africa, and in parts of the former Soviet Union they are affiliated with Muslim mosques. Religiously affiliated public schools are so common that Americans would be wise to remember that our definition of public education (schooling financed, owned, and operated by the state) is an exception to the norm. The more common definition of "public education" is schooling the state helps finance but does not monopolistically own or manage.

Wherever school systems are managed by religious organizations, it is common for parents and community leaders to organize voluntary donations to support educational programs. This is true both for domestic religious school systems in countries such as Canada and Australia and for religious organizations that help finance school systems in low-income countries. For instance, Catholics often provide assistance through Caritas, while Protestants do so through Christian Aid and World Vision. These organizations are among the largest private providers of educational assistance in the world. Among Muslims, the *Zakat* (charitable tax) is assumed to be about 2.5 percent of an individual's annual income and has financed hospitals, schools, public water supplies, and other public works for centuries. A religious foundation, called a *Waqf*, is the Koran's method for allocating personal wealth properly. Waqfs are responsible for thousands of charitable projects throughout the Muslim world. In countries with a high percentage of Muslims, the Waqfs are so common that governments sometimes dedicate a public ministry to oversee their activities. In the case of Pakistan, the central government ministry of Waqfs actually manages charitable activities, further confusing the distinction between public and private functions.[14]

Philanthropy for Education

The portion of activity allocated to education from foundations outside the United States is not clear, in part because the definition of a foundation differs from one country to another, making it difficult to monitor foundation activities accurately. However, some nations report philanthropic activity in a more complete fashion than others. For instance, about 16 percent of the philanthropy in Australia is devoted to educational purposes. In Bangladesh, education philanthropy accounts for 29 percent of charitable activities, while the share devoted to education is 25 percent in Indonesia, 10 percent in Spain, and just 4 percent in Korea.[15]

U.S.-based foundations that are engaged in international philanthropy devote about 13 percent of their giving to educational activities, compared with 11 percent for international development (including the promotion of U.S. exports, local agriculture, industry, and transport) and humanitarian relief (emergency food and medical support), and 38.5 percent for health and family planning (see Table 1).

Of the funds U.S. foundations commit to educational programs abroad, about 12 percent is allocated to projects in higher education (which make up 34% of the projects); 72 percent is allocated to graduate and professional education (23% of the projects); and 13 percent goes to support projects in K–12 education (22% of the projects).[16]

Foreign Aid as Foreign Philanthropy

Since World War II, the world's industrial democracies have allocated a portion of their public finances to assisting less wealthy nations in various

TABLE 1   International Activities of U.S.-Based Foundations by Sector, 2000

	U.S. Dollars, Millions	Percentage of Total	Number of Projects	Percentage of Total
International Affairs	169	6.9	1,416	13.9
International Development Relief	270	11.0	2,116	19.9
Health & Family Planning	944	38.5	1,192	11.0
Social Sciences	147	6.0	725	6.7
Environment	194	7.9	1,121	10.3
Arts & Culture	79	3.2	888	8.2
Science & Technology	33	1.4	126	1.2
Human Rights, Civil Liberties	130	5.3	946	8.7
Public Society Benefit	98	4.0	585	5.4
Religion	49	2.0	611	5.6
Education	337	13.7	1,091	10
Total	2,451	100	10,874	100

Source: Organization for Economic Cooperation and Development, "Philanthropic Foundations and Development Cooperation," DAC Journal 4, no. 3 (2003): Annex A.

efforts, including education. There is no legal requirement to give a certain portion of national income to foreign aid, but the industrial democracies generally agree that 1 percent of GDP is a reasonable target. This aid flows through private voluntary organizations such as CARE (an international assistance organization), bilateral organizations such as the U.S. Agency for International Development (USAID), and multilateral organizations such as the World Bank and the regional development banks.

In the years following WWII, the United States was extraordinarily generous with its assistance. In 1950, foreign aid amounted to just under 3 percent of GDP. However, the share of national income devoted to foreign aid has dropped substantially over the past 20 years. In 1997, it reached its lowest level. In terms of proportion of GDP, it fell to 0.16 percent, ranking the United States 22nd among industrial democracies in that year. The number of employees working for USAID declined from 8,200 in 1962 to about 2,000 today.[17] On the other hand, few industrial democracies have attainted the 1 percent level of philanthropic support considered to be the ideal. In 2002, Denmark committed 0.96 percent of its budget to international public

TABLE 2   International Education Activities of U.S.-Based Foundations
by Purpose, 2000

	U.S. Dollars, Millions	Percentage of Total	Number of Projects	Percentage of Total
Higher Education	39.7	11.8	372	34
Graduate & Professional Education	244	72.4	254	23
K–12*	12.9	3.8	239	22
Adult & Continuing	0.5	0.2	10	0.9
Libraries	25.8	7.7	70	6.4
Other	14.2	4.2	146	13.4
Total	337	100	1,091	100

*Does not include projects of the Open Society Institute

Source: Organization for Economic Cooperation and Development, "Philanthropic Foundations and Development Cooperation," DAC Journal 4, no. 3 (2003): Annex A.

philanthropy; Norway committed 0.89 percent, and Sweden committed 0.83 percent. Most industrial democracies commit under 0.5 percent. Of course, since the U.S. economy is the world's largest, the United States is the largest donor in absolute terms, even though foreign aid accounts for just 0.9 percent of federal government spending.

How much international public philanthropy reaches K–12 education? Only about half of the U.S. foreign aid budget is allocated to economic development or humanitarian-based relief. The other half is allocated to military, economic, and political purposes. Moreover, foreign aid tends to be allocated to a small number of strategically important countries. A significant portion of U.S. foreign aid is devoted to the Middle East, with Israel accounting for almost $3 billion a year and Egypt accounting for about $2 billion annually.

Aid for education accounts for about 6 percent of the total allocated for economic and social assistance purposes, and aid to K–12 accounts for only 3.9 percent.[18] Taking all donor nations together, support for education amounted to about $3.8 billion, the equivalent of about 8 percent of international assistance. In sub-Saharan Africa, the region that arguably needs it most, aid to education amounted to only 10 percent of the total aid allocation from the 24 industrial democracies.[19]

In terms of the transfer of resources, how does philanthropy rank in comparison to other sources? Only a small fraction of the total flow of capital to developing countries is in the form of charitable giving or development assistance.[20] In 2000, capital flows amounted to $463 billion (with $161 billion being net inflow to developing countries). Aid amounted to only 6.5 percent of this amount, and was dwarfed by the amount of capital flowing via foreign direct investment, which was 38.4 percent of the overall total. The lesson is that no matter how grandiose or important foreign aid may be in terms of public perception, as a means of resource transfer it amounts to no more than pocket change by comparison to private investment.

The Content of K–12 Philanthropy

The content of international K–12 philanthropy depends largely on the category of donor. Legal mandates and multinational executive boards determine grant content for multilateral donors. The International Labour Organization (ILO) offers training to vocational teachers. The World Health Organization (WHO) offers training to school officials on public health issues. The International Institute for Educational Planning (IIEP) offers training in educational statistics and administration. The United Nations Education, Science, and Cultural Organization (UNESCO), the UN agency officially responsible for education, offers training on special curricular issues such as civics and environmental issues and sponsors conferences on topics determined by its executive boards.[21] The budgets of multilateral grantmaking agencies are smaller than those of multilateral lending institutions; hence their impact is mostly symbolic. However, these seemingly mundane conferences can serve a useful purpose. Participating educators living under harsh dictatorships or during historical periods such as the Cold War often greatly appreciate such conferences because they are their only source of international professional exchange.

Multilateral organizations that provide loans, rather than grants, do so for quite different K–12 philanthropic initiatives. These organizations include the World Bank and its International Bank for Reconstruction and Development (IBRD), the Inter-American Development Bank (IADB), the Asian Development Bank (ADB), the European Bank for Reconstruction and Development (EBRD), and the African Development Bank (AfDB). Content is characterized by two elements. First, it must be agreed to by local government—which always has its own sense of priorities and tends to be conservative due to the need to repay the loan. Borrowing money creates quite a different set of circumstances than receiving it as a free gift.

Moreover, these types of multilateral projects are intended to leverage policy changes as well as to directly assist education. They tend to be large in comparison to other donor assistance. Projects for teacher reform may include new salary scales to reward higher performing teachers. A $500 million project to finance new educational materials in the Philippines or Indonesia may include a stipulation that the materials will be manufactured by private providers instead of the government ministry. This not only could increase the availability of relevant reading materials, but also could change or privatize the entire system of educational material distribution. A project in rural Brazil may offer new reading materials, teacher training, and curriculum modernization. At the same time, it may require a new teacher license that cannot be revoked for political reasons when a new government wins an election. Multilateral lending agency educational projects move more slowly than grant projects. It takes longer to achieve consensus on project content and design. Project disbursal also takes longer. On the other hand, these projects offer better opportunities for nonmarginal, systemwide changes. Borrowers often appreciate the opportunity to participate. This is not only because interest rates are subsidized by the international community, but because these projects often involve new managerial ideas. The analytic work undertaken prior to project approval can be deeply informative to local officials because it brings them up to date with many of the current debates over education policy in Europe and North America. This is considered very valuable.

Bilateral K–12 philanthropy is quite different than multilateral K–12 philanthropy. A bilateral agency is part of the foreign policy establishment of the donor country. Funded content thus reflects broader foreign policy goals. Such goals may lead to promotion of exports and educational areas considered to be of comparative advantage. Japan, through the Japanese International Cooperation Agency (JICA), often emphasizes electronic solutions to K–12 problems, such as the use of computers, calculators, and distance education. Canada, through the Canadian International Development Agency (CIDA), often emphasizes technical schools. France emphasizes culture and language. The United States, through USAID, has traditionally emphasized bilingual education and educational technology and is now emphasizing civics education in the transition countries. In some instances, the emphases of bilateral organizations may appear self-serving, as a solution in search of a problem. But because bilateral philanthropy is organized through foreign policy interests, and because those interests inevitably include advancing trade and political influence, such emphases are natural outgrowths of the wider circumstances involved.

As with the above institution types, organizational mandate determines the content of NGOs and charitable foundation K–12 philanthropy. In some instances the mandate may be emergency assistance. For instance, in the wake of a natural disaster, CARE or the Red Cross would fund school repair, medical assistance for schoolchildren, and textbook replacement. Church charities might be oriented toward longer-term goals, such as funding teacher training, curriculum design, or school equipment.

The Soros Foundation is one of the most interesting and influential international K–12 educational foundations. It was founded by George Soros, who migrated to the United States from Hungary after WWII. Influenced by his early experience with state socialism, Soros created the foundation in order to build and maintain "open societies."

When Eastern Europe and the former Soviet Union made the transition from party/state to democracy, the Soros Foundation spearheaded philanthropic initiatives to quickly provide experience with democratic procedures and to stabilize the democratic education of future citizens. Early programs emphasized scientific research support and new history and philosophy textbooks. Later programs have included the training of school principals, teacher retraining, policy analysis, and Step-by-Step, a program of early childhood pedagogical intervention. Assistance from the Soros Foundation flows through three streams: its worldwide network programs headquartered in New York City, its regional network programs headquartered in Budapest, and its local foundation programs.[22] The local foundations are situated in about 40 countries, including those that were formerly part of the Soviet Union, countries throughout Central Europe, as well as South Africa, Burma, Haiti, and Mongolia. In 2002, the Soros Foundation's educational assistance amounted to 21 percent of overall project commitments, or $101 million.[23]

Public and Private Philanthropy Together

For most nations, official development assistance figures are an adequate proxy for total foreign aid, as private contributions account for a relatively small share of total aid. For the United States, knowing only the public sources would be insufficient as a measure of international philanthropy. Following the tsunami catastrophe in Asia in 2004, some suggested that the U.S. response was miserly. U.S. government officials, quite rightly, responded by noting that, unlike Europe, much U.S. philanthropy flows through private, not governmental, sources.

In 2002, assistance from private sources within the United States (80% of the world's total charitable activity) added 22.6 percent to the U.S. figures for official development assistance, increasing the total amount of assistance from $13.3 billion to $16.3 billion (Table 3). On the other hand, critics of

TABLE 3   U.S. International Philanthropy, 2002

	U.S. Dollars, Billions	Percentage of Gross National Income
Public	13.3	.013
Private	3.0	.003
Total	16.3	.016

America also have a compelling point of view, for even when private philanthropy is added—or at least the figures for private philanthropy that are available—the United States only contributes about 0.016 percent of its GDP for international charity. This is hardly earth shattering.

How generous have the industrial democracies been with respect to international educational philanthropy? Considering all donor nations, educational international philanthropy from public sources in 2002 amounted to about $3.8 billion dollars, or about 8 percent of total foreign aid. This included, for instance, $1.8 billion for Africa and about $1.4 billion for Asia. The sector-by-sector breakdown of assistance illustrates the point that regardless of philanthropic purposes, which differ substantially by region, education is only a peripheral endeavor, with the highest percentage (10%) dedicated to education in sub-Saharan Africa, and the lowest (5%) dedicated to education in Europe. These figures compare unfavorably with assistance for health and population, economic infrastructure, debt reduction, and the like.

ISSUES AND DILEMMAS

Relationships between Donors and Recipients

Whether public (in foreign aid) or through private foundations, no philanthropy is neutral. Those working for foundations and governmental agencies are prone to similar influences. They act as coordinators of requests for assistance from people and institutions that by nature are at a disadvantage. This dynamic can influence their character. They may confuse their assigned position with being a personal virtue; they may feel as though they deserve to be lauded and applauded as though the support they approve were their own.

As a consequence, a complex vocabulary has developed to describe the processes by which money is controlled and approved by the recipient as opposed to the donor agency. New terminologies—"public participation," "ownership," "consultation"—have been employed to denote that the recipient was in ultimate control. For instance, the World Bank has developed new operational guidelines for its staff. These guidelines mandate a process of consultation and participation before a project can be submitted for approval by the executive board. These directives attempt to assure their management that the project is "owned" by the recipients and is not just some fancy dream of the technical staff in the donor organization. No number of administrative directives, nor any new jargon, however, can alter the fact that there is a difference in the power relationship between the donor and the recipient.

The nature of this power relationship, however, does differ with the conditions of the project. A bilateral aid agency—USAID, JICA, or the U.K.'s Department for International Development Finance (DFID)—that gives the money away in a grant is treated by the recipient as an "interested friend." Local authorities, including from the technical agencies involved, are surprisingly uninterested in the nature or content of the project. The donor agency and its staff are often treated to the illusion that what they are planning to do is exactly right, with gracious thanks all around.

Switch the terms of the project—but not the content—from a grant to a loan, however, and the nature of the relationship changes. Local technical authorities will take much more interest in the content of the project and often will debate it, regardless of how compelling the evidence offered by the donor agency to justify the project's content. Moreover, local fiscal authorities, who must give final approval for the project and who are responsible for repayment, may take a deep interest in the nature of the content and pay particular attention, for instance, to the degree of its financial sustainability. Anything that will raise salaries or ensure maintenance costs (such as computers, science labs, management information systems) will come in for particular scrutiny.

Whether a project is made on the terms of a grant or a loan may alter the nature of the relationship between local recipients and the donor agency. Agencies that lend money cannot be as cavalier about content. Because the agreement has significant financial consequences, the recipient is more careful with the donor and often considerably less obsequious.

Relationships among Donors

There are dozens of possible donor agencies in international philanthropy, even within the same sector, such as education. In instances where a nation is politically isolated, such as Zaire under the leadership of Mobutu Sese Seko or in Myanmar under the current government, few agencies will want to make donations. In these cases, the recipient will have few choices of the source or the terms of the assistance. But in other cases, such as in Tanzania in the era of President Julius Nyrere, the competition among donors was nothing short of ferocious. I recall one instance in which I participated in preparing a new World Bank loan to education. We had just completed a meeting with the permanent secretary in the Tanzanian ministry of education. As we left his office, we were greeted by the sight of three other delegations, from Britain, Germany, and Japan, all there to convince this poor official of the virtues of their particular projects. To say the least, the situation appeared odd. Here was a country listed as among the poorest in the world, with a plethora of donors all hoping to receive approval for their ideas to provide assistance.

In Tanzania, the ideas of donor agencies often clashed. According to the Swedish International Development Agency (SIDA), Tanzania did not need more secondary education; it needed Folk Development Colleges. According to the World Bank, however, Tanzania needed more secondary education. Canada's CIDA and Germany's Gesellschaft für Technische Zusammenarbeit (GTZ) commonly recommended that countries in Africa receive assistance to technical and vocational education, in spite of the evidence, often deriving from World Bank studies, that suggested that vocational and technical education was not cost effective. Because unit costs of one agency's project may differ dramatically from another, and because a poor country cannot afford to sustain the assistance of all donor projects simultaneously, one agency's conditions may be contradictory to those of another agency. It is not unusual, in fact, to find that in a very poor country, one agency's project has to be sacrificed.

All projects are expensive to prepare. Details of construction expenses in isolated regions need to be calculated with care. Salaries and other recurrent costs need to be measured. Utilization rates and management costs need to be estimated. In some instances, a project prepared by one agency will be "stolen" and financed by a second agency. A recipient country may ask one agency to prepare a project but then offer the project to a different agency, which may have easier conditions. Accusations of project preparation theft are common and are particularly problematic with agencies with similar disbursement and implementation guidelines. This is the case, for instance, between the Asian Development Bank and the World Bank, where the problems have become so serious that the agencies privately may divide up the world of economic development into spheres of interest, with one agency taking the lead in one sector and another agency taking the lead in others.

These decisions over spheres of interest may be taken without the country's permission or consent. Thus, it is common to find a situation in which a country may wish to borrow money for education but be told that education falls within the sphere of interest of a different agency. This is the case, for instance, of education in Central Asia, where senior management of the World Bank and the Asian Development Bank informally divided up sectors without the consent of the recipients.

Donors themselves have decided that more coordination is a good idea, and for the last several years they have held donor conferences in which one agency—often the World Bank—is selected to be the "coordinator." This allocation of responsibility among donors is suggested to be in the interest of the recipients. It is often not the case. By definition, increased donor coordination means fewer choices for the recipient. More competition, not less, is in the recipients' interest. Coordination also allows donors—such as the World Bank—with high visibility and therefore high levels of criticism and public protest to take a role with more leverage and yet less public vulnerability. It is quite advantageous for the World Bank to be able to say that a particular strategy is the product of consensus across many donor agencies in addition to itself, yet at the same time be asked to play the role of interagency coordinator. In this instance, the World Bank simultaneously gains political leverage and greater protection from public protest.

The Impact of International Education Philanthropy

Is the level of international education philanthropy high or low? Educational giving does not appear to be very significant when it is framed as only 8 percent of total philanthropy. However, the importance of philanthropy is more accurately captured by impact, rather than by amount of money spent. Educational philanthropy outside of the United States has, in fact, had a very large impact, for two reasons.

The first has to do with the environment of relative poverty. This can be estimated by calculating a dependency ratio, which is the monetary size of philanthropy received in a given year compared to a nation's Gross National Product (GNP), GDP, or the value of its imported goods and services. In Burkina Faso, for example, a nation of 14 million people, philanthropy accounted for 15.5 percent of GNP and 53.8 percent of GDP. In Nicaragua, philanthropy accounted for 31.6 percent of GNP and 30.8 percent of total imports. But Guinea-Bissau is perhaps the most extreme example. There, international philanthropy accounts for 410 percent of its GDP and

130 percent of the value of its imports.[24] The point here is to suggest that, though the level of resources may be small by some standards, the importance of those resources to the areas of the world where they are dedicated can be very high.

In Zambia, where over one-half of health care is provided by foreign donors, health policy is largely in the hands of those donors. Similarly, in Guinea-Bissau and other very poor countries, school systems are heavily influenced by donor policies of teacher training, curriculum reform, and textbook design. No donor agency would advertise this fact. All would portray their operations as in support of the priorities of local authorities. But the reality is that government priorities not supported by donors are meaningless because they are so unlikely to be implemented.

Thus the power of international education philanthropy exceeds its monetary investment. In some instances, donor agencies account for a large portion of all the available financial resources. Thus, in the field of education, large parts of the world are in fact recipients not just of financial assistance, but also of technical ideas stimulated by donor agencies. These include teacher merit pay in Kyrgyzstan, school vouchers in Pakistan, school-based management in Ecuador, and student loan programs to finance higher education in a dozen countries.

Content is a constant worry of the donor agencies. Has it gone too far? Is it sustainable? Is it truly "owned" by the recipients? In some instances, ownership changes as soon as there is a new election. This was the case, for instance, in Hungary, where a carefully negotiated World Bank higher education loan included tuition and other fees and a "rationalization" of small and uneconomic institutions in exchange for a significant investment in university infrastructure. The investment in university infrastructure was quite popular, but as soon as a new political party was elected, all tuition agreements were abrogated and the loan, which cost millions of dollars in preparation fees, was summarily cancelled.

While developing new democracies is the objective of much public and private international philanthropy, dealing with their impact on conditionalities has proven to be problematic. In a democracy it is more difficult to negotiate a reduction in service or an increase in the price of a service, despite compelling evidence to support it.

Conditionalities in international philanthropy raise issues other than how difficult it may be to adhere to them in a democracy. Both multilateral and bilateral donors place stronger conditions on their assistance than do U.S. foundations donating to domestic education. Some conditions placed by international philanthropic agencies have proven to be correct over time. Textbooks have traditionally proven to be among the most effective components of education philanthropy. Textbook pedagogies have usually been within the competence of local teachers; textbooks are highly valued by recipients; and the delivery of textbooks can be monitored with some degree of precision. But when the World Bank began to lend in this area, quite by accident, it was discovered that the efficiency of textbook development depended on whether or not the ministry of education held the textbook development monopoly. In no OECD country, not even the centralized systems of Japan or France, is textbook development monopolized by a ministry of education. In every case, the ministry of education will set curriculum objectives to which the textbooks must adhere, but then contract out on a competitive basis to private publishers for their development and potential purchase.

In developing and transition countries, however, education ministries claimed a monopoly over textbook development. Quality control, local authorship, market failure, and national heritage were cited as reasons. But the real reasons often had nothing to do with technical or professional issues. Rather, they had to do with the opportunity to allocate authorship to friends and relatives and to receive considerable private kickbacks from what is one of the education sector's most lucrative sources of revenue.

In the 1960s and 1970s, conflicts occurred between the World Bank and UNESCO over textbook policy, with the latter often taking the position of the recipient ministry of education. But, with the collapse of the Soviet Union and the mounting evidence from both the industrial and health sectors, where private provision of goods and services were proving to be less expensive and of higher quality, over time it became easier to force a ministry of education to relinquish its monopoly over textbook development. This is one illustration of a long-term contribution to education development of the World Bank. Ministerial monopolies over textbook development today are a rarity, a sign of progress.[25]

But there are also instances where the conditions placed on a philanthropic project can be counterproductive. As part of its overall program of macroeconomic reform, the World Bank has sometimes required nations to shift public expenditures from higher or vocational education to elementary education. While it is important to universalize basic education, is it wise or ethical for the World Bank to require such reallocation?[26]

While nations should maintain their own policies, sometimes those policies may be protectionist in nature. Should nations be allowed to maintain policies contrary to sound economic theory when they are receiving publicly funded assistance from other countries? Should locally produced textbooks, educational software, and other goods and services be protected from competition from international suppliers who may offer higher quality at a lower cost?

In some low-income countries, teacher salaries are being redesigned in accordance with the principles of performance pay in conjunction with international philanthropy. Should a philanthropic recipient be required to adhere to a policy that is still controversial in the most advanced democracies?

Disagreements over the appropriateness of certain data and policy recommendations are traditional in education. But the stakes have changed. Projects are now often designed on the basis of policy and not investment. This means that spurts of money are transferred in what are called "trenches." Trenches are released on the assurance that a recipient nation has made sufficient policy progress toward an agreed-to goal. Funds flow or can be denied on the basis of whether countries adhere to data and policy requirements mandated by donors. While it may be right for donors to place conditions on charity, what happens if those conditions are technically unsound?

Between 1962 and 1980, for instance, one condition of World Bank education assistance was that it could only be allocated to specific vocational and technical curricula. A general skills curriculum was not considered sufficiently "practical."[27] However, the views of the World Bank changed. Now the World Bank will only assist a vocational curriculum under highly specific circumstances, considering a general skills curriculum to be more "practical."

This example raises two issues. The first is that of responsibility when philanthropic conditions are technically incorrect. The second is the matter of how conditions are negotiated. With respect to the first, the question is, Who is responsible when technical conditions, believed to be correct, later prove to be incorrect? Who can a recipient hold accountable? Where the project is made on the basis of a grant, one may not consider calculability as being a very serious question. It is the donor's money to waste after all. But what should the policy be in an instance when the recipient needs to repay the cost of the (failed) project? What happens when the conditions of a loan turn out to be professionally mistaken? If all parties come to recognize that project conditions were incorrect, who becomes responsible? Who can be held accountable within the foundation or development assistance agency? Will a staff member lose his job if the conditions he negotiated turn out to be wrong? Is there a court to which local community leaders may appeal for repayment? Is there a mechanism for punishing officials who gave assurances at the time that the conditions were professionally defensible and who later changed their opinions?

Process of Project Negotiations

Educational philanthropy projects are designed on the basis of initial studies, often conducted by consultants responsible to the donor agency. These studies are then reduced to a series of proposals for assistance. The proposed projects are negotiated with the donor agency. The donor agency typically has at its disposal a wide range of expert advice. Advisors include educational statisticians, economists, policy experts, and attorneys.

Countries that receive international philanthropy for K–12 education are typically represented in negotiations by senior officials from ministries of education and finance. The latter officials confine their judgments to issues of affordability. Education officials generally do not have systematic sources of advice comparable to those available to the donor agency.

For instance, a country entering into an agreement for education aid resources might be required to make fiscal reallocations or raise elementary school tuition. Such a country is unlikely to have a source of technical or policy advice not already associated with development institutions. Such an independent source of expertise might point out that the suggested policy may be too costly, that it may generate other unintended results, or that other reforms may be more pragmatic. While, at first glance, negotiating philanthropy may not seem analogous to an adversarial legal proceeding, comparing the two situations is in fact quite illuminating. A defendant charged with a crime is offered free legal advice on the grounds that he or she deserves to be defended in a competent manner. In the case of international loan-based philanthropy, two sides negotiate a series of important policy changes to be implemented by the recipient of the philanthropy. The philanthropic organization has access to a phalanx of expertise. The recipient side does not. Yet the side that does not have access to expertise is legally responsible to repay the loan, regardless of the effectiveness of the assistance or the results of the loan conditions.

Two things result from the recipient not being "represented." One is that the intentions of the donor may be interpreted as being intrusive and hegemonic rather than altruistic. A second is that the impact of the donor projects may be compromised by recipient countries being judged as being out of compliance, when poor or unrealistic statistical indicators themselves may be the source of such noncompliance.

LESSONS LEARNED

Private philanthropy raises similar questions internationally as it does domestically. Is private philanthropy a sign of entrepreneurial enterprise in response to the demand from recipients? Or does philanthropy represent the opposite: Does it represent a failure of the wider community to take responsibility for public service? Is it a sign of a broadly held but voluntary moral code, or is it a reflection of tax and other personal incentives designed for private gain?

In wealthy democracies such as Japan and Sweden, this question is particularly pertinent. In these countries, governments have the wherewithal to implement generous and often effective social policies. They are proud of the coverage and quality of their government-provided public education systems. For the transition countries of Eastern and Central Europe and the former Soviet Union, this question is particularly painful.[28] There the state has had a monopoly on educational provision and traditionally has been known for high levels of equity and effectiveness (not efficiency), but today those qualities have declined and education systems are dependent on a high level of philanthropy. In the cases of middle-income (nontransition) countries such as Brazil, Mexico, Nigeria, and Indonesia, this question is not particularly relevant. In these countries, the state has not been particularly effective and philanthropy, both local and domestic, has been a traditional source of public goods. On the other hand, for low-income countries such as Nepal, Bangladesh, Malawi, and Bolivia, the question is also irrelevant. In these countries there is no realistic choice, other than garnering public benefits from all available sources. These states are too poor to be expected to supply public benefit in anything approaching adequacy. Hence, the issue of whether or not philanthropy is a sign of public failure for these countries is not a serious one.

Is any gift given without expectations on the part of the donor? Though all donors justify their activity on the grounds of supporting local initiative, their own interests are never neutral. For instance, the Ford and Rockefeller foundations were very active in international education in the 1960s and 1970s. Their activities have been criticized by some as upholding the capitalist system and the prescriptions of American foreign policy.[29] Others have criticized their activities for weakening recipients' free-market orientations and stimulating a sense of victimization.[30]

Some suggest that some U.S. foundations have become more professional in the delivery of programs,[31] and that others have made unique contributions to social science research, agricultural productivity, and peace.[32] For instance, one study suggested that the long-term work of the Ford and other foundations in Chile made local democracy possible.[33] In the current environment, the Soros Foundation may have been more effective than public foreign aid at invigorating the very fragile, newly opened societies of Eastern and Central Europe and the former Soviet Union.

The responsibility of donors implies a need for accountability. When philanthropy funds a large portion of a community's education activities, as it does in many parts of sub-Saharan Africa, questions of accountability are particularly important. It is not uncommon to find that donations by taxpayers in industrial democracies have been used to buy expensive automobiles, mansions, and other luxuries by local leaders instead of being allocated to their rightful humanitarian purposes. Who should be held responsible if philanthropic resources are stolen? What are the rights of taxpayers in donor nations? To what court might they appeal for reimbursement, or to have sanctions put in place against those who stole their gifts? Is there any emerging consensus or any particularly promising response to this question in law, policy, or practice?

Moral responsibility is necessary to ensure that the recipients of philanthropy do not use resources for nefarious purposes. Ethnic and religious charities, whether Irish, Hindi, Muslim, or Basque, must adhere to the condition that their projects will not precipitate social tension and will not stimulate ethnic or religious insecurity. It is one thing to argue that faith-based organizations can be more effective and more efficient than government programs of assistance. But it is quite another thing to guarantee that their philosophies will not antagonize others. This issue is especially important in education, where schools and curricula can lay down the intellectual foundations for civil conflict, civil war, and religious and ethnic aggression. Such negative results of philanthropy can be seen, for example, in cases such as donations made by foreign Muslim charities to Bosnia and Pakistan.[34] If there is any area in which more regulation over international charities is required, it is in ensuring that philanthropic educational initiatives will foster social cohesion rather than undermine it.[35]

It is also not uncommon to find philanthropic conditions that have created problems, such as resource waste or unanticipated distortions of local education systems. For instance, World Bank education policies in the 1970s caused the overexpansion of vocational education and diversified secondary curricula.[36] Regardless of whether philanthropic projects are based on loans or grants, local resources are required. It is seldom the case that foreign philanthropy is free of local cost.

Size of Philanthropy for Education

Among the most important lessons has to be the fact that education, as a competitor for philanthropic resources, is fighting a losing battle. Of the total private philanthropy from the United States, only 13 percent is allocated to education. And in spite of numerous lofty goals of "basic education for all," to which all nations subscribe, of the total assistance from public agencies across the industrial donor democracies, only about 10 percent is allocated to education. Why has education failed so dramatically to garner anything close to being a significant priority in reality? Why has the mismatch between the rhetoric and the reality not been a topic of debate?

CONCLUSION

It is true that philanthropy is not without self-interest and that donor organizations, as all organizations, have specific goals. It is true in international, just as it is in domestic, education philanthropy that all projects are associated with local opportunity costs and that these costs can deter local authorities from more important priorities. It is also true that some of the interests and goals of philanthropic organizations are mundane, duplicate local efforts, and, to avoid organizational embarrassment, are overly conservative.

Because of their fear of controversy, most philanthropic foundations and multilateral grantmaking agencies confine their programs of assistance to the least controversial content. These are classified as "supply-side" improvements. These include improvements to textbooks, curriculum, and teaching techniques. Philanthropic multilateral lending agencies, on the other hand, enter the arena of demand-based improvements. These include expanding vouchers and other choice-based methods of education financing, outsourcing of services, and privatization of educational provision.

Some ask if these outside influences distort local practice in and of themselves. From this point of view, philanthropy might be thought of as inherently intrusive. But one must not forget the value of exchanging ideas. Low- and middle-income countries often lag in matters of reform and good practice. The ideas and perspectives of philanthropic organizations can be powerful and constructive for such countries. This exposure to outside ideas can be so important for education reform that some have suggested creating a "World Bank" available for American education.[37] Such an organization would be large enough to make a nonmarginal difference to local U.S. school districts and lead philanthropy into demand-side interventions and macro-policy changes to make very significant changes.

CHAPTER 11

Strategic Giving and Public School Reform

Three Challenges

Peter Frumkin

One of the oldest and most popular targets for philanthropy is education. Going all the way back to the start of modern, large-scale giving, donors have found the idea of supporting education—in all its many forms—attractive because it offers one of the clearest and most compelling ways to increase opportunities. The approach to philanthropy outlined by Andrew Carnegie and John D. Rockefeller, stressing self-help and the search for the underlying causes of poverty, became known around the turn of the last century as "scientific philanthropy," which contrasted rather sharply with the approach to charity practiced by settlement houses and local charities.[1] These agencies sought to help the poor by meeting their immediate medical, financial, and social needs through direct-service programs located in areas of high poverty. Rockefeller and Carnegie's scientific philanthropy eschewed this kind of almsgiving, or "poor aid," and embraced the more difficult goal of removing the underlying forces that made social welfare agencies necessary. One of their favorite targets for philanthropy was education, which was pursued by Carnegie through his support of public libraries around the country and by Rockefeller through his many gifts to higher education.[2]

While the field of philanthropy has advanced and changed a great deal since the time of Carnegie's and Rockefeller's efforts to expand educational opportunity, some things have remained remarkably consistent: Donors of all sizes and persuasions are still attracted to the idea of supporting programs and organizations that are educational in nature and that promise in count-less ways to give people knowledge and skills. One of the most attractive domains within education has been the reform and improvement of public schools, which, even their most staunch supporters will concede, have not always given children in disadvantaged communities the same opportuni-ties as children in more affluent areas. Because the size and complexity of the public school system is daunting, donors have focused on small elements of the problem either by working in well-defined geographical communi-ties or on specific parts of the system, be it defined in terms of certain grades (e.g., high school years) or certain parts of the curriculum (e.g., science edu-cation).

Even with these necessary limitations, the range of interventions in the public education system has been staggering. Private philanthropy has pushed public education to change and consider new systems and practices. In the midst of all this philanthropic ferment, conceptual clarity has at times been missing. Donors have not always had the clearest objectives or the best plans to guide their giving. In this chapter, I sketch out three critical issues that education-minded donors need to confront in their giving: donors must achieve some clarity about the theory of change that guides their philan-thropy; their work must be grounded in a clear plausible model of scale; and they must select and pursue an appropriate engagement level with recipient organizations. My claim is simply that donors committed to making a dif-ference in the area of public school reform must work to address all three of these conceptual and practical challenges if they are to have a chance to overcome the substantial obstacles to change that are present.[3]

THEORIES OF CHANGE

Before embarking on a mission as complex and challenging as improving the performance of public schools, any donor would be wise to pause and think through carefully the theory of change that will guide their philanthropy. Theories of change are causal claims rendered into more explicit form. They begin with the specification of inputs into a system. In the case of philan-thropy, these inputs often take the form of grants designed to support non-profit initiatives. Philanthropic inputs fund activities and services, which can range from simple small-scale efforts to broad and ambitious programs. Change theories connect funded programs to the production of outputs or units of service, which allow donors to count and track efforts. These out-puts are connected to the intended outcomes or end states that the donor is focused on achieving on behalf of others. Outcomes represent the targets

FIGURE 1   Elements of a Theory of Change

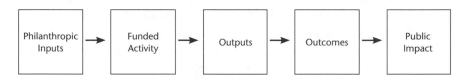

of philanthropic activity. They are the achievements realized by clients or users that allow the donor to claim mission fulfillment. The final piece in the chain is one that links the accomplishment of specific outcomes to broader social impacts. In crafting a theory of change, the objective is to make a set of plausible causal claims that can help the donor see more clearly how gifts are to be translated into results.

Theories of change can operate at many different levels—ranging from the smallest societal units to the largest ones—at which the philanthropy will work. At one end of this spectrum are theories of change that focus on the micro level through the training and development of individual leaders who might someday transform a field of practice. In school reform, this may mean funding training programs for school principals with the aim of improving the talent in the field. At the other end of the spectrum are macro-level theories that seek to bring change by shaping policy and supporting the production of new ideas.[4] Donors seeking wholesale change in public education have funded research and policy advocacy aimed at shaking up the entire field. In the middle are mesotheories of change that focus on building the organizational capacity within the nonprofit sector or networks of collaboration among similar organizations. For donors focused on education reform, this mid-level approach may entail supporting technical assistance to organizations or the support of collaboration and interaction among key organizations to form a more coherent movement. This hierarchy of change theories merely spells out for donors a set of initial choices about how to direct their giving to a particular unit of society. Choosing the right theory of change depends on a host of considerations, including the field in which the donor is working and the nature of the outcome that the donor is seeking. It involves both specifying a credible set of causal claims that will follow from the introduction of philanthropic funds and situating the effort at the right conceptual level.

Traditionally, education donors—especially institutional funders—have invested heavily on the "back end" of philanthropy, spending considerable amounts of money on evaluation and assessment aimed at measuring the impact and effectiveness of funded programs. This is due in part to the availability of test data to measure student achievement in schools, a type of performance data whose rigor and reliability—even granted its limitations—is impossible to locate in other parts of the nonprofit sector (e.g., the performing arts or homeless services). As a consequence, comparatively little time and money has been devoted to the "front end" of education philanthropy, especially when it comes to thinking systematically and creatively about the full range of interventions available in philanthropy and the underlying causal claims that are embedded in giving.[5] A well-elaborated theory of change can go a long way toward addressing this common problem.

While theories of change can illuminate the underlying logic, assumptions, and aspirations of donors, there is at least one substantial challenge that imposes itself and that continues to hover above the field, visible to all but not readily answerable by anyone. It is a problem that social scientists might term the presence of confounding variables, or "noise" in the system. This simply means that it can be difficult to actually pin down effectiveness and isolate meaningful programmatic effects related to a philanthropic intervention due to the many confounding forces that shape social outcomes. This problem is significant because it speaks to the rigor and power of philanthropic action and has implications for the credibility of claims about philanthropic effectiveness. Nevertheless, donors interested in making progress in the domain of education reform rightly continue to struggle with the whole question of how best to chart a realistic change theory, defend its underlying assumptions, and establish the robustness of its causal claims.

In almost every arena in which philanthropy operates, there are a large number of external forces that can potentially confound the causal claims that philanthropy makes. The presence of outside factors impinging on the causal chain designed by donors will vary substantially, depending on the nature and scope of the problem that is being addressed. As philanthropy aims at higher level change theories, especially those efforts to shape or change public policy, the number of potential confounding factors rises substantially. The fact that it is often difficult to draw firm causal lines starting with advocacy or basic research and changes in policy and social conditions is a function of all the complex administrative politics that surround policy implementation. In the education domain, political forces can have a profound effect on the shape of philanthropic efforts, and many of these forces are hard to predict or control. The consequences of having a plurality of confounding forces working both with and against a donor's theory of change are inescapable. It is difficult to know for sure whether the observed links—

or lack thereof—are a function of the donor's intervention or forces outside the system.

In drawing up a theory of change, donors will surely be tempted to simplify as they proceed by purposively bracketing certain complex issues and simply overlooking other elements. To a certain extent, this simplification is both necessary and productive. It allows donors to begin to sketch out the pieces of their program and how they will create change. There is, however, a substantial risk involved. Causality will tend to appear stronger and more certain than it really is. In almost all cases where philanthropic funds are used to address significant public problems, there are a large number of factors outside the theory of change that donors cannot possibly control and that will ultimately impinge on the results achieved.

Take, for example, a donor who believes that public schools are underperforming not just because of teaching and curricular shortcomings, but also because of poor management. The donor decides to establish a training program for inner-city public school principals focused on imparting strategic management skills to educators. The donor finds a partner in a local university and structures a program that will allow faculty from the business school to work with school leaders over a summer. Before going too far in the whole process, the donor decides to lay out the theory of change that is at play in this endeavor. The donor decides to start at the left-hand side of the page and sketch a box for the grant that is being contemplated to fund the start-up costs of the operation. The donor then connects this first box to a second one containing the main funded activities—the delivery of a new management training program. This second box is in turn linked to a third containing the expected outputs of the program—the delivery of a specified number of training units to a targeted group of participants. The next link is more complex, as the donor must clarify the intended outcomes of the entire effort. In this case, it turns out to be improved public school management. This relatively short-term outcome is linked to longer term outcomes, such as improved school performance and financial strength. All that is left is the final box containing the broader public impact that is being pursued. Like many other donors, the funder of this management training program hopes to see the project expanded and replicated by other funders in other communities once the program's results are publicized. Having finished this little exercise, the donors may feel buoyed and confident that everything is now in place for a successful philanthropic intervention. However, a problem lurks.

The problem with this planning and strategizing scenario is that it fails to take into account the real-world complexity surrounding philanthropic interventions, particularly those involving efforts to shape human behavior or redress complex social problems, such as uneven academic performance in schools. The most glaring problem with this logic model has nothing to do with its contents, but rather with the sense that the model represents in some way a closed system. In fact, almost every theory of change is a profoundly open system—shaped and distorted by the vast array of forces and conditions surrounding the system and shaping the ultimate plausibility of the connections claimed.

Thus, the intrepid education donor's work is not done in the case at hand. It is incumbent on anyone sketching out a logic model to take into consideration the external factors that impinge on the robustness of the causal claims being made. It may not be possible to control or even account for all of the factors, but they still need to be confronted, if for no other reason than coming to terms with the limitations of the model. In this example, external factors that lie outside the immediate control of the donor include such things as the level of support given to the endeavor by the university hosting the program and the presence or absence of competing programs that can siphon away potential participants and resources. When trying to establish the net impact of the intervention on the school performance, a whole range of competing factors must be considered, including the level of staff support the school leader enjoys in the work environment and, perhaps most critically, the local political and public funding picture that will shape the kinds of resources the school will have available to it as it moves forward. All these factors and many others will impinge on the net change in school performance.

At one level, the presence of large amounts of "noise" in philanthropic systems is disconcerting, in that it weakens the causal links that lie at the heart of all theories of change models. Part of the problem stems not from the mere presence of exogenous forces, but from the inability of philanthropy to assess the impact wrongly attributed to philanthropic interventions. In some cases, exogenous factors will be enormously important and will render claims about net philanthropic effects basically meaningless. In other circumstances, the problem of exogenous factors will be far more manageable, especially when the noise is matched up against a substantial philanthropic intervention in a narrow field of practice or a small geographic region. There is a clear connection between the problem of causality in philanthropy, the nature of the intervention being attempted, and the scope of the philanthropic program being deployed.

One interesting question that arises is whether sound philanthropic strategy demands that donors focus their giving on problems and situations

FIGURE 2   Theory of Change for School Management Program

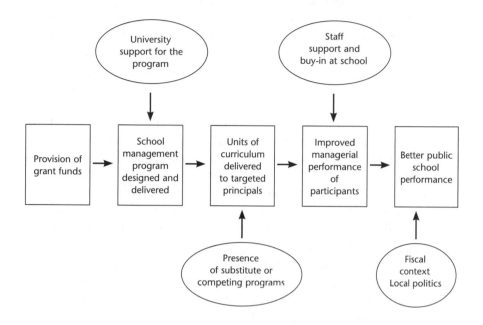

where causal links stemming from giving are strong and compelling. The attraction of such a decision is that it controls exogenous factors at the outset by guiding donors away from giving to problems where causal claims of progress are difficult to make. Although it would simplify some aspects of education philanthropy, such a decision would likely lead donors to focus on problems far too limited in character and whose solutions are far too obvious. One of the real tests of education philanthropy actually comes down to crafting interventions in areas where others have failed. These tend to be areas where there are ample amounts of noise in the form of existing support programs and where public policy can shift in an effort to address the problem. The last thing that donors should want is to remove from their potential targets the long list of intractable problems simply because they are subject to a number of interacting factors. However, when sketching a theory of change, it is important for responsible donors to confront the fact that there are many intervening and competing variables at work, some working for and others against education reform.

The presence of confounding factors could discourage a donor from trying to achieve some conceptual clarity. This is especially true if the philanthropic object at hand is public school reform, a goal that many other donors have selected but have failed to achieve. The right response in taking on a large and challenging issue like the performance of public schools is simply to act with a fair amount of humility. Some donors do not give up easily and attempt to confront these intervening forces head-on by implementing experimental evaluations with control and treatment groups, which allow some control for factors outside the program. However, these evaluations are expensive, difficult to execute effectively, and usually have some significant limitations as to how much one can gain from them.[6] Thus, while it may be possible to "control" for some of the factors that influence an education intervention, there is no real substitute for a clear understanding of the weaknesses that are inherent in much of the causal modeling that goes into philanthropy.

In the end, the real justification for a clear theory of change is not its ability to provide the framework for evaluation, although it certainly can perform that function well. The ultimate rationale for engaging in the kind of reflection and modeling described here is for public school reform–minded donors to render more clear in their own minds the objectives driving their giving. By formalizing the donor's beliefs and assumptions through the construction of a model, one meaningful step can be taken on the road toward greater strategic clarity. In some sense, it is important to judge philanthropy not just by the effects it produces or, to put it another way, for what comes out of the model. It is important also to take stock of the quality of thinking that lies behind giving and the plausibility of philanthropic intentions. A theory of change can be a telling representation of the donor's best judgment about how to address a human problem. Getting beyond the narrow measurement of the net effects of philanthropy to the underlying aspirations of donors animating giving would be productive for the field as a whole. It would reorient the field's attention from something that can often only be indirectly connected to giving, namely, the outcomes of people exposed to programs made possible by philanthropy, to something that is at the heart of responsible decisionmaking: the care with which a donor disburses philanthropic funds. This is something over which donors have complete and absolute control and for which they should be held accountable.

GOING TO SCALE

Assuming that donors are able to create coherent and compelling theories of change to guide their giving, they are still left with the difficult task of building on proven successes so as to reach as many people as possible. Being effective means more than just carrying out an initiative well and meeting the needs of a small group of people. Effectiveness also involves reaching many people and taking the social leverage that an intervention creates and amplifying it even more. Given the interest in having a real impact, donors speak frequently of taking a program to scale, going to scale, and scaling up. What exactly is meant by *scale?* At its core, the idea of scale is focused on creating a lasting and significant impact—taking the final box in the theory of change and magnifying it. Beyond the broad idea of a greater impact, the idea of scale becomes more enigmatic when it is subject to sustained scrutiny.[7] Scale has at least five overlapping meanings in philanthropy, which are in practice often collapsed. Scale can refer to 1) financial strength, 2) program expansion, 3) comprehensiveness, 4) multisite replication, and/or 5) accepted doctrine. In venturing into the field of school reform, where the problems are enormous and philanthropic resources are limited, it is critical for donors to make choices about how they want to see their work achieve meaningful scale. This means aiming for one or another conception of scale.

The first meaning of scale is related to organizational strength and sustainability.[8] Large nonprofit institutions such as museums and universities have achieved scale because they have visible institutional profiles and reputations for excellence across the nation, occupy large buildings or campuses, and possess the financial wherewithal to persist indefinitely.[9] Scale on this account is equivalent to financial strength and sustainability, often secured by endowment or by large operating budgets with dependable revenue streams. In the nonprofit sector, where financial crises are commonplace, scale means being able to withstand the test of time by being big enough to ride out the storms. Though the number of school reform groups that have gone to scale under this definition remains small, Teach For America comes to mind as one possible example. In principle, there are few obstacles to taking any single organization to scale. Though philanthropic resources are limited, if they are concentrated on a small number of organizations, there are funds available to create a new cadre of very large and durable reform-oriented organizations.

Large private foundations do not seem to embrace this notion of scale as readily as individuals, though there are some notable exceptions. Picking any single nonprofit organization as the one that will be taken to scale may appear unfair and capricious. It implies that a single donor should be able to disturb the competitive landscape and decide who wins and loses in the nonprofit arena. Few foundations want to be perceived as inequitable and heavy-handed, however. As a consequence, they shy away from tipping the scales completely in favor of one organization over another. Moreover, foundations may be less likely to bring an organization to scale because their interests are not in the organizations they fund per se, but in the specific programs and outcomes these organizations deliver. Foundations have priorities that overlap somewhat with the agendas of nonprofit organizations. When these priorities change, funders can and do find new organizations.

Another reason that individual nonprofits are not often brought to scale through the infusion of large amounts of money may be connected to efficiency concerns. While giving a nonprofit the ability to withstand the vicissitudes of the nonprofit marketplace sounds reasonable, it may not be the most efficient way to use philanthropic resources. Endowments are often established with a projected 4 or 5 percent payout on draw rate. Funding a large programmatic agenda from an endowment therefore becomes an expensive proposition. There is also the concern that taking a single organization to scale will eliminate the leverage that funders have over nonprofits because the funds will free the organization from the usual relationships of dependence. After all, if a nonprofit has enough money to conduct its programs without the continuous input of new contributions, an important performance incentive may be removed. In a field as dynamic as school reform, needs can and do change quickly. This makes maintaining a vibrant and diverse population of organizations desirable.

The second meaning of scale refers to the breadth or scope of service. Going to scale in this sense is thus roughly equivalent to program expansion and reach. When a pilot or project is launched, the goal is often to take it to scale by funding it at a higher level and by bringing the program to more people. There is a sense that a good program can never serve enough people. This is particularly in school reform, where the needs of public schools are immense and difficult to fully satisfy. As soon as an initiative seems to achieve significant results, one of the first impulses of nonprofit managers and funders alike is to ramp up the effort and find a way to identify and serve more people. In the past, the ultimate ambition has often been to get local, state, or federal funding after a small-scale program is launched with private money.

There are many powerful forces propelling nonprofits and their funders toward program expansion. First, funding scale as expansion appears fair and equitable in that it rewards past performance. Funding decisions can be justified by the results that are actually achieved. Second, expanding a program will allow it to achieve greater operational efficiency, as the marginal cost of administration will decrease as the program grows. Third, incentives are created for nonprofits to develop and deliver successful projects. If nonprofit managers know that funding to expand their programs is dependent on how well their programs work, they will work harder to make them succeed.

Fourth, it allows funders and recipients to work together over longer periods of time than they might otherwise under typical project funding.[10]

Nonprofit organizations are especially comfortable with the idea of scale as program expansion. It represents a natural way to evolve a nonprofit from a small school- or community-based organization to one that has a broader presence and impact. For nonprofit managers, aiming toward scale as program expansion is important. Because general support funding is scarce in some fields, program growth is essential to achieving some level of financial stability. Expanding programs is seen as equivalent to professional success and can be a key to advancement. Moreover, the financial incentives in the sector provide a strong correlation between budget size and salary, with managers earning more, depending on the scale of the program they oversee. As both a signal of success and a tool for advancement, scale as program expansion is thus attractive to many nonprofit organizations.

From the perspective of the funder, allowing an organization with a proven track record to expand its operations represents both a high-return activity and a relatively low-risk proposition. After all, the nonprofit has already demonstrated its ability to implement a given program. All they are seeking is funds for program expansion so that they can do more of a particular activity. This is a proposition that can be considerably less risky than the design and creation of a new initiative.

The third meaning of scale refers to a set of programs that are closely linked and that constitute a coherent set of resources for schools or communities.[11] Under this definition, the coordination problems inherent in the nonprofit sector's division of labor and proliferation of programs are overcome by bringing together under one roof an integrated set of activities and interventions. Comprehensive community-based initiatives are seen as a remedy for the problems of categorical funding, one that aims at systemwide reform. The goal of integration is an old one. Comprehensive community initiatives began in the 20th century with settlement houses. From Hull House to the modern community-focused initiatives launched by large private foundations, there does not seem to be any decrease in this type of initiative. The belief that comprehensiveness is the critical ingredient to scale emerged from years of experience with isolated project funding. Seeking to create synergies by funding integrated sets of services, many donors see scale as being closely linked to building a dominant local presence. Viewing scale as comprehensiveness is thus embedded in the idea that program links are as important as, or more important than, the creation of new programs. By focusing resources in one geographical community, some funders see bridge-building as the best way to create a sizable presence and have a more fundamental and lasting impact. In the education domain, the need for coordination and integration is as urgent as in any other domain. Too many programs operate in quiet isolation from one another, and lost synergies are commonplace.

Achieving scale by weaving together disparate programs and efforts into a cohesive whole requires that four important problems be overcome. First, interagency collaboration requires that difficult governance issues be worked out so that all parties can work together productively. Second, this approach emphasizes the goals of inclusion and diversity. Those heading such an effort must show leadership in this area and be sensitive to the heterogeneity of many community groups, programs, and networks. Third, comprehensiveness depends on the effort to gain legitimacy and support from the grassroots, not just from community elites. Fourth, any focus on collaborative strategy must address the issue of sustainability and the development of new funding streams. Inevitably, due to the size and ambition of many of these programs, government is often involved, which can be a source of support or frustration.

When a particular initiative or service model proves successful, many dissect the essential elements of the model in order to reconstruct the effort elsewhere with different personnel and under different circumstances. Replication is thus one way to achieve scale, a technique that has been tried and tested in the business sector over a long period of time.[12] Replication can proceed in two quite different ways: 1) within the organization, through a set of more or less closely linked chapters or through a franchise system linking independent organizations;[13] or 2) outside the organization, through independent efforts to create similar programs.[14]

The chapter or affiliate way of replicating services has proved critical to the expansion of many of the older and more established service and civic associations. Opening chapters in cities around the country enables an organization to achieve scale quickly, yet maintain some degree of control through centralization. Chapters are often established in a hub-and-spoke arrangement, in which funds and resources flow back and forth between the center and the periphery. One obvious problem with this approach is that it can be difficult to achieve uniformity and consistency across chapters, and thus to keep the message or mission clear and consistent. Not surprisingly, one of the biggest questions this approach raises is the amount of autonomy that should be granted to the chapters or affiliates. Some organizations have successfully implemented loose confederations, while others have long operated tightly controlled networks.

The competing-franchise approach to replication is based on the simple assumption that once a model has been established, the real work involves copying and multiplying the model in as many places as possible. Franchising has become popular with younger social entrepreneurs, who see this model as providing swift action. By licensing a "brand," nonprofits can go to scale quickly. A key challenge of the franchise approach is locating skilled people who are capable of taking a model into a new city or community and implementing it. The brand name must be protected by some form of quality assurance, for achieving consistency and measuring quality are both difficult propositions in the nonprofit sector.[15]

There are some clear difficulties to both chapter and franchise replication. Replication is not an approach that can easily be initiated or directed by funders, particularly in the education field, where local connections are prized. Moreover, public schools—with the possible exception of charter schools—are often not interested in being part of a national movement or network unless substantial financial resources are promised. Reform and school-support organizations are the more plausible targets for replication. Although funders may be able to foster some replication through the use of grants and incentives, most externally directed replication efforts will struggle with the vast unruly and idiosyncratic tide of nonprofit organizations that resist imitation and convergence. While some innovations and ideas have been replicated, large numbers of projects are unable to find any takers, even when they have shown great promise. Replication may rest on the shaky assumption that nonprofits are amenable to cookie-cutter duplication. Moreover, funders who have experimented with replication strategies have discovered that some initiatives that are successful on a small, local scale defy replication when they are taken out of their initial contexts. This is especially true when the nonprofit is working with disadvantaged populations, where trust and credibility are crucial.

Replication also ensues if the philanthropist creates a pilot or model program and then allows government or other funders to take the effort to scale. Philanthropist Eugene Lang, for example, had the novel idea of "adopting a class" of middle school students at the inner-city school he had attended years earlier. Lang promised all the students in one grade that if they worked hard and stayed in school, he would pay for their college education. When New York State got word of this offer, it did not take long before a scholarship program was devised for other disadvantaged students. This proved to be problematic. Critically missing from this public-sector imitation was the direct personal involvement that was a central part of Lang's innovative educational gift. Thus, while it is tempting to think that the replication model involves the simple multiplication of existing programs and institutions, in reality this process is more labor intensive. Embedded in many successful programs is the vision and commitment of an individual. When the program is replicated in other sites, this personal connection is often missing, and the organizations may pass from being an expression of one person's values and beliefs to a more instrumental attempt to produce certain public benefits.

A fifth dimension of scale focuses on the power of creating a new and accepted doctrine within a given field. Scale can be achieved by formulating and diffusing an idea or concept. Precipitating a major shift in a given field can have a wide-ranging and lasting impact. This shift changes the way people think about their work and carry out their programs. Creating a new doctrine is different from other forms of scale because it seeks to infiltrate broadly by changing the conceptual and intellectual frame surrounding a particular field, be it early childhood education or drug treatment. A successful effort at doctrine-building will lead to a wholesale reevaluation of a field's standard operating procedures and operational assumptions. While an operational model may be associated with a new doctrine, new ideas can and do triumph in the absence of clear applications.

Pursuing scale through doctrinal shifts appeals to funders for a number of reasons. Unlike other modes of going to scale, this approach is not limited to the boundaries of the organizations receiving funding. It is possible to propagate an idea or theory and to change service delivery models without spending money on implementation; however, one should be able to point to at least one concrete application of the doctrine. One key to successful paradigm-building involves the development and support of small networks of policy elites and nonprofit leaders. Once an idea or concept is embraced by opinion leaders, it can spread quickly throughout a field.[16] Influential doctrines have emerged from think tanks and university researchers and from practitioners who can articulate a clear theory that supports their work. One significant shortcoming to this approach to scale is that the outcomes of such efforts are hard to predict. Sometimes ideas and frameworks emerge as powerful tools for transforming practice but ultimately find no audience or willing adopters. Other times, second-rate ideas spread like wildfire within fields and are broadly adopted. The process of spreading a doctrine is not amenable to a great deal of control.

Although many funders like the idea of "going to scale," the number of initiatives accomplishing scale under any of the five definitions remains small. Only around 200,000 nonprofits out of some 1.5 million have revenues above $25,000. The number of very large and successful nonprofits is considerably smaller than 100,000 and probably closer to 10,000, the majority of which are universities and hospitals. The achievement of scale thus remains an elusive goal and one that raises a number of questions. When and why should any of these five different scale strategies be applied? Why does scale sometimes fail? Does the ideal of scale fit better in the business sector than in the nonprofit sector? Can commitments to scale and equity be embraced simultaneously? Are less successful attempts at scale simply examples of domains in which public policy should be allowed to operate? Most of these questions remain unanswered, even though scale has become a major target of organized philanthropy. Rather than engage these difficult question, it is far easier to fall back on arguments about spreading the benefits more broadly and achieving programmatic efficiencies.

DONOR ENGAGEMENT

Developing a theory of change and committing to a model for getting to scale are important, but, in assembling a philanthropic plan for contributing to the public school reform movement, donors also need to confront the challenge of crafting an appropriate and productive philanthropic style for their giving. This means thinking carefully about the issue of engagement and answering the questions of who will carry out their philanthropic work and how this work will proceed. In some cases, donors will seek the advice and counsel of family members, friends, lawyers, and consultants when executing their giving. These parties may be brought in to assist with planning or implementing a philanthropic agenda. A trend toward philanthropic disintermediation has, however, emerged in recent years: Younger donors increasingly have decided to cut out all philanthropic middlemen and instead look to themselves as the principal agents of their own philanthropy. This do-it-yourself turn is, of course, the simplest solution to the agency question in philanthropy, one that removes the threat of deviation from the donor's intent that delegating responsibility can create.[17]

Engagement styles range from a very hands-off approach in which nonprofit autonomy and expertise are privileged, to a more deeply engaged approach in which the donor and recipient work together on program development and problem-solving.[18] There are donors who are involved in all aspects of their giving and with the work of the organizations that receive their funds. Often stemming from a sense that philanthropy must be about more than check writing, involved or engaged donors want to feel a connection and offer advice and input above and beyond funds.[19] This may lead the donor to talk to and toil alongside the inner-city school leaders as they struggle to improve education under difficult circumstances. It may entail listening in on a board meeting of an education reform group that is attempting to overcome a management challenge and offering some suggestions when appropriate. It may involve the regular introduction of independent evaluators into a funded program to advise both the organization and the donor on the strengths and weaknesses of the program design and implementation. There are many ways that donors can do more than just send checks. The important questions are, Why do donors at times become engaged, and how do they go about adding value through engagement?

Why would a donor seek a high level of engagement with a recipient organization rather than simply maintain a more traditional and distanced philanthropic relationship? High-engagement donors may get involved because they want to help others help themselves and gain independence. Or they may seek a high level of engagement simply because they believe that they know better than others how to manage a project, even if they lack the specialized training and experience of the leaders within the recipient organization. This impulse to micromanage and meddle can be a product of years of managerial work in the business sector, which may have led to substantial wealth and success. It is often just a small—though sometimes unwise—leap to assume that these patterns will lead to success in philanthropy. It is also possible that the drive to engage can be related to vanity, overblown self-confidence, or a desire to impose one's will on others.

At the other extreme, an increasingly smaller number of donors are happy to withdraw from the grantmaking process and let recipient organizations do their work as they see fit. Such deference may stem from a recognition that in many cases it is the nonprofit that truly understands the problem at hand. It can also be the painful result of experience in attempting to be highly engaged, leading only to the recognition that nonprofit managers prefer to have plenty of leeway in how they operate their programs. There are other reasons to resist jumping too quickly into the philanthropic fray. Low engagement has been justified in the name of professional detachment and as a necessity for maintaining objectivity.[20] It is also far easier, and demands less time, to limit the scope of the giving relationship to pre- and postgrant evaluation rather than to expect the donor to take partial responsibility for the execution of a program or for the recipient organization's performance. In fact, the more engaged a donor is with a project the harder it may be to exit or terminate the relationship. Engagement can muddy the philanthropic waters by placing the donor into the program that is being funded, a position from which it is hard to render tough and objective judgments about quality and impact. For this reason, there are cases in which donors need to actively resist the temptation to throw themselves into the fray and get their hands dirty.

As they become more comfortable with giving, donors come to define for themselves an engagement style that fits somewhere between totally hands off and deeply engaged. For nonprofits, these decisions about style can have significant consequences. High levels of donor engagement may mean access to resources and talents of great value to the nonprofit. It may also entail a tremendous amount of extra work, as donors need to be handled and satisfied. For this reason, some nonprofits prefer to receive general operating support with as few strings attached as possible. Over time, however, almost all nonprofits learn to work with the different engagement approaches of their donors and understand that considerable variation is to be expected.

In thinking about the question of philanthropic engagement, two critical dimensions to any relationship between giver and recipient impose themselves. The first dimension is the one just described: the level of donor engagement, which can vary from very light oversight to heavy-handed control. The level of engagement will vary not only based on the style of the donor, but also on the nature of the work being carried out by the recipient. Some work, such as scientific research or the arts, makes it hard for donors to be engaged directly in the funded work simply because it requires a certain amount of independence. Other kinds of projects, such as youth programs and scholarship funds, are far more open to donor involvement and even to reengineering. After all, everyone has an opinion on how to help young people, but few people know enough about genetic research to get deeply involved. The second dimension is simpler and only describes the level of congruence or match between the values and intentions of the donor and the recipient. In some situations, donors and recipients think alike and share common aspirations, while in other cases the two parties are far apart, even if this is not apparent at the time the grant is awarded. In either event, it is possible to view congruence, overlap, and coincidence in outlook and underlying values between donors and recipients as central to the formation of a strong working relationship. When these two dimensions are joined, four types of philanthropic relationships emerge: contractual relationships in which donors and recipients simply give and get under narrowly circumscribed terms and then go their own way; delegating relationships in which donors delegate responsibility freely to those doing the work; auditing relationships in which trust is low and oversight is extensive so as to monitor the precise use of grant funds; and collaborative relationships in which the two sides work together closely to achieve a set of mutually agreed-upon goals.

At one end of the spectrum of engagement styles are the high-engagement donors who seek to collaborate and coproduce social benefits with the

FIGURE 3   Forms of Philanthropic Relationships

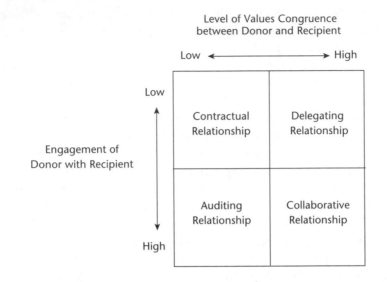

recipient organizations that they fund. Sometimes this is done by creating an operating foundation that allows the donor to actively shape the programs that are offered. Other times, higher engagement is achieved through close working relationships with nonprofit organizations that share core values and purposes. Some donors actually join the boards of the organizations they support and offer advice on planning, fundraising, and any other core function with which they feel conversant.[21] In the best cases, a strong, respectful collaboration emerges in which the skills of the donor and the recipient complement one another and contribute to improved performance.

At the other extreme of engagement approaches are donors who do little other than monitor progress, review financial statements, and ensure that the terms of the grant agreement are fulfilled.[22] Depending on how closely values are aligned, this can produce a respectful contractual relationship or a more tense auditing relationship. These auditing models often arise in smaller foundations, where large numbers of small grants are made. Unable to do more than a cursory monitoring of grantees, these underresourced foundations are led to simply set a group of procedural hurdles in place designed to maintain some semblance of accountability. Nonprofits must submit to these periodic audits and remain in compliance. Since it is far easier to monitor financial matters than mission fulfillment, it is no surprise that much of the auditing that goes on in philanthropy is over the expenditure of funds and

the accounting that accompanies this process. To really audit mission fulfillment or the production of public benefits, donors need to go to far greater
lengths and expense to collect information. It is not surprising, therefore,
that more attention is paid to getting budgets and expense reports filed than
to meaningfully and creatively assessing the mission performance of grant
recipients.

Contractual relationships are frequent in the world of corporate philanthropy, where gifts often are conveyed with relative detachment, but where
there is some assumption of alignment between values—or at least interests.
Companies that give are reluctant to get too closely connected to the organizations they support for a range of reasons. Chief among them is the fear
of exposure to negative publicity, should charitable programs backfire or fail.
While executives may want to see their employees involved in community
volunteer projects that aim to rehabilitate buildings or clean up beaches, they
may not want to get too deeply involved in designing a community program
aimed at tackling a tough problem such as crime or drug abuse. Moreover,
the focus on arts funding[23] that is often present in corporate philanthropy
makes engagement more difficult because there are few real opportunities
for company executives to help design an exhibition or design a theater production—although there are ample opportunities at each to fly the corporate banner. The engagement level of corporate donors is generally lower
than other donors for another reason: Few company foundations have large
enough staffs to really do more than process requests and focus on making
sound grant decisions. Real engagement requires a substantial commitment
of time, resources, and people, which are not always available in the context
of corporate philanthropy. Many corporate giving programs are more set up
to negotiate and structure issues related to profile and recognition than they
are to rigorously intervene in the work of nonprofits.

Engagement is a critical part of the style defined by a donor. It has implications not only for the overall fit and alignment of the giving strategy, but
also for the nonprofit organizations that are on the other side of the table.
Finding a level of engagement that both satisfies the donor and adds value
to the recipient organization is not always easy. Sometimes there will be a
misalignment between a donor who wants a lot of publicity and a cause
or organization that simply cannot mobilize the attention that is sought.
Other times, donors will want a relatively low level of engagement but end
up funding an organization that continuously seeks to draw the donor into
the organization's governance.[24] Engagement levels are thus like many other
elements of the strategic puzzle in philanthropy: They are variable and con-
textually defined by the interplay of public purposes and private values.

Engagement is something that must neither be declared by donor fiat nor postulated by a recipient. Instead, engagement needs to emerge from communication between the two parties and should aim to find a level of fit and alignment that will satisfy both sides of the philanthropic exchange.

CONCLUSION

When donors—be they individuals or institutions—choose to attempt to improve the quality of American public education, they take on a vast and complex task. What I have suggested here is that there are at least three significant philanthropic challenges that demand careful consideration as donors craft their philanthropic strategies for reforming and improving the education system. The first is the conceptual task of laying out the underlying premises that will guide the giving in the form of a simple theory of change. While there may be many roadblocks and unforeseeable bumps in the road toward reform and improvement, starting out with a clear map of how philanthropic action could, in principle, make a difference is essential. Without a theory of change, it is impossible both to plan fully or to assess meaningfully the course of a donor's giving. The second task for the donor, which should not be shrugged off as something to think about in the far-off future, relates to growth and scale. Most giving starts modestly, which is often a good idea, since many philanthropic ideas fail. However, those that show promise should be supported by a realistic scale model that will allow the donor to amplify and project the results of giving beyond its often modest starting point. The third critical element of any donor's strategic plan involves the adoption of an appropriate giving style and engagement level. School reform is a field where donors can and do get personally involved in the operational side of philanthropy. The challenge is to shape an engagement level that satisfies the donor's interests and needs while meeting the demands of the particular program. There are times when a hands-on approach will yield powerful results and times when it will be counterproductive. Good strategy involves interplay between these two scenarios.

The goal of helping to reform and improve the performance of public schools is a valuable and honorable one. In pursuing this calling, donors who bring a small measure of sound philanthropic strategy to their giving by defining a theory of change, setting out an approach to scale, and incorporating a productive engagement level will have an advantage over donors who proceed without having considered these matters.

Conclusion

Frederick M. Hess

Education philanthropy is disorderly, visible, and little studied. One consequence of this is that we both overestimate and underestimate its significance. We overestimate it because philanthropic gifts are so visible that we may focus on them—as on the tip of an iceberg—while forgetting the import of all that lies beneath the surface. And we underestimate philanthropic giving because we rarely stop to think about the ways that donors can—consciously or not—shape the politics, dynamics, and agenda of school reform.

Complicating frank discussion of these issues is the reality that philanthropists are intimidating to scholars, reformers, and practitioners. This is not because donors stifle criticism or threaten to blacklist skeptics. In fact, many prominent donors embrace consensus and try to step cautiously precisely because they are concerned about appearing to be overbearing. The truth is that much of the reticence about discussing donors may be due to caution among observers who are eager to avoid offending influential donors more than any other reason.

Such caution has the unfortunate effect of leaving important questions unasked, truths unstated, and tensions unexplored. The hope for this volume is that a group of prominent scholars, policy analysts, observers, and practitioners delving more deeply into the nexus of philanthropy and school reform would make it safer for others to start to do so.

Philanthropy plays a peculiar role in contemporary American education. In sheer size, educational philanthropy is dwarfed by state, local, and federal expenditures on public schooling. In 2004–05, U.S. taxpayers spent upwards of $500 billion on K–12 education. Meanwhile, in 2002, philanthropic foundations reported giving just $4.2 billion to educational institutions and activities of all kinds, with most of that giving going to higher education. In this volume, Jay Greene estimates that only $1 to $1.5 billion was explicitly targeted to K–12 schooling in 2002. In fact, even by the most generous estimate, no more than 40 percent of the $4.2 billion in total education giving can even be loosely linked to K–12 schooling (with the rest going to higher education, adult education, and so on). Dan Fallon, chair of the education division of Carnegie Corporation—a foundation that gave away $26 million in education support in 2004—has observed, "No one should be under the illusion that a foundation is going to create something remarkable in the shadow of a $440 billion enterprise. Our task is to help get good ideas into the marketplace so that society has good alternatives from which to choose."[1]

Unfortunately, how, or even whether, foundations adopt Fallon's sensible advice is often an open question. Foundations feel pressure to demonstrate visible and tangible contributions. Particularly in the case of foundations run by trustees, employees rarely feel empowered to champion grantees that fail to show results in a timely fashion. Living donors are eager to ensure that their largesse is invested in a meaningful and cost-effective fashion. Moreover, given the understandable desire of philanthropists and their staffs to give to children and educators that they can see, speak with, and visit, there is a natural impulse to focus on concrete programs and relatively short-term efforts.

In the public sector, however, broader public policies are essential to enabling or impeding successful innovation. Critical areas targeted by givers—ranging from teacher pay to school size to professional development—are constrained by federal, state, and local statutes. Changing educational practice, therefore, is not merely a matter of finding good programs and good educators but of changing the rules under which they work. Left unaddressed, policies and statutory constraints can leave schools and programs inflexible and unable to react to changes or adopt sensible innovations.

In the public sector, it is not enough for reform-minded donors to create promising models; instead, they must help pave the new policy path along which they wish their grantees to tread. Reform-oriented philanthropists need more than just strategy or focus. They must distinguish giving that has the potential to drive change through lethargic, outdated systems from that which does not. There is a stark difference between measures that bring new and more talented individuals into education, enable effective educators to launch new schools, and ratchet up the pressure on ineffective schools, and those that merely seek to improve curricula, enhance professional development, or forge community consensus.

Now, advocates, observers, and philanthropies have tried to provide guidance on how donors can give more effectively. That, of course, is not our focus here. While the advice provided by user-friendly monographs like *Mak-*

ing It Count: A Guide to High-Impact Education Philanthropy, A Donor's Guide to School Choice, and *Principles for Effective Education Grantmaking: Roadmap for Results in Education Philanthropy* is welcome, this kind of sensible tactical advice does not pretend to pursue the broader questions concerning the nature of donor leverage, the challenges of democratic oversight, or the relationship of private philanthropy to public schooling.[2]

KEY FINDINGS

At least eight important conclusions emerge from the chapters in this volume. Some amount to reminders of plain truths that we can too readily overlook, while others direct our attention to new questions and concerns.

First, it is vital to remember how limited the total giving that foundations are contributing to K–12 schooling is. In Jay Greene's memorable phrase, they are casting "buckets into the sea." Wielding limited resources, they must give thoughtfully and strategically if they are to make a real difference.

Second, despite the limited amount of overall philanthropy to K–12 schooling, philanthropic contributions do often represent a critical piece of the discretionary money available to support reform. Lynn Jenkins and Don McAdams point out that philanthropic giving can have a massively outsized impact—like a small rudder steering a big ship. As nationally recognized superintendents and former superintendents like Alan Bersin, Howard Fuller, and Arlene Ackerman have observed, the vast majority of existing money in schools and school districts is committed to expenditures for salary, benefits, and other routine line items. Given how state and district budgeting operates and the preexisting commitments enshrined in statutes and contracts, the amount of money available for research and development, reinvention, and reform is often exceedingly small—even in districts with annual budgets of $500 million or $1 billion. Freeing up more than a small sliver of funding to support structural changes or ambitious initiatives is exhausting and politically perilous work. Consequently, external grants loom large when it comes to executing ambitious reforms. That is why philanthropic dollars, while sparse, are so central to school reform.

Third, accountability has achieved unprecedented significance. Spurred in part by broader developments like the passage of No Child Left Behind, discussion of "program outcomes," "demonstrated effects," and "impact on achievement" is now routine. This was not always the case. Wendy Hassett and Dan Katzir explain how "new" givers are becoming increasingly sophisticated about monitoring and measuring performance. Andrew Rotherham,

Bryan Hassel, and Amy Way make clear that some foundations have recognized that credible, independent research can be an important lever in public policy debates. Peter Frumkin explains how evaluation not only can help donors assess the results of prior decisions, but also can play a formative role in shaping strategy. Raising the question of where this all may lead is Steve Heyneman's observation that international givers have found that loans yield more accountability than grants—presumably because recipients are disciplined by the realization that they will have to repay the money. Heyneman's analysis suggests that efforts to promote accountability may foster new and nontraditional forms of philanthropic giving, such as the hybrid "venture philanthropy" model that has been pioneered by the San Francisco–based NewSchools Venture Fund.

Fourth, as Tom Loveless reminds us, it matters not only how strategically foundations pursue their reform agendas but what educational ideas and beliefs are at the heart of those agendas. The world of philanthropy has been consumed in recent years by the emphasis on focus and accountability. Business school jargon like "leverage" and "venture capital" has become a sign of seriousness. While a welcome development in many respects, this does pose the risk that fundamentals may be overlooked or brushed aside by those taken with their strategic vision. Tom Loveless's chapter suggests that most foundation program officers—especially those who have not themselves been educators—doubt the importance of "old-fashioned" values like student discipline, testing, teacher content, knowledge, and basic skills. This raises important questions as to just what principles grantmakers are embracing and what those mean for the content of philanthropic reform. For all the talk about strategic giving, Loveless's findings suggest that the foundation staff are committed to particular notions of teaching and learning that are at odds with the thinking of most parents and teachers.

Fifth, several contributors hint that one result of philanthropic support is the elevation of certain grantees to new levels of influence via a process I'll term the "American Idol" effect. At any given time, there are hundreds or thousands of education reforms playing out across the nation's landscape. Attracting support from a large, nationally recognized foundation can launch one of these struggling, aspiring efforts to center stage. The resources, spotlight, and national credibility that visible major donor support can provide to districts, superintendents, and reform proposals can help turn them into national causes. Philanthropic funding gives models visibility and a pedigree, attracting both journalists to profile them and evaluators to document their effects. Since education reforms have a long history of working, at least on a small scale in pilot sites, and since evaluators are often positively disposed to a particular reform, it is probably not a surprise that the cycle triggered by the philanthropic gift often ends by turning senior district officials into national avatars for the heralded reform. The attention of prominent professors has helped transform the former leaders of reform efforts in New York City's District 2, Chicago, Houston, San Diego, and other school systems into iconic figures.[3]

As one superintendent forlornly wondered, "Where do I go to get my guru? . . . If the foundations aren't supporting you, even though you're improving achievement, how do you get on their radar screen?"[4] The handful of nationally celebrated superintendents and former superintendents are almost all champions of one or another reform model embraced by leading givers, while less established superintendents see the benefits of adapting the favored models or finding their own sponsor. Now, none of this is ill intentioned, nor is it necessarily harmful. If the donors are promoting sensible and effective reforms, such pressure is all to the good. So recognizing this pattern is not to decry it but to suggest that the ability of foundations to elect the "American Idols" of education reform deserves far more attention than it has received.

Sixth, their own successes have given select philanthropists a degree of celebrity that magnifies the impact of their giving. Business superstars like Bill Gates, Michael Dell, and Michael Milken have fame (and sometimes notoriety) that can help command the attention of major media and public officials, even apart from their wealth. Even Stephanie Sanford, senior policy officer at the Gates Foundation, has remarked, "We didn't fully anticipate the impact and value of [Gates's] voice when he spoke out on high schools; we weren't prepared for the impact of his celebrity."[5]

Again, this is not entirely new. In large part, it has simply not been discussed. When Andrew Carnegie in the 19th century—or Bill Gates in the 21st century—threw his celebrity and reputation behind a particular reform proposal, it helped to focus the agenda in a way that even a large gift from a minor figure could not. Leading educational philanthropists like Eli Broad or Jim Barksdale also have extensive personal relationships in the worlds of politics and industry that can help attract attention to their efforts. Some donors are reticent about the public spotlight, but the aura of celebrity donors is a real and significant phenomenon.

Seventh, in some policy areas, just a handful of foundations may play a huge role in funding reform efforts and advocacy. In this volume, we see this phenomenon most clearly in the case of choice-based school reform. Bryan Hassel and Amy Way show that the Gates and Walton foundations fund over 80 percent of nonprivate school choice. To observe the reality of this oligopoly is not necessarily to pass judgment on it. Such a concentration could lend coherence, provide stable leadership, and ensure the presence of a patron committed to quality, or it could stifle unpopular critiques, eliminate unconventional ideas, and shut out promising entrepreneurs.

The concentration of influence is particularly evident in the case of high school reform, where the nation's largest education philanthropist, the Gates Foundation, is intensely focused. It seems safe to estimate that the foundation is providing well over two-thirds of all philanthropic giving to high school reform, creating the possibility that one donor will be largely responsible for the shape of modern-day high schools. Multiple voices and strategies are likely to emerge only to the extent that Gates chooses to fund them, while other strategies are likely to be neglected without the foundation's momentum, fame (and notoriety), and resources. The point is not to challenge the value or appropriateness of the Gates Foundation efforts, but to encourage scholars, journalists, and policymakers to keep a sharp eye on the agenda and actions of dominant funders.

Finally, determining to pursue a strategy of "high-leverage" giving is not as simple or straightforward as some suggest. Analysts have proffered at least two strategies for rethinking what "leverage" means. One approach, posed by Jay Greene, is to consider the degree to which a gift will redirect the future use of public funds. By Greene's calculations, a $1 million gift that helped launch a charter or small high school and thereby influenced $1 million per year in future public funding would have much greater leverage than a $1 million gift that produced an annual shift of $500,000 in future public spending. A second approach, which I have proposed elsewhere, focuses on whether the gift is helping to change the incentives that shape the way district officials, school leaders, and teachers behave.[6] In this light, opening a small school would likely not be a high-leverage activity because it would not compel educators to do anything differently, while promoting educational competition, advancing hard-edged accountability, or linking pay to performance would be high leverage. The point is not that one or another perspective is necessarily "right," but that each can deepen our appreciation of what leverage entails and implies.

To suggest how the Greene and Hess approaches might yield different verdicts on leverage, consider the New Vision Schools initiative in New York City. In the past few years, New Vision Schools has launched 75 "New Century" high schools with the support of $30 million from the Gates Foundation, Carnegie Corporation, and other funders. Because these schools will henceforward be funded by tens or hundreds of millions of dollars in annual per-pupil funding, Greene's analysis would label the reforms a model of high-leverage giving. On the other hand, because nothing in the New Vision approach changes the incentives or regulations under which district educators operate—except insofar as such changes are adopted on a school-by-school basis—I would describe it as low leverage. The point is not that either Greene or I is right—both perspectives are probably instructive in some ways and limited in others—but that bland exhortations to embrace "high-leverage giving" should be taken with a grain of salt.

FIVE CHALLENGES

This is where I would typically list a series of recommendations distilled from the contributions to this book. In this case, that seems decidedly inappropriate. For one thing, the lack of serious inquiry into educational philanthropy means that we just don't understand enough to permit clear or simple answers. For another, the desirability of various reform strategies depends on the aims, intentions, and values of philanthropists and the public. Rather than offering pat answers, I'll discuss five key challenges that confront philanthropists, policymakers, and the public. In nearly every case these challenges are aggravated by the nature, ambition, and tactics of the emergent "new" givers. While not as satisfying as simple solutions, transparency and straight talk can serve as vital first steps in imaginative problem-solving and democratic accountability.

The Challenge of "Strategic" Giving

Donor attempts to promote coherent reform efforts can clash with desire to foster diverse ideas and entrepreneurial approaches. An open market that embraces experimentation would be messy, full of failures, and uncoordinated. However, if funders reject faddism, new and effective approaches can flourish. Of course, this approach often works at cross-purposes with the level of focus and strategic vision embraced by the new givers. How donors can advance strategic visions of reform without stifling entrepreneurial efforts is an open question.

The urgency of the question is highlighted by the experiences of some of the leading givers themselves. After all, in the early 1980s, no expert in the technology sector foresaw that Bill Gates and Paul Allen would succeed with Microsoft where hundreds of competitors would fail. Even careful attention to "outcomes" would have failed to distinguish the Gates-Allen enterprise from scores of other aspiring software firms. Ultimately, it wasn't a coordinated effort to identify the most promising enterprise but the competition of a free market that elevated Microsoft. Carried too far, or executed without sufficient appreciation for the strengths of the marketplace and the American system, strategic giving is akin to trying to select the "best" enterprise and ensure its broad adoption. While the urge is understandable, given the limited dollars available to philanthropists and the commensurate desire to promote high-leverage activity, all parties should take care to resist the temptation toward hubris.

Strategic giving can hold traps for recipients as well as donors. Even highly focused giving can create constituents who will become advocates. Whether funding a new teacher pay system, reading program, or design for middle schools, support forges a group of district educators and community members with a stake in the program's survival. District personnel may see it as a way to procure extra resources, advance their professional career, or as a measure of their importance. Community members may see it as symbolically important—a statement that their school is important or notable—or as a way to secure extra resources for their children's programs.

Whatever the specifics of a given case, major philanthropic district initiatives routinely boast testimonials from participants, attract positive news coverage, produce favorable evaluations by researchers hired by supporters, and thus become a cherished part of the school district firmament. Over time, programs find constituencies, start to claim district support, and can pile up gradually alongside (or atop) one another. With time, even a collection of "focused" initiatives can make it more difficult for districts to maintain coherence and focus on the future. The gradual accretion of such gifts, even if pursued in a disciplined manner, can weigh down a district with conflicting constituencies, each with their own favorite program. None of this is insuperable, as Richard Colvin documented in the case of San Diego. There, superintendent Alan Bersin opted to sever ties with several district funders rather than accept their restrictions on his management strategy. Nonetheless, the weight of accumulated initiatives and grant conditions poses one more constraint on burdened district officials and educators engaged in urban reform.

The Political Economy of Evaluation

Philanthropists, reformers, and practitioners agree about the desirability of program evaluation and enhanced accountability. When it comes to ensuring the quality and utility of those evaluations, however, attention to technical issues has generally been accompanied by inattention to professional realities that undercut their value.

In theory, everyone engaged in school reform supports hard-hitting program evaluation. Foundation staff want to know what's working, practitioners want feedback on how to refine their efforts, and evaluators want to maintain professional respect and produce credible research. They all want to do the right thing. At the same time, these individuals often find themselves anything but disinterested about what it means "to do the right thing" when it comes to evaluating philanthropic initiatives. Steve Heyneman, for instance, explains how the very dynamic of philanthropy can "influence the character" of international grantors and grantees, with donors often feeling a personal attachment to the projects they fund.

Foundation staffers who have committed millions of dollars to particular programs and provided them with very public endorsements have made a professional commitment and put their foundation's prestige on the line. They may worry that reversing their course (or changing course) will embarrass the foundation or its trustees. Quite naturally, with the best of intentions, program officers may regard criticism skeptically and be certain that any disappointments reflect imperfect implementation rather than fundamental misjudgments or flaws in the design of the reform.

It's no surprise that practitioners and reformers are emotionally and professionally invested in their programs and regard them as effective. What is surprising is that a lot of these practitioners are right—pilot programs frequently impress, due in substantial part to the advantages of impassioned leadership, extra resources, exceptional faculty, and a common culture forged by a shared bond.[7] Documentation of the success of a pilot effort can open the door to additional resources and opportunities. Affirmation by a "respected" scholar magnifies the benefits. At the same time, negative findings from an evaluation—or even explicit recognition that a program's success may be due to factors that cannot be systematically replicated—can feel like a rebuke. If made public, criticism can be read as a critique of the grantee's personal judgment or professional wisdom, may devastate their ability to attract public or private support, and, at a minimum, may incline donors to look elsewhere rather than place new bets on a questionable venture. Consequently, program designers and practitioners have both personal and professional reasons to quietly address criticisms of program effects or cautions regarding design, while trumpeting the more positive elements of an evaluation.

Researchers themselves compete fiercely for the right to evaluate high-profile reform initiatives. Almost without exception, the evaluators are hired by funders or grantees. This poses some obvious complexities. Winning access to individual schools, districts, and foundations is a delicate process, one that requires careful attention to building relationships. Because results for educational evaluations are typically equivocal, it is only natural that evaluators attentive to their professional future would take care not to present results in an unnecessarily critical manner. Most evaluators are selected, at least in part, because they are perceived as being sympathetic to the reform in question. Moreover, leading evaluators have often achieved that status based on their previous work, meaning that they are frequently asked to evaluate reforms designed in accord with models they have helped develop or refine. Concern for their prospects and reputations usefully pushes researchers to take care in data collection and analysis, but can also encourage them to be exceedingly careful about issuing bluntly critical assessments that may give pause to potential clients. Leading institutional evaluators hired for their professional neutrality often maintain that reputation by issuing sophisticated evaluations couched in enough cautions that they can be interpreted either positively or negatively. This lack of clarity has traditionally prevented evaluators from having to term a given initiative a "failure," while permitting grantors and practitioners to selectively cull reports for indicators of "success." Glossy, enthusiastic dissemination of selected findings can leave policymakers and the public with a skewed take on what evaluations actually report. Finally, the evaluators of a promising new reform are at the center of an important development. If they torpedo its significance, attention will likely shift elsewhere and they will marginalize themselves and the fruits of their work. In the end, there is every incentive for evaluators to suggest that the subject of their research is significant and promising, while allowing that much work remains and that future efforts will require continued observation and analysis.

Promisingly, the increasing availability of student achievement data and the effort to devise established standards for educational evidence hold the possibility of altering the political economy of evaluation in constructive ways. The transparency of achievement results makes it easier for skeptics to assess the effects of initiatives and allows disinterested parties to more readily assess advertised benefits. Efforts to establish clear standards for what constitutes permissible evidence will help ensure that evaluations are judged by consistent rules and reduce the wiggle room that can permit program supporters to spin results in the most favorable light. Only time will tell whether these trends will actually reshape the political economy of evaluation or whether donors, educators, researchers, and entrepreneurs will themselves devise new safeguards.

The Lure of Geniality

Philanthropists give to K–12 education for the best of reasons: to be good citizens and give our children a more promising future. The last thing many givers want is for these efforts to provoke controversy. In fact, Marquette University professor and former superintendent Howard Fuller has noted that many major donors insist on collaboration and consensus, a recipe for what Fuller terms "illusionary change."[8] The frequent result is that these donors have traditionally deferred to the sensibilities of those invested in the status quo. Unsurprisingly, most have favored conventional experts and consensual solutions, while shying away from structural reforms that challenge established arrangements regarding hiring, evaluation, compensation, management practice, and school choice.

Foundations that publicly embrace structural reforms like charter schooling, school choice, test-based accountability, performance-based compensation, or the recruitment of nontraditional leaders can raise eyebrows among teachers unions and established education groups. Unless grantors and grantees carefully accommodate concerns and play down the radicality of their activities, they can find themselves on the firing line. Bryan Hassel and Amy Way document how this plays out in the case of giving to choice-based education, where most funders explicitly reject the notion that they are seeking to make education "competitive." Similarly, Wendy Hassett and Dan Katzir explain how The Broad Foundation has carefully tended its relations with school districts to avoid conflicts that might result from its support for charter schooling or nontraditional superintendents.

Faced with the possibility that they will be assaulted for their civic efforts, it is easy for donors to soft-pedal the larger implications of the initiatives they are backing and to give in conventional, inconspicuous, educator-directed ways that do not provoke criticism. This reality puts another spin on the gentle treatment that foundations receive, discussed in the introduction to this volume. The reality is often an amiable gentleman's agreement—akin to the famous "Horace's Compromise" once depicted by Ted Sizer—in which foundations agree not to push too hard and the educational establishment agrees not to find fault.

The result is what Robin Pasquarella, president and CEO of the Seattle Alliance for Education, has called "Band-Aid giving." Referring to donors who seek to patch structural problems by supporting highly touted new programs or making feel-good contributions, Pasquarella has observed, "They're random acts of kindness. There's nothing wrong with that. . . . It just doesn't change anything." Sometimes it can be worse than that. At times, these Band-

Aids can sap energy from more fundamental efforts to refashion schooling, allow policymakers and district officials to hold off on tough-minded measures, or undermine coherence and focus.[9]

Mobilizing districtwide reform or pursuing structural change requires foundations to be more accepting of conflict and criticism than has been the historic norm. Reform ambition on the scale of the Annenberg Challenge or the Gates Foundation's high school initiative simply cannot be brought to fruition through consensus. Change on that scale requires overturning too many comfortable arrangements and angering too many constituencies. As Harvard University public policy professor Ronald Heifetz, author of *Leadership Without Easy Answers*, and his colleagues have observed, "For foundations [to assert public leadership] they must become accustomed to setbacks, uncomfortable public pressures, and a time frame that tries the patience of both foundation executives and stakeholders. What's required is leadership that views controversy and conflict as allies rather than obstacles in achieving reform."[10]

Donors that take bold steps in areas where school districts are ill equipped or not inclined to lead and where caution stays the hand of public officials deserve to be lauded (and, of course, scrutinized). However, in the end, the lessons these grantors take from these initiatives, how they tout them, and whether they are willing to forthrightly pose these initiatives as challenges to the status quo may matter more than the results of pilot programs themselves.

The philanthropic community is in the midst of a slow, awkward evolution from the earnest efforts epitomized by the Annenberg Challenge to a savvier, more politically aware approach. As Raymond Domanico, author of a Fordham Foundation study of the Annenberg Challenge effort in New York, concluded, "This was a non-confrontational approach to reform. The Annenberg Challenge was not set up to challenge the status quo; rather it relied upon much the same set of relationships and processes that had yielded the status quo in large public school systems."[11] Today's donors have struck out on a different course, still seeking to avoid confrontation but intent on building outside as well as inside traditional school systems. How successfully they will negotiate that balance remains to be seen.

Pipelines vs. Programs

Donors have a continual choice between supporting "programs" or supporting "pipelines." Programs, which are far more common, are ventures that directly involve a limited population of children and educators. Pipelines, on the other hand, primarily seek to attract new talent to education, keep those individuals engaged, or create new opportunities for talented practitioners to advance and influence the profession. Pipeline ventures break down barriers, open doors, and create opportunities and flexibility. By seeking to alter the composition of the educational workforce, pipelines offer foundations a way to pursue a high-leverage strategy without seeking to directly alter public policy.

Pipeline initiatives, like Teach For America (TFA), the National Board for Professional Teaching Standards (NBPTS), Troops to Teachers, the New Teacher Project, and New Leaders for New Schools do not expect to reshape a teaching force of more than three million through their numbers alone. Rather, they aim to change the face of educational leadership, create new educational advocates and entrepreneurs, and remake the culture of teaching. Many of the benefits of these efforts will be felt downstream, when they have drawn talented teachers and principals, retained high performers, or seeded alumni across schools of education, school reform organizations, and state government. Pipeline ventures have an impact on children and schools less directly than do reading programs or computer labs, but they permit donors to give for a clear and potentially high-impact venture without explicitly engaging public policy.

Of course, as discussed above, foundation staff have traditionally preferred school programs and heralded educators to initiatives with a more indirect impact on children. Andrew Rotherham, Bryan Hassel, and Amy Way explain why most foundations give to individual schools while shying away from research and policy. Moreover, for the new givers, supporting identifiable programs and people readily complements their emphasis on demonstrable results. The fact that pipleine ventures like TFA or NBPTS have a tenuous and hard-to-demonstrate short-term impact on student achievement, coupled with the reality that many of the long-term benefits may manifest themselves outside the classroom, makes it is easy to underestimate the actual benefits. The challenge is that donors are disinclined to support pipeline programs, are unlikely to fully appreciate the potential benefits, and are embracing accountability frameworks that may reinforce these existing biases. Just as givers must become more sophisticated in their thinking about "leverage," it is vital that they fully appreciate the value of pipelines as well as programs.

Balancing Performance and Patience

Finally, the risk of underestimating the long-term benefits of efforts like NBPTS raises an explicit challenge of its own. The new focus on disciplined management strategies and measurable results in the near term is a healthy corrective for philanthropies that have too often leaped to support glitzy programs or the latest fad. However, a laudable focus on performance metrics, like math and reading achievement gains, can morph into an excessive and exclusive fascination with short-term outcomes. That said, the kinds of lapses evident during the technology boom and bust of the late 1990s remind us of the dangers of placing too great an emphasis on near-term, visible results and insufficient weight on investing with patience. Jane Hannaway and Kendra Bischoff's chapter describes how philanthropic investments in Teach For America and the National Board for Professional Teaching Standards—whatever their near-term effects on student achievement—have profoundly reshaped the way America tackles the teacher-quality challenge. Scholars have been able to identify only a limited direct impact of either TFA or NBPTS on student learning, but the impact these programs have had on the educational workforce, state policy, public debate, and distinct initiatives have been profound.

Leslie Lenkowsky relates a historic parallel when he points out that Carnegie Corporation's support for Gunnar Myrdal's research on the education of black children was regarded by the foundation as a failed grant during the 1940s. It was only later, when Myrdal's work proved seminal in changing educated opinion and affecting judicial rulings on school segregation, that its value was clear.

There is a healthy tension for grantors: attend to outcomes but balance this concern for accountability with appreciation for the power of ambitious strategies that may not demonstrate near-term effects. In addressing this tension, grantors need to measure progress using a broad array of appropriate metrics—not merely test scores or graduation rates. In the case of Teach For America, for instance, in addition to direct effects on achievement, it would make sense to consider the quality of applicants, the effect on interest in teaching, the future pursuits of TFA alumni, and a bevy of similar measures. In the end, the sensible embrace of accountability must not become a stifling or dogmatic exercise in bean-counting.

THE IMPORTANCE OF DEMOCRATIC SCRUTINY

High-leverage private giving intended to change public policy raises concerns that some private individuals may exert an unhealthy and disproportionate influence on democratic institutions. At the same time, a free society demands that private resources and commitment be the primary engine of social improvement. The key, ultimately, is to encourage civic engagement while ensuring public accountability through transparency and scrutiny.

Absent such scrutiny, calls for more formal or aggressive federal regulation have mounted. In 2005, for instance, the senior Republican and Democratic members of the Senate Finance Committee promised to introduce legislation designed to regulate the tax-exempt sector. A series of congressional hearings in 2004 and 2005 investigated tax-exempt giving. Increased federal data collection could make a great deal of sense, especially if the journalistic and scholarly communities fail to provide meaningful scrutiny of philanthropic giving in education. After all, tax-exempt status is a public policy privilege bestowed on givers. Abuses and improprieties by tax-exempt foundations obviously call for appropriate federal action.

It would be regrettable, however, if these deliberations were regarded as an opportunity to promote a more intrusive role for Congress or the executive branch. Such measures would strike at the openness and flexibility of the American system, and the attendant ability of individuals to find patrons for new and better ideas—all in a dubious attempt to eliminate the inevitable unruly dissonance that ensues. After all, so long as we disagree on how to improve our schools, we are going to disagree on what sensible remedies or giving will look like. The goal—for educators, policymakers, or philanthropists—should not necessarily be more "rational" giving, but more considered giving. Philanthropists should pursue giving that increases the flow of talented and entrepreneurial people into education, demonstrates the promise of vigorous efforts to reinvent schooling, upends anachronistic arrangements, and makes the case for thoughtful policy reforms. That will require more attention to strategy, results, and accountability than has traditionally been the case, but it certainly does not call for a more active governmental involvement.

When, as Tom Loveless shows, philanthropies are encouraging public schools to adopt reforms that are at odds with public preference, it is indisputable that the public and its elected officials must be engaged in assessing those efforts, debating results, and questioning key assumptions. My hope is that this volume can serve as a small part of such an effort to promote transparency and encourage public scrutiny, rendering more formal proposals unnecessary.

Nearly two hundred years ago, Alexis de Tocqueville traveled the United States and famously declared, "Nothing, in my opinion, is more deserving of our attention than the intellectual and moral associations of America. The political and industrial associations of that country strike us forcibly; but the others elude our observation, or, if we discover them, we understand them imperfectly, because we have hardly ever seen anything of the kind."[12]

Gazing upon this cacophony of associations and private endeavors, de Tocqueville marveled,

> Americans of all ages, all conditions, all minds constantly unite. . . . Americans use associations to give fetes, to found seminaries, to build inns, to raise churches, to distribute books, to send missionaries to the antipodes; in this manner they create hospitals, prisons, schools. Finally, if it is a question of bringing to light a truth or developing sentiment with the support of a great example, they associate. Everywhere that, at the head of a new undertaking, you see the government in France and a great lord in England, count on it that you will perceive an association in the United States.

Ultimately, for de Tocqueville, the genius of America amounted to "the infinite art with which the inhabitants of the United States managed to fix a common goal to the efforts of many men and to get them to advance to it freely."[13] That "infinite art" of cooperation among free, independent-minded individuals and organizations has served our nation well for more than two centuries. As we strive to prepare a new generation of Americans for the challenges of the 21st century, let us keep faith with that proud heritage of voluntary and private endeavors.

CONCLUSION

American K–12 schooling is a wonder of statutes, regulations, legal guidelines, licenses, organizational routines, contractual provisions, and political pressures. In truth, the prohibitions and restrictions are so dense that most education reform is about tinkering with curricula, pedagogies, training, and management routines—creating a constant whir of activity but changing little of substance. Yet, it need not be this way. De Tocqueville reminds us of the essential role that philanthropists and entrepreneurs have so often played in American life. Reform-minded philanthropists have the independence and flexibility to pursue the changes that educators cannot. Because policymakers and officials have trouble imagining what they have never seen and are understandably hesitant to advocate for brand-new measures, foundations can play the critical roles of modeling programs that would otherwise remain unexplored and helping new, entrepreneurial individuals find their way into the world of schooling. Ultimately, however, the likelihood is that these programs and these talented individuals will be stranded like jalopies along a rutted road if the policy environment remains hostile and treacherous.

As Richard Colvin detailed, the new donors have learned the importance of focusing on the sustained, lasting results of their generosity. Bill Porter, executive director of Grantmakers for Education, has explained that high-impact givers are asking themselves, "Once your grant dollars are done, how do you sustain the change? Whose dollars are going to fill the vacuum? . . . The ultimate in sustainability is changing the policy. We can build some interesting teacher training programs, for instance, or we can try to change licensing programs for all teachers in the state." In a sector where even the most generous gifts are no match for the money routinely spent on outdated and outmoded systems, the "new" education philanthropy's influence will ultimately turn on its ability to change politics and policy.

One of America's great strengths is the ability to weave together the idealistic and the pragmatic in ways that serve our common interests. America's great successes have come not from central planning or intricate programs for social betterment, but from the noisy cacophony of free men trying, failing, cooperating, and competing. Philanthropy has always been an integral part of that pageant. As the industrious, the fortunate, and the compassionate give something back, they help ensure that unheralded individuals will have a chance to make their mark. Especially in the world of public schooling, where district bureaucracies, state statutes, and entrenched cultures can fiercely resist fundamental change, philanthropy, in all its scattered, untidy variety, has the chance to ensure that there is a competition of ideas.

Of course, the price of this diversity is fragmentation and a persistent fascination with the new, the different, and the glib. Recognizing these perils, a new generation of donors has sought to discipline their clients and their giving by managing more intensively and introducing a new emphasis on results and accountability. This development, if pursued sensibly and with care, may help funders avoid faddism without degrading the ability of philanthropists to nurture those tender but potentially vital shoots that might not otherwise find any sunlight in the old-growth forests of American schooling.

Whether the new emphasis on accountability plays out as desired, however, it is clear that we need to forge a new social compact between educational philanthropists and the public. The fact that donors are conducting self-evaluations and strategic assessments is laudable but not sufficient. The centrality of philanthropic efforts, the influence of select funders, and a growing commitment to high-leverage giving suggests the need for rigorous, public debate over objectives, strategies, and performance.

Such debate inevitably entails critiques that may seem incomplete, wrongheaded, or unfair—especially to foundations used to gentle treatment. Only this kind of scrutiny, however, will flag blind spots, wishful thinking, or ineffective spending. The point is not that skeptics are always right, but that most efforts to change policy or organizations enjoy mixed results. The value of skeptics is that they raise unpleasant issues. Whether or not the foundation personnel agree with such assessments, they are essential to forestalling the hubris and groupthink that may otherwise ensnare would-be reformers. Open, honest, and skeptical discussion is the linchpin in the democratic compact that welcomes philanthropic attempts to reform public institutions—but on the condition that all of us, as a community, observe, consider, and ultimately pass judgment on the handiwork of our benefactors.

Notes

Introduction

Frederick M. Hess

1. Loren Renz and Steven Lawrence, "Foundation Growth and Giving Estimates: 2004 Preview," *Foundation Today Series: 2005 Edition* (New York: The Foundation Center): 1.
2. Polling data as reported by The Gallup Organization in Karlyn Bowman, "Opinion Pulse," *The American Enterprise* (June 2005): 60–62.
3. James M. Ferris, *Foundations and Public Policymaking: Leveraging Philanthropic Dollars, Knowledge, and Networks* (Los Angeles: University of Southern California, Center on Philanthropy and Public Policy, 2003): 5.
4. Ellen Condliffe Lagemann, *Private Power for the Public Good: A History of the Carnegie Foundation for the Advancement of Teaching* (New York: College Board, 1999); Ellen Condliffe Lagemann, *The Politics of Knowledge: The Carnegie Corporation, Philanthropy, and Public Policy* (Chicago: University of Chicago Press, 1992); Gerald Jonas, *The Circuit Riders: Rockefeller Money and the Rise of Modern Science* (New York: W. W. Norton, 1989).
5. See, for example, Chester F. Finn Jr. and Kelly Amis, *Making It Count: A Guide to High-Impact Education Philanthropy* (Washington, DC: Thomas B. Fordham Foundation, 2001); Raymond Domanico, ed., *Can Philanthropy Fix Our Schools? Appraising Walter Annenberg's $500 Million Gift to Public Education* (Washington, DC: Thomas B. Fordham Foundation, 2000).
6. Kevin Bolduc, Phil Buchanan, and Judy Huang, *Listening to Grantees: What Nonprofits Value in Their Foundation Funders* (Cambridge, MA: Center for Effective Philanthropy, 2004); Grantmakers for Education, *Principles for Effective Education Grantmaking: Roadmap for Results in Education Philanthropy* (Portland, OR: Grantmakers for Education, 2005); Brian C. Anderson, *A Donor's Guide to School Choice* (Washington, DC: Philanthropy Roundtable, 2004).
7. "A Private Gift for Public Education," *New York Times*, December 21, 1993.
8. William Celis, "Annenberg to Give Education $500 Million over Five Years," *New York Times*, December 17, 1993; Frederick M. Hess, "Re-Tooling K–12 Giving," *Philanthropy* (September/October 2004); Chester E. Finn Jr. and Marci Kanstoroom, "Afterword: Lessons from the Annenberg Challenge," in *Can Philanthropy Fix Our Schools? Appraising Walter Annenberg's $500 Million Gift to Public Education*, ed. Raymond J. Domanico (Washington, DC: Thomas B. Fordham Foundation, 2000).
9. The Foundation Center, "Top 50 U.S. Foundations Awarding Grants for Elementary and Secondary Education, circa 1998," The Foundation Center's Statistical Information Services, 2000.

10. The Foundation Center, "Top 50 U.S. Foundations Awarding Grants for Elementary and Secondary Education, circa 2002," The Foundation Center's Statistical Information Services, 2004; The Foundation Center, "Top 50 Recipients of Foundation Grants for Elementary and Secondary Education, circa 2002," The Foundation Center's Statistical Information Services, 2004.
11. Michael T. Hartney, "Funders Leaving the Field," *Philanthropy* (September/October 2004): 33.
12. Frederick M. Hess, "Re-Tooling K–12 Giving," *Philanthropy* (September/October 2004): 27–33.
13. Bill Gates, National Governors Association/Achieve Summit, Prepared Remarks, February 26, 2005.
14. Alan Richard, "Miss. Offered $50 Million for Student Incentives," *Education Week*, March 30, 2005; Emily Wagster Pettus, "Former Netscape Chief Executive Offers $50 Million to Boost Mississippi Education," *New York Times*, March 23, 2005; Emily Wagster Pettus, "Barksdale Won't Fund Scholarships," *New York Times*, May 31, 2005.
15. Ronald A. Heifetz, John V. Kania, and Mark R. Kramer, "Leading Boldly: Foundations Can Move Past Traditional Approaches to Create Social Change Through Imaginative—and Even Controversial—Leadership," *Stanford Social Innovation Review* (Winter 2004): 21–31.
16. Penny Cockerell, "Computer Giants Join in $130 Million State Education Project," Associated Press, November 12, 2003.
17. Peggy Anderson, "Public Schools, Private Billions and the Best of Intentions," Associated Press, May 17, 2005. Available online at http://www.cnn.com/2005/EDUCATION/05/17/gates.on.education.ap/index.html
18. Frederick M. Hess, "Rethinking America's Schools: Frederick M. Hess Responds," *Philanthropy* (March/April 2005): 23–24.
19. Peggy Anderson, "Public Schools, Private Billions and the Best of Intentions," Associated Press, May 17, 2005. Available online at http://www.cnn.com/2005/EDUCATION/05/17/gates.on.education.ap/index.html
20. Kevin Bolduc, Phil Buchanan, and Judy Huang, *Listening to Grantees: What Nonprofits Value in Their Foundation Funders* (Cambridge, MA: Center for Effective Philanthropy, 2004): 6.

Chapter 1
A New Generation of Philanthropists and Their Great Ambitions

Richard Lee Colvin

1. Bill Gates, "What's Wrong with American High Schools," *Los Angeles Times*, March 1, 2005.
2. Michael Bailin, "Institution and Field Building at The Edna McConnell Clark Foundation," *Venture Philanthropy 2001: The Changing Landscape*. Retrieved April 2, 2005, from www.venturepp.org
3. Denise Jarrett Weeks, "Collected Wisdom," *Northwest Education Magazine*. Retrieved April 2, 2005, from http://www.nwrel.org/nwedu/09-02/overview.asp

4. The Future of Philanthropy Project, "U.S. Philanthropy by the Numbers." Retrieved April 2, 2005, from http://www.futureofphilanthropy.org

5. *The Broad Foundations: The First Thirty Years, 1974–2004* (Los Angeles: The Broad Foundation, 2004).

6. Laura Hipp, "Barksdale Pledges $50M for Students," *Clarion-Ledger*, March 23, 2005.

7. Michael T. Hartney, "A Powerhouse Charter-Funder Aims for the Next Level," *Philanthropy* (September/October 2004). Retrieved from http://www.philanthropyroundtable.org/magazines/2004/SeptOct/Powerhouse.htm

8. The Foundation Center, "Distribution of Foundation Grants by Subject Categories, circa 2002." Retrieved April 2, 2005, from http://fdncenter.org/fc_stats/pdf/04_fund_sub/2002/10_02.pdf

9. The Foundation Center, various tables. Retrieved April 2, 2005, from http://fdncenter.org/fc_stats/gs_subject.html

10. *Lessons and Reflections on Public School Reform* (Radnor, PA: The Annenberg Foundation, 2002). Retrieved April 2, 2005, from http://www.annenbergfoundation.org/other/other_show.htm?doc_id=212527

11. *Lessons and Reflections on Public School Reform* (Radnor, PA: The Annenberg Foundation, 2002). Retrieved April 2, 2005, from http://www.annenbergfoundation.org/other/other_show.htm?doc_id=212527

12. "Vartan Gregorian Responds on Behalf of the Annenberg Challenge," *Philanthropy* (March/April, 2005). Retrieved from http://www.philanthropyroundtable.org/magazines/2005/marapr/coverstory.htm

13. "Vartan Gregorian Responds on Behalf of the Annenberg Challenge," *Philanthropy* (March/April, 2005). Retrieved from http://www.philanthropyroundtable.org/magazines/2005/marapr/coverstory.htm

14. Becky A. Smerdon, American Institutes for Research, presentation to the 2005 Hechinger Institute-AERA Research Symposium, April 11, 2005, Montreal, Canada.

15. The Foundation Center, various tables. Retrieved April 2, 2005, from http://fdncenter.org/fc_stats/gs_subject.html

16. Ford Foundation, "A Foundation Goes to School: The Ford Foundation Comprehensive School Improvement Program, 1960–1970" (New York: Ford Foundation, 1972): 40.

Chapter 2
Buckets into the Sea: Why Philanthropy Isn't Changing Schools, and How It Could

Jay P. Greene

1. I actually examined the 31 largest foundations, according to The Foundation Center, but excluded The Wallace Foundation because I could not find any education grants in their 2002 990 filing. All of their grants appeared to support arts programs, not K–12 education. Recent information from Amy Way, an author in this volume, suggests that the difficulty in locating education grants from The Wallace Foundation may be due to a change in the foundation's name. Exclusion or inclusion of The Wallace Foundation would not substantively change the results.

2. The 2002 990 forms were the most recent ones generally available for foundations on the GuideStar website (http://www.guidestar.org/search/). The filing used for The Walton Family Foundation was for 2003 because it was available electronically and could be coded more easily. Using the 2002 filing for that foundation would not substantially change the results.

3. My coding of grants is necessarily imperfect. Not all organizations provide sufficient information to know the exact purpose of each grant, so coding requires drawing fine lines and making judgment calls. While there may be a fair chance of error in the coding of any particular grant, the overall findings are very unlikely to be affected by these individual errors.

4. *Digest of Education Statistics, 2003*, Table 166 (Washington, DC: National Center for Education Statistics, 2004). Retrieved February 25, 2005, from http://nces.ed.gov/programs/digest/d03/tables/dt166.asp

5. *Digest of Education Statistics, 2003*, Table 37 (Washington, DC: National Center for Education Statistics, 2004). Retrieved on February 25, 2005, from http://nces.ed.gov/programs/digest/d03/tables/dt037.asp

6. *Top 50 U.S. Foundations Awarding Grants for Elementary and Secondary Education, circa 2002* (Washington, DC: The Foundation Center, 2004). Retrieved February 25, 2005, from http://fdncenter.org/fc_stats/pdf/04_fund_sub/2002/50_found_sub/f_sub_b20_02.pdf

7. *Foundation Giving Trends, 2003*, Table 12 (Washington, DC: The Foundation Center, 2004).

8. "The Forbes 400: The Richest in America," *Forbes*, September 2002.

9. *Top 100 Foundations by Asset Size* (Washington, DC: The Foundation Center, 2005). Retrieved February 25, 2005, from http://fdncenter.org/research/trends_analysis/top100assets.html

10. Greg Winter, "In the Schools: Those Bake Sales Add Up, to $9 Billion or So," *New York Times*, November 15, 2004.

11. *Total GDP 2003* (Washington, DC: World Bank, 2005). Retrieved February 25, 2005, from http://www.worldbank.org/data/databytopic/GDP.pdf

Chapter 3
The "Best Uses" of Philanthropy for Reform

Leslie Lenkowsky

Emily Spencer assisted with the original version of this chapter, which was prepared for the Thomas B. Fordham Foundation.

1. *Giving USA 2005* (Glenview, IL: Giving USA Foundation, with the Center on Philanthropy at Indiana University, 2005): 20; Josefina Atienza and Jennie Altman, *Foundation Giving Trends: Update on Funding Priorities* (New York: The Foundation Center, 2005): 4.

2. Josefina Atienza and Jennie Altman, *Foundation Giving Trends: Update on Funding Priorities* (New York: The Foundation Center, 2005): 8.

3. The phrase is Andrew Carnegie's. He estimated that most of the gifts made at the time he wrote (1889) were not made well. See Andrew Carnegie, "The Gospel of Wealth," in

The Gospel of Wealth and Other Essays by Andrew Carnegie, ed. Edward C. Kirkland (Cambridge, MA: Harvard University Press, 1962).

4. Robert Bremner, *American Philanthropy*, 2nd ed. (Chicago: Chicago University Press, 1988): 7.

5. Lloyd P. Jorgensen, *The State and the Non-Public School: 1825–1925* (Columbia, MO: University of Missouri Press, 1987): 5.

6. Sheldon S. Cohen, *A History of Colonial Education: 1607–1776* (New York: John Wiley & Sons, 1974): 157.

7. Lawrence A. Cremin, *American Education: The Colonial Experience: 1607–1783* (New York: Harper & Row, 1970): 178.

8. Cremin, *American Education,* p. 177.

9. Cremin, *American Education,* p. 180.

10. Cotton Mather, "Essays to Do Good," in *Making the Nonprofit Sector in the United States: A Reader*, ed. David Hammack (Bloomington, IN: Indiana University Press, 1998): 59.

11. Cremin, *American Education,* p. 342.

12. Lloyd P. Jorgensen, *The State and the Non-Public School: 1825–1925* (Columbia, MO: University of Missouri Press, 1987): 8.

13. Eric Anderson and Alfred A. Moss Jr., *Dangerous Donations: Northern Philanthropy and Southern Black Education, 1902–1930* (Columbia, MO: University of Missouri Press, 1999): 4.

14. Anderson and Moss, *Dangerous Donations,* p. 5.

15. Barry Karl and Stanley Katz, "Foundations and Ruling Class Elites," *Daedalus* 116 (1987).

16. Ellen Condliffe Lagemann, *The Politics of Knowledge: The Carnegie Corporation, Philanthropy and Public Policy* (Middletown, CT: Wesleyan University Press, 1989): 123–146.

17. Diane Ravitch, *The Great School Wars: New York City, 1805–1973* (New York: Basic Books, 1974): 35.

18. Ravitch, *The Great School Wars,* p. 63; Timothy Walch, *Parish School: American Catholic Parochial Education from Colonial Times to the Present* (New York: Crossroad Publishing, 1996): 42.

19. Mary J. Oates, *The Catholic Philanthropic Tradition in America* (Bloomington, IN: Indiana University Press, 1995): 153.

20. 268 U.S. 510 (1925).

21. Diane Ravitch, *Left Back: A Century of Failed School Reforms* (New York: Simon & Schuster, 2000): 174.

22. Robert J. Havighurst, "Foundations and Public Education in the Twentieth Century," in *Private Philanthropy and Public Elementary and Secondary Education: Proceedings of the Rockefeller Archive Center Conference held on June 8, 1979,* ed. Gerald Benjamin (New York: Rockefeller Archive Center, 1980): 9.

23. Ravitch, *Left Back,* p. 186.

24. Diane Ravitch, *The Troubled Crusade: American Education, 1945–1980* (New York: Basic Books 1983): 251.

25. According to data from the National Center for Education Statistics, approximately 5.3 million schoolchildren were enrolled in private elementary and secondary schools in 2001–02. Of these, 47.1 percent were in Catholic schools, 36 percent in schools operated by other religious denominations (Evangelical Lutherans, Seventh Day Adven-

tists, Southern Baptists, Jewish, Christian and others), and 16 percent attended nonsectarian schools. Stephen P. Broughman and Kathleen W. Pugh, *Characteristics of Private Schools in the United States: Results from the 2001–2002 Private School Universe Survey* (Washington, DC: U.S. Department of Education, National Center for Education Statistics, 2004): Table 1.

26. *Giving USA 2000* (Glenview, IL: Giving USA Foundation, with the Center on Philanthropy at Indiana University, 2000): 84.

27. The phrase is derived from the French *école normale,* or model school.

28. Edith Nye MacMullen, *In the Cause of True Education: Henry Barnard and Nineteenth-Century School Reform* (New Haven, CT: Yale University Press, 1991): 160.

29. Frederick M. Binder, *The Age of the Common School, 1830–1865* (New York: John Wiley & Sons, 1974): 81.

30. Paul H. Mattingly, *The Classless Profession: American Schoolmen in the Nineteenth Century* (New York: New York University Press, 1975): 214.

31. Mattingly, *The Classless Profession,* p. 93.

32. Mattingly, *The Classless Profession,* p. 73.

33. Cremin, *American Education,* pp. 169–171.

34. Patricia Albjerg Graham, *Community and Class in American Education, 1865–1918* (New York: John Wiley & Sons, 1974): 112.

35. Lagemann, *The Politics of Knowledge,* p. 86.

36. Raymond Fosdick, *The Story of the Rockefeller Foundation* (New York: Harper, 1952): 254.

37. Cf. James D. Koerner, *The Miseducation of American Teachers* (Boston: Houghton Mifflin, 1963). Koerner was president of the Council for Basic Education when he wrote this book, but shortly afterward became a program officer with the Alfred P. Sloan Foundation.

38. Arthur Bestor, *Educational Wastelands: The Retreat from Learning in Our Public Schools* (Urbana: University of Illinois Press, 1953): 231.

39. Bestor, *Educational Wastelands,* p. 138.

40. National Commission on Excellence in Education, *A Nation at Risk: The Imperative for Educational Reform* (Washington, DC: Government Printing Office, 1983): 30.

41. Thomas Toch, *In the Name of Excellence: The Struggle to Reform the Nation's Schools, Why It Is Failing, and What Should Be Done* (New York: Oxford University Press, 1991): 139.

42. Joel Spring, *The American School: 1642–1996,* 4th ed. (New York: McGraw-Hill Companies, 1997): 64.

43. Ravitch, *The Great School Wars,* p. 12.

44. Ravitch, *The Great School Wars,* p. 12.

45. Spring, *The American School,* p. 200.

46. Ellen Condliffe Lagemann, *Private Power for the Public Good: A History of the Carnegie Foundation for the Advancement of Teaching* (Middletown, CT: Wesleyan University Press, 1983): 95.

47. Lagemann, *Private Power for the Public Good,* p. 106.

48. Nicholas Lemann, *The Big Test: The Secret History of the American Meritocracy* (New York: Farrar, Straus and Giroux, 1999): 32.

49. John A. Valentine, *The College Board and the School Curriculum: A History of the College Board's Influence on the Substance and Standards of American Education, 1900–1980* (New York: College Entrance Examination Board, 1987): 86.

50. Lagemann, *Private Power for the Public Good,* p. 207.

51. Lagemann, *Private Power for the Public Good,* p. 191.

52. Lagemann, *Private Power for the Public Good,* p. 198.

53. Gilbert Sewall, *Necessary Lessons: Decline and Renewal in American Schools* (New York: Free Press, 1983): 32.

54. Joel Spring, *The Sorting Machine: National Education Policy since 1945* (New York: David McKay Company, 1976): 116.

55. Paul Woodring, *Investment in Education: An Historical Appraisal of the Fund for the Advancement of Education* (Boston: Little, Brown, 1970): 139.

56. Lagemann, *The Politics of Knowledge,* p. 231.

57. Spring, *The American School,* p. 329.

58. See Shalom M. Fisch and Rosemarie T. Truglio, eds., *"G" Is for Growing: Thirty Years of Research on Children and Sesame Street* (Mahwah, NJ: Lawrence Erlbaum Associates, 2001).

59. Paul Nachtigal, *A Foundation Goes to School: The Ford Foundation Comprehensive School Improvement Program, 1960–1970* (New York: Ford Foundation, 1972): 40.

60. National Commission on Excellence in Education, *A Nation at Risk,* p. 24.

61. Bremner, *American Philanthropy,* p. 45.

62. Jorgensen, *The State and the Non-Public School,* p. 13.

63. Bremner, *American Philanthropy,* p. 67.

64. Mann, quoted in Frederick M. Binder, *The Age of the Common School, 1830–1865* (New York: John Wiley & Sons, 1974): 49.

65. Jorgensen, *The State and the Non-Public School,* p. 23.

66. Ravitch, *The Great School Wars,* p. 21.

67. David C. Hammack and Stanton Wheeler, *Social Science in the Making: Essays on the Russell Sage Foundation, 1907–1972* (New York: Russell Sage Foundation, 1994): 12.

68. David Benjamin Jones, "Playground Association of America: A Thwarted Attempt at the Professionalism of Play Leaders" (Ph.D. diss., University of Oregon, 1989): 1.

69. Judith Sealander, *Private Wealth and Public Life* (Baltimore: Johns Hopkins University Press, 1997): 148.

70. George S. Bobinsky, *Carnegie Libraries: Their History and Impact on American Public Library Development* (Chicago: American Library Association, 1969): 15–16.

71. William W. Cutler III, *Parents and Schools: The 150-Year Struggle for Control in American Education* (Chicago: University of Chicago Press, 2000): 153.

72. Morris Isaiah Berger, *The Settlement, the Immigrant and the Public School: A Study of the Influence of the Settlement Movement and the New Migration upon Public Education: 1890–1924* (New York: Arno Press, 1980): 84–88.

73. Daniel C. Humphrey, "Teach Them Not to Be Poor: Philanthropy and New Haven School Reform in the 1960s" (Ph.D. diss., Teachers College, Columbia University, 1992): 205.

74. Ravitch, *The Great School Wars;* Martin Mayer, *The Teachers Strike* (New York: Perennial, 1969).

75. Peter Dobkin Hall, "A Historical Overview of the Private Nonprofit Sector," in *The Nonprofit Sector: A Research Handbook,* ed. Walter Powell (New Haven, CT: Yale University Press, 1987): 7.

76. See the "I Have a Dream" website for more information, http://www.ihad.org.

77. See the Children's Scholarship Fund website for more information, http://www.scholarshipfund.org.

78. Steven L. Schlossman, "Philanthropy and the Gospel of Child Development," in *Private Philanthropy and Public Elementary and Secondary Education: Proceedings of the Rockefeller Archive Center Conference held on June 8, 1979,* ed. Gerald Benjamin (New York: Rockefeller Archive Center, 1980): 23.

79. See the School Development Program website for more information, http://www.info. med.yale.edu/comer/about/overview.html. See also James P. Comer, Norris M. Haynes, and Edward T. Joyner, "The School Development Program," in *Rallying the Whole Village: The Comer Process for Reforming Education,* ed. James P. Comer, Norris M. Haynes, Edward T. Joyner, and Michael Ben-Avie (New York: Teachers College Press, 1996): 1–26.

80. See the "Perry Preschool Project," at the High/Scope Education Research Foundation's website, http://www.highscope.org/research/RESPER.HTM.

81. Bremner, *American Philanthropy,* pp. 60–61. See also Stephen O'Connor, *Orphan Trains: The Story of Charles Loring Brace and the Children He Saved and Failed* (Boston: Houghton Mifflin, 2001).

82. Robert D. Putnam, *Bowling Alone: The Collapse and Revival of American Community* (New York: Simon & Schuster, 2000): 386–387.

83. America's Promise: The Alliance for Youth, *Report to the Nation* (Alexandria, VA: America's Promise, 2000): 9.

84. Mark Dowie, *American Foundations: An Investigative History* (Cambridge, MA: MIT Press, 2001): 105–140.

85. Mark Greenberg and Michael C. Laracy, *Welfare Reform: Next Steps Offer New Opportunities,* Policy Paper No. 4 (Washington, DC: Neighborhood Funders Group, 2000): 8.

Chapter 4
How Program Officers at Education Philanthropies View Education

Tom Loveless

Appreciation is extended to Alice Henriques for research assistance and data collection, Public Agenda for allowing the use of their survey questions, and Steve Farkas for helpful advice in conceptualizing this project. Andrew Kelly and Rick Hess offered helpful advice on earlier drafts. Errors are the author's.

1. Steve Farkas and Jean Johnson, *Different Drummers* (New York: Public Agenda, 1997): 8.

2. Farkas and Johnson, *Different Drummers,* p. 15.

3. Farkas and Johnson, *Different Drummers,* p. 16.

4. Ford Foundation, "A Foundation Goes to School: The Ford Foundation Comprehensive School Improvement Program, 1960–1970" (New York: Ford Foundation, 1972); Edward J. Meade, "Recalling and Updating 'Philanthropy and Public Schools: One Foundation's Evolving Perspective,'" *Teachers College Record* 93, no. 3 (1992): 436–462; Bruno Manno and John Barry, "When Education Philanthropy Goes Awry," *Seven Studies in Education Philanthropy* (Washington, DC: Thomas B. Fordham Foundation, 2001).

5. Chester E. Finn Jr. and Marci Kanstoroom, *Can Philanthropy Fix Our Schools?* (New York: Thomas B. Fordham Foundation, 2000): 52.

6. Meg Sommerfeld, "Annenberg School Program Yields Millions, but Gets Mixed Results." Retrieved June 27, 2002, from http://philanthropy.com

7. Frederick M. Hess, "Re-Tooling K–12 Giving," *Philanthropy* (September/October 2004): 27.

8. Theodore E. Lobman, "Public Education Grantmaking Styles: More Money, More Vision, More Demands," *Teachers College Record* 93, no. 3 (1992): 382–402.

9. Milbrey W. McLaughlin, "The RAND Change Agent Study: Ten Years Later," in *Educational Policy Implementation,* ed. Allan R. Odden (Albany: State University of New York Press, 1991): 143–155; Tom Loveless, *The Tracking Wars* (Washington, DC: Brookings Institution Press, 1999).

10. Alfie Kohn, *The Schools Our Children Deserve* (Boston: Houghton Mifflin, 1999).

11. Howard Gardner, *The Disciplined Mind: What All Students Should Understand* (New York: Simon & Schuster, 1999).

12. E. D. Hirsch Jr., *The Schools We Need and Why We Don't Have Them* (New York: Doubleday, 1996).

13. Jean Johnson and Steve Farkas, *Getting By: What American Teenagers Really Think about Their Schools* (New York: Public Agenda, 1997).

14. Diane Ravitch, *The Troubled Crusade* (New York: Basic Books, 1983): 231.

15. Maisie McAdoo, "Buying School Reform," *Phi Delta Kappan* (January 1998): 364–369.

16. Wei Wei Cui, "Reducing Error in Mail Surveys," *Practical Assessment, Research & Evaluation* 8, no. 18 (2003); Joseph R. Hochstim, "A Critical Comparison of Three Strategies of Collecting Data from Households," *Journal of the American Statistical Association* (1967): 62, 976–987; Thomas W. Mangione, Ralph W. Hingson, and Jane Barrett, "Collecting Sensitive Data: A Comparison of Three Survey Strategies," *Sociological Methods and Research* 10, no. 3 (1982): 337–346; A. Walaker and Joseph D. Restuccia, "Obtaining Information on Patient Satisfaction with Hospital Care: Mail Versus Telephone," *Health Services Research* (1984): 19, 291–306; Edith de Leeuw, *Data Quality in Mail, Telephone and Face to Face Surveys* (Amsterdam: TT-Publikaties, 1992)

17. Cui, "Reducing Error in Mail Surveys"; Hochstim, "A Critical Comparison of Three Strategies of Collecting Data from Households," pp. 62, 976–987.

18. Farkas and Johnson, *Different Drummers*, p. 15.

19. Farkas and Johnson, *Different Drummers*, p. 29.

Chapter 5
Philanthropy and Urban School District Reform: Lessons from Charlotte, Houston, and San Diego

Lynn Jenkins and Donald R. McAdams

1. Center for Reform of School Systems, *We Are Going to Fix This! Charlotte's School Board Makes a Long-Term Commitment to Equity and Student Achievement* (Houston: Center for Reform of School Systems, unpublished case study, 2004).

2. Donald R. McAdams, *What School Boards Can Do: Reform Governance for Urban Schools* (New York: Teachers College Press, 2006).

3. Donald R. McAdams, *Fighting to Save Our Urban Schools . . . and Winning! Lessons from Houston* (New York: Teachers College Press, 2000); Donald R. McAdams, "Houston ISD: An Improving Accountability System to Support Whole Systems Change," in *Urban School District Accountability Systems,* ed. Donald R. McAdams et al. (Houston: Center for Reform of School Systems, 2003); Donald R. McAdams and Betsy Breier, *It Takes a*

City: Building a High Performance School District in Houston (Houston: Center for Reform of School Systems; unpublished case study prepared for The Broad Institute for School Boards, 2004).

4. American Institutes for Research, *Evaluation of the Blueprint for Student Success in San Diego City Schools* (Palo Alto: American Institutes for Research, 2003): Figure 1.1, pp. 1–5.

5. Frederick M. Hess, ed., *Urban School Reform: Lessons from San Diego* (Cambridge, MA: Harvard Education Press, 2005); Amy M. Hightower, *San Diego's Big Boom: District Bureaucracy Supports Culture of Learning* (Seattle: University of Washington, Center for the Study of Teaching and Policy, 2002); Christine Campbell, *San Diego City Schools: Breaking Eggs: Omelet or Scrambled?* (Houston: Center for Reform of School Systems, unpublished case study prepared for The Broad Institute for School Boards, 2002); Linda Darling-Hammond et al., *Building Instructional Quality: "Inside-Out" and "Outside-In" Perspectives on San Diego's School Reform* (Seattle: University of Washington, Center for the Study of Teaching and Policy, 2003).

6. The survey asked respondents to include only major gifts and grants designed to support improvements in teaching and learning, district operations, and other school reform initiatives, and to exclude gifts for construction or renovation of facilities, gifts in kind, and gifts to support student events (concerts, travel, etc.).

7. Southwest Educational Development Laboratory, *Philanthropic Support for Public Education in the Southwest Region* (Austin: SEDL, 2000).

8. Ford Foundation, *Request for Proposals: Collaborating for Educational Reform Initiative* (New York: Ford Foundation, 1997), as cited in Susan J. Bodlilly, Joan Chun, Gina Ikemoto, and Sue Stockly, *Challenges and Potential of a Collaborative Approach to Education Reform* (Washington, DC: RAND Education, 2004): xvii.

9. Bodlilly et al., *Challenges and Potential,* p. 65.

10. Interview with Margaret Carnes, managing director, Charlotte Advocates for Education, January 2005.

11. Interview with Deborah Antshel, executive director, Charlotte-Mecklenburg Public Schools Foundation/Office of Strategic Partnerships, January 2005.

12. Charlotte-Mecklenburg Schools, "BellSouth Foundation Makes the First Major Contribution to the Charlotte-Mecklenburg Public Schools Foundation," Press Release, 2004.

13. Kerry White, "Local Funds Playing Larger Roles in Reform," *Education Week*, May 26, 1999.

14. Interview with Michelle Pola, executive director, Houston A+ Challenge, January 2005. Additional information was gathered from the organization's website, www.houstonaplus.org.

15. The TLI is a 100-point index based on the Texas Assessment of Academic Skills, or TAAS, which was the state-mandated assessment during this period.

16. Pedro Reyes and Joy Phillips, *2002 Annenberg Evaluation Report [Year 3]: Lessons Learned on Urban School Reform* (Austin: University of Texas, 2002).

17. Reyes and Phillips, *2002 Annenberg Evaluation,* p. 3.

18. Bob Schwartz, president of Achieve, as quoted in Meg Sommerfield, "What Did the Money Buy? Critics Question the Effectiveness of Annenberg Grants for Education," *Chronicle of Philanthropy* 12, no. 14 (2000).

19. Holly Holland, *Whatever It Takes: Transforming American Schools, The Project GRAD Story* (New York: Teachers College Press, 2005): 3.

20. Project GRAD, *Working to Close the Achievement Gap* (Houston: Project GRAD, 2004).

21. Project GRAD costs, on average, about 5 to 7 percent on top of a district's annual per-student expenditure in the public schools where it operates. Information provided by Tina Breska-Medlin, director of development, Project GRAD Houston, January 2005.

22. Quoted in Project GRAD press release, "New Book Documents Project GRAD's Educational Initiatives in Houston," January 7, 2005.

23. Holland, *Whatever It Takes*, p. 5.

24. As quoted in Holland, *Whatever It Takes*, p. 11.

25. This evaluation process is described in a Project GRAD publication entitled *Working to Close the Academic Achievement Gap* (Houston: Project GRAD USA, 2004). Additional information is available on the MDRC website at www.mdrc.org.

26. Interview with Carol Hoey, assistant superintendent, Community Relations Department, Houston Independent School District, January 2005.

27. Interview with Dot Woodfin, director, Character Education Program, Houston Independent School District, January 2005.

28. The district uses a variety of reading assessments, including the Stanford Diagnostic Reading Test. At the time this case was written, it was in the process of selecting districtwide mathematics assessments.

29. Interview with Mary Hopper, chief academic officer, San Diego City Schools, February 2005.

30. In 2003, the district received an additional $6 million from the Hewlett Foundation and nearly $20 million from Gates and Carnegie, targeted to high school reforms. We do not examine these additional philanthropic efforts in this study, however, because they fall at the very end of our study period and because it is too early to evaluate either their implementation or their impact.

31. Chris Moran, "Report Card on Reform Just So-So," *San Diego Union-Tribune*, May 13, 2003.

32. Frederick M. Hess, "Lessons from San Diego," *The Education Gadfly*, April 28, 2005. A more detailed account of San Diego's successes and failures under the leadership of Alan Bersin can be found in Frederick M. Hess, ed., *Urban School Reform: Lessons from San Diego* (Cambridge, MA: Harvard Education Press, 2005).

33. Hess, "Lessons from San Diego."

34. Christine Campbell, *Philanthropic Due Diligence* (Seattle: University of Washington, Center on Reinventing Public Education, 2002).

35. Respondents were asked to include only major grants/gifts designed to support improvements in teaching and learning, district operations, and other school reform initiatives, and to exclude gifts for construction or renovation of facilities, gifts in kind, and gifts to support student events (concerts, travel, etc.).

Chapter 6
Philanthropy and Labor Market Reform

Jane Hannaway and Kendra Bischoff

1. Dennis R. Young, "Complementary, Supplementary, or Adversarial? A Theoretical and Historical Examination of Nonprofit-Government Relations in the United States," in *Nonprofits and Government: Collaboration and Conflict*, ed. Elizabeth Boris and C. Eugene

Steuerle (Washington, DC: Urban Institute Press, 1999); Elizabeth Boris and C. Eugene Steuerle, eds., *Nonprofits and Government: Collaboration and Conflict* (Washington, DC: Urban Institute Press, 1999).

2. *No City Left Behind* conference, Philadelphia, Pennsylvania, October 13–16, 2004.

3. Richard Murnane, *Impact of School Resources on the Learning of Inner City Children* (Cambridge, MA: Ballinger, 1975); David J. Armor, Patricia Conry-Oseguera, Millicent Cox, Niceima King, Lorraine McDonnell, Anthony Pascal, Edward Pauly, and Gail Zellman, *Analysis of the School Preferred Reading Program in Selected Los Angeles Minority Schools* (Santa Monica: Rand Corporation, 1976).

4. Daniel Goldhaber, Dominic J. Brewer, and Deborah Anderson, "A Three-Way Error Components Analysis of Educational Productivity," *Education Economics* 7, no. 3 (1999): 199–208; Eric A. Hanushek, John F. Kain, and Steven G. Rivkin, "Why Public Schools Lose Teachers," *Journal of Human Resources* 39, no. 2 (2004): 326–354; Ronald Ferguson, "Teachers' Perceptions and Expectations and the Black-White Test Score Gap," in *The Black-White Test Score Gap*, ed. C. Jencks and M. Phillips (Washington, DC: Brookings Institution Press, 1998); S. Paul Wright, Sandra Horn, and William Sanders, "Teachers and Classroom Heterogeneity: Their Effects on Educational Outcomes," *Journal of Personnel Evaluation in Education* 11, no. 1 (1997): 57–67; Steven G. Rivkin, Eric A. Hanushek, and John F. Kain, "Teachers, Schools, and Academic Achievement," *Econometrica* 73, no. 2 (March 2005): 417–458.

5. Rivkin, Hanushek, and Kain, "Teachers, Schools, and Academic Achievement," pp. 417–458.

6. Dale Ballou and Michael Podgursky, *Teacher Pay and Teacher Quality* (Kalamazoo, MI: W. E. Upjohn Institute, 1997); Drew H. Gitomer, Andrew S. Latham, and Robert Ziomek, *The Academic Quality of Prospective Teachers: The Impact of Admissions and Licensure Testing* (Princeton, NJ: Educational Testing Service and ACT, Inc., 1999).

7. Richard Ingersoll, "The Problem of Underqualified Teachers in American Secondary Schools," *Educational Researcher* 28, no. 2 (1999): 26–36.

8. In education, state certification refers to state licensing to teach. We distinguish that from national board certification, which is designed to certify that an individual possesses certain skills and knowledge.

9. Hamilton Lankford, Susanna Loeb, and James Wycoff, "Teacher Sorting and the Plight of Urban Schools: A Descriptive Analysis," *Educational Evaluation and Policy Analysis* 24, no. 1 (2002): 37–62.

10. Daniel Goldhaber and Emily Anthony, *Teacher Quality and Student Achievement* (ERIC Clearinghouse on Urban Education). (New York: Teachers College, Institute for Urban and Minority Education, 2003).

11. Eric A. Hanushek, "The Economics of Schooling: Production and Efficiency in Public Schools," *Journal of Economic Literature* 24, no. 3 (1986): 141–178.

12. Rob Greenwald, Larry Hedges, and Richard Laine, "The Effect of School Resources on Student Achievement," *Review of Education Research* 66, no. 3 (1996): 361–396.

13. Richard Murnane, *Impact of School Resources on the Learning of Inner City Children* (Cambridge, MA: Ballinger, 1975); Linda Darling-Hammond, "Teacher Quality and Student Achievement: A Review of State Policy and Evidence," *Education Policy Analysis Archives* 8, no. 1 (January 2000): Available online at http://epaa.asu.edu/epaa/v8n1/; Steven G. Rivkin, Eric A. Hanushek, and John F. Kain, "Teachers, Schools, and Academic Achieve-

ment," *Econometrica* 73, no. 2 (March 2005): 417–458.

14. Ronald F. Ferguson, "Paying for Public Education: New Evidence on How and Why Money Matters," *Harvard Journal on Legislation* 28 (Summer 1991): 465–498; Ronald F. Ferguson and Helen F. Ladd, "How and Why Money Matters: An Analysis of Alabama Schools," in *Holding Schools Accountable: Performance Based Reform in Education*, ed. Helen F. Ladd (Washington, DC: Brookings Institution Press, 1996); Robert P. Strauss and Elizabeth A. Sawyer, "Some New Evidence on Teacher and Student Competencies," *Economics of Education Review* 5, no. 1 (1986): 141–148; Robert P. Strauss and William B. Vogt, *It's What You Know, Not How You Learned to Teach It: Evidence from a Study of the Effects of Knowledge and Pedagogy on Student Achievement*, Paper presented at the annual meeting of the American Educational Finance Association, Cincinnati, Ohio, March 2001; Ronald G. Ehrenberg and Dominic J. Brewer, "Did Teachers' Verbal Ability and Race Matter in the 1960s? Coleman Revisited," *Economics of Education Review* 14, no. 1 (1995): 1–21; James S. Coleman, *Equality of Educational Opportunity* (Washington, DC: U.S. Government Printing Office, 1966).

15. Daniel Goldhaber and Dominic J. Brewer, "Evaluating the Effect of Teacher Degree Level on Educational Performance," in *Developments in School Finance 1996*, ed. J. William Fowler (Washington, DC: National Center for Education Statistics, 1997); David Monk and Jennifer King-Rice, "Multi-Level Teacher Resource Effects on Pupil Performance in Secondary Mathematics and Science: The Role of Teacher Subject Matter Preparation," in *Choices and Consequences: Contemporary Policy Issues in Education*, ed. Ronald Ehrenberg (Ithaca, NY: ILR Press, 1994).

16. David H. Monk, "Subject Area Preparation of Secondary Mathematics and Science Teachers and Student Achievement," *Economics of Education Review* 13, no. 2 (1994): 125–145.

17. Daniel Goldhaber and Dominic Brewer, "Does Teacher Certification Matter? High School Teacher Certification Status and Student Achievement," *Educational Evaluation and Policy Analysis* 22, no. 2 (2000): 129–145.

18. National Center for Education Statistics, "Teacher Quality: A Report on the Preparation and Qualifications of Public School Teachers" (Washington, DC: U.S. Department of Education, 1999).

19. Hamilton Lankford, Susanna Loeb, and James Wycoff, "Teacher Sorting and the Plight of Urban Schools: A Descriptive Analysis," *Educational Evaluation and Policy Analysis* 24, no. 1 (2002): 37–62. These findings are based on data from New York; analysis on data from Texas does not show the same pattern.

20. Eric A. Hanushek, John F. Kain, and Steven G. Rivkin, "Why Public Schools Lose Teachers," *Journal of Human Resources* 39, no. 2 (2004): 326–354.

21. William H. Baugh and Joe A. Stone, "Mobility and Wage Equilibration in the Educator Labor Market," *Economics of Education Review* 3 (Summer 1982): 253–274; Eric A. Hanushek and Richard R. Pace, "Who Chooses to Teach (and Why)?" *Economics of Education Review* 14 (June 1995): 107–117; Richard J. Murnane, Judith D. Singer, and John B. Willett, "The Influences of Salaries and Opportunity Costs on Teachers' Career Choices: Evidence from North Carolina," *Harvard Educational Review* 59 (1989): 325–346; R. Mark Gritz and Neil D. Theobold, "The Effects of School District Spending Priorities on Length of Stay in Teaching," *Journal of Human Resources* 31, no. 3 (1996): 477–512.

22. Lankford, Loeb, and Wycoff, "Teacher Sorting and the Plight of Urban Schools," pp. 37–62. However, a few exceptions are beginning to develop, for example, Los Angeles and New York City.

23. That said, there have been some recent notable attempts at reform. For example, Denver has instituted a merit pay plan, though critics argue it is a very watered-down model.

24. Carnegie Forum on Education and the Economy, *A Nation Prepared: Teachers for the 21st Century* (Washington, DC: Task Force on Teaching as a Profession, 1986).

25. The members included: Lewis M. Branscomb, chief scientist at IBM; Alan Campbell, vice president of ARA Services; Mary Futrell, president of NEA; John Gardner, founder of Common Cause and former secretary of HEW; Fred Hechinger, education editor for the *New York Times;* William Honig, California state superintendent; James B. Hunt, attorney and soon-elected governor of North Carolina; Vera Katz, Oregon's speaker of the house; Thomas Kean, governor of New Jersey; Judith Lanier, education dean, Michigan State University; Arturo Madrid, founding president of Tomas Rivera Center; Shirley Malcom, director of Science Education AAAS; Ruth Randall, Minnesota's commissioner of education; and Albert Shanker, president of AFT.

26. Carnegie Forum, *A Nation Prepared,* p. 2.

27. Carnegie Forum, *A Nation Prepared,* p. 3.

28. Carnegie Forum, *A Nation Prepared,* p. 117.

29. Carnegie Forum, *A Nation Prepared,* p. 118.

30. Observers give Mary Futrell great credit for keeping the NEA productively involved.

31. NBPTS Annual Reports.

32. Interestingly, funding for NBPTS was zeroed out in 1994 in Gingrich's "Contract with America" but reinserted in the budget in the Senate Appropriations Committee.

33. Source: NBPTS.

34. Terry Branstad is the former governor of Iowa and a member of the NBPTS board from 1989–92.

35. Daniel Goldhaber, David Perry, and Emily Anthony, "The National Board for Professional Teaching Standards (NBPTS) Process: Who Applies and What Factors Are Associated with NBPTS Certification," *Educational Evaluation and Policy Analysis* (Winter 2004); Andrew Rotherham, "Credit Where It's Due," *Education Week,* March 30, 2005, pp. 34, 48.

36. Daniel Goldhaber and Emily Anthony, *Can Teacher Quality Be Effectively Assessed?* (Unpublished working paper, The Urban Institute and University of Washington, 2004).

37. Wendy Kopp, *One Day, All Children* (New York: Public Affairs, 2001).

38. One of the original team members, who was in charge of designing TFA's summer training program, was Kim Smith, who was a cofounder and now serves as CEO of the New-Schools Venture Fund.

39. In lieu of a monetary contribution, Morgan Stanley offered Teach For America office space in their Manhattan building. This space served as the organization's headquarters for the next five years. TFA estimates that this donation, along with the use of their phones and office equipment, saved them $500,000 per year.

40. Union Carbide was the first corporation to show serious interest in Teach For America. In addition to contributing money, the corporation gave Kopp legal advice and pro-

vided advisors as she made the transition from a subsidiary of Princeton to a freestanding nonprofit organization.

41. The six original sites were: Rural Georgia, Los Angeles, New Orleans, New York City, Eastern North Carolina, and South Louisiana.

42. Linda Darling-Hammond, "Who Will Speak for the Children? How 'Teach For America' Hurts Urban Schools and Students," *Phi Delta Kappan* 76, no. 1 (1994): 21–34.

43. They required that TFA cut its budget by $1 million and that its teachers obtain the education grant award that all Americorps volunteers received at the completion of service. Kopp argued that her teachers were earning regular salaries, not stipends, and did not need the grant, but agreed to meet this requirement.

44. Margaret Raymond, Stephen Fletcher, and Javier Luque, *An Evaluation of Teacher Differences and Student Outcomes in Houston, Texas* (Stanford, CA: Center for Research on Education Outcomes, 2001).

45. Kane, Parsons, & Associates, *Principal Satisfaction with Teach For America Teachers* (June 2004). The survey included 515 telephone interviews with principals in all 20 TFA regions in the 2003–04 school year. The final data reflect a 52 percent representative sample of principals across TFA regions and school types.

46. Paul T. Decker, Daniel P. Mayer, and Steven Glazerman, *The Effects of Teach For America on Students: Findings from a National Evaluation* (Mathematica Policy Research, June 2004).

47. Cynthia Skinner, *Creating a Force of Leaders to Eliminate Educational Inequity: Teach For America's Study of Alumni Career Trajectories,* Paper presented at the annual meeting of the American Educational Research Association, Montreal, 2005, Teach For America.

Chapter 7
Choosing to Fund School Choice

Bryan C. Hassel and Amy Way

1. Jim Hopkins, "Wal-Mart Heirs Pour Riches into Education Reform," *USA Today*, March 11, 2004.

2. Foundation Center, "Top 50 Foundations Awarding Grants for Elementary and Secondary Education, circa 2002." Available online at http://www.fdncenter.org/fc_stats/

3. Foundation Center, "Top 50 Foundations Awarding Grants for Elementary and Secondary Education, circa 2002." Available online at http://www.fdncenter.org/fc_stats/

4. This category was a combination of Greene's categories for small public schools, vocational and alternative public schools, and public early college schools.

5. For this category, we analyzed Greene's list of research grants and identified those related to school choice.

6. Bryan Hassel and Alex Medler, *A New Bet for Better Schools?* (Washington, DC: The Philanthropy Roundtable, 2004).

7. Raymond Domanico et al., *Can Philanthropy Fix Our Schools? Appraising Walter Annenberg's $500 Million Gift to Public Education* (Washington, DC: Thomas B. Fordham Foundation, 2000). Available online at http://www.edexcellence.net/doc/annenberg.pdf

8. Brian C. Anderson, *A Donor's Guide to School Choice* (Washington, DC: The Philanthropy Roundtable, 2004).

10. Anderson, *A Donor's Guide to School Choice.*
11. Anderson, *A Donor's Guide to School Choice.*
12. Anderson, *A Donor's Guide to School Choice.*
13. Anderson, *A Donor's Guide to School Choice.*
14. Bryan Hassel, *Jumpstarting the Charter School Movement* (Washington, DC: The Philanthropy Roundtable, 2004).
15. E-mail correspondence with Joan Lange, Challenge Foundation
16. Children's Scholarship Fund, http://www.scholarshipfund.org/index.asp
17. Invent PA, Pennsylvania Department of Community and Economic Development website, http://www.inventpa.com/default.aspx?id=267
18. California Charter Schools Association, http://www.charterassociation.org/cnt_association_staff.asp
19. John E. Chubb and Terry M. Moe, *Politics, Markets, and America's Schools* (Washington, DC: Brookings Institution Press, 1990).
20. Harvard University, Program on Education Policy and Governance, http://www.ksg.harvard.edu/pepg/
21. Linda Shaw, "Gates' Donation Supports Charter Schools," *Seattle Times,* September 10, 2004. Available online at http://seattletimes.nwsource.com/html/education/2002031753_charter10m.html
22. Burt Hubbard, "$7 Million Was Twice What Candidates Raised for State Races," *Rocky Mountain News,* January 3, 2005.
23. EdVoice, http://www.edvoice.org/edvoice/ev_advisory_board.html
24. John J. Miller, *Strategic Investment in Ideas: How Two Foundations Reshaped America* (Washington, DC: The Philanthropy Roundtable, 2003).
25. John J. Miller, *Strategic Investment in Ideas: How Two Foundations Reshaped America* (Washington, DC: The Philanthropy Roundtable, 2003); Frederick M. Hess, *Revolution at the Margins: The Impact of Competition on Urban School Systems* (Washington, DC: Brookings Institution Press, 2002).
26. Christine W. Letts, William Ryan, and Allen Grossman, "Virtuous Capital: What Foundations Can Learn from Venture Capitalists," *Harvard Business Review* 75, no. 2 (March/April 1997).
27. Caroline Hendrie, "Leaders May Disband New Charter School Organization," *Education Week,* November 5, 2003. Available online at http://www.edweek.org/ew/articles/2003/11/05/10charter.h23.html; Caroline Hendrie, "New Group to Push For Charter Schools," *Education Week,* July 28, 2004. Available online at http://www.edweek.org/ew/ewstory.cfm?slug=43charter.h23
28. Caroline Hendrie, "Charter Schools: California Rivals," *Education Week,* September 10, 2003. Available online at http://www.edweek.org/ew/articles/2003/09/10/02charter.h23.html
29. American Institutes for Research and SRI International, *The National School District and Network Grants Program: Year 2 Evaluation Report* (Seattle: Bill & Melinda Gates Foundation, April 2004). Available online at http://www.gatesfoundation.org/Education/ResearchAndEvaluation/
30. Education Commission of the States publishes a 50-state summary of school choice provisions. See *School Choice State Laws: 50-State Profile* (Denver: Education Commission of the States). Available online at http://www.ecs.org

31. John Wirt, Susan Choy, Patrick Rooney, Stephen Provasnik, Anindita Sen, and Richard Tobin, *The Condition of Education 2004* (NCES 2004-077) (Washington, DC: U.S. Department of Education, National Center for Education Statistics, 2004), Indicator 25. Available online at http://nces.ed.gov/programs/coe/2004/section4/indicator25.asp

Chapter 8
Teaching Fishing or Giving Away Fish? Grantmaking for Research, Policy, and Advocacy

Andrew J. Rotherham

The author thanks Kate Blosveren for her invaluable research assistance.

Disclosure: During the past three years, the author has received philanthropic support for various projects from the following foundations: The Annie E. Casey Foundation, the Bill & Melinda Gates Foundation, The Broad Foundation, The Joyce Foundation, NewSchools Venture Fund, the Pisces Foundation, Smith Richardson Foundation, The Rodel Foundation, and The William and Flora Hewlett Foundation.

1. David Tyack and Larry Cuban, *Tinkering Toward Utopia* (Cambridge, MA: Harvard University Press, 1995).
2. Interview with Paul Hill, December 22, 2004.
3. Frederick M. Hess, "Retooling K–12 Giving," *Philanthropy* (September/October 2004). Hess estimates $1.2 based on the Foundation Center. Jay Greene, in this volume, estimates somewhat higher.
4. Because this chapter represents a very baseline analysis, it uses a broad definition of research and policy development that encompasses original and applied research as well as policy development and policy advocacy. Though there are obviously essential distinctions between these different types of work, all are ultimately intended to influence the public policymaking process either directly or indirectly.
5. Tyack and Cuban, *Tinkering Toward Utopia*.
6. Eric Patashnik, "After the Public Interest Prevails: The Political Sustainability of Policy Reform," *Governance* (April 2003).
7. Frank R. Baumgartner and Bryan D. Jones, *Agendas and Instability in American Politics* (Chicago: University of Chicago Press, 1993).
8. James Pierson and Rebecca Rimel, "Foundations and Public Policy," *Philanthropy* (January/February 2005).
9. Paul T. Hill, *Education Philanthropy for the 21st Century* (Washington, DC: Thomas B. Fordham Foundation, 2001).
10. Interview with Bruno Manno, January 4, 2005.
11. Interview with Chester E. Finn Jr., February 7, 2005.
12. Organizational Research Services, *Theory of Change: A Practical Tool for Action, Results and Learning* (Baltimore: The Annie E. Casey Foundation, 2004).
13. See Jay Greene, "Buckets into the Sea: Why Philanthropy Isn't Changing Schools, and How It Could," in this volume.
14. Based on an author survey of the 51 largest grantmakers to elementary and secondary education.

15. Interview with Bill Porter, January 5, 2005.

16. Interview with Stephanie Saroki, February 6, 2005.

17. Interview with Chester E. Finn Jr., February 7, 2005.

18. Interview with Mike Kirst, January 4, 2005.

19. Frederick M. Hess, "Science and Nonscience: The Limits of Scientific Research," *The Education Gadfly*, February 17, 2005.

20. See Leslie Lenkowsky, "The 'Best Uses' of Philanthropy for Reform," in this volume.

21. Greene, "Buckets into the Sea."

22. Walton does support policy advocacy organizations like the Black Alliance for Educational Options. However, the primary thrust of their funding is direct support for schools and school choice options.

23. Interview with Gregory McGinity, January 4, 2005.

24. Interview with Daniel Fallon, December 30, 2004.

25. For a timeline of these events, see Whitney Garrison, "A Timeline of Congressional Oversight," *Philanthropy* (July/August 2004). Available online at http://www.philanthropy roundtable.org/magazines/2004/julyaugust/timelinejulyaugust.htm

26. For an overview of current issues see, for instance, Adam Meyerson, "Congress and Charitable Reform," *Philanthropy* (January/February 2005).

27. Interview with Sue Urahn, February 18, 2005.

28. Interview with Daniel Fallon, December 30, 2004.

29. Michael W. Kirst, Gail Meister, and Stephen R. Rowley, "Policy Issue Networks: Their Influence on State Policymaking," *Policy Studies Journal* (December 1984).

30. Richard Magat, *The Ford Foundation at Work: Philanthropic Choices, Methods, and Styles* (New York: Ford Foundation, 1979).

31. Interview with James A. Kelly, February 14, 2005.

32. James A. Kelly, *Looking Back, Moving Ahead: A Decade of School Finance Reform* (New York: Ford Foundation, 1980).

33. Kelly, *Looking Back, Moving Ahead.*

34. Magat, *The Ford Foundation at Work.*

35. The William and Flora Hewlett Foundation website. Retrieved February 9, 2005, from www.hewlett.org

36. Interview with Mike Smith, December 28, 2004.

37. Interview with Milton Friedman, May 27, 2005.

38. John J. Miller, "Strategic Investment in Ideas: How Two Foundations Reshaped America" (Washington, DC: The Philanthropy Roundtable, 2003).

39. Miller, "Strategic Investment in Ideas."

40. Interview with Joe Williams, March 20, 2005.

41. Interview with Joe Williams, March 20, 2005.

42. Andrew Rich, "War of Ideas: Why Mainstream and Liberal Foundations and the Think Tanks They Support Are Losing in the War of Ideas in American Politics," *Stanford Social Innovation Review* (Spring 2005).

43. The Washington, DC, program was passed by Congress, and the Colorado program was subsequently declared unconstitutional under that state's constitution.

44. Foundation Center and Gates Foundation figures.

45. Hess, "Retooling K–12 Giving." Hess estimates $1.2 million, based on the Foundation Center. Jay Greene, in this volume, estimates somewhat higher.

46. Barbara Dudley, "It's Time to Rein in the Power of the Biggest Donors," *Chronicle of Philanthropy* (October 21, 1999).
47. In addition, controversial issues overshadow other giving. For instance, while Walton is roundly criticized by voucher opponents for its giving to school choice organizations, it's little noted that, according to the most recent data in the Foundation Center's Foundation 1000, Walton also gave more than $5 million to historical societies and museums in 2002, including more than $1 million to the National Museum of Women in the Arts and almost a million dollars to the National Council of La Raza.
48. Foundation Center data and Spencer Foundation website, www.spencer.org. It is important to note that this refers to grants awarded in 2002–03. These grants may be paid out over a one- to five-year period. These figures do not include individual fellowship awards.
49. www.spencer.org
50. www.spencer.org
51. Interview with Kim Smith, January 21, 2005.
52. Interview with Daniel Fallon, December 30, 2004.

Chapter 10
The International Dimension

Stephen P. Heyneman

1. U.S. education does not seem to have succeeded in garnering philanthropic resources much better than has education internationally. Philanthropic assistance to education within the United States is only 25 percent of the total level of available philanthropy, and only about 4 percent of the total is directed to K–12 education. (See Jay Greene's chapter in this volume.)
2. Organization for Economic Cooperation and Development (OECD), "Philanthropic Foundations and Development Cooperation," *DAC Journal* 4, no. 3 (2003): Annex A, p. 3.
3. In many parts of the former Soviet Union, income received by schools and universities is taxed by the government, in essence treating them as profit-making businesses. Recipients of private charitable support—including schools, universities, and NGOs—are taxed on the bases of their grants unless individual exceptions can be negotiated with tax authorities. Because tax policy is so idiosyncratic, grantmaking in transition societies is deeply problematic.
4. Carol C. Adelman and Ronen Sebag, *International Grantmaking by U.S. Foundations* (Indianapolis: Hudson Institute, 2003).
5. OECD, "Philanthropic Foundations and Development Cooperation," p. 63.
6. The Organization for Economic Cooperation and Development is a data-gathering and policy-research organization serving its member states. Its member states include only the world's most economically advanced democracies. It makes no policy and has no authority to sanction. Nevertheless, its analytic papers and reports are widely read and are influential.
7. OECD, "Philanthropic Foundations and Development Cooperation," p. 16.

8. Andreas Schluter, Volker Then, and Peter Walkenhorst, *Foundations in Europe: Society, Management and Law* (Gutersloh, Germany: Bertelsmann Foundation Publishers, 2001): 52.

9. Carol C. Adelman and Ronen Sebag, *International Grantmaking by European Foundations* (Indianapolis: Hudson Institute, 2003): 59.

10. Britain is the exception, where virtually all foundations are grant making.

11. Schluter et al., *Foundations in Europe*, p. 85.

12. OECD, "Philanthropic Foundations and Development Cooperation," p. 66.

13. Stephen P. Heyneman, "From the Party/State to Multi-Ethnic Democracy: Education and Social Cohesion in the Europe and Central Asia Region," *Educational Evaluation and Policy Analysis* 21, no. 4 (July 2000): 345–361.

14. Gail Richardson, "Islamic Law and Zakat: Waqf Resources in Pakistan," in *Islam and Social Policy*, ed. Stephen P. Heyneman (Nashville: Vanderbilt University Press, 2004).

15. OECD, "Philanthropic Foundations and Development Cooperation," p. 37.

16. These figures do not include the projects of the Open Society Institute of the Soros Foundation. In spite of the legal registration of the parent foundation in the United States, the local foundations that disbursed the funds are registered within the 40 countries of the foundation's operations.

17. Curt Tarnoff and Larry Nowels, *Foreign Aid: An Introductory Overview of U.S. Programs and Policy* (Washington, DC: Congressional Research Service, 2004): 15.

18. Tarnoff and Nowels, *Foreign Aid*, p. 10.

19. Organization for Economic Cooperation and Development, *Education at a Glance: 2002* (Paris: OECD, 2002): 67.

20. The net flow of capital is the amount of capital that is shifted from one part of the world to another, minus the flow of capital in the opposite direction. For instance, the net flow of capital to developing countries is the gross amount less the amount developing countries pay for debt service.

21. The governance of most United Nations organizations is on the basis of one country/one vote. There are two exceptions: The ILO governance is through a "tripartite" arrangement in which power is shared equally between governments, labor unions, and private businesses. With the Multilateral Development Banks, governance is on the basis of equity-owned shares.

22. Global network programs include postgraduate scholarships and fellowships; regional network programs include assistance to the Central European University, the Higher Education Support Program, Street Law, English language, and K–12 policy reform.

23. Soros Foundation, *Annual Report* (New York: Soros Foundation, 2002).

24. Hafiz A. Akhand and Kanhaya L Gupta, *Foreign Aid in the Twenty-First Century* (Boston: Kluwer Academic, 2002).

25. Stephen P. Heyneman, *The Role of Textbooks in a Modern System of Education* (Geneva: UNESCO/International Bureau of Education, forthcoming).

26. Stephen P. Heyneman, "The History and Problems in the Making of Education Policy at the World Bank: 1960–2000," *International Journal of Education Development* 23 (2003): 315–337.

27. Heyneman, "The History and Problems in the Making of Education Policy at the World Bank," pp. 15–37.

28. Transition countries include those with centrally administered economies. These include not only the 15 republics of the former Soviet Union, but all the nations of

Central and Southern Europe, Algeria, Egypt, Mongolia, Vietnam, Laos, Kampuchea, Eritrea, Guinea-Bissau, Guinea-Conakry, the People's Republic of China, Cuba, Mozambique, Somalia, Syria, and Iraq.

29. Edward Berman, *The Influence of Carnegie, Ford, Rockefeller Foundations on American Foreign Policy* (Albany: State University of New York Press, 1983).

30. Heather MacDonald, *The Burden of Bad Ideas* (Chicago: University of Chicago Press, 2000).

31. Ellen Condliffe Lagemann, *Philanthropic Foundations: New Scholarship, New Possibilities* (Bloomington, IN: University of Indiana Press, 1999).

32. Warren Weaver, *U.S. Philanthropic Foundations: Their History, Structure, Management and Record* (New York: Harper and Row, 1967).

33. Jeffrey Puryear, *Thinking Politics: Intellectuals and Democracy in Chile, 1973–1988* (Baltimore: Johns Hopkins University Press, 1994)

34. Stephen P. Heyneman, "From the Party/State to Multi-Ethnic Democracy: Education and Social Cohesion in the Europe and Central Asia Region," *Educational Evaluation and Policy Analysis* 21, no. 4 (July 2000): 345–361; Stephen P. Heyneman, "Education, Social Cohesion and the Future Role of International Organizations," *Peabody Journal of Education* 78, no. 3 (2003): 25–38.

35. Heyneman, "Education, Social Cohesion and the Future Role of International Organizations," pp. 25–38.

36. Heyneman, "The History and Problems in the Making of Education Policy at the World Bank," pp. 315–337; Stephen P. Heyneman, "Foreign Aid to Education: Recent U.S. Initiatives: Background, Risks, and Prospects," *Peabody Journal of Education* 80, no. 1 (2005): 107–119.

37. Stephen P. Heyneman, "Suppose There Were a World Bank for American Education?" *Education Week*, December 8, 2004, pp. 31, 44.

Chapter 11
Strategic Giving and Public School Reform: Three Challenges

Peter Frumkin

1. Rockefeller was explicit in his desire to avoid charity. After an early meeting, one of the founding trustees wrote a memo for the board setting out key principles for The Rockefeller Foundation, the first of which was "Individual charity and relief are excluded" and the last of which was "As between objects which are of an immediately remedial or alleviatory nature, such as asylums for the orphan, blind, or cripples, and those which go to the root of individual or social ill-being and misery, the latter objects are to be preferred." Raymond Fosdick, *The Story of The Rockefeller Foundation* (New York: Harper, 1952): 22–23.

2. For a history of the Carnegie Corporation, see Ellen Condliffe Lagemann, *The Politics of Knowledge: The Carnegie Corporation, Philanthropy, and Public Policy* (Chicago: University of Chicago Press, 1989). For a history of its founder, see Peter Krass, *Carnegie* (New York: Wiley, 2002). Ronald Chernow, in *Titan: The Life of John D. Rockefeller* (New York: Vintage, 1999), provides a full account of Rockefeller's life and philanthropy.

3. A fuller discussion of these and other elements of philanthropic strategy can be found

in Peter Frumkin, *Strategic Giving: The Art and Science of Philanthropy* (Chicago: University of Chicago Press, forthcoming).

4. In Mark Dowie, *American Foundations: An Investigative History* (Cambridge, MA: MIT Press, 2001), a critic of foundations argues that institutional philanthropy has been too cautious and supportive of the status quo and that the opportunity that foundations have to alter the political order has largely been missed.

5. On the interplay of philanthropic experience and creativity, see Ruth Tebbets Brousseau, "Experienced Grant-makers at Work: When Creativity Comes into Play," in *Practice Matters: The Improving Philanthropy Project,* eds. Patricia Patrizi, Kay Sherwood, and Abby Spector (Working Paper Series) (New York: Foundation Center, 2003). Brousseau suggests that there are five "foundations of creativity" in philanthropy: the presence of a motivating belief and core values; a set of cognitive skills that could be deployed to do the work more effectively; a high level of interpersonal competence that facilitates good working relationships; an ability to cross boundaries and operate in different settings; and sense of journey and adventure.

6. For a history of attempts to measure philanthropic impact, see Peter Dobkin Hall, "A Historical Perspective on Evaluation in Foundations," in *Foundations and Evaluations,* eds. Marc T. Braverman, Norman A. Constantine, and Jana Kay Slater (San Francisco: Jossey-Bass, 2004): 27–50.

7. Estelle James, "How Nonprofits Grow: A Model," in *The Economics of Nonprofit Institutions: Studies in Structure and Policy,* ed. Susan Rose-Ackerman (New York: Oxford University Press, 1986): 185–195.

8. Tom David, "Reflection on Sustainability" (Reflections Paper Series) (Woodland Hills, CA: California Wellness Foundation, 2002). He notes that sustainability can be a complex goal in philanthropy: "Sometimes we [the California Wellness Foundation] continue to fund something because *we* believe it should be sustained rather than because there is genuine demand for it, perhaps to validate our initial judgment and subsequent investment of dollars. This is a particular risk of initiative-style grantmaking, where the source of the idea is the foundation itself. It can be difficult for a foundation to acknowledge failure when such efforts prove unsustainable."

9. For an interesting discussion of the role of endowments in higher education, see Henry A. Hansmann, "Why Do Universities Have Endowments?" *Journal of Legal Studies* 19, no. 1 (1990): 3–42.

10. Edward A. Martenson and Joel Podolny, "Strategic Issues for the Arts: The Impact of Foundations on the Strategic Outlook of Arts Organizations," *National Arts Stabilization Journal* 2, no. 3 (1999): 35–37.

11. I owe this conceptualization of scale to Christine W. Letts.

12. Jeffrey L. Bradach, in *Franchise Organizations* (Boston: Harvard Business School Press, 1998), gives a fine overview of the principles and practices of franchise organizations in the business world. While there are substantial difference between companies and nonprofits, some of the core issues transfer relatively directly.

13. Geraldo J. Espinoza, "Note on Buying a Franchise" (Boston: Harvard Business School Press, 1990).

14. Richard H. DeLeon, *Replication: A Strategy to Improve the Delivery of Education and Job Training Programs* (Philadelphia: Public/Private Ventures, 1990).

15. On the many challenges to successful program replication and for a typology of replication strategies, see Replication and Program Services, *Building from Strength: Replica-*

tion as a Strategy for Expanding Social Programs That Work (Philadelphia: Replication and Program Services, 1994). This study was based on a broad set of interviews with leaders across the nonprofit sector and found that replication "does not typically occur as a result of deliberate public policy, but more often as a private entrepreneurial effort that is in essence analogous to starting a new business. That is, replication happens because a champion (usually the creator and initial operator of the program prototype) finds financial backers, develops a plan to market his or her product, and takes it to new localities" (p. i). Interestingly, this study found that "more often than not, the program replicated did not have in hand research evidence that proved their effectiveness. Their attractiveness was more often based on a combination of widespread local need for the program to meet a particular problem or need; widespread recognition of the particular program being replicated because of aggressive marketing or media attention; and the champion's ambition, fundraising ability and marketing savvy" (p. i).

16. Barry D. Karl and Stanley N. Katz, "The American Philanthropic Foundation and the Public Sphere, 1890–1930," *Minerva* 19, no. 2 (1981): 236–270.

17. Peter Frumkin, "Fidelity in Philanthropy: Two Challenges to Community Foundations," *Nonprofit-Management & Leadership* 8, no. 1 (1997): 65–76; Ronald Chester, "Cy Pres: A Promise Unfulfilled," *Indiana Law Journal* 54, no. 407 (1979).

18. Christine W. Letts and William Ryan, "Filling the Performance Gap: High-Engagement Philanthropy—What Grantees Say about Power, Performance, and Money," *Stanford Social Innovation Review* 1, no. 1 (Spring 2003): 26–33. Letts and Ryan focus on high-engagement philanthropy, which they define as "a performance-centered strategy where alignment, reliable money and strategy coaching are used together to convert a grantmaking relationship into an accountability relationship that uses power to improve performance."

19. Peter Frumkin, "The Face of the New Philanthropy," *Responsive Community* 13, no. 3 (2000): 41–48.

20. Careful selection of grantees can reduce the need for heavy engagement later on. For a short list of what grantmakers need to consider before making a grant, see Elizabeth Lurie, "What Foundations Look for in Grant Proposals," *Philanthropy* 140 (1988).

21. The idea of a close and engaged relationship between funder and recipient has been likened to the typical relationship between a venture capitalist and the start-up firm receiving investment funds. See Christine W. Letts, William P. Ryan, and Allen Grossman, "Virtuous Capital: What Foundations Can Learn from Venture Capitalists," *Harvard Business Review* 75, no. 2 (1997): 36–44.

22. Reading and interpreting financial statements requires practice and skill. For an introductory guide, see Louise Stevens, "The Earnings Shift: The New Bottom Line Paradigm for the Arts Industry in a Market-Driven Era," *Journal of Arts Management, Law, and Society* 26, no. 2 (1996): 101–113.

23. Margaret J. Wyszomirski, "Philanthropy and Culture: Patterns, Context and Change," in *Philanthropy and the Nonprofit Sector in a Changing America*, ed. Charles T. Clotfelter and Thomas Ehrlich (Bloomington: Indiana University Press, 2001): 461–480.

24. Engagement is often constrained by institutional identity. A discussion of the way leaders and boards negotiate roles can be found in Center for Effective Philanthropy, *Foundation Governance: The CEO Viewpoint* (Cambridge, MA: Center for Effective Philanthropy, 2004). See also F. Warren McFarlan, "Working on Nonprofit Boards: Don't Assume the Shoe Fits," *Harvard Business Review* 77, no. 6 (November 1999): 65–80.

Conclusion

Frederick M. Hess

1. Frederick M. Hess, "Re-Tooling K–12 Giving," *Philanthropy* (September/October 2004): 27–33.
2. Chester E. Finn Jr. and Kelly Amis, *Making It Count: A Guide to High-Impact Education Philanthropy* (Washington, DC: Thomas B. Fordham Foundation, 2001); Brian C. Anderson, *A Donor's Guide to School Choice* (Washington, DC: The Philanthropy Roundtable, 2004); Grantmakers for Education, *Principles for Effective Education Grantmaking: Roadmap for Results in Education Philanthropy* (Portland, OR: Grantmakers for Education, 2005).
3. Warren Simmons, remarks presented at the American Enterprise Institute conference, "With the Best of Intentions," Washington, DC, April 25, 2005.
4. Arlene Ackerman, remarks presented at the American Enterprise Institute conference, "With the Best of Intentions," Washington, DC, April 25, 2005.
5. Stephanie Sanford, remarks presented at the American Enterprise Institute conference, "With the Best of Intentions," Washington, DC, April 25, 2005.
6. Hess, "Re-Tooling K–12 Giving," pp. 27–33.
7. Richard F. Elmore, "Getting to Scale with Good Educational Practice," *Harvard Educational Review* 66, no. 1 (Spring 1996): 1–26.
8. Howard Fuller, "With the Best of Intentions," remarks presented at the American Enterprise Institute conference, Washington, DC, April 25, 2005.
9. Hess, "Re-Tooling K–12 Giving," pp. 27–33.
10. Ronald A. Heifetz, John V. Kania, and Mark R. Kramer, "Leading Boldly: Foundations Can Move Past Traditional Approaches to Create Social Change through Imaginative—and Even Controversial—Leadership," *Stanford Social Innovation Review* (Winter 2004): 28.
11. Raymond Domanico, "Introduction: An Unprecedented Challenge," in *Can Philanthropy Fix Our Schools? Appraising Walter Annenberg's $500 Million Gift to Public Education,* ed. Raymond Domanico (Washington, DC: Thomas B. Fordham Foundation, 2000): 1.
12. Alexis de Tocqueville, *Democracy in America,* trans. Harvey C. Mansfield and Delba Winthrop (Chicago: University of Chicago Press, 2000): 180.
13. De Tocqueville, *Democracy in America,* p. 489.

About the Contributors

Kendra Bischoff is a research assistant in the Education Policy Center at the Urban Institute. Before moving to Washington, DC, she served as an Americorps volunteer in a New Mexico high school. She began a doctoral program in sociology in the fall of 2005.

Richard Lee Colvin is director of the Hechinger Institute on Education and the Media at Teachers College, Columbia University. Before joining the institute, he was a reporter for the *Los Angeles Times*, where he wrote principally about state and national education policy issues and won a number of national awards. He also wrote about education for two other newspapers and has contributed to a number of education publications. He was a 2000–01 Michigan Journalism Fellow at the University of Michigan.

Peter Frumkin is a professor of public affairs at the Lyndon B. Johnson School of Public Affairs, University of Texas at Austin, where he is director of the RGK Center for Philanthropy and Community Service. Before joining UT, he was an associate professor at Harvard's John F. Kennedy School of Government. Frumkin has lectured on philanthropy at numerous universities and served as a consultant to foundations and individual donors on strategy and evaluation. He is the author of *On Being Nonprofit* and has authored numerous articles on nonprofit management and all aspects of philanthropy. He is now completing a book, *Strategic Giving*, to be published next year.

Jay P. Greene is an endowed chair and head of the Department of Education Reform at the University of Arkansas. He is also a senior fellow at the Manhattan Institute for Policy Research. His book, *Education Myths*, was published in August 2005. He has also recently conducted research on high school graduation rates, school choice, social promotion, and special education.

Jane Hannaway, an organizational sociologist whose work focuses on the study of educational organizations, is director of the Education Policy Center at the Urban Institute. She has also been a senior researcher with the Consortium for Policy Research in Education and served on the faculty of Columbia, Princeton, and Stanford universities. She has authored or coauthored four books and numerous papers in education and management journals and has twice served as vice president of the American Educational Research Association.

Bryan C. Hassel directs Public Impact, a North Carolina–based education policy and management consulting firm. He consults with foundations, nonprofits, and government agencies on improvement methods for K–12 education. His recent efforts have focused on helping philanthropists invest strategically in charter schooling and on authoring the Philanthropy Roundtable's *Jumpstarting the Charter School Movement*. He is author of *The Charter School Challenge: Avoiding the Pitfalls, Fulfilling the Promise*, coauthor of *Picky Parent Guide: Choose Your Child's School with Confidence, the Elementary Years, K–6*, and coeditor of *Learning from School Choice*.

Wendy Hassett is a policy analyst at The Broad Foundation. She has formerly served as development coordinator at George Washington University, manager of operations at Voter.com, and education coordinator in the White House Fellows Office.

Frederick M. Hess is director of education policy studies at the American Enterprise Institute (AEI) and executive editor of *Education Next*. His books include *Common Sense School Reform, Leaving No Child Behind?, A Qualified Teacher in Every Classroom?, Revolution at the Margins, Spinning Wheels, Bringing the Social Sciences Alive*, and *Urban School Reform*. His work has appeared in scholarly and popular publications, including *Teachers College Record, Phi Delta Kappan, Social Science Quarterly, Philanthropy, Urban Affairs Review*, and *Education Week*. He serves on the review board for The Broad Prize in Urban Education and the research advisory board for the National Center for Educational Accountability. Before joining AEI, he was a public high school teacher and a professor of education and politics at the University of Virginia.

Stephen P. Heyneman worked at the World Bank for 22 years. His numerous roles included researching education quality and design policies, managing external training for worldwide senior officials in education policy, and being responsible for lending strategy, first for the Middle East and North Africa and later for Europe and Central Asia. In 1998, he was appointed vice president in charge of international operations of an education consultant firm in Alexandria, Virginia. Heyneman was appointed professor of international education policy at Vanderbilt University in Nashville in 2000.

Lynn Jenkins is director of research for the Center for Reform of School Systems in Houston. She previously worked as a freelance writer and researcher on a wide range of education policy, research, and assessment projects, and as a researcher and writer at the Carnegie Foundation for the Advancement of Teaching. Jenkins also directed reporting and writing assessment activities for the National Assessment of Educational Progress and reporting activities for the National Adult Literacy Survey projects at Educational Testing Service in Princeton, New Jersey. She is the author and coauthor of numerous reports based on educational assessments and research.

Dan Katzir, managing director at The Broad Foundation, has worked with numerous school districts, universities, corporations, and community organizations to improve leadership in urban K–12 schools. He is former executive director of the UCLA School Management Program, a university-based nonprofit school leadership initiative. Katzir was previously the founding regional director in Los Angeles for Sylvan Learning Systems, chief operating officer for Teach For America, and a consultant with Bain & Company, an international management consulting firm.

Leslie Lenkowsky rejoined the faculty of Indiana University as professor of public affairs and philanthropic studies and director of graduate programs for the Center on Philanthropy after stepping down in 2004 as chief executive officer of the Corporation for National and Community Service, the entity that administers Americorps, Learn and Serve America, and the National Senior Service Corps. Before joining the George W. Bush administration, Lenkowsky served as a director of the corporation, appointed by President Bill Clinton. He also has served as president of the Hudson Institute and of the Institute for Educational Affairs, as deputy director of the U.S. Information Agency, and as research director at the Smith Richardson Foundation. He is a fellow at the National Academy of Public Administration.

Tom Loveless is director of the Brown Center on Education Policy and senior fellow in governance studies at the Brookings Institution. His research focuses on education policy and the politics of education reform. He is author of *The Tracking Wars*, coeditor of *Stability and Change in American Education* and *Bridging the Achievement Gap*, and editor of *The Great Curriculum Debate* and *Conflicting Missions?* He authors *The Brown Center Report on American Education.* Loveless was previously a sixth-grade teacher in California and associate professor of public policy at Harvard's John F. Kennedy School of Government.

Donald R. McAdams is president of the Center for Reform of School Systems. He previously served as a member of the Houston Independent School District Board of Education, including two terms as board president. McAdams has served on numerous national commissions, advisory committees, and boards, and has written numerous articles and columns for newspapers, trade publications, and academic journals. He is the author of *Fighting to Save Our Urban Schools . . . and Winning!* and *What School Boards Can Do.* Previous positions include research professor, University of Houston; president, McAdams & Faillace, Inc.; executive vice president, American Productivity & Quality Center; president, Texas Independent College Fund; president, Southwestern Adventist College; and associate professor of history, Andrews University.

Andrew J. Rotherham is cofounder and codirector of Education Sector, a senior fellow at the Progressive Policy Institute, and a member of the Virginia Board of Education. He is the author of numerous articles and papers about education and coeditor of two books on education policy. He serves on advisory boards and committees for organizations that include the American Academy for Liberal Education, The Broad Foundation, the National Governors Association, and NewSchools Venture Fund. Rotherham is chairman of the board of the National Council on Teacher Quality and a board member of the Cesar Chavez Public Charter High School for Public Policy and the Charter School Leadership Council. He previously served at the White House as special assistant to the president for domestic policy during the Clinton administration.

Amy Way is a research associate at Public Impact, a North Carolina–based education policy and management consulting firm. She has carried out research on a wide range of school choice–related issues and has conducted an evaluation of a choice-oriented foundation's effort to scale up high-quality charter schools. Way played a major role in developing the definitive research synthesis that examines what is known about school professional development, Learning Point Associates' *Designing Effective Professional Development Experiences*.

Index